Advances in
Clinical Child Psychology
Volume 18

ADVANCES IN CLINICAL CHILD PSYCHOLOGY

A Continuation Order Plan is available for this series. A continuation order will bring delivery of each new volume immediately upon publication. Volumes are billed only upon actual shipment. For further information please contact the publisher.

Advances in

Clinical Child Psychology

Volume 18

Edited by

THOMAS H. OLLENDICK

Virginia Polytechnic Institute and State University
Blacksburg, Virginia

and

RONALD J. PRINZ

University of South Carolina
Columbia, South Carolina

Plenum Press • New York and London

The Library of Congress cataloged the first volume of this title as follows:

Advances in clinical child psychology, v. 1–

New York, Plenum Press, ©1977–

v. ill. 24 cm.
Key title: Advances in clinical child psychology. ISSN 0149-4732

1. Clinical psychology—Collected works. 2. Child psychology—Collected works.
3. Child psychotherapy—Collected works.
RJ503.3.A37 618.9'28'9   77-643411

ISBN 0-306-45143-3

©1996 Plenum Press, New York
A Division of Plenum Publishing Corporation
233 Spring Street, New York, N.Y. 10013

Printed in the United States of America

Contributors

Melanie J. Bonner

Department of Psychology, Virginia Polytechnic Institute and State University, Blacksburg, Virginia 24061

Patricia Chamberlain

Oregon Social Learning Center, 207 East 5th Avenue, Eugene, Oregon 97401

Marnie Filer

Ferkauf Graduate School of Psychology and Department of Epidemiology and Social Medicine, Albert Einstein College of Medicine, Yeshiva University, Bronx, New York 10461

Jack W. Finney

Department of Psychology, Virginia Polytechnic Institute and State University, Blacksburg, Virginia 24061

Sharon L. Foster

California School of Professional Psychology, San Diego, California 92121

Ross W. Greene

Pediatric Psychopharmacology Unit, Massachusetts General Hospital and Harvard Medical School, Boston, Massachusetts 02114

Andrea M. Kulberg

California School of Professional Psychology, San Diego, California 92121

Charles R. Martinez, Jr.

California School of Professional Psychology, San Diego, California 92121

Craig S. Neumann

Department of Psychology, Emory University, Atlanta, Georgia 30322

Donald P. Oswald

Department of Psychiatry, Medical College of Virginia, Virginia Commonwealth University, Richmond, Virginia 23298

Matthew R. Sanders   *Behaviour Research and Therapy Centre,
                          Department of Psychology, University of
                          Queensland, Brisbane, Queensland 4072,
                          Australia*

Nirbhay N. Singh   *Department of Psychiatry, Medical College
                          of Virginia, Virginia Commonwealth Uni-
                          versity, Richmond, Virginia 23298*

Ada Spitzer   *Department of Parent and Child Nursing,
                          University of Washington, Seattle, Washing-
                          ton 98195*

Elaine F. Walker   *Department of Psychology, Emory Univer-
                          sity, Atlanta, Georgia 30322*

Carolyn Webster-Stratton *Department of Parent and Child Nursing,
                          University of Washington, Seattle, Washing-
                          ton 98195*

Thomas Ashby Wills   *Ferkauf Graduate School of Psychology and
                          Department of Epidemiology and Social
                          Medicine, Albert Einstein College of Medi-
                          cine, Yeshiva University, Bronx, New York
                          10461*

Preface

As in past volumes, the current volume of *Advances in Clinical Child Psychology* strives for a broad range of timely topics on the study and treatment of children, adolescents, and families. Volume 18 includes a new array of contributions covering issues pertaining to treatment, etiology, and psychosocial context.

The first two contributions address conduct problems. Using qualitative research methods, Webster-Stratton and Spitzer take a unique look at what it is like to be a parent of a young child with conduct problems as well as what it is like to be a participant in a parent training program. Chamberlain presents research on residential and foster-care treatment for adolescents with conduct disorder. As these chapters well reflect, Webster-Stratton, Spitzer, and Chamberlain are all veterans of programmatic research on treatment of child and adolescent conduct problems.

Wills and Filer describe an emerging stress–coping model that has been applied to adolescent substance use and is empirically well justified. This model has implications for furthering intervention strategies as well as enhancing our scientific understanding of adolescents and the development of substance abuse.

Foster, Martinez, and Kulberg confront the issue that researchers face pertaining to race and ethnicity as it relates to our understanding of peer relations. This chapter addresses some of the measurement and conceptual challenges relative to assessing ethnic variables and relating these to social cognitions of peers, friendship patterns, and peer acceptance.

Neumann and Walker explore the connections between childhood neuromotor soft signs and adult psychopathology, taking into account child behavior problems. The exciting line of research being conducted under Walker's direction provides a strong foundation for the chapter.

Addressing the psychosocial aspects of attention-deficit hyperactivity disorder (ADHD), Greene analyzes how a goodness-of-fit perspective aids in understanding classroom adjustment of children with ADHD. The chapter recognizes the importance of the interpersonal (i.e., teacher–student) and ecological dynamics influencing children's adjustment at school.

The last three chapters have implications for delivery of child mental health services. The chapter by Bonner and Finney provides a cogent psychosocial model for conceptualizing children's health status and related treatment needs. From a treatment perspective, Sanders addresses psychosocial aspects of children's health problems with respect to behavioral family intervention and also reviews some of the other new applications of this mode of treatment. Oswald and Singh analyze some of the emerging trends in child and adolescent services, including innovative programs, and offer recommendations for future public policy.

THOMAS H. OLLENDICK
RONALD J. PRINZ

Contents

Chapter 1. Parenting a Young Child with Conduct
Problems: New Insights Using Qualitative Methods   1

Carolyn Webster-Stratton and Ada Spitzer

1. Introduction 1
2. Qualitative versus Quantitative Research 2
3. Reliability and Validity in Qualitative Research 4
4. Types of Qualitative Research 6
5. Grounded Theory—Methodology 7
   - 5.1. Step 1. Open Coding 8
   - 5.2. Step 2. Axial Coding (Hypothesizing and
     Categorizing) 8
   - 5.3. Step 3. Selective Coding and Theoretical
     Integration 9
6. Why Do Qualitative Research on Conduct Problems? 11
7. Study 1. The Meaning of Having a Child with Conduct
   Problems: "Families under Siege" 13
   - 7.1. Participants 14
   - 7.2. Analysis 15
   - 7.3. The Child's Profile 16
   - 7.4. Impact of the Child on the Family System:
     "The Ripple Effect" 21
   - 7.5. Impact of the Child on the Family's Relationships
     with the Community 25
   - 7.6. Theoretical Integration—Living with a Conduct-
     Problem Child: An Experience of Learned
     Helplessness 28
   - 7.7. Discussion 31
8. Study 2. Parents Undergoing Therapy: An Experience of
   Gaining Knowledge and Control 34
   - 8.1. Participants 35
   - 8.2. Phase I. Alternating Despair and Hope 35
   - 8.3. Phase II. Tempering the Dream 37
   - 8.4. Phase III. "Making the Shoe Fit" 41
   - 8.5. Phase IV. Coping Effectively 42
   - 8.6. Discussion 46

9. Three-Year Follow-Up: Moving beyond the Intervention—
    "The Work Continues" 47
    9.1. Participants 48
    9.2. Parenting Attitudes and Behavior 49
    9.3. Relationships with Other Parents 53
    9.4. Parents' Sense of Self 55
    9.5. Discussion 58
10. Conclusion 59
11. References 60

Chapter 2. Community-Based Residential Treatment
for Adolescents with Conduct Disorder   63

Patricia Chamberlain

1. Overview 63
    1.1. Research on Environmental Mediators of
          Delinquency 65
    1.2. Association with Peers 66
    1.3. Background and Applications of the Oregon Social
          Learning Center Treatment Foster Care Model 67
    1.4. The Oregon Social Learning Center Treatment Foster
          Care Model 68
2. Pilot Studies on the Efficacy of the Oregon Social Learning
    Center Treatment Foster Care Programs 70
    2.1. Treatment Foster Care as a Treatment for
          Delinquency 70
    2.2. Treatment Foster Care as a Treatment for Severe
          Emotional Disturbance 71
    2.3. Gender-Related Considerations in Conducting
          Community-Based Treatments for Adolescents 73
    2.4. Gender Differences in Responsiveness to Treatment
          Foster Care 75
    2.5. Mediators of Male Delinquency: A Clinical Trial 77
3. Conclusions 85
4. References 87

Chapter 3. Stress–Coping Model of Adolescent
Substance Use   91

Thomas Ashby Wills and Marnie Filer

1. Introduction 91

2. Theoretical Models of Adolescent Substance Use 93
    2.1. Stress–Coping Model 93
    2.2. Competence and Resiliency Models 97
    2.3. Deviancy Model 98
3. Overview of Research Methods 100
4. Stress and Substance Use 103
    4.1. Convergent Assessments of Stress and
          Substance Use 103
    4.2. Causation of Negative Life Events 104
    4.3. Moderating Effects of Attitudes 105
5. Coping and Substance Use 105
    5.1. Assessment of Coping 105
    5.2. Analysis of Coping–Substance Use Relationships 108
    5.3. Moderation Effects of Active and Avoidant Coping ... 109
    5.4. Effects of Coping over Time 110
    5.5. Coping Functions of Substance Use 110
6. Stress-Buffering Effects of Support and Competence 111
    6.1. Buffering Effects of Parental Support 111
    6.2. Buffering Effects of Academic and Social
          Competence 113
7. Temperament, Stress, and Coping Patterns 115
    7.1. Temperament and Stress–Coping Factors 116
    7.2. Temperament, Self-Control, and Conduct Disorder ... 118
8. Current Conclusions and Further Directions 119
9. References 124

Chapter 4. Race, Ethnicity, and Children's Peer Relations   133

Sharon L. Foster, Charles R. Martinez, Jr., and Andrea M. Kulberg

1. Introduction 133
2. Defining and Measuring Ethnicity 135
3. Ethnicity-Related Social Values and Practices 137
    3.1. Hispanic Children 138
    3.2. African-American Children 140
    3.3. Asian-American Children 142
    3.4. Anglo-American Children 144
4. Social Cognition and Perceptions of Peers 145
    4.1. Attributions 146
    4.2. Stereotypes, Biases, and Intergroup Attitudes 147
5. Friendship, Peer Acceptance, and Ethnicity 152
    5.1. Cross- and Same-Race Friendship and Interactional
          Preferences 153

5.2. Correlates of Peer Acceptance and Rejection 156
6. Conclusions, Implications, and Future Directions 163
7. References 166

Chapter 5. Childhood Neuromotor Soft Signs, Behavior
Problems, and Adult Psychopathology   173

Craig S. Neumann and Elaine F. Walker

1. Introduction 173
2. Soft Signs of Neuromotor Dysfunction in Children 174
   2.1. Determinants of Soft Signs 176
   2.2. Developmental Changes in Soft Signs 177
3. The Relation between Childhood Neuromotor Functions
   and Behavior Problems 177
   3.1. Childhood Neuromotor Soft Signs and Clinical
        Psychopathology 179
4. The Emory Study of Precursors of Adult Psychopathology .. 180
   4.1. Subjects 181
   4.2. Procedures and Measures 182
   4.3. Findings 184
5. Conclusions 193
   5.1. Neurodevelopmental Processes 195
   5.2. Directions for Future Research 197
6. Appendix: Neuromotor Rating Scale 198
7. References 199

Chapter 6. Students with Attention-Deficit Hyperactivity
Disorder and Their Teachers: Implications of a
Goodness-of-Fit Perspective   205

Ross W. Greene

1. Introduction 205
2. Compatibility Equations 207
   2.1. Student–Teacher Compatibility 209
   2.2. Teacher–Treatment Compatibility 214
   2.3. Student–Treatment Compatibility 216
3. Implications for School-Based Assessment and
   Intervention 220
4. Implications for Applied Research 222
5. Implications for Teacher Training 224

6. Summary 225
7. References 225

Chapter 7.   A Psychosocial Model of Children's Health Status

231

Melanie J. Bonner and Jack W. Finney

1. Background and Objectives 231
   1.1. Overview of Children's Health Status 231
   1.2. Objectives 233
2. Primary Child Variables Associated with Health Status 233
   2.1. Perceptions of Control 234
   2.2. Coping and Stress 235
   2.3. Child Psychopathology 237
   2.4. Child Health Care Utilization 239
3. Secondary Variables Associated with Health Status 240
   3.1. Symptom Appraisal, Interpretation, and Labeling ... 240
   3.2. Concepts of Health and Illness 241
   3.3. Relationships among Primary and Secondary
        Variables 243
   3.4. Summary 245
4. Parental Factors That Influence Children's Health Status ... 246
   4.1. Health Beliefs and Behaviors 246
   4.2. Family Functioning 247
   4.3. Parental Psychopathology 248
   4.4. Parental Health Care Utilization Patterns 250
5. Socialization of Health Behaviors 252
   5.1. Family Context 252
6. Social Learning Processes: Reinforcement and Modeling ... 253
   6.1. Reinforcement of Illness Behaviors 253
   6.2. Direct Modeling of Health Behaviors 254
   6.3. Social Learning and Coping Responses 257
   6.4. Social Learning and Control Perceptions 261
   6.5. The Coping–Control Relationship 261
7. Maternal Negative Affect and Socialization of Illness
   Behavior 262
   7.1. The Influence of Maternal Negative Affect on
        the Coping–Control Relationship 264
8. Learned Illness Behavior: Recurrent Abdominal Pain
   as an Exemplar 266
   8.1. Recurrent Abdominal Pain and Social Learning 266

	8.2.	Recurrent Abdominal Pain and Maternal Negative Affect	266
	8.3.	Recurrent Abdominal Pain and Child Psychopathology	267
	8.4.	Recurrent Abdominal Pain and Primary Care Utilization	268
	8.5.	Recurrent Abdominal Pain and Coping and Control	269
	8.6.	Interventions: Implications of the Theoretical Model	270
	8.7.	Recurrent Abdominal Pain: Summary	272
9.	Conclusion		273
10.	References		276

Chapter 8.   New Directions in Behavioral Family Intervention with Children   283

Matthew R. Sanders

1.	Introduction		283
2.	What Is Behavioral Family Intervention?		284
	2.1.	Conceptual Framework	285
	2.2.	Therapeutic Options	286
	2.3.	Consultation Skills	288
3.	Applications with Health-Related Problems		288
	3.1.	Pain Management	288
	3.2.	Chronic Food Refusal	293
	3.3.	Infant Sleep Disturbance	296
	3.4.	Relatively Neglected Areas	297
4.	Applications with Childhood Anxiety Disorders		298
	4.1.	Overview	300
5.	Applications with Conduct-Problem Children		300
	5.1.	Effectiveness	300
	5.2.	Enhancing Treatment Outcome	304
	5.3.	Overview	307
6.	Applications with Maritally Distressed and Remarried Families		307
	6.1.	Children in Conflictual Marriages	307
	6.2.	Children in Remarried Families	309
7.	Issues and Future Directions		310
	7.1.	The Importance of Process Variables	310
	7.2.	Intervening across Multiple Settings	313

7.3. Applying High-Power Interventions 314
7.4. Dealing with Educational and Learning Problems 315
7.5. Applications That Combine Individual and Family-
      Focused Interventions 315
7.6. Rural and Isolated Families 316
7.7. Toward a Public Health Perspective on Family
      Intervention 316
7.8. The Role of the Media in Family Intervention 317
8. Conclusion 318
9. References 320

Chapter 9. Emerging Trends in Child and Adolescent Mental Health Services   331

Donald P. Oswald and Nirbhay N. Singh

1. Introduction 331
    1.1. Child Mental Health Services Reform 331
    1.2. Estimates of Need 332
    1.3. Barriers to Appropriate and Effective Services 333
    1.4. Social and Demographic Trends 335
2. New Directions 336
    2.1. The Importance of "Place" 336
    2.2. Development of Home-Based Services 338
    2.3. Systems of Care in the Community 340
    2.4. Key Features of Systems of Care 342
    2.5. Applications of the Systems of Care Approach 344
    2.6. Evaluation of Systems of Care 347
3. Alternative Approaches 349
    3.1. Therapeutic Foster Care 350
    3.2. Day Treatment Programs 350
    3.3. Prevention Programs 351
    3.4. Developments in Inpatient Care 351
    3.5. Beyond Systems of Care 352
4. Emerging Issues 353
    4.1. Impact of National Health Care Reform 353
    4.2. Managed Care and Mental Health Services 353
    4.3. The Role of the Private Sector 353
    4.4. School-Based Services 354
    4.5. Meeting the Mental Health Needs of Children in
          Primary Care Settings 354
    4.6. Focus on Severe Emotional Disturbance 355

    4.7. Awareness of Diversity and Cultural Sensitivity   355
    4.8. Development of Transition Services   356
    4.9. Implications for Child Mental Health Training
          Programs   356
    4.10. Where Does the Future Lie?   358
5. References   360

Index   367

Advances in
Clinical Child Psychology

Volume 18

1

Parenting a Young Child with Conduct Problems

New Insights Using Qualitative Methods

CAROLYN WEBSTER-STRATTON AND ADA SPITZER

1. Introduction

What is qualitative research? Why should we do it? After all, isn't quantitative research the only "legitimate" method of scientific research—objective, verifiable, and methodologically rigorous? Does qualitative research have scientific integrity? Is it reliable? Valid? Generalizable? Can it add anything new to the findings of quantitative research? Is it publishable? After all, haven't psychology journals adhered almost exclusively to quantitative models of research? Why have they published so little qualitative research?

These are some of the questions that the first author of this paper asked herself when the second author, her doctoral student at the time, suggested that they undertake a qualitative analysis of parents' experiences living with their conduct-problem children. In part, these questions and concerns arose out of the first author's lack of familiarity with qualitative research. She had not studied this approach in her graduate training in psychology, nor had she read many articles using qualitative approaches in the psychological journals. At her student's urging, the professor put aside her discomfort with qualitative methods and reluctantly began the first of what was to become a series of three studies. She was motivated in part by a desire to learn about qualitative methods, particularly procedures grounded in theory.

CAROLYN WEBSTER-STRATTON AND ADA SPITZER • Department of Parent and Child Nursing, University of Washington, Seattle, Washington 98195.

Advances in Clinical Child Psychology, Volume 18, edited by Thomas H. Ollendick and Ronald J. Prinz. Plenum Press, New York, 1996.

This endeavor on the part of two researchers who do not profess to be experts on qualitative research resulted in a firm belief that the assumptions and methods of qualitative research can and should be incorporated with quantitative methods to help advance our understanding of families of children with conduct problems. This new line of research has convinced us that however much we have learned from traditional (quantitative) research about child conduct disorders and their treatment, our understanding of them remains in a sense superficial without the insights to be gained from qualitative research. For while quantitative research can tell us the number and types of behavior problems in children, it cannot tell us the meaning of those problems for the family. While it can tell us the relative effectiveness of treatment programs in behavioral terms (e.g., 30% reduction in parental criticisms or child deviance), quantitative research cannot tell us what actually occurs during treatment from the parents' perspective, namely, the experience of treatment in terms of internal changes and the meaning of treatment in parents' lives.

This chapter, then, has a twofold purpose: to provide an overview of qualitative research, emphasizing the techniques and procedures of grounded theory, and to illustrate the application and usefulness of qualitative research through our findings from three studies of families of children with conduct problems. These studies were based on parents' perspectives at three different points in time: (1) prior to intervention, (2) throughout the 20-week therapy process, and (3) 2 to 3 years after intervention.

2. Qualitative versus Quantitative Research

On its simplest level, the term "qualitative research" refers to types of research that produce findings arrived at by nonquantitative methods. It refers to methods of documenting, analyzing, and interpreting attributes, patterns, characteristics, values, and meanings of specific contextual or "gestaltic" features of the phenomenon under study (Leininger, 1985; Clarke, 1992). Typically, it stresses open-ended approaches to data gathering and inductive or intuitive approaches to analysis. But on a more profound level, qualitative research stems from a philosophical position that humans construct their subjective reality and that there are multiple realities as opposed to a single, objective truth. To understand the decisions and actions of individuals, we must understand the complex meanings they give to the reality they perceive (Berger & Luckman, 1966), and to understand a phenomenon, we have to see how it is experienced by the subject. Qualitative research accords a central role to subjective reality (or, more accurately, subjective realities) and therefore recognizes the importance of understanding contexts such as families, life events, social circumstances, cultures. This approach has its roots in the scientific disciplines of sociology and anthropology. Essentially, the goal is to document and interpret as fully as possible the phenomenon under study *from the subject's point of view* and *in its particular contexts*.

Qualitative research is considered to be of dubious value by some quantitative researchers, for it seems to defy all the traditional principles of quantitative research. For example, it is seen as overly subjective; its methods of interviews and participant observation are unreliable because they are not standardized, producing results that are of questionable validity and difficult to replicate. Certainly, if qualitative research is pursued without proper understanding of its underlying research principles, or by a researcher who is not sensitive to the phenomenon as it emerges or who is insufficiently analytical in its interpretation, the research may well lack validity. Yet the same accusation could be made of quantitative researchers who misinterpret statistical significance or fail to provide information on the clinical significance of findings. So let us put value judgments aside, and first describe some general contrasts between qualitative and quantitative research.

In many ways, the assumptions and methods of qualitative research may appear to be irreconcilable with those of quantitative research. For example, traditional quantitative researchers emphasize the importance of starting from theory and working deductively via a set of hypotheses using a carefully worked out design, standardized methods of data collection, randomized experiments, and statistics. Qualitative researchers, on the other hand, do not start with a theory or with a set of hypotheses to be tested; rather, they begin with broad, open-ended questions that become more focused in the process of data collection and analysis. Hypotheses are arrived at inductively, and are confirmed or rejected in light of the accumulating data. For these researchers, there are no standardized questions, no statistical analysis. While the quantitative researcher attempts to manipulate the variable of interest, such as how the intervention (the independent variable) influences a particular parent behavior (the dependent variable), the qualitative researcher attempts to assess the overall meaning of the phenomenon in its natural context, as perceived by those who are experiencing it. Theory emerges late in the process, as a result of the researcher's insights and based on induction or intuition. Thus, whereas quantitative research is context-free, emphasizes deterministic or causal explanations, and aspires to objective knowledge via numerical methods and deductive logic, qualitative research is inherently subjective, inductive, and context-sensitive, stressing the importance of describing, interpreting, and understanding the meanings of phenomena.

It is our contention that these types of research should not be in competition; each serves different purposes. Quantitative methodology has a well-deserved role in advancing our knowledge, for quantitative data and statistical analysis help to establish and verify facts. Qualitative research offers the promise of advancing our understanding by giving new dimensions and depth to factual knowledge, embedding fact in culturally relevant meaning, and perhaps providing rich clues for new lines of investigation. By pursuing both approaches to the phenomenon we wish to understand, we stand a better chance of overcoming the deficiencies and biases of each.

3. Reliability and Validity in Qualitative Research

Though qualitative research is often criticized as lacking in scientific rigor or integrity; there are criteria for evaluating its scientific integrity. Because the methods and aims of qualitative research are inherently different from those of quantitative research, the criteria for evaluating the scientific integrity of qualitative research must differ accordingly. For example, take the scientific principle of replicability. Applied to quantitative research as is customary, this criterion means that the experiment can be reproduced in successive experiments with identical results. To do this, the investigator must re-create the original conditions and control any extraneous variables that may impinge on the phenomenon under study. The research is credible only if it is reproducible. In qualitative research, however, the social and psychological variables that impinge on the phenomenon under investigation are notoriously difficult to control. Furthermore, these variables are by no means regarded as "extraneous"; rather, they are the vitally important subjective reality that the qualitative researcher seeks to understand. Thus, qualitative research almost by definition defies the criterion of reproducibility. Moreover, because grounded theory depends on the researchers' creative interaction with the data, it is unlikely that two researchers would come up with the same theory. In fact, the question of replicability is not especially relevant to qualitative research, in which the point of theory generation is to offer a new perspective on a phenomenon, a useful way of looking at it.

Nonetheless, the usual canons of "good science" do apply to qualitative research, but simply require modification (for a succinct overview of these canons, see Gortner & Schultz, 1988, p. 204). Foremost among these canons are reliability and validity. Guba (1981) and Lincoln and

Guba (1985) have suggested the term *trustworthiness* in reference to reliability and validity in qualitative research. The trustworthiness of any given qualitative research study can be assessed in terms of four factors: credibility, transferability, dependability, and confirmability.

Credibility refers to having confidence in the truth of the findings. Glaser and Strauss (1967) and Strauss and Corbin (1990) state that the credibility of a qualitative study is a matter of how the investigators derived their conclusions. As a first step in assessing the credibility of the conclusions, the reviewer has to ask whether the subjects are appropriate informants for the investigation and whether the data they offer are true presentations of the area of concern. In our studies, for example, the subjects were parents of conduct-problem children; they were considered reliable informants for research on the experience of parenting a child with conduct problems, the process of parent training intervention, and the long-term subjective results of intervention. The perspectives that these parents provide must be accepted as accurate representations of that realm.

The second factor in trustworthiness, transferability, is concerned with the degree to which the results are context-bound (Sandelowski, 1986). Research is considered trustworthy to the degree to which it adequately represents a particular cultural, social, or economic group. In our studies, our sample consisted of both mothers and fathers of conduct-problem children from different socioeconomic levels (one third welfare, one third lower and middle class, and one third upper class); the children had a variety of behavioral problems, and the parents exhibited different approaches to child-rearing. Therefore, the range of data was considered sufficient to provide the basis for assessing relevancy to a wide cross-section of socioeconomic groups representing primarily Caucasian mothers and fathers.

Dependability, the third criterion of trustworthiness, is defined by Lincoln and Guba (1985) as the reliability of the investigator's coding of data. In our studies, dependability was determined by subjecting a random sample of transcripts to analysis by two independent coders who were expert therapists. These coders were asked to review the categories, read the transcripts, and code the data using the derived categories. Approximately 80% reliability was achieved, and any areas of disagreement were discussed and a decision made as to the most appropriate category.

The last dimension of trustworthiness is confirmability. This dimension is defined as the ability of an independent reviewer to conduct a formal audit of the various study procedures (Lincoln & Guba, 1985). In our studies, one of the investigators served as a reviewer by auditing the various study procedures step by step. Validity checks were conducted throughout the stages of data collection and data analysis. A first-order validity check of the investigator's interpretation was carried out during the collection phase through continuous feedback from the interviewees. Data were repeatedly compared and contrasted. To clarify concepts or validate the investigator's perceptions, parents were often asked to explain their ideas or to comment on other parents' ideas. In a second-order validity check, the importance of the various categories of the experience was validated against a standard question: "How is this for you, and how are you doing now?"

4. Types of Qualitative Research

There are many different types of qualitative research: grounded theory; ethnography; phenomenological, historical, philosophical inquiry; and conversational analysis. All have similar purposes, but each has its own rules of evidence, inference, and verification, and all differ in terms of the degree to which the researcher is permitted to interpret the data and the degree of importance given to theory building. For example, ethnography, with its roots in anthropology, has traditionally been used in the study of different ethnic groups to understand their cultural systems, behaviors, and meanings (Sanday, 1983). It uses extensive fieldwork and participant-observation methods (i.e., to become part of the subculture one is studying) to discover how culture shapes people's behavior and their interpretation of their experience. The goal is to produce a factual and rich description and analysis of life in a particular culture or subcultural group. Ethnography contributes explanatory theories of culture, cultural behavior, and cultural meanings. Phenomenological studies examine how people perceive their world and make sense of an experience (C. T. Beck, 1990; Spiegelberg, 1976) with the goal of describing lived experience rather than defining, categorizing, explaining, or interpreting it by means of theories. In contrast to ethnography, phenomenology does not attempt to make interpretations or to generate explanatory theories, but simply to describe experiences as they are lived by people (i.e., without judgment).

Grounded theory is a qualitative method originally developed by sociologists Glaser and Strauss (1967) in a study of dying. Grounded theory research is aimed at initiating new theory and/or reformulating and clarifying existing theory. This method begins with systematic techniques to study the phenomenon and gather data, and moves inductively through data verification and analysis, allowing the researcher to abstract qualitative data into concepts or categories and to generate a theory or conceptual framework (Strauss, 1987). The theory emerges from the data and remains grounded in the data, hence the term "grounded theory." While this method has systematic and rigorous procedures and techniques designed to provide analytical process precision (described below), it also relies on the researcher's inquiring, analytical mind. The researcher is not expected to be a neutral observer or a tabula rasa—rather, the qualitative researcher brings to the interviews the general perspective of her discipline as well as her own theoretical perspectives. This process is perhaps inevitable in all research, but in qualitative research this inevitability is acknowledged and valued. The qualitative researcher starts with a set of experiences he or she wants to explore, rather than a hypothesis to prove or disprove. Thus, the researcher actively forms questions, seeks data, asks new questions based on the data, and interacts with the data by checking out hunches and formulating concepts. It is this process that results in "discovery"—discovering and conceptualizing the essence of complex interactional processes— and a grasp of another's subjective reality. The theory that emerges should present a new way of understanding the observations from which it is generated.

5. Grounded Theory—Methodology

For our qualitative studies, we chose the method of grounded theory (Glaser & Strauss, 1967; Strauss, 1987). One of the reasons we chose grounded theory is that by virtue of its emphasis on theory (in contrast to other qualitative methods), and by virtue of the place of theory in its processes (emerging, not a priori), it had the potential to offer new insights into a problem that we had previously studied extensively via quantitative methods. Second, as mentioned earlier, because grounded theory incorporates a systematic set of procedures to help develop an inductively derived theory about the phenomenon under study, it promises greater scientific integrity than other qualitative methods. In this method, the researcher abstracts qualitative data into concepts and categories. Constant comparison of data units is used to find similarities and variations within categories, to link categories in a hierarchical mode, and to form working hypotheses as to the theoretical nature of these links (Lincoln & Guba, 1985). By constantly comparing and contrasting the data, the researcher attempts to guard against premature commitment to a set of analytical categories, a liability in quantitative research as well as in other types of qualitative research.

The data-coding process used in grounded theory involves three stages: (1) open coding, (2) axial coding, and (3) selective coding.

5.1. Step 1. Open Coding

In the first phase of analysis, transcriptions are analyzed separately and subjected to open coding (Strauss, 1987). The initial codes are the result of breaking the data into small, meaningful units. Each discrete incident, idea, event, or name is coded as a concept. Dozens of codes are added as needed throughout the analysis and are entered into the computer. This step represents the most detailed phase of the coding, but is also the most generative because it becomes the basis of future theoretical sampling and tells the researcher what to focus on in the next interview.

5.2. Step 2. Axial Coding (Hypothesizing and Categorizing)

Whereas open coding breaks apart the data and allows one to see them in terms of minute categories, axial coding is the first step in putting the data together. To take a humble analogy, consider opening a new jigsaw puzzle: You open the box, separate the pieces, mix them up, then sort them by color, design, and shape and begin to fit the pieces back together. In axial coding, the initial codes arrived at during open coding are compared and contrasted to detect similarities and differences among them (Hutchinson, 1986). When the researcher perceives an overriding category that encompasses two or more codes, these codes are grouped together as dimensions of one axial code. It must be emphasized that this grouping is not determined a priori. For example, after hearing many parents talk in diverse ways about feeling trapped by their children, we generated a category "held hostage" that encompassed a number of specific situations originally coded as separate (e.g., unable to go to the grocery store, unable to socialize). As in open coding, one source of names for categories is the words or phrases used by the parents themselves; these are called "in vivo" codes. For example, one parent's expression "under siege" was used to summarize parents' feelings about living with their children when they first sought help.

Axial coding strengthens the density of the categories by "specifying varieties of conditions, strategies, and consequences that are associated with the appearance of the phenomenon referenced by the category" (Strauss, 1987, p. 64).It is at this point that the researcher's intuition and sensitivity concerning following up on meaningful categories for families become critical. Taking the aforementioned example of the category "held hostage," the researcher develops a hunch about the potential importance of this phenomenon for families and proceeds to analyze this category preintervention, during therapy, and at follow-up. The researcher must continually reflect on the data and the categories, comparing one informant to another, comparing each informant to emerging categories, each category to other categories, and categories to the literature. Each axial category is in a sense the result of the researcher's "hunch" about the process; each hunch is then subjected to examination in light of all the data, which validate or invalidate the hunch, that is, the category. In this stage of data analysis, the researcher proceeds with axial coding and at the same time continues open coding. This process is what "grounds" the theory—the categories and the proposed relationships among categories are provisional until they have been verified over and over again in light of the data.

5.3. Step 3. Selective Coding and Theoretical Integration

The third phase of analysis, selective coding, is a process of focusing selectively on higher-order categories that seem to make sense (and in doing so disregarding or discarding other categories). Open coding is refined as codes identified early in the process either do not hold up under scrutiny or are not generated in successive data and are therefore discarded. As selective coding proceeds, the relationships or connections among the core categories are explored and integrated. This integration is similar to axial coding, but done at a more abstract level of analysis; it is a process of "weaving the fractured data back together again" (Glaser, 1978, p. 116). The goal in this phase of analysis is to reduce the number of categories by creating higher-order categories, to explicate the relationships among these categories, and to develop a theory. It has been called "theoretical integration" (Glaser, 1978).

For example, from our initial study, we developed the core categories of parents "treading water" (denying the problem), problem recognition, self-blame, "nothing works," and mounting anger and loss of control. This process led us to the theory of learned helplessness, which then became the basis for further qualitative analysis as we sought to determine how parents overcame these feelings and began to cope more effectively. In this phase of analysis, the researcher is translating categories into an analytical "story," trying to capture the process in a conceptual framework. It may become apparent that some components of the process are absent or incomplete, which means that the researcher is driven to collect more data, selected on the basis of what is already known about the problem. This is called "theoretical sampling." For example, we learned from our pretreatment interviews how families perceived their experiences with other parents whose children were behaviorally normal and with teachers, but we did not have much information on how their extended family members had reacted to their difficulties. This led us to "theoretical sampling"—that is, conducting additional selective interviews with families to explore and expand this missing link in the theory evolving around lack of family support, increasing isolation, and eventual learned helplessness.

The qualitative research—specifically, grounded theory—presented in this chapter is based on individual interviews of parents of conduct-problem children prior to therapy, group sessions and individual interviews during therapy, and follow-up interviews several years later. Since we had videotaped all interviews and therapy sessions, we had a rich set of longitudinal data on each family. Transcriptions of interviews and therapy sessions were initially entered into a computer and formatted for use with Ethnograph (Seidel, Kjolseth, & Seymour, 1988). Ethnograph is a computer software program that provides the researcher with a convenient means of storing and sorting through the massive amounts of data that accrue in qualitative research interviews. The computer serves as the index cards, scissors, and glue for breaking apart, sorting, and reassembling the data. For example, once the interview is transcribed into the computer, it is formatted into 40-character lines, allowing each line of transcript to be sequentially numbered and providing an empty right side of the page for coding.

In open coding, the data were approached across families at three time periods: before, during, and after treatment. This procedure allowed the investigators to study each family separately across the various intake and therapy sessions, as well as to compare and contrast different families' responses as they moved through the different phases of the intervention program. Parents' own words often supplied the codes for this phase of analysis. The Ethnograph program allowed us to sort through every transcript for every occurrence of a given code—for example, every transcript in which a parent talked about feeling trapped. In axial coding, the categories were analyzed for similarities and differences in parents' behaviors, comparisons from one parent to another, and changing viewpoints as the invention program advanced. As the categories were examined more closely, it became clear that the parents described their responses in terms of different phases. For example, in the beginning, we were struck by parents' reluctance to admit their child's and their own problems and the length of time it had taken them to seek assistance. We termed this phenomenon "treading water." Once we had coded and developed categories based on the first set of transcripts, we analyzed a second set of randomly chosen transcripts according to the categories we had developed to continue to search for properties of categories, and to compare each category and subcategory for different patterns and recurrent themes; these categories and subcategories were validated and any new codes identified. In the third phase of coding, selective coding and theoretical integration, we sought to link categories to causal relationships; for example, the difficult and aggressive child leads to the parents' feeling of being held hostage and to eventual alienation from the community. The phases that had become obvious during axial coding evolved into a description of the sequential process by which parents moved from "treading water," to problem recognition, to learned helplessness, and to eventual effective coping strategies following treatment. This coping theory is the "cement" that integrates all the components of the theory and is the basis for the analysis at 3-year follow-up.

6. Why Do Qualitative Research on Conduct Problems?

Despite the volume of quantitative research showing correlations between child conduct problems and the more coercive styles of parental discipline, it is far from clear whether there is a causal relationship (and, if there is, which factor is cause and which is effect). This question is part of a larger question, namely, what it is like to parent a child with conduct problems. Apart from anecdotal information, we know very little about how parents experience their conduct-problem children, how they perceive and react to the problematic behavior over time, and what difficulties they encounter as they try to cope with the behavior. This is a question ideally suited to the methods of qualitative research, for it is a matter of understanding these parents' subjective reality.

Moreover, the literature contains comparatively little discussion of the impact of child conduct problems on the family system—that is, how the child's conduct problems affect relationships within the family (e.g., relationships between parents, or relationships of parents with other siblings)—or of their impact on relationships between the family system and outside systems or agencies (e.g., relationships with grandparents, with schools, with other families). While there is research to indicate that families of conduct-problem children experience high rates of major and minor life stressors (e.g., Forgatch, Patterson, & Skinner, 1988; Patterson, 1982; Wahler & Dumas, 1984; Webster-Stratton, 1988, 1991), marital stress (e.g., Furey & Forehand, 1985; Schaughency & Lahey, 1985; Webster-Stratton, 1989; Webster-Stratton & Hammond, 1988), and social isolation or lack of social support (Dumas & Wahler, 1985; Wahler & Dumas, 1984; Webster-Stratton, 1985a,b), it is unclear exactly how child conduct problems may contribute to these stresses. We know very little *from the parent's point of view* of the difficulties parents encounter as they try to cope with the child's conduct problems and simultaneously manage the stresses within the family system as well as the accompanying stresses in their relationships with agencies and individuals outside the family. This lack of insight into the meaning of child conduct problems in the lives of families—the *lived reality* and gestalt of conduct problems—is not surprising, given that the research has been largely quantitative. The first of our qualitative studies is a first step, we hope, in addressing that gap in our understanding of child conduct problems.

The area of child conduct problems has a second gap, namely, in understanding the subjective experience of undergoing treatment. Despite documented effectiveness for various types of parent training programs, the literature contains little discussion of such intervention programs from the parent's point of view. The large body of research to date has been quantitative in nature, focusing on static outcome measures such as reductions in rates of negative parental discipline (e.g., criticisms, physical force) and child deviant behaviors (e.g., hitting, noncompliance). To put it a little differently, while the end product of parent training has been well researched, the process has not. We know little about the actual processes of change brought about by such programs. Yet there are many questions to be answered concerning the intervention process: What happens when parental behaviors, attitudes, and practices are challenged and modified by a parent training program? What emotional, social, and cognitive changes accompany the process of behavioral change (i.e., parenting practices)? What difficulties do parents undergo as they work with the concepts presented in the program? How do these changes affect the family system—that is, what kinds of impact does the program have on different family members and on their relationships and interactions? In fact, our ignorance regarding what happens when parents' attitudes and practices are challenged is profound, particularly with regard to the consequences when the intervention raises cultural, family, or personal lifestyle issues. As these questions are matters of process rather than outcome and subjective rather than objective reality, they are more amenable to qualitative research rather than quantitative.

A third area that we felt qualitative research could help us explore was understanding long-term effects of intervention. While our quantitative follow-up data have enabled us to predict which families would relapse and which would maintain treatment successes at a given follow-up point, they did not provide information on how parents perceived and experienced those relapses and/or successes, nor did the data provide information on what impact intervention had had for the children and their families. What was it like to end treatment? How are the families generally coping several years later? What kinds of successes or failures have their children had? How did the parents react to relapses in their children's behavior? What are their perceptions about intervention in retrospect? In the face of relapses, did they consider treatment to have been useful? How could the intervention program have better prepared them for their experiences following intervention? What do the families feel they still need?

In sum, we felt that qualitative research would complement our quantitative research by allowing us to examine three areas: the impact of the conduct-problem child on her or his parents' lives, the subjective experience of undergoing therapy, and the meaning that the experience of therapy has for parents from a longer-term perspective. The scope of our data allowed us to describe the rich process of cognitive, emotional, and social changes that parents underwent from the initial intake interview to a follow-up point 3 years later. To answer the question posed at the start of this chapter, qualitative research on conduct problems in families is inherently valuable for the new knowledge it yields—what it can reveal that quantitative research cannot. But perhaps the most important reason for doing qualitative research is a practical one: We cannot successfully treat children with conduct problems unless we know more about these families' subjective experiences prior to therapy, in therapy, and afterward.

7. Study 1. The Meaning of Having a Child with Conduct Problems: "Families under Siege"

As stated earlier, we had conducted a number of quantitative studies of the families who came to our clinic and had accumulated a large body of data indicating that these parents of conduct-problem children were depressed, stressed, angry, critical, and inclined to use physical forms of discipline (Webster-Stratton, 1994). Our quantitative research had revealed that prior to intervention, over 23% of the mothers and 6% of the fathers were experiencing mild to moderate depression (i.e., a score of over 13 on the Beck Depression Inventory) (A. T. Beck, 1972); 65% of mothers and 36% of fathers were experiencing high levels of stress (i.e., a score above 294, or in the 90th percentile on the Parent Stress Inventory) (Abidin, 1993); 39% of mothers and 11% of fathers had high levels of anger (i.e., a score of above 9 on the Brief Anger–Aggression Questionnaire) (Maiuro, Vitaliano, & Cohn, 1987). Of those parents who were married or had been living with a partner for more than 3 months, nearly half (51%) reported significant distress in their relationship with their partner (scores of less than 100 on the marital adjustment scale and/or experiences with spouse abuse) (Locke & Wallace, 1959). According to our independent observations of family behavior in the home, parents were highly critical in their communication with their children (i.e., a mean of one critical statement every 2 minutes). In telephone interviews regarding discipline, 48% of mothers reported that they "frequently" yelled, hit, and spanked their children.

We also had accumulated considerable data regarding the children's behavior. Based on parent reports of child misbehaviors, over 99% of the children were more than 1 standard deviation above the norm for conduct problems on the Eyberg Child Behavior Inventory (ECBI) (Eyberg & Ross, 1978), and over 75% of mothers and 67% of fathers reported that their children were highly aggressive, defiant, and/or noncompliant— that is, they exhibited behaviors that translated into externalizing *T*-scores above 90% on the Child Behavior Checklist (CBCL) (Achenbach & Edelbrock, 1991). On home observations, children were observed to exhibit an average of 18 deviant behaviors per half hour.

These quantitative data, however, could take us only so far and no further. It did not help us understand the experiences families had prior to entering our intervention program or how long the behavior problems had been occurring. Neither did it provide insights into the impact their children's problems had on their intra- and extrafamilial relationships. Moreover, such static data on parent and child behavior did not tell us how these parents perceived the relentless process of trying to parent a difficult child. Our first study, carried out prior to families entering treatment, is described in some detail to illustrate our beginning efforts at using grounded theory methods and to show how these qualitative data enriched our understanding of these families and the parents' experiences.

7.1. Participants

One of the major differences between the methods of quantitative and qualitative research concerns sample size. We did not know in advance how many subjects our study would involve, for with grounded theory the researcher keeps interviewing new subjects until he or she has developed a conceptual framework that is integrated and testable and explains the phenomenon to his or her satisfaction. Ultimately, our sample consisted of 57 families (57 mothers and 20 fathers) of young children with conduct problems. Criteria for study entry were: (1) the child was between 3 and 7 years old; (2) the child had no debilitating physical impairment, intellectual deficit, or history of psychosis, and was not in treatment at the time of referral; (3) the primary referral problem was child misconduct (e.g., noncompliance, aggression, oppositional behaviors) that had been occurring for more than 6 months; and (4) parents' reports of their child's behavior problems were clinically significant according to the ECBI.

Of these families, 73% were headed by couples and 26% by single mothers (only a portion of fathers participated in the interviews). The mean age was 34.1 for the mothers and 35.9 for the fathers. Family social class, as determined by the Hollingshead and Redlich (1958) Two Factor Index, varied across a wide range: Class 5 ($N = 6$), Class 4 ($N = 18$), Class 3 ($N = 16$), Class 2 ($N = 20$), Class 1 ($N = 17$). The sample of children included 57 boys and 20 girls, with a mean age of 4 years and 10 months. The mean number of behavior problems reported at pretreatment according to the ECBI was 21.3 ($SD = 5.6$), indicating that the children were clearly in the clinic range according to Eyberg and Ross (1978) (for nonclinic range: mean $= 6.8$, SD $= 3.9$).

7.2. Analysis

Each couple or single parent underwent an extensive intake interview lasting 3–4 hours. Information was elicited about the effects of the child's antisocial behaviors on the family system as well as the parents' feelings, thoughts, and attitudes toward themselves as parents. Transcriptions from videotapes of these interviews were computer formatted for use with Ethnograph (Seidel et al., 1988).

In the first phase of data analysis, ten transcripts selected at random were analyzed separately and subjected to open coding (Strauss, 1987), resulting in Level 1 codes. Customarily in this type of research, analysis of the first interview would influence further data collection and interviews, but because we already had all the interviews on videotape, we randomly determined a starting point. These codes were the result of breaking the data into small meaningful units; often the informant's words provided the code. For example, the parent was asked, "Tell me what your child is like at home." The parent's description of the child would be coded line by line using such categories as "aggressive to animals" or "violent with sister." Once the ten transcripts had been coded, it became apparent that these Level 1 codes could be grouped into three major domains: the profile of a conduct-problem child, the impact of the child's conduct problems on the family system, and the family's relationships with the broader community.

In the second (axial) phase of analysis, the Level 1 codes were constantly compared and contrasted to detect similarities and differences; codes that represented dimensions of an overriding category were grouped together. Selected categories were then subjected to axial coding (Strauss, 1987) to strengthen the density of these categories (Strauss, 1987). Specifically, these categories were analyzed in regard to the child's profile, certain focal points in the family system, and the characteristics of the developing parental pattern of discipline. Axial analysis was used to develop and validate the core categories. Next, a second set of 30 randomly chosen transcripts were analyzed according to the categories to validate the existing codes and to develop any additional codes as necessary.

In the third (selective) phase of coding, the relationships among the core categories were explored. Codes that did not hold up under analysis were discarded. Selected interviews were conducted to fill in any gaps in the data. The analysis indicated that the relationship of child conduct problems to parenting styles took the form of a complex, multilevel process in which parents felt increasingly ineffective or helpless at parenting their conduct-problem children. The transcripts and videotapes of over 50 intake interviews with mothers and fathers were subjected to this third phase of analysis.

7.3. The Child's Profile

In order to understand the meaning of living with a conduct-problem child, it was crucial to understand first how these children are perceived by their parents. We had a wealth of data on these children's behavior, as reported by their parents and teachers as well as by independent observers. But what did their parents *think* and *feel* about that behavior and, more generally, about their child? Certainly there are a variety of emotional and psychological reactions one can have to problematic behavior, such as anger, guilt, embarrassment, empathy, apathy, sympathy, rage, indifference, and sadness, and a variety of cognitive responses (or nonresponses), such as denial, rationalization, projection, and distortion. We wanted to know whether there are certain emotional, psychological, and cognitive reactions that are typical of parents of children with conduct problems. Insight into their perspective, or at the very least awareness of it, is crucial for those of us who are working with these parents, because it is parents' perceptions of their child, the meanings they attribute to the child's behavior, and the feelings they have as a consequence of those attributions that shape their reactions to the child in general and to conduct problems in particular, not to mention their attitudes toward parenting and toward intervention.

7.3.1. Child as Tyrant, Parent as Victim

When asked to name their child's dominant characteristic, these parents specified *aggression*. Children with conduct problems were described by their parents as both verbally and physically aggressive toward family members and abusive of pets. Parents reported that their children intentionally harmed these targets with no evidence of remorse or regret.

> Mother: I don't know if you have suffered the physical abuses—I have. Just a few weeks ago, he threw his booster seat in my face and hit my jaw. And he thought it was funny! . . . . He was acting up, and I think he had already had one Time Out for yelling and screaming and interrupting us at the table. And I said, "Fine, you are going upstairs now. You are not having dessert." And he just flew into a rage. He picked up a metal fork and threw it with all his force, and hit me—barely missed my eyes. There was blood on my forehead. I was screaming, I was hysterical. And I was terrified, I mean, to see that type of behavior, that type of rage.

> Mother: She tells me she is going to run away from home and that she wants to leave. She told her father she wished he was dead so that way he won't wake up . . .

Frequently, parents recounted incidents in which their children had been destructive to the house or household objects. This aggression extended outside the family as well. Parents reported that their children were aggressive toward other children in day care settings, at friends' homes, and toward strangers in public places. Sometimes this aggression was sexual in nature: pulling down other children's underwear, touching children in their genital areas, using sexually provocative language, and so on. Parents described having to be always on guard, for their own sake and to ensure the other children's emotional and physical safety.

> Mother: He is so violent with his sister. He split her lip a couple of times. And he almost knocked her out once when he hit her over the head with a five-pound brass pitcher. He's put plastic bags over her head. Even things that you wouldn't think could be dangerous, you have to make sure and keep out of his reach.

They were also concerned that younger siblings would develop similar patterns of aggressive behaviors by watching their older brother or sister. In the face of this verbal, emotional, and physical aggression, parents reported feeling victimized and tyrannized. The ever-present possibility of abuse left them feeling deeply insecure when around their children. Clearly, they experienced their child as the one in charge, the family member who "called the shots."

A second well-known characteristic of children with conduct problems is their noncompliance and defiance. Parents in our study gave vivid descriptions of the arguments that they would get into with their children, which usually ended up in screaming fights. Parents could get their children to comply only by expending an enormous amount of energy.

> Mother: He just digs his heels in: "That's it, I am not wearing these socks! Forget it, I'm not going!" And he is right. He's gone to school in his pajamas, without lunch, in the pouring rain without any coat. "I've made up my mind, Mom, that's it!" he'll say to me. He will explain to me, "Mom, we

are done with this discussion . . . ." He doesn't have any easygoing bone in his body. He is not ever going to say, "Okay, I'll put that turtleneck on." It's going to be, "I will do something but only on my terms . . . I will do nothing that you want me to do and furthermore I'll throw such a tantrum and throw this cereal bowl all over the wall, so you will be late, and mad at me when you clean it up . . . ." He enjoys that power.

Perpetually faced with these continually defiant reactions, these parents typically felt exhausted. In short, these children controlled the entire family by virtue of the power they commanded through their resistance.

7.3.2. Hyperactivity and Distractibility

A third well-known trait of conduct problem children is their hyperactivity and distractibility. Many of these parents talked about their children's high-intensity temperaments. They described their children as highly active, easily "wound up," overexcited, loud, wild, and out of control since birth.

> Father: He's mentally fine, but his emotions are twisted in some ways— he doesn't seem to have the normalities that a lot of kids have. I look at my nieces and nephews and, while they have their moments, most of the time they can listen and talk. But with Keith he goes off into outer space and won't come back—he's not even on this planet! He's crazy, running around the house screaming, jumping on the bed, and goes into a fit of hyperactivity trying to accumulate as many things wrong as possible in that time. To get him under control we have to restrain him until he's so worn out, he's exhausted.

Moreover, they felt that their children had trouble listening and concentrating even for brief periods of time. They reported that when they made requests of their children, their children often "tuned them out" or got so distracted by their surroundings that they forgot what the parents had requested. They described their children as unable to sit still to play on their own and constantly demanding attention. The consequences for the parents were twofold: exhaustion and anxiety. These parents never get a break or quiet moment during the day. And, because their children's activity level is so high, their safety and even their survival is a major parenting issue.

> Mother: From 15 months he started running and destroying everything in sight and has not stopped since then. Keeping him alive became paramount. Once he crawled out of his car seat and over the seat when I was going 50 miles an hour and he hit the door and it flew open. He was so reckless that I could not shower unless he was in his crib asleep. I could not have him out of my sight for a minute. Life with him was a nightmare. One time I put him in his room for a nap, and turned on the shower. And I hear this frantic banging on my door, and it was my neighbor telling me that his second floor window was open—he had thrown a book on the roof and was going to get it. And so from 25 months to 3, it was this incredible desire to keep him alive. We couldn't afford one mistake.

Many parents were concerned about their child's inability to learn from experience. Too often, they had seen their child suffer the negative consequences of a particular behavior, yet go on to repeat the same self-defeating behavior later.

> Father: I am concerned because he is so experimental. If you tell him (or explain to him) not to do something, that guarantees he will try it at least one more time. He's so impulsive he doesn't think out the consequences of what he does. He has a kind of destructive curiosity which will get him into big trouble if he is still doing that as a teenager.
>
> Mother: I'm concerned because he makes a mistake and we talk about it, but there is no carryover to the next situation. He still makes the same mistake. Then when I try to talk about it with him, he has this blank face with rolling eyes and I get scared that a kid this young is tuning me out.

Similarly, they would describe having tried to help the child understand a problem, only to be met with either a blank expression or a deliberately defiant continuation of the troublesome behavior. This led parents to worry about their child's future.

7.3.3. Developmental Problems

Aside from the characteristics unique to children with conduct problems, parents reported various developmental problems that are common among children between 3 and 8 years of age. However, the intensity with which their children experienced these problems made their parents' experiences far from normal. For example, sleeping and eating problems are typical of children at this age. Yet one parent reported:

> Mother: One day we tried just to wait him out. At 6:00 I said, "We've got to go to bed." Six A.M.! We waited all night and he never did go to sleep.

Parents described how, when they tried to get their children to bed at a certain time, which is a normal area of conflict for parents and children at this age, their children would become noncompliant and defiant.

> Father: You have to follow them every step of the way to get them to go to bed. And then, once they are in bed, they're either turning on the light and getting up and playing with their toys, or else sneaking around the house. They won't stay put. I found the only thing that I can do to really control that is: I take a chair down at the end of the hall, part it in front of their door, and sit and read a book. Then they'll settle down and go to sleep.

Normal eating problems were exacerbated by the conduct-problem child's high activity level, lack of concentration, and inability to sit in the same place for a long period of time.

> Father: A meal at our house is like a circus. It's like two rats out of a sack. One goes one way and one goes the other. He'll run around the table. He'll take a bite of food, he'll sit down half on the chair, take another bite of food, and then run off and chew it and run around.

They also described resorting to various extreme measures in order to achieve some semblance of family mealtimes.

> Mother: He is so hyperactive at meals that even at age 4 we keep him in a high chair to get him to eat. We joke about how we have to break his legs to get him in the high chair. We are just so determined to have a family meal where he is not running around and causing havoc.

Transitions are difficult for many children between the ages of 3 and 7 years. Yet for these conduct-problem children, this common developmental problem was extreme; almost any change in routine was reported by the parents to result in defiant behavior. At the root of this problem is the child's inability to adapt.

> Mother: Transitions are really hard for him. We try to give him warnings, like bedtime is in 10 minutes. And then sometimes you get a temper tantrum getting his teeth brushed. Because even though he's had warnings, it hasn't assimilated that we mean, you are going to bed, we're going to turn the light off. He thinks he can still play.

A fourth developmental problem reported by these parents concerned fears. Whereas it is commonly believed that conduct-problem children exhibit externalizing but not internalizing behaviors, interviews with parents indicated that these children also exhibited many internalizing problems such as fears and suicidal thoughts.

> Father: He has night fears. It's been awful. It started about a year ago, but it got really bad about 4 months ago. The toys started moving their heads, and the stuffed animals . . . and then I had this long conversation with him in the bathtub the other day, and he is scared of thunder and lightning and it comes every night. He thinks that the thunder and lightning can throw bowling balls down from the roof and they can come and get him . . . it took about 20 minutes to get through that conversation. He has anxiety in his room—he lays awake for hours. We give him flashlights—sometimes he'll be awake at 2 or 3 in the morning from anxieties.
>
> Father: He often talks about wanting to die and how he wants to kill himself. Like the other day he was angry because he got pulled out of swim lessons for not keeping his hands to himself and he said, "It's so terrible, I should just die."

7.3.4. Unpredictability: Child as "Jekyll and Hyde"

Along with reporting the negative aspects of their children's behaviors, most parents talked about their children's personalities as having positive aspects. For instance, parents often portrayed their children as particularly sensitive and reactive to others' moods.

> Mother: He doesn't like to see anybody upset. It really bothers him. He just becomes very emotional. Say if I'm upset, he really catches on to it. Or if my husband and I are having a disagreement, he'll immediately start hollering at my husband to side with me, to get him to stop screaming.

While this sensitivity presented a challenge for the parents, it was also seen as a positive characteristic, a special gift as it were. Many parents described their children as having unique cognitive abilities and being more developmentally advanced than other children in their age group. One parent characterized her child as a "Jekyll and Hyde," an apt label for the child who is at times highly tyrannical, destructive, and defiant, and at other times loving, intelligent, understanding, and sensitive to others' emotions.

> Mother: He is like a "Jekyll and Hyde." Sometimes he can be sweet, charming, loving, easy to get along with, he's a very good-natured child. But then there's the other side of him which emerges—an angry, hostile, aggressive, hurting child, who will do violent things to try to get his way. He is rough with animals and mean with little children, and he is very noncompliant. By the time he is ready to be loving again, you are fed up.

Although the personality profile of the conduct-problem child that emerged from our interviews with parents was a mixture of negative and positive characteristics, certainly the negative predominated. It was the unpredictability of these negative behaviors that seemed to cause parents so much stress. Behavior problems might arise any time, any place; parents had to be always on their guard. Thus, ironically, the child's positive characteristics contributed to the parents' stress, since without a positive side there would have been no unpredictability. A "Jekyll and Hyde" child was harder to cope with than a mere "monster" child would have been.

> Father: We have these stressful times where he is very defiant and argumentative, we all lose our temper and perhaps he finally gets a swat. Then there is this emotional breakdown followed by big make-up sessions where he tells us he loves us. It is an emotional roller coaster.

In summary, it is evident from these descriptions that conduct-disordered children are not only nonreinforcing to their parents, but actually physically and emotionally punishing. Parents' feelings of victimization were amplified by their uncertainty about how their children might respond at any moment.

7.4. Impact of the Child on the Family System: "The Ripple Effect"

Our quantitative research had informed us about the high level of family stress, particularly marital distress. Because quantitative measures do not reveal anything about causality, however, we did not know how these parents' stress was related to their experience of living with a conduct-problem child. Our qualitative data revealed that the conduct-problem child's behavior introduces significant stresses into her or his family system and, moreover, that these stresses have a cumulative effect on the parents. Parents' descriptions of the impact on their lives of their child's conduct problems suggested an image of ripples in a pond that widen until eventually the entire pond is affected. The child's behavior has consequences that radiate outward from the child in ever-widening circles, affecting first the parents, then the marital relationship, then other siblings, then the extended family, and then the family's relationships with the community.

7.4.1. Impact on Parents' Relationship

We have already described the impact of the child's behavior on his or her parents individually—namely, the experience of being tyrannized or victimized. But the couple's relationship also is affected. The relationship between the parents is dominated by the need to continually monitor and discipline the child. Very little time and energy are left for parents to devote to themselves or to each other.

> Mother: One of the things that is so frustrating is that he has consumed our lives. Since he's been born, 99% of our conversation is about Matthew and what we are going to do to deal with his behavior problems. We don't have a life—everything revolves around Matthew.

Except in the unusual situations in which the father was the primary caretaker, the mother was the one who spent the most hours "under siege" with the conduct-problem child. Furthermore, mothers often took on a disproportionate sense of responsibility for the child. Typically, this imbalance created a situation in which mothers were exhausted and beleaguered, desperate for some time alone, with little energy to spare for husbands. And yet at the end of a long day with a conduct-problem child, mothers needed to share these feelings with their partners, especially when they blamed themselves for the day's problems.

The father, on the other hand, typically spent less time with the child and therefore had a less intense, somewhat easier relationship with the child. This difference between the mother–child and father–child relationships was potentially a source of relief and perspective and typically created conflict in the parents' own relationship. Observing their partner engaged in long episodes of cajoling and yelling at the child, fathers often questioned these approaches and were critical of the mothers' discipline or any inconsistency.

> Father: On a micro level if my son gets my wife upset, she doesn't distinguish between him and me. If it's a weekday and I've had a hard day at work I have limited resources when I get home at night. I may try to smooth the waters a little, but I'm often not successful and sometimes I get concerned about the way he is treated. I feel real angry about it, but I haven't done anything.

We commonly heard fathers express the belief that their wives were "too easy" and "not tough enough." These criticisms were bolstered by their awareness that they did not have the same kinds of problems with their children that their partners experienced. Mothers, in turn, felt resentful if fathers had an easier time with the child. Fathers often reported feeling left out and unsure how to contribute. Their subsequent guilt and confusion discouraged rather than encouraged communication between the couple. Frequently, fathers' distress was so great that they withdrew from the situation or avoided discussions with their partners about the children. Of course, these kinds of responses from fathers exacerbated the mothers' anger and frustration, thereby undermining the support system potential in the couple's relationship.

The result of this dynamic was a polarization of the couple:

> Mother: I always feel that if you [looking at husband] took a bigger role in parenting we could do it together and share the role. I feel it is you against "us" [mom and the children]. I want it to be "us" and "them."
>
> Father: Since our son was born, you [looking at his wife] have become really obsessed with parenting. Even during the pregnancy, you were always reading really big books about how to parent and trying to be supermom. I am not willing to put my mind, body, and soul into parenting all day and night. I'm going to have walls and boundaries. You are constantly attached— even when we go out for time alone, what do you talk about? Nothing but the kids! I finally made it a rule when we are out with friends not to talk about the children. The separation in our relationship began when he was born.

In this last example, the father's experience of parenting a conduct-problem child has distorted his thinking about the relationship. The normal estrangement a husband feels at birth (feeling outside the mother–child bond) becomes, upon reflection, a permanent condition. He projects onto the past what he feels now, a "rewriting" of the couple's history that only increases the emotional estrangement. Consequently, this couple experiences a loss of intimacy due not only to the practical constraints of too little time and too little privacy for a sex life, but also to the intense feelings of guilt, anger, frustration, and resentment that result from perceiving the relationship in terms of estrangement.

The sense of loss of control that parents felt in their parenting role seemed to spill over into their own relationship, resulting in a paralyzing depression and a sense of hopelessness. Instead of the relationship being a protective factor, a zone of relief from the stress of parenting a conduct-problem child, it was permeated by that stress and developed its own stressful dynamics.

> Mother: She [child] doesn't allow us to talk together—with the kids we don't get enough time together. As far as a romantic sexual-type relationship, for the past 4 years, it's been shot to hell! We don't have time to talk, we don't have time to pull in together, and, you know, just have a relationship.

7.4.2. Impact on Siblings

As described by these parents, living with a conduct-problem child has both a direct and an indirect impact on siblings. The direct impact lies in the child's aggressive behavior, which is often directed toward siblings, as discussed earlier. The indirect impact lies in siblings' relationships with their parents, especially their parents' expectations for them. Most parents felt that the constant, extraordinary degree of attentiveness required to manage the conduct-problem child's behavior left them with very little time or energy to attend to siblings. Stretched to the limits, they felt unable to tolerate misbehavior from more than one child. They expected siblings to be model children who always act responsibly and under control.

> Mother: What happens in our family dynamic is that our non-problem child always has to be responsible. Wrongly, but you know, because life with his brother is so incredibly complicated, he is expected to act like a 40-year-old and think like a 40-year-old. The consequences for him are great. I expect too much of him, I expect him to act, to use his head every minute of every day about dangers for his brother—that's more than an 8-year-old should have to contend with. Because life with his brother is so dangerous for everybody and because we try to control his brother's behavior, we are constantly on him to control his. And that is hard . . . he never gets to have a bad day, he never gets to throw a tantrum, he never gets to do anything because we are so maxed out on his brother, there's nothing left for him. He has to shut up, behave, and not talk to us about any of his concerns and problems.

Or because these parents felt so beleaguered, they placed the siblings in a shared parenting role, expecting them to care for the conduct-problem child. With siblings expected to act as adults and sometimes as parents, normal familial roles are distorted. The shift in the normal balance of power that occurs when a child becomes a tyrant and parents become victims is extended further; the family system is turned on its head.

It is obvious that these parental expectations place an unfair burden on the sibling in terms of age-inappropriate responsibilities. Moreover, these expectations are likely to create a sense of resentment on the part of the sibling toward the misbehaving child. In many families, the "good sibling" was becoming as difficult as the conduct-problem child by mimicking the problematic behaviors, a predictable result of the excessive parental attention given to the problem child.

> Mother: He definitely requires a lot of attention. And basically what we are feeling now is a backlash from giving him so much attention, that my older one, who used to be my "great kid," is now acting up and being sneaky and starting to get that way.

7.4.3. Impact on Extended Family

These parents also reported that their children's conduct problems had become a source of tension between themselves and *their* parents and/or siblings (i.e., between the parents and grandparents or between the parents and aunts and uncles). It seems that grandparents often attributed the child's misbehaviors to a lack of good parenting. Many parents reported that their parents (the child's grandparents) were always giving advice about how they "should" handle the problems. Typically, they advocated a stricter approach to misbehavior.

> Mother: When Grandma comes to visit about once a month, he [child] just goes ape. He starts terrorizing the cats, he starts throwing his toys, he starts going ape. And he has a real hard time when Grandpa is there. And Grandpa likes him, but Grandma thinks we should "nail the little sucker a good plant a couple of times on the rear end."

On the other hand, sometimes the children did not behave as badly with grandparents as they did at home with their parents, a fact that these parents interpreted as further evidence of their own failure as parents.

7.5. Impact of the Child on the Family's Relationships with the Community

Eventually, the child's conduct problems "rippled outward" to affect the family's relationships with professionals, teachers, and other parents in their community. In general, these relationships become characterized by negative feedback to the parents: stigmatization, social isolation, and rejection.

Parents felt rejected and isolated by teachers' and day-care providers' reactions to their children's misbehaviors. The children's aggression and defiance created problems with their peer group at school, causing other children to cry or misbehave and generally increasing the level of aggression in the classroom. Understandably, teachers became more disapproving and punishing toward these children. Parents frequently reported that they had been asked by teachers to find another day care or school for their child because their child was unmanageable and consumed too much of the teacher's time. Some families had been asked to leave half a dozen day care centers by the time their child was 5 years old.

> Mother: It started when he was 18 months old. He was always the most aggressive, the most outgoing, the loudest child in every group he's ever been in. And I remember after his first day at day care—I picked him up and I got a phone call. It was on my answering machine—I mean the teacher

never confronted me in person and she just said she didn't think it was going to work—he was terrorizing other children and really being a disruptive force to her preschool. And I had to drop that day care. So you know, no notice—and it's just been like that from that point. I remember getting a phone call on my answering machine, and with it one of the teachers asking me to call back—I was just holding my breath, wondering if she was going to tell me to take him out . . . . I would come back after 3 hours and just the expression on her face—it was this horrified, painful expression.

Mother: He's 3 years old and he's always on probation. The teacher just greeted me with one of those really painful expressions I'm so familiar with: "Your son did this." Then you would hear stories of how your son had to have two people release him from a choke hold on another child or how he was pouring water on someone's head. They told me not to bring him back. I was just so embarrassed.

Moreover, as children's antisocial identity was established, they frequently became targets of other children's ridicule and rejection.

A further "ripple effect" was that the disproportionate amount of teacher time devoted to the child's behavior problems resulted in resentment by parents of other children in the school or day care and complaints to teachers and principals.

Mother: I've never been to a school meeting when I haven't been trashed. I can't stand to go to one more meeting and have them tell us what they are not going to do for us. After they got rid of us—well it was like we were disposable and we never heard from them again.

This intense negative feedback compounded the parents' feelings of isolation and lack of support.

Mother: The principal came up to me and said your boy is a very sick boy and is going to need many years of psychoanalytic counseling—I feel all the teachers knew this and set us up in the school so we couldn't win. I felt everyone else in this kindergarten were on this raft while we were swimming around trying to clutch to get on. We said we'll pay for books and I'm helping out twice a week in class and I'm offering to be a personal aide and we'll pay for a social skills teacher—and everywhere we'd go around the raft and try to get on someone would step on our fingers.

Yes, and we even sent away for literature to provide ADD handbooks for the teachers which were never read. By the end of the school year, we started realizing that the kindergarten raft was sailing away, and when they told us not to come back, we felt we were left drowning in the water.

Faced with this stigmatization and confused by their child's behavior, these parents had sought help from a variety of professionals, such as pediatricians, psychologists, counselors, and psychiatrists. In general, they were frustrated in this quest. Parents had received conflicting opinions regarding the seriousness of their child's problems and conflicting advice about how to deal with them. Many parents reported being told that their child was "normal," that she or he would soon "outgrow" the problems, and that they should just "loosen up" and "be patient." Far from being reassuring, this advice caused parents to blame themselves for overreacting to the problem behaviors or confused them, since in their experience the behavior was not normal.

> Mother: I've talked to our pediatrician about it. I went and saw a counselor, and I've talked to him about it. And everyone basically told me, "Oh, he's just a normal kid." Well, I mean our life at home is not normal . . . and they say, "he is just like a normal 4-year-old . . . nothing is wrong with your child." And he goes, "I wouldn't worry about it." And he kept telling me, "I wouldn't worry about your kid, I would worry about the ones that are quiet and compliant and do everything they're told." So you know I was just pulling my hair out—while they are trying to make you happy and realize that you don't have a weird child—but that's not what I wanted to hear. I wanted to hear step one, two, three, four . . . and I really don't know what to do.

Other professionals would tell them to "be more consistent and get stricter control" of their children's problems. The net result, regardless of the type of advice given, was to make the parents feel at fault and confused about how to cope with the situation.

As the "ripples" spread, these parents experienced increasing isolation from other parents in their neighborhoods and in their schools. Parents felt a lack of connection with and support from parents of "normal" children. They thought that if they were honest about their difficulties, they would encounter indifference.

> Mother: Basically I feel I am really in a minority. Because of all the other mothers I've talked to . . . they've never been hit. I mean to me it's unimaginable not to be slapped and kicked. And I have a friend. I was telling her about it and she says, "What? Your son hits you? My daughters never hit me." I mean other parents look at me like I just walked off another planet. So I feel very isolated. I feel like no one is like me! No one has my situation.
>
> Mother: There's always the fear that if you share with somebody what your child is like, somebody will assume it's your fault, and think you screwed up as a parent. Or they'll reject you and say, "God, I don't want to hear about this!"

Or, worse yet, the parents feared reprisals in terms of the impact this information could have on others' perceptions of them or their child. The tremendous amount of negative feedback these parents received from other parents bred feelings of stigmatization. This lack of empathy was often perceived as rejection or condemnation. When they invited other children to come over to their house to play with their child, they were turned down. Their children seldom received invitations to birthday parties or to play at another child's house. Typically, after one experience with their child, a babysitter would not want to come back.

> Mother: She has run off three babysitters. No one wants to babysit her. I mean, one day she was jumping on the bed, pulled down the curtains, threw pillows all over the place, wouldn't mind the babysitter. We came home, everything was trashed. And the babysitter said, "Look what this child did."

Parents even felt rejection from strangers in grocery stores, parks, and restaurants.

> Mother: There have been times when he has been aggressive enough that I've seen a look in other people's eyes that just makes me feel horrible to the core. One day I took him to the children's museum by myself, and by the time we left, maybe 45 minutes later, I was really an emotional wreck because I'd seen a look and posture in the other parents there that showed repulsion on their part. And I felt that as a couple, we were really being rejected. And I literally saw other people come into a play area and, seeing we were there, just turn their own child away.

As a result, parents reported becoming more and more insular. Frequently, they reported having stopped taking their children to grocery stores and restaurants in order to avoid having to deal with possible tantrums and negative behavior in these public places.

> Mother: I won't take him shopping with me because he throws temper tantrums, and with child abuse laws the way they are now you can't discipline him in public any more. So I won't take him. I won't even take him to a restaurant.

This apprehension of blame and rejection from extended family members and from the community led parents to feel more and more isolated.

> Mother: There is huge isolation. My mother doesn't understand, my stepfather is hypercritical, and other parents think it's awful—rarely do we get support. Other parents walk in our house and look at the holes and think, "My God, what kind of children live here, obviously these parents are letting things run amok." Isolation has been a huge issue for me, I don't think anyone else understands. Nobody has a child like him.

In sum, they felt stuck with a child who was noncompliant and aggressive—a tyrant at home, a terror at school and in the community—with no support or understanding from others.

7.6. Theoretical Integration—Living with a Conduct-Problem Child: An Experience of Learned Helplessness

When professionals and lay people alike look at families of conduct-problem children, certain judgments are commonplace: The parents are at fault for their child's misbehaviors, the parents might resolve their child's problems if only they were more committed as parents or used more effective discipline strategies. But these judgments are off base.

Persons outside these families usually have only a superficial view of what these parents have experienced and of the cumulative effects of the child's behaviors—we see the situation within the context of our own generally positive experiences of child-rearing. Such an approach is insensitive to the disrupting process that parents go through while raising a child with conduct problems. We haven't experienced what it is like to feel "held hostage" by a tyrannical child. Nor have we experienced the complexities of the "ripple effect."

Unfortunately, research has done little to correct these misperceptions. Quantitative data such as mean scores of parental critical statements toward their children, number of spankings per day, and mean depression or marital scores do not help us understand subjective realities or the context of the phenomenon. Such data may even bolster common misperceptions of these parents as incompetent and blameworthy.

Qualitative data, on the other hand, allow us to understand the phenomenon within its context and to explore links between phenomena. In the third step of grounded theory analysis, theoretical integration, the researcher is permitted to have "hunches" about the data and to make "intuitive leaps." Findings from this qualitative study led us from the open and axial coding of interviews with parents (as described earlier) to integrating the recurring themes into a theory, namely, that of learned helplessness (Seligman, 1975). Although this theory was not original with us, this study did for the first time reveal how the theory applies to the phenomenon of parents living with a conduct-problem child. For example, the recurring themes of unpredictability, isolation, victimization, self-blame, and despair over not being able to change the situation that we found in our data are also the hallmarks of learned helplessness. We have described the three phases of the process that parents went through (treading water, problem recognition, and learned helplessness) in a longer version of this paper published elsewhere (Webster-Stratton, 1994).

The basic premise of the learned helplessness theory (Seligman, 1975) is that during contact with an uncontrollable situation, an organism learns that outcomes and responses are noncontingent (Abramson, Seligman, & Teasdale, 1978; Maier & Seligman, 1976; Seligman, 1975). As parents realized that their child's behavior problems were not going to disappear, they coped with their feelings of self-blame by launching into a variety of discipline approaches with their child. Parents reported seeking help from books, from courses, and from various professionals. They reported trying a range of discipline strategies such as teaching, yelling, criticism, spanking, Time Out, taking away privileges, and positive reinforcement. After several years of struggling to control the child's behavior problems with only limited success, if any, they began to believe they were doomed to be ineffective in changing their children's behaviors. In fact, typically, the children's misbehaviors were often gradually escalating under what parents perceived as their own best efforts. Parents reported reaching a point at which they believed that "nothing works."

> Father: I get agitated easily, I mean, this has been 4 years of this. And I am 42 years old, and I've just about had it. So now I'm kind of at my wit's end, like what to do. Because nothing is working.
>
> Mother: Both of us are professionals and we work with people a lot and we've had a lot of resources. We've been in counseling since he was 3 years old and seen several psychologists and psychiatrists and we've worked very hard, but haven't gotten very far. He's still got the same traits and that's scary.
>
> Mother: I'm stuck here—it will never get any better, this child is going to be a delinquent, I know it. I'm going crazy and I need help. Maybe I should give up because I'm going down in a sinking ship.

They felt helpless and inadequate in their parenting roles and, more generally, as human beings. Moreover, their extended family members, teachers, professionals, and other parents seemed to confirm these feelings of ineptness.

The transition from intense feelings of inadequacy to learned helplessness was evident in parents' reports of feeling overwhelmed, even paralyzed, by their children's behavior problems. Parents talked at times as though they believed their children were "out to get them." As the embattled parents felt increasingly helpless, they began seeing their children as the powerful ones. In an inversion of the usual power structure, the children were controlling their parents' lives. Thus, the parents became victims and the children oppressors. In response to their sense of victimization, the parents' anger increased, as if in an effort to regain control and power in the relationship. Additionally, however, these powerful feelings of anger were coupled with fears of losing control of their own behavior with their children and control of their sanity.

> Mother: I was ready to just walk away from everybody. It was just too much—his screaming, the temper tantrums all day. And I thought I was completely loony bins. I felt like a real failure as a human being . . . There are times when he just drives me to destruction. . . .

Sometimes parents reported that they did lose control of themselves and used excessive physical punishment. Such out-of-control reactions further inflamed their self-blame, setting in motion a vicious cycle of anger, loss of control (ineffective parenting), and guilt. These reactions and feelings, in turn, further aggravated the child's aggressive responses. Eventually, the fear of their own angry responses led parents to give up even trying to discipline their child and to withdraw, which in turn brought on depression.

> Mother: It's like he pushes, and pushes, and pushes me . . . I feel real helpless . . . and what I do is, rather than react appropriately, I shut down. I mean it's like I'm in shock. That's when I feel really incompetent. . . . I have truly never questioned my own sanity, as I have with the kind of episodes I told you. It really overwhelms me—it scares me.

Another characteristic of the learned helplessness experienced by these parents, and one that was very difficult for them to accept, was a sense of having invested for so long in their child with little or no "return" for their investment in terms of joy and pleasure in their parent–child relationship. This situation, in which parents experienced few rewards for the difficult work of parenting, created a sense of paradox and despair for parents in that the discrepancy between what they were "putting in" and what they were "getting out" was just too great.

> Mother: I've noticed other mothers and families, and they really enjoy their little girls and their little boys, because it's a real different situation for them. And it's not like that for me. I don't have that real enjoyment.

7.7. Discussion

As mentioned earlier, learned helplessness theory posits that when people undergo experiences in which they have no control over what happens to them, they develop certain motivational, cognitive, and emotional deficits. The motivational deficit is characterized by retarded initiation of voluntary responses, the cognitive deficit by a belief or expectation that outcomes are uncontrollable, and the emotional deficit by depressed affect (Abramson et al., 1978; Maier & Seligman, 1976; Seligman, 1975). Parents of conduct-problem children learn through repeated experience that regardless of what parenting strategy they use (e.g., Time Out, spanking, explanation, positive reinforcement), the child's aversive behavior remains constant. In other words, the outcome is not affected by their actions. Moreover, on those rare occasions when they were able to influence their child's behavior, these parents came to feel that there was no predicting which parenting strategy would produce a particular outcome. For example, Time Out might be effective at one time, but not at a different time—even in response to the identical problem behavior. Thus, they feel there is no discernible relationship between their actions and the outcome.

Abramson et al. (1978) distinguish between universal and personal helplessness. In universal helplessness, the person believes that neither he nor she nor anyone can solve the problem, whereas in personal helplessness the person believes that while the problem is solvable, he or she lacks the skills to solve it (i.e., low self-efficacy expectations). Analysis of the attributions of the parents of conduct-problem children in our study revealed that these parents had developed a sense of personal helplessness. Parents constantly compared their child-rearing skills to those of other parents and came to believe that unlike other parents, they were incapable of controlling their child's behavior. These internal comparisons were reinforced by feedback from family members, teachers, and other professionals, who also attributed the child's behavior or problems to their lack of parenting skills—thereby increasing their sense of personal helplessness.

Our qualitative data amplified our quantitative findings concerning depression among this population of parents, revealing very low levels of self-esteem or high levels of depression or both. This finding is explained by learned helplessness theory, which asserts that people who feel personally helpless show lower self-esteem than do those who experience their helplessness as universal (Abramson et al., 1978). A related hypothesis advanced by Bandura (1982, 1985, 1989) may also help explain this finding. He proposes that self-efficacy beliefs are central to an individual's transactions with the environment. For example, in his view, a parent may understand how to do Time Out with an aggressive child, but be unable to do it because of self-doubts. In addition, Bandura (1989) has suggested that the relationship between self-efficacy and performance is bidirectional. Self-efficacy beliefs are enhanced or decreased, respectively, by success or failure experiences. The parents in our study reported feeling ineffective due to their repeated failure experiences trying to parent their difficult conduct-problem children. Thus, they stopped trying.

According to the theory, learned helplessness varies in terms of generality, chronicity, and intensity of the problem (Abramson et al., 1978; Kofta & Sedek, 1989; Mikulincer & Casopy, 1986; Miller & Norman, 1979). The helplessness felt by these parents was extreme in all three respects. With regard to generality, these parents of conduct-problem children felt inadequate in other areas of their lives beyond child-rearing, such as in their marital relationship and relationships with teachers, other parents, and professionals in the community. Many felt isolated, stigmatized, and even rejected. Thus, their sense of helplessness had become somewhat globalized rather than remaining specific to the child. With regard to chronicity, these parents reported waiting endlessly for their child's problems to disappear before they even began to try to control them—and when they did try to handle them, they were usually unsuccessful. Most had therefore experienced chronic helplessness for several years. With regard to intensity, the high intensity at which these parents experienced these problems evolves from the importance our society places on successful child-rearing and a harmonious family. Abramson et al. (1978) have suggested that intensity of helplessness will be higher to the extent that the event about which the person feels himself helpless is highly preferred or valued. It is not difficult to understand the intense feelings of helplessness that can occur when parents develop the conviction that they lack the skills for rearing behaviorally normal children.

As discussed earlier, we knew from our quantitative studies that parents were stressed, depressed, angry, out of control, and critical with their children. We had not information, however, about the interaction of these factors, their relation to the child's behavior problems, and their subjective meaning for the parents. It is one thing, for example, to know that parents are angry or depressed as measured on a standardized scale, and quite another thing to hear how they feel "held hostage" by their children and to know that their attitudes and feelings are similar to those of a prisoner of war (i.e., learned helplessness). It is one thing to know that they are more critical in their communication than parents of "normal" children, but when we also know that they blame themselves and have low self-esteem, we interpret their critical behavior in a light different from, say, that in which we interpret the behavior of parents with strong self-images who are critical of their children. Thus, our qualitative findings, and especially the theory that arose from our findings, add meaning to our quantitative findings by helping us to see the gestalt of these families. Understanding parents' sense of victimization and their feelings of isolation and stigmatization as the ripple effect spreads from the family to community puts the quantitative data "in context." Understanding how the unpredictability of their children's conduct problems contributes to their feelings of helplessness and their difficulty with providing consistent parenting gives us new insights into these parents.

This qualitative analysis has important implications for treatment. Not only does this theoretical formulation contribute a new viewpoint regarding the development of conduct problems in families, but also the description itself should help sensitize therapists to the long history that these parents have already experienced prior to seeking help for their problems. Moreover, learned helplessness and low self-efficacy beliefs can be reversed by experiences of success. Teaching effective parenting skills undoubtedly starts a reversal process; it begins to give parents some expectation that they will eventually be able to control outcomes (i.e., their children's behaviors). These findings also reveal the importance of enhancing social support (reversing these parents' experience of isolation and stigmatization) by involving partners and, if possible, teachers in the intervention. Indeed, these findings suggest that group-based therapeutic approaches would be particularly helpful for these parents in that the group experience counteracts their isolation, normalizes some of their experiences, and can provide support.

8. Study 2. Parents Undergoing Therapy: An Experience of Gaining Knowledge and Control

From our first qualitative study, we learned a great deal about what parents of conduct-problem children experience within their families and communities. What about their experience in therapy? Our quantitative research had shown that compared to waiting-list controls, families in our parent training program showed significant decreases in parental anger, stress, and depressive symptoms immediately posttreatment; only 20% of mothers and 10% of fathers still reported depression or stress in the abnormal range (i.e., about the 90th percentile). Moreover, home observations of parent–child interactions indicated a significant decrease in parental critical statements, an increase in praise statements and a significant reduction in child deviant behaviors. In this study (Webster-Stratton, 1994), over 70% of mothers and 75% of fathers perceived their children to be in the normal range as measured by the CBCL, that is, a T-score below 63 (Achenbach & Edelbrock, 1991).

These results attest to the value of the intervention, in terms of parents' emotional states (anger, stress, depression) and behavior (criticisms, praise). But this is very limited information indeed about the impact of therapy, particularly about the therapeutic process. We wanted to know more than the outcome of the intervention; we wanted to know what parents experienced during the intervention, the broad range of interwoven emotional, cognitive, and interpersonal effects not necessarily captured by our usual quantitative measures and not necessarily reflected in behavioral outcomes. In part, this need to know more about parents' subjective experience of therapy was a matter of good practice; that is, we wanted to understand what difficulties parents experienced as they worked with the concepts presented in the program so that we might improve our intervention. But also, in light of our first qualitative study, we wanted to know the extent to which their attempts to change their parenting practices affected the family system and their relationships and with those outside the family. And, knowing what we now know about the isolation, anger, guilt, despair, and helplessness experienced by these parents, we wanted to know how the process of undergoing our intervention affected these feelings and perceptions. Consequently, our second qualitative study was an analysis of the subjective reality of intervention, the process of change as experienced by parents in our intervention program.

8.1. Participants

Subjects were parents of conduct-problem children (ages 3–7). In the study, 20–24 weekly meetings of five different groups of parents (totaling 40 mothers and 30 fathers) were videotaped, and 16 therapist consultations with 37 mothers and 30 fathers were audiotaped half-way through the parent intervention program and upon termination of the program. Transcriptions of these videotapes and audiotapes provided the data for this study.

The data suggest that in learning to cope more effectively with life as the parent of a conduct-problem child, parents went through several phases. First, their attitude seemed to oscillate between despair and irrational hope. Next, as they gradually came to realize that their child's problems were chronic, their anger, guilt, and resistance gradually decreased. In this phase, most families were able to change their expectations and settle for a less than total recovery of the family and the child; we called this phase "tempering the dream." This phase was followed by a third phase in which the parents worked at "fine-tuning" or tailoring the program to their own particular needs; we called this phase "making the shoe fit." Finally, by the end of the intervention, many parents had reached a phase of "coping effectively." As these phases (and the prior phase of "acknowledging the problem") have been described in detail in an earlier paper (Spitzer, Webster-Stratton, & Hollinsworth, 1991), we will describe them only briefly here in order to illustrate the type of findings that arose from our qualitative data.

8.2. Phase I. Alternating Despair and Hope

8.2.1. Reexamining the Blame and Guilt

As parents participated in the parent training program and learned new parenting strategies such as play skills, effective reinforcement, and nonviolent discipline approaches, their guilt over their previous use of punitive approaches, their regret about their earlier lack of parenting knowledge, and their failure to use these new approaches more consistently with their children (unfortunately, new sources of guilt!) were recurring themes.

> Session 6
> Mother: These sessions have helped me feel a whole lot better about having more control about what's going on. I guess my biggest problem is that I feel

> guilty when I am not doing the right things and when I am going back to my
> other habits. I know we're not handling those [behavior problems] right,
> especially when he starts piling a lot of them at once. I tend to lose it com-
> pletely and just scream hysterically at him and spank him, which I don't
> want to be doing.

The guilt arose, of course, from a desire to attribute blame. Initially,
parents were preoccupied with identifying who should be blamed for
the child's problems. While some externalized the child's problems and
blamed the child's personality on an absent parent, teachers, or society
in general, other parents internalized the child's problems and attributed
them to their own personal inadequacies or lack of parenting skills.
During treatment, as parents viewed the videotaped examples of other
parents interacting in different ways with children of different temperaments, and as they listened in group to other parents' accounts of their
family's interactions, they began to reexamine the blame. Their guilt
began to give way to a realization that children with difficult temperaments demand higher degrees of parental supervision. They began to
reframe their parenting goal as successful socialization of whatever type
of child one had been given. Children with conduct problems simply
required different parenting skills. With this new mind-set, parents
were able to think more constructively about their child, focusing on
which parenting techniques would work best to bring out her or his
prosocial behaviors and personality strengths and which strategies
would decrease his or her aggression and noncompliance. Thus, the
focus of parents' attitudes gradually shifted from assigning blame for
their child's problem (and feeling guilt) to attempting to understand and
manage the behavior problems.

8.2.2. Finding "Magic Moon Dust"

While parents initially expressed guilt over their failure to control
their child's misbehaviors, as they began to learn new parenting strategies they reported feelings of excitement, even exhilaration, over the
prospect of improving their interactions with their children.

> Session 3
> Father: I have this weird feeling that after 3 weeks in this class, my son is
> instantly better. Through bad habits and exhaustion I was using too much
> power. So I backed off and we don't have the power struggles any more.

Most parents, after completing the first four programs (Play, Learning,
Praise, and Tangible Rewards), experienced a major shift in their perception of their children's behaviors. They began to notice and appreciate
their child's positive behaviors and deemphasize the negative.

Session 6
Mother: By keeping track of praises I was able to be aware of all the positive things he does. It is so easy to get bent up and think, "He can't do anything right." All of a sudden you start listening to yourself saying, "You did a nice job there. Thank you!" Once I started to be specific in my praises, I noticed how many areas he is really trying to do right. You start thinking, "He's capable. He's probably been doing this a lot longer than I was willing to listen or give him credit for."

Session 6
Father: Once it got into a more positive cycle and I had more patience because I wasn't getting all this negative stuff all the time, I found myself willing to put up with some shenanigans, not let him get away with it but also not go through the roof because I wasn't at the end of my rope after a day of many positives.

On reflection, it became obvious to us that the parenting techniques that we were teaching were all too often perceived by parents as "magic moon dust" that could cure all their child's problems. The immediate relief that they experienced as their child made initial improvements led them to believe that their child's problems would be easily solved. Moreover, they sometimes seemed to believe that these changes in their children's behavior would alleviate other family problems. They anticipated a "total cure." In this phase, parents did not consider the possibility that their child's behavior might regress or that improvement might cease at some point. Moreover, parents did not comprehend the long-term commitment and the sheer amount of work that would be necessary to sustain these initial improvements.

8.3. Phase II. Tempering the Dream

In the next phase, parents faced the fact that there are no magical solutions and realized that they would need to "temper the dream" by adjusting their hopes and expectations. Three categories were identified in the data as part of tempering the dream: "apparent setbacks," resistance, and "no quick fix."

8.3.1. Apparent Setbacks

Soon after parents started to apply what they were learning in the program, unexpected changes started to take place in the child's conduct problems, in the parents themselves, and in the family system. Some of these changes were in conflict with the parents' expectations for the program, resulting in anxiety and anger in some cases. Three common themes characterized these apparent setbacks: role reversal within sibling relationships, conflicted parenting, and child's regression despite parents' hard work.

Role reversal was evident when parents reported that as the target child's behavior improved, the behavior of the sibling (mostly the younger child) became more deviant.

Session 8
Mother: Our younger child, who has always been the one that's hard to get ready for bed, is cooperative lately. Boom! He's the first one ready because he knows if there's extra time, I'll play Legos with him. Now the older child, who has always been easy to get into bed, is dragging his feet. Try dragging a chunky 8-year-old up the stairs to bed.

As parents put into practice with the target child the strategies taught in the program, they observed that the other children in the family began demanding the same degree of attention, thus further taxing these parents' already depleted resources and energy. Often, the other children's demands took the form of noncompliance and deviance, with the result that parents felt more discouraged because they had made headway on one child's conduct problems only to have them surge elsewhere.

Conflicted parenting occurred when one partner participated actively in the program while the other parent did not participate, was critical of the program, or was invested in maintaining the status quo. These differences in level of participation led not only to debate as to the best way to handle the child's misbehavior, but also to conflicts within the couple's relationship. Thus, at this stage, the intervention seemed to some parents to increase marital stress. Conflicted parenting also operated in some cases in which a single parent had a former spouse, a boyfriend, or a grandparent involved in raising the child but not participating in the program.

Session 8
Mother: Now, what's happening is he goes to his father's house for one or two nights a week and his father doesn't reinforce him at all. And I tried to explain to him the sticker charts are not to be used as punishment, and he just sort of says, "Yeah, yeah, yeah, I know this stuff."

Regression, the third type of setback, occurred when the child's behavior seemed to regress despite the parents' hard work. Their hopes raised as a result of initial improvements, anticipating success and desperate for some relief, parents made no allowances for limited progress or for actual regression in the children's behavior. Therefore, when parents encountered regressions, their reaction was one of disbelief, depression, and even anger.

Session 9
Mother: In the last two weeks, we've had a 75 to 85% regression. Complete—well, almost complete—reversal to where she was before this class began.

I'm not certain why. I was really sick; maybe that had something to do with it. All of a sudden, out of the blue, she's had some real bad episodes, and last week it was every day. It's like we've never been in this class. And the time before that—up through Christmas—was wonderful. I mean both of us had to hold him down to get him dressed on Saturday, amidst screaming and kicking and spanking.

Session 9
Mother: I really feel that I give a lot. I see myself giving a lot of praise, a lot of attention, a lot of the right things. I know a lot of the times that I'm doing the right things, but then I get *so* burned out. I feel like I'm doing *so* much that I know is good and I'm not getting enough back. Sometimes I get so burned out and totally worn out. I'm tired of doing all these right things. I'm just tired of parenting.

These emotions arose from a perceived lack of congruence between the parent's hard work at implementing the program's strategies and the child's failure to improve—so much work, so little progress. In some cases, as shown in the next example, the parents felt that the children actively resisted their efforts to change the family dynamics.

Session 6
Mother: This morning I told him, "Well, you just did a really great job on your homework, I'm just real pleased, you just got it done, and like now you don't have to run." And he goes, "Yeah, yeah, right mom, yeah, yeah, right." And I'm getting mad. Almost a sarcastic feedback, like well, I've heard it several times in the past couple of weeks. It's almost like he's hip to the fact that I am praising him, it's like he doesn't buy it.

8.3.2. Resistance

In general, parents did not have realistic expectations concerning the demands the program would impose on them and their family life. They wanted and expected the program to lighten their burden, to decrease the amount of effort involved in parenting a child with conduct problems; instead, it was putting more demands on them, adding to the burden they felt. This was only for the short term, of course, but that was how most of them were focused. Along with anger at these setbacks, they expressed resistance when they discovered that favorable changes in their child's behavior could be brought about and maintained only to the extent that they were willing to continue investing time and energy in implementing the program; to some, this investment was excessive. Although most parents accepted the rationale of the program, during this phase many exhibited resistance to parts of the program, especially those parts that demanded extra effort. Frequently, this resistance was manifested in parents' failure to complete the weekly homework assignment. When asked about the homework, parents would give excuses such as lack of time, forgetting the assignment, too much stress at home and at work, procrastination, and difficulty being motivated.

Sometimes parents resisted homework assignments involving interactions with their children because they perceived their children as controlling. It was as though the parent did not want to do anything that would cede further control to the child. In cases in which the child was verbally abusive of the parent, parents were even less inclined to spend time with their child. There was no reinforcement for doing so.

> *Session 5*
> Mother: I feel like I am being held hostage some of the times by the kids, with some of the things we've tried. When I was doing the playtime with the kids, I began to feel abused in that I would always be the bad guy, and Laars would always be doing something to the bad guy. He loves this time, but he orders me around. He is using words: "Do what I tell you," "I am going to decide what we are gonna do today." "I hate you. You are stupid, Mommy, you are not nice . . ." So far, the videos said let the child lead the way, and he does not seem to want to do much more than have this real negative interaction. What it does to me is make me not want to do this playtime. For me there is no reward. The more I realize the right things to do, the more the wrong things loom huge to me. And I'm feeling really discouraged by that.

8.3.3. No Quick Fix

The combined effect of the setbacks and resistance was apparent in a deterioration of the "total cure" myth and a dissipation of the "magic moon dust" phase. Parents gradually came to understand that there was no quick fix or cure for their child's problems or for their family as a whole. It was not a matter of a "flaw" in their child that could be "fixed" like a broken arm or a faulty heart valve.

> *Session 13*
> Mother: I think we've seen them improve, but it'll vary. If things are going bad, they generally go bad all day. There are some days when nothing works and I can't say a single positive thing. But there are other days, and more of them when the kids are doing better. You can kind of tell when you wake him up. I'll go wake him up, I'll rub his back a little bit. If he wakes up rolls over and hugs me, I know it's a good morning. And if he says, "Leave me alone," it's going to be tough.

Parents realized that although their child's behavior would improve, as would their overall parent-child interaction, the child's temperament and associated problems were long-term. The chronic nature of the problems would continue to exact a heavy toll from parents, requiring them to monitor the child continuously. This acknowledgment of the duration of the child's problems constituted a change in parental perceptions, and it was necessary in order for them to make a long-term commitment both to the intervention and to the principles taught in the program.

Session 8
Father: I've had a couple of horrible weeks. I feel like I have to be "on" all the time. I think I have to be telling myself to just try and mellow out, and it's difficult.

8.4. Phase III. "Making the Shoe Fit"

In this phase of learning to cope more effectively with their children's problems, parents began a process of "making the shoe fit"—that is, tailoring the concepts shown in the standardized videotape examples to their own family situations and parenting style. This phase was a critical determinant of parents' degree of success in implementing the program. Data indicated that failure to tailor the program resulted in diminished success because of parents' inappropriate expectations, either for themselves or for their children. Two categories of "making the shoe fit" were identified in the data: understanding parenting techniques and generalizing parenting techniques.

8.4.1. Understanding Parenting Techniques

The analysis indicated that in general, parents acquired a good understanding of the rationale for the parenting principles and techniques presented in the videotapes. However, some difficulties were apparent concerning their understanding how to implement specific approaches in a realistic and age-appropriate manner.

For example, reinforcement menus were developed by some parents with inappropriate expectations and without concern for the child's developmental stage or the frequency and type of misbehavior. More specifically, parents demonstrated difficulties around the timing of the reward (i.e., how long the child should wait before getting the reward), the type of behaviors to choose for reinforcement, and the cost for each behavior (e.g., 2 points = sharing, 5 points = extra reading time, 25 points = visit to the zoo).

Another parenting technique that posed difficulties for many of these parents was reducing the number of commands and giving the child adequate opportunity to comply with a command. Having come to expect noncompliance, parents had compensated with frequent repetitions of their commands (chain commands). This had become a habit, almost a reflex, which they found difficult to stop.

Session 7
Father: I am the kind of a person that is very directive. I direct my son in almost everything he does, and so I am having a hard time dropping down the number of commands.

Issues of unrealistic expectations, failing to consider the child's developmental status or type of misbehavior, also arose with regard to implementation of Time Out. For example, some parents had a hard time finding an appropriate place for Time Out in their home, or at any rate gave this as an excuse for not using Time Out with their children. Others overused Time Out for child misbehaviors that should have been ignored or for behaviors that were actually age-appropriate. Sometimes it was difficult for parents to know which strategy (Command, Time Out, Ignore, Consequences, Distraction) should be used in response to a particular misbehavior or a new situation.

8.4.2. Generalizing Parenting Techniques

Data indicated that some parents, in the process of "making the shoe fit," had difficulties generalizing the particular parenting techniques shown in the videotape scenarios to other children, other problems, and other settings. They did not readily see how a given parenting strategy could be used with different behaviors across different age groups. For example, without help from the therapist, some parents could not take the concept of the Ignore technique, which is demonstrated on the videotape as a response to tantrums, and generalize its use to a response to whining and swearing.

Parents also expressed difficulties understanding how to use the techniques in different settings. They commonly struggled with the use of Time Out and Ignore in public settings, and with more than one child.

> Session 10
> Mother: He usually is just fine, but it's the minute that you get him into a store. Like yesterday at the store, he was going up to people, poking his hand and stopping them from moving, or grabbing them like grabbing women's skirts from behind. And the hard thing in the store you can't take him out and put him in the car for Time Out.

Interestingly, parents had less difficulty generalizing the techniques when their training involved group discussions. Presumably, the parent group sharing and problem solving provided a rich array of examples of parents applying the concepts in different situations, which helped enhance parents' ability to generalize the concepts—that is, to learn the skills.

8.5. Phase IV. Coping Effectively

In this phase of treatment, parents began to exhibit effective cognitive and emotional coping strategies: They could express empathy for their children's problems, understand their children's developmental needs, experience their own vulnerability without feeling victimized, and laugh at their own responses. As they discovered that they could cope successfully with the daily hassles of having a conduct-problem child, they gained confidence in themselves and in their ability to cope with future problems. In this phase, parents expressed the conviction that they would survive their children's and their own relapses. Having reframed their child's behavior problems in terms of temperament rather than malevolence or their own failure as parents, they became experts at managing and responding to their children's special needs, which allowed them to act as their children's advocates in the larger community. Four categories of coping effectively were identified in the data: coming to terms with the hard work, accepting and respecting their child and themselves, self-refueling, and getting support.

8.5.1. Coming to Terms with the Hard Work of Parenting

By this phase, parents had realized that they had "high-maintenance," temperamentally difficult children. They came to terms with the reality that their children's problems are chronic, characterized by the unpredictable relapses, constant vulnerabilities to changes in routine, and the emergence of new behavior problems whenever the children entered new settings such as school. They faced the fact that these problems require parents to invest an exorbitant amount of time and energy in the hard work of constantly anticipating, monitoring, and problem-solving, and that this investment would be required of them for many years. During this phase, parents were able to manage their anger and grief related to their hoped-for "ideal" child, to accept their child's difficulties, to appreciate their strengths, and to invest themselves in committed parenting.

> Session 15
> Mother: I'm continually watching at home: How can we avoid these problems? How can we avoid the activating event? How can I derail something before it explodes? Okay now, cool it down. They're getting excited. Let's break it up.

> Session 15
> Father: He still has these fits, but they are farther apart and less severe— not as violent as they used to be. He relapses, but they're still not like they used to be.

8.5.2. Accepting and Respecting Their Child and Themselves

In this phase, parents indicated empathy, understanding, and acceptance of their child's particular temperament and sensitivity to the child's developmental struggles. Part of gaining this empathy for the child was parents being able to see beyond their own frustration and anger, to understand the child's feelings and perspective.

> *Session 20*
> Father: You know, something we haven't talked about specifically in this parenting class, although it is in everything you've talked about, is respecting children and their space in the world. You know they should be treated as equal human beings—it doesn't mean you don't set limits and all that stuff, but it means you know that they're human beings and as deserving of respect as you are.

They accepted their child's need for independence and realized their child needed to have opportunities to learn from mistakes. They also understood the importance of their patience and support in the child's developmental process.

> *Session 20*
> Mother: In the last three weeks I've noticed a synthesis of all the sessions we've had, and me basically changing the way I interact with Hannah in a dramatic way—spontaneously. Now when I interact with her I tend to look at her eyes and I realize I can't remember my parents ever doing that. I'm giving her more space and time—more room to make mistakes, screw up, and make messes. I'm trying to give her more independence, when she wants to do something let her do it, rather than saying you're going to spill the milk all over the floor. It's fine if she spills the milk, she'll learn what happens and we've actually been getting on really well.

Coping effectively meant that parents not only had to come to understand and accept their child's temperament and difficulties, but also had to accept their own imperfections as parents. They no longer berated themselves for their anger and impatience, but saw their emotional responses as normal ones and understood their need to maintain personal self-control. In the next example, the father is able to stop his angry response, to see his daughter's viewpoint, and then to recognize her capacity to help him cope.

> *Session 20*
> Father: I went into the bathroom to get Sara to finish brushing her teeth and there was a puddle of water on the floor and a roll of wet toilet paper and I was angry and ready to lose it and said, "This is it!" as I threw the toilet paper. You know what she said? "Dad, don't talk to me like that. You know you can scare me." Normally she would have cried, but now I think she was thinking of my point of view.
> I said, "You're right, and I'm sorry. I'm real tired and it's wet in here." I felt saved by her.

8.5.3. Self-Refueling

Along with becoming more knowledgeable and confident in their parenting skills and more accepting of and able to manage their own emotions, coping parents also realized the importance of caring for themselves as individuals and couples. As the blame, guilt, fear, and anger subsided and the child's behavior improved, parents were able to get babysitters so that they could spend time away from the children. Parents expressed the view that taking time for themselves and being with their partners was a "refueling" process that allowed them to gain a more positive perspective and to maintain the energy they needed for coping with their child's problems.

Session 13
Mother: If I'm grading my kids for controlling their aggression and for compliance and good behavior, I need to ask myself, "How many times do I lose it?" "How am I doing in keeping my temper and my anger, and how well am I doing in rerouting my thinking when I'm short-circuiting?" I need to keep track of that and reward myself. Hey, it's okay to get an ice cream cone or treat yourself to a babysitter for an hour or buy a new blouse. Hey, it dawned on me that my behavior needs to be measured, too, since that's what we're really all discussing, how we can change to effect change in our children. Well, I even mentioned that to the kids and David was really cute, and said, "Well, Mom, we can move our sticker charts over on the refrigerator and make room for you too."

Gradually, parents also experienced some "refueling" through their children. As their efforts began to pay off, parents began to experience their children as reinforcing.

Session 14
Mother: I started in the mornings, instead of yelling at them to wake up because I had to go to work and rushing around, I wake them both up by giving them a back rub and then I wake them up real gently and they just love it. Now they come up to me and say,"Mom, we need positive strokes." About two weeks ago they came up when I was sitting and started rubbing my arm and said, "You need positive strokes, Mom." So they are reciprocating now, which I thought was really interesting.

8.5.4. Getting Support

During this phase, parents no longer felt isolated and stigmatized because of their child's problems and their own parenting, but rather had found support. The parents indicated that the parent group provided a safe place where they could be honest about their difficulties and allow themselves to be vulnerable. Often, to their surprise, they found that the other parents all had had similar experiences and felt similar emotions. Thus, the parent group provided a much-needed sense of connection with other parents.

Session 14
Father: Out of all the thousands of people that you meet from day to day and you have dealings with them, I feel very fortunate to have this class and this

group of people that has really enlightened and enriched my life. And, ah, it's going to make me a better person from knowing everyone here.

Session 24
Father: Even when this program is finished, I will always think about this group in spirit.

Session 18
Mother: This group's all sharing—and it's people that aren't judging me, that are taking risks and saying, "Ellen, have you tried this? Or considered you are off track?" You know we're all putting a lot into this and my feeling is the more we as individuals put into it, the more we get out of it. It's the turning point—every class has been building stronger and stronger. I know we're going to make it—I'm going to make it—the boys are going to make it. The three of us are going to live happily ever after–we're going to have our problems.

8.6. Discussion

We had known from our quantitative research that generally families would show significant posttreatment reductions in depression, stress, and anger and more positive parenting interactions with their children. In this qualitative research, we were interested not in treatment *outcome* but in treatment *processes*. The process experienced by the parents who were enrolled in this videotape parent training program was one of gradually gaining the knowledge and control to effectively cope with the stresses resulting from having a conduct-problem child. But this overview of the process as seen in terms of its end point—an overview that might have been inferred after all, from our earlier quantitative data—does not adequately reflect the nature of the process. As this study revealed, on their trajectory toward effective coping, parents went through considerable struggles and setbacks. Far from being a linear process, it involved many up and downs, surges and reversals, and although the outcome was indeed positive, the same was not always true of the process at any given moment.

This study revealed that the process parents undergo while in treatment involves radically different phases. This understanding of the process is vital for those of us involved in intervention with these families, for if we can anticipate these phases, we can not only prepare ourselves to deal with them, but also prepare our clients for them. For example, we can help temper their expectations, help them understand and cope with resistance, and provide them with strategies for countering their self-blame or discouragement when setbacks occur. Moreover, it is important to remember that from *within* the process, that is, from the standpoint of those who are undergoing therapy, a positive trajectory may not be evident. In fact, at many points, parents could see only that the behavior had not substantially changed and their own role was as difficult as ever. If anything, in light of the raised expectations that are the natural result of being in a treatment program, their situation seemed to them worse and they felt more discouraged.

As hoped, we learned a great deal from this qualitative study about the particular emotional experiences and cognitive restructuring during treatment that are responsible for parents' new ability to cope by the end of the program. Experiencing new hope, having those hopes dashed by setbacks and regression, then experiencing anger at the child, at oneself, and at the therapists; experiencing empathy and support, moving from discouragement, even despair, to recommitment—these were key emotional steps in the process. Reframing the child's behavior problems as a matter of temperament and developmental phase; abandoning blame and guilt as a model and substituting the need for special parenting skills; incorporating the ideas of self-care and ongoing support as elements in one's own stability and well-being; arriving at a view of oneself as competent, though imperfect, rather than a victim or a failure—these are the cognitive shifts that we discovered. We found that in general, these emotional and cognitive changes occurred in a certain sequence and were interwoven in complex ways, which suggests that they cannot be rushed—for instance, parents were not ready to empathize with and respect their child until they had first gone through the "tempering the dream" phase; they were not motivated to generalize the techniques ("making the shoe fit") until they had first gone through the stages of unrealistic hopes and disillusionment. Those of us involved in parent training need to be attuned to these stages in the treatment process. Our empathy and our effectiveness depend upon it.

9. Three-Year Follow-Up: Moving beyond the Intervention— "The Work Continues"

The purpose of this third qualitative study was to explore through interviews the subjective experience of parents in the 3 years following completion of the parent training program. Our quantitative data obtained 3 years posttreatment indicated sustained improvements in parenting behaviors and child behaviors (within normal limits) for two thirds of the sample; however, 25% of children were reported by their parents and teachers as continuing to have behavior problems that put them in the clinic range for aggressive behaviors. But these numerical data did not help us understand what meaning these parents assigned to their own parenting efforts and their child's successes or failures. It did not tell us how families had coped with any child relapses that had occurred since completing the intervention, how they felt about their child's successes or problem behaviors and their progress in managing them, how they were coping with school-related difficulties. It told us nothing about how they perceived their experience in the treatment program in retrospect, and what it was like to end treatment. We were interested in the relationships within the family and the family's relationships with the community: Did these parents continue to experience a sense of isolation or stigma because of having a difficult child? We were especially anxious to learn whether the cognitive restructuring and emotional adjustments that had occurred over the process of treatment had been maintained. These questions led us to our third qualitative study, which is currently in progress.

9.1. Participants

We randomly selected for interview a subset of 10 parents who represented both single-parent and married families. We plan to continue to interview more families at longer intervals posttreatment. In these interviews, parents talked about their fears regarding the ending of the parent group program 3 years earlier.

> Mother: My immediate feeling was being cut loose. I felt very vulnerable. It was scary because it had been so wonderful to be with the other parents. Because that was the first time I had ever been around parents that had kids like mine. That was so reinforcing. I remember feeling terribly vulnerable when I left and being afraid that I wouldn't be able to continue . . . I wouldn't remember what to do. I was nervous. Over time I realized I had incorporated a lot of the basic stuff.

Parents feared that once the program was over they would not be able to maintain their efforts or would not know what to do when a new behavior problem came up. Their feelings of vulnerability returned. They felt worried about relapses and were uncertain of their own skills. Parents who had not seen the dramatic changes in behavior that others had seen were worried that their child's behavior would not continue to improve without the help of the group sessions.

> Mother: I was afraid we couldn't maintain the changes without the support of the group and having to go in and report each week. I felt a sense of loss of the group, because we had developed really good relationships and I knew that I would miss those people.

The ending of the parenting groups represented a loss of support, not just from the therapists who had provided assistance in troubleshooting behavior problems but also from the parent group who had provided so much moral support. How did these parents cope with the loss of support, the challenges posed by their children's behavior, the sense of vulnerability? The qualitative data gathered in these interviews revealed a number of common themes in parents' subjective experience posttreatment, themes that fell into three categories: parenting attitudes and behavior, relationships with other parents, and parents' sense of self.

9.2. Parenting Attitudes and Behavior

9.2.1. Taking It Moment by Moment

All the parents told stories of the successes and improvements that had been made in their children's social skills over the subsequent years. In many cases, improvements were slow in coming.

> Mother: It took a long time for the principles in the program to really have an effect. The first year afterwards, things were still very hard—to travel, to go somewhere else, the level of aggression was still very high for her. It takes a long time to get results—like three years. Now you can see the results.

Yet rather than feeling frustrated at the slow pace of change, these parents felt proud and confident of their own and their children's accomplishments. Their newfound pride has, it appears, two sources: First, they had learned to look for and celebrate the positive in their children's behavior.

> Mother: I have learned with these kids to take each moment by moment. I used to look at the day as a 24-hour unit—now I celebrate the wonderful moments with him when they come. And we have more wonderful moments all the time.
>
> Mother: Someone gave me a journal, but I hate to write because I do so much of it at work. Instead I record the neat things that happen with my children, and there are times I'll go and read it. For example, times when my kids are really insightful or funny or when they do something I feel good about, I record it. I've been doing that for three years now and it's wonderful.

They noted the contrast between this perspective on their children and their perspective before treatment.

> Mother: I think what can happen is you could be so overwhelmed with the intensity of the difficult times that you don't see the good times. I know that was happening when I went to the parenting clinic.

A second and more complex source of pride in their children's successes arose from their own newfound sensitivity to their children's temperament and emotional state. The interviews reflected parents who had learned to read the cues in a situation and to decide what the optimal approach would be. To use a metaphor, over time they had become sensitive barometers to their children's reactions and had decided to adapt to the weather, rather than disregard the weather or act as though it were different.

> Mother: I don't make as many plans. I sort of wait and see how the day is going.
> Mother: We really try to look at the right time for doing something. He's supposed to read to me every night, but I can sense if it's not going to be successful and he needs to be doing something else. At one time I might have forced him—but now my motto is "seize the moment."

9.2.2. Becoming a Strategist: See the Big Picture

Related to their new determination and ability to adapt to their child's state-of-the-moment, these parents had maintained their grasp on the principles behind behavior management and had refined their sense of how to apply the skills within their family. In short, they had become "expert strategists."

> Mother: It's the ability to first analyze, then internalize some of those parenting coping skills that make life easier.
> Mother: We're more skilled, which helps a lot. I think skills with high-maintenance kids are worth their weight in gold because it's still tough with skills. I can pull out things such as charts and I know ways of distancing the battle. Things are better in that respect.

They were able to anticipate potential problems with their children and to head them off with preventive approaches; they had parental "radar" constantly on the alert. As one parent put it, they had become "constantly vigilant" so as to help their children stay out of trouble. They had learned how to structure each day so as to increase the likelihood that their children would behave positively and to decrease the potential for misbehavior.

This did not mean they let their children do whatever they wanted—quite the contrary. Most parents found that they needed to structure their children's time, to establish clear expectations of what was expected and clear descriptions of the consequences for not complying. Attending to their children's need for behavioral guidance required not only vigilance but also steadfastness and rigor.

> Mother: He is such a volatile kid, I have found that I have to be incredibly structured. Everything is: "If you do this, then you can do this." You know, "When you follow the rules this week, then on Friday you get to rent a tape," which is a big reward for him. It's constant: "When you get your shoes on in the morning then you can watch TV." It works. For example, to get him into bed at night, I had to develop a set of structured steps, and now he's incorporated them so it's not an issue.
> Mother: I have to be constantly vigilant, keep ahead of him because he acts before he thinks.

Like the long-range planner, parents seemed to have developed a wide-angle view—to be cognizant of their long-range goals and to choose the most effective parenting strategy in accordance with not only the desired behavior but also the larger goal.

> Mother: I try to take more time for him now. My housekeeping suffers because I'm a single parent and I can't do everything. But in the big picture, you know, the messy house doesn't matter that much.

This ability to be a strategist requires that parents see the big picture as well as be attuned to the moment-by-moment interactions. As one parent put it, she now had a blueprint for decision making that helped her feel in control, on track.

> Mother: I can head off probably 80% of the problems with the parenting techniques I learned. I have a set of principles now that I work from—a blueprint.

9.2.3. Coping with Relapses

All the parents talked about times when their children had relapses in their behavior. It was common for them to feel a sense of panic and even fear that all their prior efforts had been useless. Yet they described a variety of ways of coping with these relapses.

> Mother: I remember this time my son got into this horrible cycle—worse than before we went to the parenting clinic. I was afraid all the gains we had made were lost—we were in a negative cycle and I was panicked. I was resentful because I had done so much for him, like taking him to miniature golf and McDonald's, and then when we got home he went crazy because there was something he didn't like. He was very destructive—throwing things everywhere because he couldn't get what he wanted. But then I realized he can only focus on the feeling of the moment. Later I also realized he had been good all day—that it was only one night.

In this example, the parent dealt with her reaction to her son's relapse by reflecting on his temperament and recognizing that he is an impulsive child who cannot focus on his earlier pleasure at the positive experiences with her. Once she reminded herself that her child can deal only with the feeling of the moment, in this instance anger, she was able to diffuse some of her feelings of anger toward him for his ungratefulness. Second, she placed the event in context, objectified the situation, realizing that for most of the day his behavior had been good. Many of the parents talked about their conscious cognitive work at deemphasizing the negative moments with their children and focusing on the positive times.

Third, parents coped with relapses by reframing them as normal or natural. By understanding that relapses were to be expected, they were better able to prepare themselves to deal with them as well as to decrease their panic and fear. They also reframed the way they perceived these regressions by treating them as "learning experiences."

> Mother: I remember that learning is a process of making mistakes, and a little kid doesn't know everything you do as an adult. Sometimes this is so obvious, but when you live every day with a little character that's running around it is easy to forget.

Yet another coping strategy was reframing the relapses as challenges that, with their newfound sense of competence as parents, they felt prepared to meet.

> Mother: My life is more stressed now because of working full time and the step kids moving in. But the way I feel about parenting is that I know what to do, whereas before I'd be so frustrated and discouraged and think nothing would ever change.

Having learned new skills and behavioral principles, they began to feel optimistic and competent with their parenting approaches, especially as they saw improvements in their children's behavior problems. They felt confident that they had the skills to do what was necessary to help teach their child some new social behavior.

> Mother: Now when he relapses, I just assume there will be a way to problem-solve it. And I have ideas instead of going around finding books everywhere. Like I'll go to the teacher and say, "Okay we need to work out a plan," and I feel like it's manageable.

Some parents turned to the parenting clinic for support when their children relapsed. Paradoxically, this revived and strengthened their sense of competence, for they perceived it as a resource they knew how to utilize—one of their strategies for coping.

> Mother: His behavior went downhill really fast when we separated. So I went to the parenting clinic, as it felt like a place to go for resources and support, and it's really worked. I've had to eat all my words about my fears— I guess we have more skills and my child has more skills now.

Involvement in school activities was another skill that parents mentioned.

> Mother: There is no doubt that my being active in PTSA helped our kid, and you don't have to be working in the classroom, but if you're working outside the home it does behoove you to find a way to be active in school activities so that they recognize you're going to be there. I call up if he gets a demerit slip and his story isn't consistent with the writing on the slip. I call up and find out the teacher's perspective, and I write a note. One time I wrote a note to the principal that resulted in a meeting of the recess teachers. That in the long run supports my son and other kids. You need to know what is happening in school.

Sometimes parents even talked about their own relapses and how they were able to get themselves back on the program.

> Mother: My husband and I used to fight over how to handle our daughter. In the group, we agreed on how to handle her behavior. I had to learn to

stop interrupting and correcting my husband even if I disagreed. Well, yes-
terday I didn't support him, and he was really upset with me. So this goes
deeper than parenting, more about loyalty and remembering to be supportive to the other.

Other parents talked about how they had attempted to slow down the
pace of life for themselves and build in restful times so that they are
"refueled" and ready for the relapses when they happen.

> Mother: I've been divorced for six years now, and I used to think I had to
> be doing all these social things when I didn't have the kids. Now at least one
> night a week I come home, read the paper, do laundry, and rest—I try to use
> that time so that when my kids are with me I have the energy for them and
> can give them attention. I wouldn't be able to give them the attention they
> need if I didn't take time for myself. So that's one means of support for me.

9.3. Relationships with Other Parents

9.3.1. Moving Forward: Building Networks and Finding Support

All the parents we interviewed talked about the importance of their
parent training group and the tremendous support that the group had
given them. Just knowing that other parents had children who were also
challenging and difficult to manage helped to "normalize" their problems, to take away the stigma. Hearing those parents' week-by-week
struggles with their children's behavior helped defuse their guilt, anger,
and frustration. Over the subsequent years, these memories of the other
families in their group provided a kind of mental relationship that
helped them to survive the tough moments of self-doubt and the isolation.

Because of this positive experience in the parent training group, all
the parents we interviewed had attempted to get involved in or even set
up other parent support groups in subsequent years. Several parents
had become involved in CHAD, an organization for parents of attention-
deficit disorder children; others had joined school parent organizations;
one had started her own parent support group in her community; another joined the adoptive parents support group; another had joined a
Parents' Corps of Little League; several others continued to meet with
parents from their group and to call them on the phone for support.

> Mother: My husband talks about missing the group. More than me be-
> cause I keep in touch with more people that give me feedback. But now that
> we are going to ADD group, that's nice for my husband.

In general, parents seemed to derive the most support from other parents who openly acknowledged the difficulties of parenting and were
nonjudgmental.

> Mother: I've hooked up with other parents that have children like mine and it's been incredibly helpful. One friend of mine has kids just like mine and we have our club, "The Dark Side of Erma Bombeck," because you have to have humor in this. We have one rule that you can call any time. She and I have really gotten ourselves through this. And she's the one I talk to most often. But some other parents who have adopted kids, I talk to them too.

In addition, many parents had kept up their connections with the therapists by periodically calling about a concern. In some cases, this was only once or twice a year; in others, it was more often. Regardless of the frequency of contact, knowing that the parenting clinic was available appeared to provide important psychological and emotional support.

> Mother: I keep in touch with the therapist at the clinic by phone. So I'm not really feeling the loss. That's been positive. I feel like there's continuity and I still see it as a resource. I've stayed close to the people in the class.
> Mother: When I've been frustrated and not able to solve problems, I call up the parenting clinic, and I felt like there's this forever, underlying support there.

Almost all the families requested follow-up sessions or a refresher course. They saw this supplementary training as a helpful way to troubleshoot new issues as the children grew older.

> Mother: I think for these type of kids and bumbling parents trying to deal with this it would be nice to have follow-ups or refresher classes. I think we hit the same issues as the children get older, only at an upgraded level.

9.3.2. Dealing with Isolation and Stigma

One of the few negative notes in these parents' accounts of the years since the intervention was the rejection they felt from parents of well-behaved children.

> Mother: The hardest thing for me is the judgment of other people. I grew up being well liked, and now all these people are passing judgment on me as a bad person because of my kids' behavior.

All had continued to experience the pain of other parents refusing to let their children play together. All still felt judged by other parents even though their children were behaving much better at home and at school.

> Mother: Our neighbors won't let their kids play with my children because they think we're horrible people. One thing for me that has been particularly hard is the messages I've gotten from other parents at school, much more than neighbors and stuff. I mean the neighbors come over to my house and realize I'm an okay person, that I'm not one of those dysfunctional single mothers. But at school those parents really don't want their children playing with my children.

Even worse, these parents continued to experience alienation from their extended family members. They felt misunderstood and unsupported, which led to anger; at the same time, they felt embarrassed about their children's behavior. These complex feelings led them to avoid contact with other family members.

> Mother: The messages I get today are that I am a bad parent because of the way my kids act. And I know deep down I'm not. But when you get these messages, I get them from my family, my extended family! I have given up going to family reunions because my kids are always the ones in trouble and it's not worth it. It's too hard.

Their anger about their family's lack of support seemed to have lessened, however, as they realized it was due to a lack of understanding. They seemed to have moved beyond their anger, having learned not to position themselves in vulnerable situations and to look for their support elsewhere.

> Mother: I get no support from my family with this issue. They just don't get it. It's like if you haven't had cancer you don't know what it's really like. I'm convinced some of my closest friends think it's my fault—they could do better. I've wanted to say so many times, "You walk in my shoes and then make a judgment." I think the big thing is having friends who have kids like mine.

9.4. Parents' Sense of Self

9.4.1. Maintaining and Building Self-Esteem

As they reflected on their experience in the parenting program, these parents talked about their experience as a kind of "crossroads" or watershed, a time when they moved from feeling victimized and helpless to realizing that there were ways of coping more effectively with their child's problems.

> Mother: I look back on my experience with the parenting clinic as a crossroads. I have told people, "I shudder to think where we would be now without having gone through that." I felt such a profound sense of failure as a parent. I didn't know what to do. I was going to let him go and live with his dad forever. I couldn't handle it.
>
> Mother: In the beginning we didn't have the skills. And that isn't to say we aren't intelligent. We are both highly educated, hard-working people; it's just that we didn't have the skills, and now we know how to use them.

One of the themes from these interviews 3 years after treatment that was markedly different from our earlier interviews while the parents were still in the program was the parents' emphasis on conscious efforts to maintain and build their self-esteem. In the face of the feelings of blame and stigma from extended family and other parents, these parents had to work hard at reaffirming their own worth.

> Mother: My friend and I who have children who are more challenging, we laugh at other parents who think they're such good parents when they're in fact the ones who have really easy kids. I think one of the biggest challenges when you have this kind of child is to feel okay as a parent—because you do not get those messages from other people. That's just the reality.

For these mothers, a key strategy for maintaining a strong sense of self was periodically distancing themselves literally and figuratively from their conduct-problem child.

> Mother: I'm not a natural mother—so I needed help to learn the skills, and it's still a lot of work. Getting some space and time for myself helps immensely. Talking to friends and getting away from the children helps me regroup.
> Mother: I think he needs other adults in his life besides me. I think he needs time away as much as I need time away.

This theme is distinct from the "refueling" discussed earlier. Whereas the purpose of refueling was to renew one's resources as a parent (i.e., so as to be able to give more to the child), here the emphasis was on time apart as a means of maintaining and strengthening the parent's sense of identity as something other than a parent. These parents recognized the importance of having a strong sense of self apart from parenthood in order to function well as a parent.

> Mother: I still feel ownership and get embarrassed by him. That's one place I'd like to work at. I need a little more separateness . . . . Even though I know it isn't true, I still feel that if I was a better parent he would be better. I know that isn't true, but my gut still says it is, so I wish I could have a little bit more gut distance from him so I could feel a little happier myself. If I got that distance I'd deal with him better and it would all work better, but I haven't been able to make that jump yet.
> Mother: I have to create my own reward system. I realized I have to establish an identity other than parenthood. I mean I very much identify myself as a single parent, but I take great pride in my work. I go off with other women when I don't have the kids.

This literal and figurative distancing, a form of establishing boundaries, allowed these mothers to depersonalize their child's behavior problems and to put them in a wider developmental context.

> Mother: When he misbehaves, I am able to keep it in the context of a learning experience for him, a need for me to be consistent and to think. I ask myself, "What does this really mean? Is this something I should just let ride? How significant is it?" I don't blame myself now.

9.4.2. Grieving, Accepting, and Changing Expectations

Three years after treatment, while these children's behavior problems had improved (according to teacher and parent reports they were within normal range) on standardized measures, they were still very much a challenge to manage.

> Mother: He's still volatile. He can escalate from zero to hundred in the snap of a finger and be that way for hours. He will throw furniture and take the room apart and totally wipe me out. Because I came from a mellow, laid-back family—and he's got a different temperament. He cannot wait one minute for dinner or anything.

Parents still talked about what they had thought their parenting experiences would be like in comparison with the reality. As had been true in our earlier interviews, there was a sense of parents grieving over the hoped-for child, the harmonious home life, the easy road.

> Mother: You know, you grow up thinking you are going to be a certain type of parent—and I had wonderful parents. Well, you know I've had to learn that in our family we're not going to sit around the table and have wonderful discussions—they cannot sit still for more than five minutes.
> Mother: Parenting is work. I wish it would be more fun and less work.
> Mother: I still put a lot of time into parenting and probably a lot more than I have the energy for or a lot more than most people, but now I'm enjoying it a lot more, that's the difference. But it takes a lot of time.
> Mother: I still want to be a sweet, nice mom—like Donna Reed. Why do I have to speak sharply—unless I go to him and say his name and get his attention he won't have heard me.

As these examples reveal, grieving over the hoped-for child and hoped-for home life also implies the loss of a certain hoped-for sense of self as parent. The conduct-problem child challenges a parent's sense of competence; these parents had to adjust their expectations of themselves as well as their child.

But balancing this theme of loss was a strong theme of acceptance. As mentioned earlier, parents had come to accept their children's temperament and therefore viewed their behavior differently.

> Mother: He used to be out of control all the time, almost daily with him. Well, now it happened maybe twice a year, or three times. Other people would come in and say he was totally outrageous, but I don't consider it totally outrageous. I have a different standard of what outrageous is than if I had my nieces and nephews as children.

With this acceptance of their child came greater acceptance of themselves as parents—self-respect and, at times, celebration of self for having made the necessary accommodations.

> Mother: I think I have had to do a lot of grieving about these children not being the kids I thought I would have. But I feel a bit better about me as a parent today. I don't feel great, because, you know, this culture measures parenting in terms of how your child behaves and my kids do not get high scores in that area . . . but it's so much better now.
> Mother: I have the handles I need to help him, but I think we're going to

have a hard life along the road. I don't see it ever being easy. I don't think he is going to have an easy life. He just doesn't have the temperament to have an easy life. Yes, I wished for that and I still wish for that, and I wish there was a cure but I don't think there is. It is better now than it was.

Mother: This indicates how far I've come. Last summer another woman and myself took eight kids camping, and five of them were on Ritalin. That was so empowering for me. First of all, as women to be able to go camping . . . second, that we're taking eight kids and five of them challenging kids, and we did great. So I guess that's a real measure that I'm feeling a lot better about being a parent.

9.5. Discussion

Our third qualitative study indicated that generally parents are coping well, are maintaining their parenting skills, and are feeling optimistic and in control of the situation. This is in contrast to our interviews 3 years earlier, which were full of themes of blame, loss of control, and helplessness. Parents no longer felt "under siege" by their children; they had taken charge. Nonetheless, the interviews indicated that children's behavior was still problematic and that parents were having to devote a great deal of mental, physical, and emotional energy providing an optimal environment for their temperamentally difficult children and in maintaining their self-esteem.

Mother: I hope that we one day can start operating from automatic and it doesn't take so much time and effort. I know parenting is always going to take a lot of effort, but I wish it didn't have to be such focus. But I have an idea for what to do—that's probably a real important thing.

Largely, this work was being done without the support of extended family, parents of older children in their children's classrooms, or their teachers.

The theory that emerged from our qualitative research on these ten families is that despite continuing stigmatization and stresses in managing ongoing child behavior problems at home and school, parents were still coping and had maintained a sense of competence—in fact, more so than immediately posttreatment. They had developed emotional and cognitive coping strategies to manage problem situations. Such coping strategies involved "seeing the big picture" and focusing on the long-range goals and overall positive improvements in the child rather than the moment-to-moment, specific negative behaviors; reading their children's behavioral cues and anticipating their reactions; reframing child behavior relapses as normal; organizing their daily routines so as to bring out the best in their child; building supportive parent networks; and promoting their own self-acceptance. These data imply that one of the most powerful ways to help these parents is not to focus exclusively on child behavior improvements, but to focus as well on their ability to normalize their experience, to adjust their expectations, and to self-refuel. We are currently continuing this study with a larger representation of families 3–5 years posttreatment in order to determine whether these patterns hold true. It is important that we interview families whose children are doing well at home and school as well as those whose parents and teachers are still reporting child-conduct problems that have reverted to pretreatment levels. By continuing this study, we hope to learn more about the meaning of coping for these families—that is, how some families were able to move from feeling helpless to believing in their ability to cope with their difficult children and stressful lives while others were not coping well.

10. Conclusion

What have we learned from these three studies that we did not know from our quantitative research? In each of the three studies, we have seen the importance of understanding parents' subjective realities (e.g., feeling victimized or helpless) as well as understanding context (e.g., ripple effects involving teachers and community responses) in order to give enhanced meaning to parents' decisions and actions. Each of the three studies has shown us a different advantage of qualitative research. For example, the first study helped us grasp the gestalt of the child's conduct problems—namely, the child as tyrant, the sense of victimization experienced by parents, the isolation and stigmatization of the family. From this study there emerged the theory of learned helplessness regarding families with conduct-problem children. The second study helped us understand the processes families experience during treatment as they gain knowledge and control, resist new ideas, cope with setbacks, experience a support network of parents, and arrive at a new view of themselves as competent. Here, we found a conceptual framework of four phases that families will experience while engaged in treatment. Our third study is helping us to refine this theory regarding parents' coping strategies as we examine how they maintain their sense of competence in the face of relapses (in some cases, to pretreatment levels) and continuing stigmatization. This qualitative research using grounded theory methods has fleshed out our quantitative studies with meaning by providing a theoretical framework through which we can interpret and, in turn, test our quantitative data.

These qualitative studies not only enhance our understanding but also have important implications for treatment. The first study suggests the importance of treatment programs that enhance social support by involving fathers and teachers and that reduce stigmatization by creating new supportive networks of parents with similar children. The second study helps therapists not only to anticipate phases that parents will be likely to experience during parent training, but also to prepare families for them. The third study suggests possible ways to broaden our interventions so that our support extends beyond training parents in parenting skills—for example, by preparing families for what lies ahead with their children, by encouraging their efforts to share the burden of responsibility through supportive groups and friendships, and by emphasizing aspects of the intervention that promote self-care, self-acceptance, and empowerment. Short-term efforts are clearly insufficient: We need to educate society at large in order to reduce the stigmatization and isolation that these families face in their day-to-day encounters.

> Mother: The challenges keep changing and with different kids, but now I know ways to attack each one as it comes up. I don't think anymore when old things come up again, "God! we failed," or, "I thought we had taken care of that, it didn't work." I don't look at it that way; rather, it's just going to be challenges all the way, and we'll just keep applying what we have learned.

The challenges certainly continue for them and for the therapeutic community.

ACKNOWLEDGMENTS

This research was supported by the NIH National Center for Nursing Research Grant No. 5 RO1 NR01075-10 and to National Institute of Mental Health ADAMHA Research Scientist Development Award Level II No. 1 KO2 MH00988-03. Thanks to Dianna Brehm for qualitative interviews with families at follow-up and especially to Deborah Woolley Lindsay for her review, feedback, and critical insights concerning this chapter. Correspondence concerning this chapter should be sent to Carolyn Webster-Stratton, Parenting Clinic, Box 354801, School of Nursing, University of Washington, Seattle, WA 98195.

11. References

Abidin, R. R. (1993). *Parenting stress manual*. Virginia: Pediatric Psychology Press.

Abramson, L. Y., Seligman, M. E. P., & Teasdale, J. D. (1978). Learned helplessness in humans: Critique and reformulation. *Journal of Abnormal Psychology, 87*, 49–74.

Achenbach, T. M. & Edelbrock, C. S. (1991). *Manual for Child Behavior Checklist and Revised Child Behavior Profile*. Burlington, VT: University Associates in Psychiatry.

Bandura, A. (1982). Self-efficacy mechanism in human agency. *American Psychologist, 37*, 122–147.

Bandura, A. (1985). *Social foundations of thought and action: A social cognitive theory*. Englewood Cliffs, NJ: Prentice-Hall.

Bandura, A. (1989). Human agency in social cognitive theory. *American Psychologist, 44*, 1175–1184.

Beck, A. T. (1972). *Depression: Causes and treatment*. Philadelphia: University of Pennsylvania Press.

Beck, C. T. (1990). Qualitative research: Methodologies and use in pediatric nursing. *Issues in Comprehensive Pediatric Nursing, 13*, 193–201.

Berger, P. L., & Luckman, T. (1966). *The social construction of reality: A treatise in the sociology of knowledge*. Garden City, NY: Doubleday.

Clarke, L. (1992). Qualitative research: Meaning and language. *Journal of Advanced Nursing, 17*, 243–252.

Dumas, J. E., & Wahler, R. G. (1985). Indiscriminate mothering and contextual factors in aggressive–oppositional child behavior: "Damned if you do and damned if you don't." *Journal of Abnormal Child Psychology, 13*, 1–17.

Eyberg, S., & Ross, A. (1978). Assessment of child behavior problems: The validation of a new inventory. *Journal of Clinical Psychology, 16*, 113–116.

Folkman, S., & Lazarus, R. S. (1988). Coping as a mediator of emotion. *Journal of Personality and Social Psychology, 54*(3), 466–475.

Folkman, S., Lazarus, R. S., Dunkel-Schetter, C., DeLongis, A., & Gruen, R. J. (1986). Dynamics of stressful encounter: Cognitive appraisal, coping, and encounter outcomes. *Journal of Personality and Social Psychology, 50*, 992–1003.

Forgatch, M. S., Patterson, G. R., & Skinner, M. (1988). A mediational model for the effect of divorce on antisocial behavior in boys. In E. M. Hetherington & J. D. Aresteh (Eds.), *Impact of divorce, single parenting, and step-parenting on children* (pp. 135–154). Hillsdale, NJ: Erlbaum Associates.

Furey, W. H., & Forehand, R. (1985). What factors are associated with mothers being more subjective and less objective in evaluating their clinic-referred child's behavior? Unpublished manuscript.

Glaser, B. (1978). *Advances in the methodology of grounded theory: Theoretical sensitivity*. Mill Valley: Sociological Press.

Glaser, B., & Strauss, A. (1967). *The discovery of grounded theory: Strategies for qualitative research* New York: Aldine.

Gortner, S., & Schultz, P. (1988). Approaches to nursing science methods. *Image, 20*, 22–23.

Guba, E. G. (1981). Criteria for assessing the trustworthiness of naturalistic inquiries. *Educational and Technology Journal, 29*, 75–92.

Hollingshead, A. B., & Redlich, F. C. (1958). *Social class and mental illness*. New York: John Wiley.

Hutchinson, S. (1986). Grounded theory: The method. In P. L. Munhall & C. J. Oiler (Eds.), *Nursing research—A qualitative perspective* (pp. 11–130). Norwalk CT: Appleton-Century-Crofts.

Kofta, M., & Sedek, G. (1989). Repeated failure: A source of helplessness or a factor irrelevant to its emergence? *Journal of Experimental Psychology: General, 118*, 3–12.

Leininger, M. (1985). Nature, rationale, and importance of qualitative research methods in nursing. In M. M. Leininger (Ed.), *Qualitative research methods in nursing*. Toronto: Grune & Stratton; Harcourt, Brace, Jovanovich.

Lincoln, Y. S., & Guba, E. G. (1985). *Naturalistic inquiry*. Beverly Hills: Sage Publications.

Locke, H. J. & Wallace, K. M. (1959). Short marital adjustment and prediction tests: Their reliability and validity. *Marriage and Family Living. 21*, 251–255.

Maier, S. F., & Seligman, M. E. P. (1976). Learned helplessness: Theory and evidence. *Journal of Experimental Psychology, 105*, 3–46.

Maiuro, R. D., Vitaliano, P. P., & Cohn, T. S. (1987). A brief measure for the assessment of anger and aggression. *Journal of Interpersonal Violence, 2*, 251–255.

Mikulincer, M., & Casopy, T. (1986). The conceptualization of helplessness: A phenomenological structural analysis. *Motivation and Emotion, 10*, 263–277.

Miller, I., & Norman, W. (1979). Learned helplessness in humans: A review and attribution-theory model. *Psychological Bulletin, 86*, 93–118.

Patterson, G. R. (1982). *Coercive family process*. Eugene, OR: Castalia Press.

Sanday, P. (1983). The ethnographic paradigm(s). In J. Van Maanen (Ed.), *Qualitative methodology* (pp. 19–35). Beverly Hills: Sage Publications.

Sandelowski, M. (1986). The problem of rigor in qualitative research. *Advances in Nursing Science, 8*(3), 27–37.

Schaughency, E. A., & Lahey, B. B. (1985). Mothers' and fathers' perceptions of child deviance: Roles of child behavior, parental depression, and marital satisfaction. *Journal of Consulting and Clinical Psychology, 53*, 718–723.

Seidel, J. V., Kjolseth, R., & Seymour, E. (1988). *The Ethnograph*. Littleton, CO: Qualis Research Associates.

Seligman, M. E. P. (1975). *Helplessness: On depression, development, and death*. San Francisco: Freeman.

Spiegelberg, H. (1976). *The phenomenological movement*, Vols. I & II. The Hague: Martinus Nijhoff.

Spitzer, A., Webster-Stratton, C., & Hollinsworth, T. (1991). Coping with conduct-problem children: Parents gaining knowledge and control. *Journal of Clinical Child Psychology, 20*(4), 413–427.

Strauss, A. L. (1987). *Qualitative analysis for social scientists*. Cambridge: Cambridge University Press.

Strauss, A., & Corbin, J. (1990). *Basics of qualitative research: Grounded theory procedures and techniques*. London: Sage Publications.

Wahler, R. G., & Dumas, J. E. (1984). Changing the observational coding styles of insular and noninsular mothers: A step toward maintenance of parent training effects. In R. F. Dangel & R. A. Polster (Eds.), *Parent training: Foundations of research and practice* (pp. 379–416). New York: Guilford Press.

Webster-Stratton, C. (1985a). Comparison of abusive and nonabusive families with conduct-disordered children. *American Journal of Orthopsychiatry, 55*(1), 59–69.

Webster-Stratton, C. (1985b). Predictors of treatment outcome in parent training for conduct disordered children. *Behavior Therapy, 16*, 223–243.

Webster-Stratton, C. (1988). Mothers' and fathers' perceptions of child deviance: Roles of parent and child behaviors and parent adjustment. *Journal of Consulting and Clinical Psychology, 56*(6), 909–915.

Webster-Stratton, C. (1989). The relationship of marital support, conflict and divorce to parent perceptions, behaviors, and childhood conduct problems. *Journal of Marriage and the Family, 51*, 417–430.

Webster-Stratton, C. (1991). Stress: A potential disruptor of parent perceptions and family interactions. *Journal of Clinical Child Psychology, 19*, 302–312.

Webster-Stratton, C. (1994). Advancing videotape parent training: A comparison study. *Journal of Consulting and Clinical Psychology, 62*, 583–593.

Webster-Stratton, C., & Hammond, M. (1988). Maternal depression and its relationship to life stress, perceptions of child behavior problems, parenting behaviors, and child conduct problems. *Journal of Abnormal Child Psychology, 16*(3), 299–315.

Webster-Stratton, C., & Herbert, M. (1994). *Troubled families—Problem children*. Chichester: Wiley.

2

Community-Based Residential Treatment for Adolescents with Conduct Disorder

Patricia Chamberlain

1. Overview

Given that some adolescents will inevitably be in need of out-of-home placement, placing them in a local community-based program vs. a more restrictive institutional setting has numerous advantages for the teenagers and their families. Primary among these advantages is that the adolescents are not isolated from family members and others with whom they may have important relationships. Community-based care is also less costly than institutional alternatives, and the opportunities for generalization of treatment effects are probably greater when treatment is conducted in a minimally restrictive setting close to home. Community protection factors come into play, however, in the making of programming decisions for adolescents with severe conduct problems and delinquency. Can local citizens be reassured that placing teenagers in an unlocked setting is a reasonable decision, given the potential damage they might do to property or, worse, the risk that they will commit crimes against persons? The effectiveness of the supervision provided to adolescents in community-based treatment settings is central to the issue of program effectiveness and to the level of community acceptance of noninstitutional attempts to address adolescent crime and aggression.

Another key variable in the success of community-based programs

Patricia Chamberlain • Oregon Social Learning Center, 207 East 5th Avenue, Eugene, Oregon 97401.

Advances in Clinical Child Psychology, Volume 18, edited by Thomas H. Ollendick and Ronald J. Prinz. Plenum Press, New York, 1996.

for adolescents with conduct problems is the effectiveness of control strategies and disciplinary methods. There is a need for disciplinary methods that get adolescents' attention, that can be implemented consistently and fairly, and that work on helping adolescents change aggressive and destructive patterns of behavior. Control of criminal activities and violent behavior is an obvious priority for programs, for both community protection and therapeutic reasons.

The two most widely used residential community-based models of treatment and control of delinquency currently practiced in the United States are peer-mediated group work methods (e.g., Craft, Stevenson, & Granger, 1964; Vorrath & Brendtro, 1985) and adult-mediated behavioral models (e.g., Phillips, Wolf, & Fixsen, 1973). These two models use very different discipline strategies and hypothesize different mechanisms for achieving therapeutic change. Peer-culture approaches provide opportunities and motivation for change through therapeutic group work, including peer confrontation and determination of discipline. Behavioral models stress the use of contingency management systems and promotion of positive relationships with mentoring adults. The relative effectiveness of these two models has not been tested. For that matter, the literature on community-based residential care models in general is largely descriptive, with little research conducted on either program outcomes or treatment process variables. A 1994 report on the effectiveness of residential care from the United States General Accounting Office concluded (p. 4) that:

> not enough is known about residential care programs to provide a clear picture of which kinds of treatment approaches work best or about the effectiveness of treatment over the long term.

That same report identified 11 key elements that were thought to be important for program success: (1) developing individual treatment plans; (2) participation of a caring adult; (3) building self-esteem; (4) planning for postprogram life; (5) teaching social, coping, and living skills; (6) coordinating services; (7) involving the family; (8) enforcing a strict code of discipline; providing (9) postprogram support; (10) a family-like atmosphere; and (11) a positive peer culture. With the two possible exceptions of discipline and parent involvement, there is little or no empirical evidence that supports the use of any of these elements. With over 600,000 children and adolescents living in residential care in the United States (Allen, 1991), this method of service delivery deserves empirical attention.

In this chapter, a family-based treatment foster care (TFC) model for adolescents with severe conduct problems and delinquency will be described, along with results from preliminary studies on its feasibility and effectiveness. Data from an ongoing study that compares staff assumptions, patterns of association and influence with peers and adults, and daily supervision and discipline practices that take place in TFC and group care (GC) programs will also be presented. A brief review of some key studies on the development and correlates of delinquency that inform clinical interventions is first presented.

1.1. Research on Environmental Mediators of Delinquency

Programmatic longitudinal research on developmental models of antisocial behavior and severe conduct problems has come a long way toward specification of mediators, antecedents, and the general topography of chronic conduct problem syndromes. For example, a number of studies have found that poor parental discipline practices strongly relate to subsequent development of antisocial behavior in children, even after controlling for significant contextual factors such as social class and educational level (Elder, Caspi, & Downey, 1983; Huesmann, Eron, Lefkowitz, & Walder, 1984). Poor and punitive discipline has also been shown to relate to self-destructive behavior in the next generation (e.g., Yesavage, Becker, & Werner, 1983; Yesavage & Widrow, 1985) and to criminal behavior (McCord, 1988; Widom, 1989).

As pointed out by Cappell and Heiner (1990), the use of aggressive or violent discipline in the family of origin is neither a necessary nor a sufficient condition for generating aggressive discipline methods in one's own family. Nevertheless, correlation evidence consistently supports the notion of cross-generational transmission of harsh discipline practices (e.g., Egeland, Jacobvitz, & Papatola, 1987; Herrenkohl, Herrenkohl, & Toedter, 1983; Simons, Whitbeck, Conger, & Chyi-In, 1991). Studies of the prediction of delinquency typically implicate poor parental discipline practices as an antecedent to the development of antisocial patterns (reviewed in Rutter & Giller, 1984). The clinical implication for application to adolescents with conduct problems is that within the context of their daily experiences, youths would benefit from exposure to consistent, nonviolent, nonphysical, non-anger-based discipline methods that are perceived by them to be fair and appropriate to the infraction.

The lack of effective supervision has also been linked with later delinquency in several well-conducted longitudinal studies. For example, in their reanalysis of the Gluecks' data (Glueck & Glueck, 1950), Laub and Sampson (1988) found that lack of maternal supervision, discipline that was harsh and erratic, and low parental attachment were key predictors of serious and chronic delinquency. Wilson (1987) found that for families living in high-crime neighborhoods, 80% of parents who were lax supervisors vs. 30% of strict supervisors had delinquent sons. Farrington (1978) found that poor parental supervision and harsh discipline at age 8 were significant precursors of aggression and violence in adolescence. Studies using adolescent self-report generally support the findings from the longitudinal studies. Several studies found that delinquency was lower for adolescents with higher levels of parental supervision (e.g., Campbell, 1987; Cernkovich & Giordano, 1987; Streit, 1981; E. L. Wells & Rankin, 1988).

One may conclude from this body of literature that poor parental supervision, along with harsh punitive discipline, relates to the later development of adolescent conduct problems and delinquency. The direction of these relationships is not entirely clear because of the possibility that children with difficult temperaments make it harder for parents to carry out such parenting tasks as supervision and discipline. Also, the predictive relationship of supervision to delinquency may arise partly from the fact that good supervision implies a certain level of family organization and involvement in the child's daily activities. Good supervision practices imply that the family has implicit or explicit rules about matters such as where the child is allowed to go, with whom she or he may associate, and what times he or she is expected home. To maintain good supervision, parents must have some degree of success at dealing with rule violations. At any rate, it seems clear that treatment programs designed to remediate severe conduct problems and criminal behavior in adolescents should be characterized by well-conceptualized and implemented supervision and discipline strategies.

1.2. Association with Peers

The link between supervision and adolescent conduct problems has been shown to be mediated in large part by the powerful social influence of the peer group (e.g., Elliott, Huizinga, & Ageton, 1985). An adolescent who is poorly supervised is more likely to associate with, and be influenced by, antisocial peers. In a study comparing after-school supervision of 10- to 16-year-old youths, Steinberg (1986) found that children whose parents did not know their whereabouts were more susceptible to negative peer pressure than were youths who were directly supervised by adults or youths whose parents knew where they were after school hours. Lax supervision in combination with rejection by normal peers puts children at risk for association with peers with nonconventional or deviant orientations (e.g., Dishion, Patterson, Stoolmiller, & Skinner, 1991; Patterson & Stouthamer-Loeber, 1984).

Association with deviant peers has been shown to be a strong predictor of delinquent activity and drug use. For example, findings from the large-scale National Youth Study (Elliott et al., 1985) showed virtually no risk for delinquency given no association with deviant peers, regardless of the youth's level of bonding with family or school. These authors suggested that popular peer-culture, group-oriented treatment approaches ". . . may actually be contributing to the maintenance and enhancement of delinquent friendship cliques" (Elliott et al., 1985, p. 149). In support of this notion, they cite results from evaluations of street worker programs with delinquent gangs (e.g., Klein, 1969, 1971; Miller, 1962) that suggest that delinquency increased relative to the level of intensity of the group-oriented intervention (i.e., the greater the intensity, the greater the delinquency). Whether or not antisocial behavior is reinforced by association with a delinquent peer group, as has been suggested by some work (e.g., Banducci, 1967; Gold & Andres, 1978; Reese & Palmer, 1970), or can be ameliorated by peer-mediated treatments, is an empirical question that deserves careful attention given the implications for treatment programs and the costs to states and communities of conducting community-based programs. This question, along with the desire to examine the potential impact of theoretically grounded process variables such as supervision and discipline, motivated us to conduct a controlled clinical trial comparing TFC to GC approaches, preliminary results of which are presented in later sections of this chapter.

1.3. Background and Applications of the Oregon Social Learning Center Treatment Foster Care Model

In the mid-1970s, the Oregon Social Learning Center (OSLC) was funded by the National Institute of Mental Health to compare the effectiveness of parent training family therapy to a "treatment as usual" community control condition for adolescents referred from the juvenile justice system. To qualify for inclusion, youths had to have three or more arrests, one of which was for a nonstatus offense (i.e., an offense that is not age-related). The goal of this study was to transfer and adapt the parent training methods that had been developed and tested with younger aggressive children to an adolescent population evidencing problems of delinquency. We were not long into this process when it became apparent clinically that the problems being presented were much more complex and severe than we had faced previously. The occurrence of frequent family crises posed a major problem in terms of trying to implement our parent-mediated model of treatment. Families would come to sessions week after week wanting to debrief issues such as missing jewelry, their latest visit from the police, or the expulsion of their teenager from school. Therapists had great difficulty fitting the skills-training agenda into session time. In clinical staff meetings, we lamented our inability to put forth our therapeutic agenda. Usually, the target adolescent and frequently his or her siblings were engaged in a virtual nonstop cavalcade of rule-violating activities at home, at school, or both. Most families perceived as unresponsive any attempt to ignore or minimize the importance of these activities or to suggest that session time be proportioned between crises and ways of stopping them. The results of this study (Bank, Marlowe, Reid, Patterson, & Weinrott, 1991) showed that although there was a statistically significant effect on the rates of adolescent offending in follow-up, the clinical significance of the improvements seemed minimal, especially given the large amount of clinical supervision and number of family sessions (i.e., almost 1 year of treatment).

In 1983, the State of Oregon put out a request for proposals for community-based residential programs designed to prevent incarceration in the state training school. We wanted to design a program model that allowed us to use what we had learned from our own and others' previous work with antisocial children and their families. Even though we had been humbled by our work with multiple offenders, we remained convinced that the family provided the best setting, and perhaps the only setting, for effective socialization of children. We wanted to find ways to stop, or at least slow down, teenagers' high-rate offending and rule-breaking behaviors so we could begin to work on skill building and development of prosocial relationships. We thought that minimizing contact with peers who were also engaging in criminal behavior would help us achieve these aims.

1.4. The Oregon Social Learning Center Treatment Foster Care Model

The TFC program model (Chamberlain, 1994) uses community families specially selected and intensively trained and supervised to provide placements for adolescents. One child is placed in each home to minimize the child's association with deviant peers. Each week, program participants and their families (biological, step, adoptive, or other aftercare resource) receive therapy, and the child's progress and problems at school are closely monitored. Frequent home visits during which parents and youth have opportunities to practice program procedures are a key part of family treatment. Each youth has an individualized treatment plan that is translated into everyday practice through a point and level system implemented by the treatment foster parents. This plan is continuously revised as new targets emerge throughout treatment. Case managers coordinate all aspects of treatment and work with county parole/probation officers. Since 1983, using this model, we have treated over 150 teenagers referred by the courts. The average placement lasts 6 months. Components of the TFC program model and case examples are described fully in Chamberlain (1994).

In 1986, we adapted the model to work with children and adolescents referred for severe emotional disturbance from the Child and Adolescent Treatment Program at the Oregon State Hospital (Chamberlain & Reid, 1991). These youngsters had spent the previous year in the hospital and were ready for community placement. Unfortunately, community placements for this population of youngsters were scarce, with most group programs allowing at most one or two slots for referrals from the hospital. We applied for and received a federal grant from the Department of Health and Human Services, Children's Bureau, to examine whether TFC was a viable community-based placement option for youngsters making the transition out of the hospital. Those referred had no family aftercare resource or were not thought to be ready to return home. Referred cases were randomly assigned to TFC or to "treatment as usual" in the community. These children and adolescents had chaotic histories, as evidenced by their having had an average of five previous out-of-home placements and few aftercare family resources, and most had histories of mental illness in their families. In addition, the children themselves had all demonstrated that they were a significant danger to themselves or others, or both, presenting serious safety and clinical concerns to programs that agreed to admit them.

Not surprisingly, it was difficult to recruit suitable TFC homes for these youngsters. We attempted to find adults who had experience with severely emotionally disturbed children, who were stable, and who were willing to work with the program to provide daily treatment to the child placed with them. Many excellent foster parents were not suitable for this program. Some of these parents were inexperienced in dealing with severe child problems; some had a great deal of love to give, but were not willing to work actively and consistently toward specific behavior goals for the child. The program used a team approach to address unanticipated problems in a timely manner through the case manager, the TFC parents, and the program therapists. A key factor in selection of foster families was whether we felt they could work well within this team approach.

Components of the program included (1) extensive preservice training for TFC parents; (2) ongoing supervision and support for foster parents, including daily telephone contact and weekly meetings; (3) daily management of the child in the community and the home using an individualized behavioral program; (4) individual child treatment, including weekly sessions and on-call crisis intervention; (5) promoting family (or relative) contact and conducting family treatment when possible; (6) case management services; (7) school programming, including consultation to the schools and crisis intervention; and (8) psychiatric consultation.

These youngsters had fewer family resources available to them than those we had previously treated for delinquency. In many cases, their parents were deceased, hospitalized, or in prison. Although we made considerable effort to find extended family members who might provide for their care following participation in the TFC program, most (85%) were placed in long-term foster care settings in aftercare.

2. Pilot Studies on the Efficacy of the Oregon Social Learning Center Treatment Foster Care Programs

2.1. Treatment Foster Care as a Treatment for Delinquency

The effectiveness of TFC as a diversion from placement in locked (i.e., state training school) settings was first tested on the initial 16 cases we treated from 1983 to 1985 (Chamberlain, 1990). These first 16 consecutive referrals were matched by computer using records from the State Children's Services Division (CSD) to subjects who had participated in one of the other ten statewide diversion programs that were funded in 1983. Experimental (E) and matched control (C) subjects were comparable on a number of family risk factors, including percentages of families living below poverty level, divorced, with parents hospitalized, incarcerated or convicted of felonies, or with siblings institutionalized. There was a difference in the percentage of cases who were adopted (E = 31%, C = 0%). No differences in child risk factors, including being victims of physical or sexual abuse, suicide attempts, running away, felonies, or dangerousness to self or others, were found. School adjustment variables also showed no differences between E and C groups.

The number of days that youth were incarcerated in the state training schools was tracked for 1 year prior to diversion-program placement and for 2 years following program completion using the CSD service records the agency used to request payment on the cases. The number of days in placement was also tracked. Prior to treatment, 12 of the 16 participants in the experimental group had been incarcerated, as had 12 of the 16 comparison group participants. The average number of days incarcerated for participants in the two groups did not differ reliably [E = 22.9 (SD = 29.2), C = 14.9 (SD = 24.4)]. No difference was found for the amount of time in placement for subjects in the two groups [E = 142 days (SD = 78), C = 146 days (SD = 112)]. Of the experimental participants, 12 (75%) completed treatment, 3 (19%) were incarcerated and did

TABLE 1
Incarceration Rates

Group	Days incarcerated (mean)		Number of subjects incarcerated (mean)		
	Year 1	Year 2	Year 1	Year 2	Year 1 + 2
Experimental (N = 16)	86.4	44.3	6	7	8
Comparison (N = 16)	159.9	66.8	14[a]	10	15[b]

[a]E < C (χ^2 = 6.53, p < 0.01).
[b]E < C (χ^2 = 5.56, p < 0.02).

not complete, and 1 (6%) ran away. For comparison participants, 5 (31%) completed, 4 (25%) were incarcerated during the placement, and 7 (44%) ran away. The rate of successful vs. unsuccessful program completion was significantly different (χ^2 = 6.15, p < 0.03).

Incarceration rates posttreatment also indicated more favorable outcomes for the TFC condition. Table 1 shows number of days incarcerated for years 1 and 2 follow-up and prevalence of incarcerations for participants in each group. Beyond treatment considerations, cost is an important factor in the selection of community programming. At the estimated cost of $75 per day (probably an underestimate) for incarceration in the state training school, the experimental participants cost the State of Oregon approximately $122,000 less in follow-up than did the comparison subjects. In year 1, experimental participants spent 46% fewer days incarcerated than did comparison participants, and 34% fewer days in year 2. The relation between the number of days in placement and subsequent incarceration was significantly related for participants in the experimental group (r = 0.72, p = 0.001), but not for those in the comparison group (r = 0.04). These results encouraged us to continue to develop our TFC model and to adapt it to other populations of youngsters who needed alternatives to living in institutional settings.

2.2. Treatment Foster Care as a Treatment for Severe Emotional Disturbance

Study participants were 8 males and 12 females referred by state hospital outreach teams. Data on their demographic and risk factor characteristics are presented in Table 2. Outreach teams consisted of multi-disciplinary staff (e.g., psychiatrists, social workers, psychologists, edu-

TABLE 2
Demographic and Risk Factor Data from State Hospital Study Sample

Demographic and risk factors	TFC (experimental) (N = 10)	Treatment as usual (control) (N = 10)
Mean age (years) at referral and (range)	13.9 (9–18)	15.1 (12–17)
Mean number of previous placements and (range)	5.1 (1–10)	5.0 (1–12)
Percentage with risk factor:		
Failed adoptions	30%	0%
Siblings institutionalized	20%	30%
Siblings in foster care	50%	40%
Mental illness in family	80%	90%
Family available for aftercare	0%	20%
Family violence	80%	90%
Youth charged with felony	30%	30%
Sexually abusive	40%	20%
Sexually abused	80%	70%
Suicide attempts	60%	20%
Multiple runaway	60%	80%

cators, occupational therapists) who worked with each case. Referred cases were all judged to be ready for community placement. After referral, cases were randomly assigned to TFC or "treatment as usual" in their communities. Participants had been hospitalized an average of 240 days during the year prior to referral.

The average length of time from the date of referral to placement outside the hospital differed (i.e., $p = 0.05$) for the experimental (TFC) and control (treatment as usual) groups [E mean = 81 days (SD = 42), C mean = 182 days (SD = 136)]. All 10 experimental participants were placed in family settings, while only 7 of the control cases left the hospital during the 2-year study period. Of the 7 control cases placed outside the hospital, 4 were placed in families and 3 went to residential care settings.

Given that a child was placed in a community setting, the next step was to look at how well the placements maintained. For the following placement, youths in the experimental group spent an average of 288 days (SD = 138) living in their communities. Three youths were rehospitalized. Of the 7 control participants, 2 were rehospitalized during the 1-year follow up, and the group mean for days living in the community was 261 (SD = 157). Although there was no difference between the two groups in the amount of time spent in communities for children who were placed outside the hospital, these results indicated that the TFC model was a viable option for this population of severely disturbed children.

These early studies demonstrated the promise of the TFC approach; however, both used small samples. In order to further examine the potential and limitations of the approach, we were interested in conducting programmatic research on the model. Toward this goal, we have begun to examine how males and females respond differently to TFC and the clinical implications for gender-specific programming.

2.3. Gender-Related Considerations in Conducting Community-Based Treatments for Adolescents

Relative to the amount of research conducted on male samples on treatment effectiveness and life course development of antisocial patterns, there are few published studies that focus on females. Zoccolillo (1993) attributes this dearth to four factors: (1) the perception that the presence of severe conduct problems in the female population is relatively rare; (2) arrest and imprisonment rates are lower for females than for males, and much research is initiated from the criminal justice system; (3) the DSM-III-R criteria for conduct disorders (American Psychiatric Association, 1987) were derived largely from studies on boys; and (4) girls with severe conduct problems are likely to be found outside criminal justice or psychiatry, and this circumstance leads to underestimates of the prevalence and seriousness of the problem. Yet several studies document that outcomes are poor for females who were antisocial as adolescents. For example, Robins and her colleagues have shown that while males who were antisocial as adolescents are more likely to engage in criminal activities as adults, females are more at risk for diverse types of poor outcomes. Robins and Price (1991) found that regardless of other types of psychiatric problems, conduct problems in females predicted poor long-term outcomes such as internalizing disorders, early pregnancy, psychiatric hospitalization, and high use of social services.

Lewis, Yeager, Cobham-Portorreal, Klein, Showalter, and Antony (1991) followed up a sample of adolescents 7–12 years after they were incarcerated and found that while fewer females than males had been arrested, of 21 females studied, only 6 had completed high school, 4 were prostitutes, 19 had attempted suicide, 15 had serious drug problems, 13 had been involved in seriously violent relationships, and 1 had died.

The study by Warren and Rosenbaum (1987) of 159 females who had been involved with the California Youth Authority also yielded a negative prognosis. Even though most of these subjects were status offenders as teenagers, as adults, only 4% of these women had not been arrested at least once, and 60% were incarcerated at least once. Zoccolillo and Rogers (1991) examined long-term outcomes for 55 white, middle-class, adolescent females who had been hospitalized for severe conduct problems. At 2–4 years postdischarge, they found a mortality rate of 6% (twice the national rate), a 35% pregnancy rate (compared to an 8% state rate), and a high rate of dropout from high school. Although many of these girls had comorbid emotional disorders, the authors concluded that it was the presence of severe conduct problems that contributed to their poor long-term prognoses.

Given the seriousness of adult outcomes for antisocial girls, not to mention the potential harmful effects on the next generation (e.g., Andres, Brown, & Creasey, 1990; Merikangas & Spiker, 1982; Westen, Ludolph, Misle, Ruffins, & Block, 1990), it seems strange that females have been nearly ignored by life-course and clinical researchers alike. There is evidence that after reaching adolescence, girls as a group are also shortchanged by service delivery systems in that they tend not to receive mental health, social service, and educational services as often as their male counterparts (Offord, Boyle, & Racine, 1991). It is unclear whether the reason for this neglect is that services for girls don't exist, girls don't seek out services as often as boys, or service providers are biased against treating girls. Utilization rates for adolescent females were found to be lower than for any other group (i.e., younger females and younger and older males).

Although adolescent females use fewer services, they are more likely than males to be incarcerated for minor offenses (Chesney-Lind, 1988), even though they tend to commit fewer and less serious offenses than males (Ageton & Elliott, 1978). Chesney-Lind's review showed that despite the relatively minor nature of their criminal offending, more adolescent females than males nationwide end up in adult jails. One consequence of this lack of attention to study and treatment of female adolescents is that agencies and practitioners have little if any guidance available to them in their attempts to provide appropriate programming for females with severe conduct problems.

After our first TFC program had been operating for only 1 year, we began to get referrals for females. Typically, these young women had contact with both the criminal justice and the mental health system. Although our program model was based on research conducted with largely all-male samples, we decided to admit females beginning in 1984. By early 1992, in TFC, we had treated 37 females referred by the juvenile courts.

2.4. Gender Differences in Responsiveness to Treatment Foster Care

We examined initial risk factors, in-program adjustment, and outcomes for 88 consecutive referrals (53 males, 35 females) for severe delinquency (Chamberlain & Reid, 1994). Sample characteristics are summarized in Table 3 with respect to pretreatment risk factors, age, arrest, and

TABLE 3

Pretreatment Risk Factors, Age, Arrest, and Placement Histories

Demographic and risk factors	Males (N = 53)		Females (N = 35)	
	Mean (SD)			
Age at intake (years)	14.54	(1.50)	14.80	(1.45)
Age at first offense (years)	11.91	(2.22)	12.89	(1.32)[a]
Number of prior placements	2.52	(7.64)	4.26	(4.79)[a]
Total arrests	10.84	(5.87)	8.43	(4.12)[a]
	N	(%)	N	(%)
Family risk factors				
One-parent family at intake	30	(57%)	17	(52%)
Income < $10,000	28	(53%)	17	(52%)
Parents ever divorced	41	(77%)	31	(87%)
Three or more siblings	15	(28%)	10	(29%)
Siblings institutionalized	11	(21%)	9	(26%)
Adopted	5	(9%)	7	(20%)
Mother hospitalized	5	(9%)	3	(9%)
Father convicted	8	(15%)	6	(18%)
Family violence	35	(66%)	26	(74%)
Abuse				
Victim of physical abuse	27	(51%)	12	(34%)
Victim of sexual abuse	6	(11%)	17	(49%)
Perpetrator of sexual abuse	8	(15%)	0	(0%)[a]
Child risk factors				
Attempted suicide	3	(6%)	10	(29%)[a]
Two or more runaways	29	(56%)	30	(86%)[a]
Charged with felony	47	(89%)	18	(51%)[a]
Firesetting	8	(15%)	1	(3%)
Serious drug/alcohol problem	23	(43%)	18	(51%)
Chronic truancy	41	(77%)	29	(83%)
Less than 1 year below grade level	24	(45%)	22	(63%)
Mean total risk factors	6.96	(2.3)	7.34	(2.4)
(of 19 measured)				

[a] $p < 0.05$.

placement histories. Several reliable gender differences were found. Males were younger at the age of their first arrest by almost 10 months. Compared to females, males had more arrests at intake and more felonies. Females had been placed outside their homes more often than males; this finding is in line with other research that suggests that families of females with antisocial behavior tend to be more disrupted and have more conflict than families of antisocial males (e.g., Henggeler, Edwards, & Borduin, 1987; Morris, 1964; Widom, 1978). Significantly more females than males had been sexually abused, while males were more often perpetrators of sexual abuse. Females were more likely to have attempted and to have run away multiple times.

Overall, females appeared to have more severe emotional disturbance than males who were referred to our program. It was somewhat surprising to us, as we began to gain experience placing and treating TFC cases, that seasoned foster parents were less willing to provide placements for females than for males. Surely females were less likely to pose certain risks, such as physical violence or serious criminal activities, to foster families than were their male counterparts. Nonetheless, foster families who had provided care for both sexes tended to prefer males. It was this situation, in part, that motivated us to conduct research on patterns of behavior problems in care, as well as differential outcomes for males and females. The realization that our program model had been designed on the basis of research that identified treatment needs of males also led us to question the appropriateness of the model for treating adolescent females.

In terms of program outcomes, completion rates were found to be comparable for boys and girls who were admitted to our TFC program: 71% of males and 73% of females completed. Analysis of data on official arrests during the year following treatment showed that both sexes had significant drops in arrest rates compared to pretreatment levels. We found significant gender differences, however, when we examined the occurrence and patterns of daily problem behaviors while the youths were in TFC. To study daily behavior problem occurrence, we used the Parent Daily Report (PDR) Checklist measure (Chamberlain & Reid, 1987), which was administered to the TFC parents 5 times a week by telephone. For all cases, data on the PDR Checklist were aggregated by month (based on 20 cells) to yield monthly mean rates.

During the first month of placement in TFC, males demonstrated a reliably higher rate of daily problems than their female counterparts ($p = 0.04$). By the 6th month of placement, however, females displayed significantly more behavior problems than males ($p = 0.005$). For males, the rates of behavior problems dropped over time, improving as they progressed in their placements. For females, the opposite pattern occurred;

they were getting worse over time. Females typically began their placements showing relatively few overt behavior problems. As they became more accustomed to life in the TFC home, their rate of daily problem manifestations increased. This pattern increased the probability that girls would be rejected in their foster homes. Foster parents reported feeling as though they had made a positive start but were failing as time went on. This study (Chamberlain & Reid, 1994) has led us to believe that treatment programming for girls should focus on variables additional to those emphasized in treatment models designed for males. For example, due to their early histories of sexual abuse and more numerous and severe family disruptions, females with severe conduct problems might require more time to establish family relationships in which they feel it is "safe" to express their negative emotions. A key issue for these adolescent females seems to be that their tendency to lash out at people close to them interferes with their ability to establish and maintain supportive relationships.

Another problem that often causes disruptions or failures of adolescent females in residential care is their involvement with highly deviant males who are usually older. Although studies by Rutter and his colleagues (Quinton & Rutter, 1984; Rutter, 1989) demonstrated that relationships with supportive, nonabusive males predicted positive adjustment for females who had been institutionalized as adolescents, their results are somewhat mixed: While the females' delinquency decreased, their daily displays of anger increased. It may be that expression of anger is a positive mechanism for change, especially given that these young women are living in safe, nonabusive environments. Learning to deal with anger in nondestructive ways is certainly a treatment goal for most of these girls. These findings point out the need for clinical intervention studies that examine treatments specifically tailored for adolescent females. A study is under way that focuses on what are thought to be key mediators of treatment effectiveness for males.

2.5. Mediators of Male Delinquency: A Clinical Trial

In 1990, we began conducting a study in which 12- to 18-year-old boys with severe and chronic delinquency who have been referred by the local juvenile court have been randomly assigned to treatment in GC or TFC. Participants have an average of 13.7 official arrests prior to inclusion in the study and are an average of 14 years 10 months old. Data from confidential self-reports of delinquent activities yield much larger numbers of offenses committed. Subjects reported that during the 6-month period immediately prior to baseline, they had committed an average of 12.9 criminal offenses in their communities. This is a "deep end" population in terms of their level of delinquency, and they reflect the State of Oregon's commitment to use community-based treatment programs as an alternative to incarceration in the state training schools. So far, the study includes 60 subjects. The final sample of 90 participants will be completed during 1995 or early 1996.

In addition to assessing short- and long-term delinquency and mental-health-related outcomes of the subjects participating in the study (Chamberlain, 1991), we are also examining the treatment process employed. Specifically, we hypothesized that the amounts and types of supervision, discipline, and patterns of association with delinquent and nondelinquent peers and adults would predict outcomes. Data on these and other treatment process variables were collected from program care providers prior to the boys' placements. After youths had been placed in the program for 3 months, boys and caretakers were assessed on actual supervision and discipline given and received and on adult and peer association and influence patterns. Initial findings will be presented in a subsequent section. First, we present a general description of the TFC model as well as results from preliminary studies on the model.

2.5.1. Differences in Assumptions and Methods of Practice in Treatment Foster Care and Group Care

The basic theories that underlie various treatment approaches presumably relate to hypothesized mechanisms of change and to methods of practice. As was previously discussed, however, there is an alarming lack of research in the area of residential care and virtually no work that ties theory and practice to outcomes. Colton (1989a, b) argued that the little research that has been conducted on residential care has overemphasized child characteristics, paying insufficient attention to characteristics of treatment environments.

GC programs in our preliminary study all used a peer-centered treatment approach and had from 6 to 15 boys in residence. TFC homes used a behavioral, adult-mediated model and had one boy placed in each home. Both program models treated 12- to 18-year-old males who were designated for out-of-home placement by the court because of severe and chronic delinquency. Cases were randomly assigned to GC or TFC placements.

Table 4 summarizes demographic characteristics and arrest data for the sample of study boys. An examination of risk factors assessed at baseline showed comparability between the two groups on 17 of 19 variables. The groups differed significantly with respect to perpetration of sexual abuse (TFC > GC) and low academic performance (GC > TFC).

We examined the differences in the TFC and GC program models at

TABLE 4
Demographic Characteristics and Arrest Data

Demographic and risk factors	GC	TFC
Mean age at first arrest (years)	12.10	12.53
Mean age at intake (years)	14.8	14.11
Mean number of arrests	14.2	13.3
Percentage with risk factor:		
Single-parent families	40%	35%
Adopted	5%	17%
Mom hospitalized/mental	13.6%	8.3%
Dad hospitalized/mental	0%	0%
Dad convicted of crime	25%	38%
Mom convicted of crime	27%	25%
Documented physical abuse	10%	6%
Documented sexual abuse	15%	0%
Perpetrated sex offense	13%	18%
Siblings in residential care	15%	11%
Family income < $10,000	25%	25%
Past suicide attempt	10%	0%
Committed felony	100%	78%
Chronic truancy	77%	59%
Multiple runaways	80%	67%
Arrested for firesetting	30%	20%

two levels: (1) staff beliefs or assumptions about how the programs ran and (2) actual daily practices. Beliefs and assumptions were assessed by interviewing key program staff prior to any youth participation. We interviewed line staff rather than program administrators because we focused on daily program operations and what youth could expect to experience as participants in TFC and GC models. In the group home settings, the staff member with the most tenure was selected for the interview. In TFC, the foster parent who provided the primary care for the adolescent was selected to participate in the interview. Next, after youths had been placed for 3 months, actual program practices were examined. In both treatment settings, we interviewed boys and their primary adult caretakers about key aspects of their daily routines.

2.5.2. Assessment of Staff Assumptions

An ecological interview was developed with the aim of defining staff beliefs or assumptions about what factors were important for program success, what types of therapy were expected to relate to what types of changes, and what daily supervision, discipline, and peer and adult association patterns boys were exposed to as part of their treatment programs. Interviews were conducted prior to boys' placement in the programs and took approximately 2.5 hours to complete. Programs and foster families were paid $100 per interview to participate.

Table 5 summarizes staff impressions of who they thought were major influences on boys' success in their respective programs. Staff in GC and TFC programs differed in terms of how much influence they felt adults had on boys' success ($F[1,32] = 6.29$; $p = 0.017$). A score was calculated that measured the difference between the relative influence of adults and peers within each program model. In TFC, staff perceived that adults were much more influential than peers ($F[1,27] = 7.37$; $p = 0.011$). In GC, adults were seen as being only slightly more influential than peers—less than a 1-point difference on a 10-point scale vs. more than a 3-point difference in TFC.

Staff assumptions about supervision and discipline practices looked different for the two program models. In comparison to adults in GC, adults in TFC thought that boys spent less time per day without adult supervision ($F[1,32] = 4.1$; $p = 0.05$). Three aspects of discipline were examined: who decides when discipline is needed, who decides what the discipline will be, and who administers the discipline. In GC, while adults reported that they retained a good measure of control, their scores were significantly lower than those in TFC on a composite score that summarized these three aspects of discipline (GC mean = 0.67; TFC mean = 1.0; $F[1,32] = 8.78$; $p = 0.005$).

Not surprisingly, boys in GC were expected by staff to spend more time with peers than those in TFC ($p = 0.003$). Boys in TFC were thought to spend more one-on-one time with a program adult ($p = 0.0002$). A

TABLE 5
Adult Perceptions of Influences

Questions and respondents	GC adults		TFC adults	
	Mean	SD	Mean	SD
Who influences boy's success?				
Peers	6.9	(2.0)	5.8	(2.1)
Caretaking adults	7.7	(1.0)[a]	8.7	(1.4)[a]
Difference score (caretaker influence minus peer influence)	0.75	(2.3)[b]	3.3	(2.5)[b]

[a,b]Scores with the same superscript are significantly different at the 0.05 level.

summary score represented how much individual adult contact relative to peer contact boys were expected to experience in the two program models and yielded a significant difference, revealing more adult contact in TFC and more peer contact in GC ($p = 0.0002$). These results point out the different assumptions that underlie peer-mediated and adult-mediated program models. Data on staff assumptions were consistent with the two contrasting theories in terms of patterns of adult and peer influence, level of supervision, and implementation of discipline practices.

2.5.3. Assessment of Program Practices

After 3 months in their respective programs, participating youths and their primary program adult caretakers were interviewed in person and through a series of five follow-up telephone interviews. The telephone interview was a modified version of the PDR Checklist that has been used in numerous longitudinal (e.g., Patterson, 1986; Patterson, Capaldi, & Bank, 1990) and clinical outcome studies in the United States (e.g., Weinrott, Bauske, & Patterson, 1979), Canada (Hunt, Day, & Levene, 1991), and Italy (Pastorelli, 1995). The PDR Checklist has also been adapted for use with children and adolescents. The checklist is easy to administer, requiring a 10-minute telephone contact, and is used to obtain information about the occurrence or nonoccurrence during the prior 24-hour period of a list of problem behaviors associated with conduct problems and aggression. The PDR Checklist has been shown to have good psychometric properties, to relate well to more molecular data, such as home observations, and to be sensitive to clinical change (Chamberlain & Reid, 1987; Patterson, Chamberlain, & Reid, 1982). Inter-interviewer reliabilities are high, ranging from 0.85 to 0.98, and interviewer training can be accomplished in 30–60 minutes.

Each boy and his adult caretaker were interviewed separately on five occasions within a 2-week period using the PDR Checklist. In addition to getting information on problem behavior occurrence, we asked about supervision and discipline administered and received and about patterns of adult and peer contact. For each substantive area under investigation, we calculated three scores: the boy's report, the adult caretaker's report, and the discrepancy between the two. We arbitrarily defined the discrepancy score as being the adult report score minus the boy report score so that a positive discrepancy score indicated that the adult was reporting more incidents than the boy and a negative score indicated that the boy was reporting more incidents. All scores reflected the average rate per day and were based on five days of data from each agent. The PDR Checklist measure used is shown in Figure 1.

PARENT DAILY REPORT CHECKLIST

Week of:_____
YOUTH:_____ (#_____) PDR Caller:_____
FOSTER PARENT:_____ (#_____) PHONE:_____

BEHAVIORS	SU	M	TU	W	TH	
Arguing						SUN/Rec time:
Back-talking						Unsupervised time:
Bedwetting						
Competitiveness						
Complaining						
Defiance						
Destructive, vandalism						MON/Rec time:
Encopresis						Unsupervised time:
Fighting						
Irritability						
Lying						
Negativism						
Boisterous/rowdy						TUE/Rec time:
Not minding						Unsupervised time:
Staying out late						
Skipping meals						
Running away						
Swearing/obscene lang.						
Tease/provoke						WED/Rec time:
Depression/sadness						Unsupervised time:
Sluggish						
Jealous						
Truant						
Stealing						
Nervous/jittery						
Short attention span						THU/Rec time:
Daydreaming						Unsupervised time:
Irresponsibility						
Marijuana/drugs						
Alcohol						
School problem						

TOTAL POINTS: ____ ____ ____ ____ ____

TOTAL POINTS LOST: ____ ____ ____ ____ ____
    Friday: Total Points_____   Points Lost_____   Recreation Time_____
    Saturday: Total Points_____   Points Lost_____   Recreation Time_____
                                                                  Total Recreation Time_____

ANYTHING POSITIVE/NEGATIVE HAPPEN?
SUNDAY   _____
MONDAY   _____
TUESDAY   _____
WEDNESDAY _____
THURSDAY   _____

Figure 1. Modified PDR Checklist used in the GC vs. TFC study.

TABLE 6
PDR Checklist Data on Problem Behavior Occurrence

| | GC | | TFC | |
Respondent	Mean	SD	Mean	SD
Adult-reported	3.7	(2.3)	3.6	(1.7)
Boy-reported	6.6	(3.9)[a]	2.9	(2.3)[a]
Discrepancy score	−2.88	(4.4)[a]	0.69	(0.69)[a]

[a] $p < 0.05$.

2.5.4. Occurrence of Boys' Problem Behaviors

Adult caretakers in both the TFC and the GC program reported that boys engaged in an average of just under 4 problem behaviors from the PDR Checklist per day. In Table 6, these data are shown along with boy report data. As can be seen in this table, boys in GC and TFC differed reliably on how many problem behaviors they said they had engaged in, with GC boys reporting over twice the rate reported by TFC boys. The discrepancy score was significantly different in both magnitude and direction. In GC, there was more disagreement between adults and boys than there was in TFC ($p = 0.02$). In TFC, the positive discrepancy score reflected the higher rates of problem occurrence reported by adults than by boys, whereas a negative discrepancy score in GC reflected the opposite ordering of problem behavior rates. These results suggest either that adults in TFC are more vigilant trackers of problem behavior or that boys in GC engage in more problem behaviors that their caretakers do not observe, or both.

2.5.5. Supervision and Discipline Given and Received and Patterns of Adult Contact

In both program models, adults reported less unsupervised time than boys did (see Table 7). In GC, adults reported that they spent just over 3 hours per day with boys, while in TFC, adults reported spending over 5 hours with boys ($p = 0.03$). When asked about the amount of unsupervised time that boys experienced, adults in both program models underestimated amounts compared to boys' reports, but this difference was much larger for GC ($p = 0.04$).

In an effort to measure actual discipline given and received, boys and adults were both asked if a consequence was given (or received) for each misbehavior reported on the PDR. Adults in GC reported that they

TABLE 7
Adult Contact/Supervision (Mediators)

	GC		TFC	
Respondent	Mean	SD	Mean	SD
Average number of minutes with caretaker				
Adult caretaker report	189	$(139)^a$	311	$(134)^a$
Boy report	188	(134)	266	(174)
Difference score	1.6	(98.6)	45	(174)
Average number of minutes without adult supervision				
Adult caretaker report	7.8	$(12.3)^a$	23.2	$(25)^a$
Boy report	78.8	(90)	35.1	(46)
Difference score	−71	$(93)^b$	−11	$(31)^b$

^{a,b}Scores with the same superscript are significantly different at the 0.05 level.

provided a consequence for problem behaviors 34% of the time, while TFC adults provided consequences for 62% of boys' problem behaviors ($p = 0.05$). GC boys reported that they received consequences only 15% of the time, and TFC boys reported that 37% of their problem behaviors received consequences ($p = 0.05$). Even though boys in both conditions reported receiving fewer consequences than adults say they gave, boys in TFC appear to be receiving more consistent daily discipline than GC boys.

Finally, the amount of contact and relative influence of negative peers was assessed in the two models. Because, by the very nature of GC, boys in this model spend more time with delinquent peers, we were interested in assessing how much time boys in both groups were spending associating with nonprogram delinquent peers. For GC, adults reported that such association occurred only very rarely (mean = 1 minute per day). In TFC, adults said that boys spent an average of 33 minutes per day with delinquent peers. Boys' reports gave a different picture. GC boys reported that on average, they spent 18 minutes per day with nonprogram delinquent peers; TFC boys reported spending an average of 4.5 minutes per day (N.S.). The two groups of boys' self-ratings of how influenced they were by negative peers were significantly different (GC > TFC; $p = 0.05$).

Regardless of placement condition, the way in which measures of supervision, discipline, and association patterns with adults and peers relate to outcomes such as self-reports and official reports of delinquen-

TABLE 8
Mediating Variables and Delinquency Outcomes

Variable	Placement + 6 months (N = 50)	Placement + 12 months (N = 39)
	Self-reports of criminal activities	
Deviant peers	0.37[a]	0.45[a]
Supervision	−0.36[a]	−0.23
Discipline	−0.12	−0.24
	Official arrests	
Deviant peers	0.37[a]	0.16
Supervision	−0.31[a]	−0.23
Discipline	−0.34[a]	−0.40[a]

[a] $p < 0.05$.

cy is of theoretical interest. Preliminary correlations among constructs measuring these mediating variables and delinquency outcomes indicate that there appear to be reliable associations between scores on these mediating variables and outcomes (see Table 8). These data should be interpreted with caution because they represent results from just over half the total sample size (i.e., 90). The direction of the relationships for the three hypothesized mediators was as expected for both self-reports and official reports of offenses; contact with deviant peers potentiated criminal activity while effective supervision suppressed it.

3. Conclusions

Community responses to adolescent delinquency are typically characterized by a mixed agenda: Hold the individual responsible for his or her actions, protect the community, and at the same time provide a rehabilitative experience. The selection of placement settings that address these goals is influenced by factors such as the current political climate (e.g., three strikes), the community program's capabilities, and what resources are available. Residential group care (GC) settings have the appeal of providing a uniform, standardized response to adolescent delinquency. The treatment foster care (TFC) setting is more likely to be perceived as varying depending on the characteristics, strengths, and weaknesses of the individual foster parents. This chapter describes a foster care program model that uses a systematic approach, grounded in social learning theory, for treating adolescents with severe delinquency. The TFC approach appears to have numerous advantages over GC the foremost of which is the separation of the teenager from peers who have similar problems. The data presented indicate that TFC parents are better supervisors, provide more consistent discipline, and spend more time with and have more positive influence on the youths placed with them than do GC staff. Further, boys in TFC report less influence from peers with similar problems, a feeling that is borne out of the correlations between association with deviant peers and self-reports of criminal activities at 6 and 12 months postplacement.

TFC programs now exist in most states, and there are several sites in Canada and Europe. This program model has received increased attention as an alternative to group residential care and institutionalization (Rivera & Kutash, 1994; Meadowcroft, Thomlison, & Chamberlain, 1994). Like other models of residential care, TFC is now widely used, yet empirical evidence to support its effectiveness is sparse.

In reviews of the residential care literature (e.g., Small, Kennedy, & Bender, 1991; K. Wells, 1991), descriptions of various characteristics of placement living settings are discussed. Key dimensions, such as level of restrictiveness, amount and type of supervision and discipline, importance of peer relations, and types and amounts of transactions with adults are seen as being important elements in treatment planning. While the residential care literature contains several excellent descriptions of the therapeutic milieus (e.g., Redl & Wineman, 1957) along with theoretically grounded hypotheses about what are the salient change mechanisms, no data exist that directly connect the influence of these factors on adolescents' adjustment with the adolescents' progress in care, let alone their postplacement outcomes. Studies such as the one described in this chapter are needed not only to begin to examine the characteristics of effective residential care models, but also to begin to sort out what types of problems are responsive to various forms of treatment.

To the extent that salient aspects of residential care models can be assessed and matched with the treatment needs of referred youths, the basis for making placement decisions will be improved. Specific, clinically relevant criteria that can be used for placement of children and adolescents in various forms of residential treatment are lacking (K. Wells, 1991). Research is needed that can clarify when residential care is indicated and which kinds of children/adolescent problems are likely to benefit from which types of residential treatment. As it is now, placement decisions are often made solely on the basis of availability of a bed space in a crisis atmosphere. All too often, this "place and hope" strategy results in failure.

4. References

Ageton, S. S., & Elliott, D. S. (1978). *The incidence of delinquent behavior in a national probability sample of adolescents* (Report No. 3). The National Youth Survey. Boulder, CO: Behavioral Research Institute.

Allen, M. (1991). Crafting a federal legislative framework for child welfare reform. *American Journal of Orthopsychiatry, 61*(4), 610–623.

American Psychiatric Association (1987). *Diagnostic and statistical manual of mental disorders,* 3rd. ed.—revised. Washington, DC: Author.

Andrews, B., Brown, G. W., & Creasey, L. (1990). Intergenerational links between psychiatric disorder in mothers and daughters: The role of parenting experiences. *Journal of Child Psychology and Psychiatry, 31*(7), 1115–1129.

Banducci, R. (1967). The effects of mother's employment on the achievement, aspirations, and expectations of the child. *Personnel and Guidance Journal, 46,* 263–267.

Bank, L., Marlowe, J. H., Reid, J. B., Patterson, G. R., & Weinrott, M. R. (1991). A comparative evaluation of parent training interventions for families of chronic delinquents. *Journal of Abnormal Child Psychology, 19*(1), 15–33.

Campbell, A. (1987). Self-reported delinquency and home life: Evidence from a sample of British girls. *Journal of Youth and Adolescence, 16*(2), 167–177.

Cappell, C., & Heiner, R. B. (1990). The intergenerational transmission of family aggression. *Journal of Family Violence, 5*(2), 135–152.

Cernkovich, S. A., & Giordano, P. C. (1987). Family relationships and delinquency. *Criminology, 25,* 295–321.

Chamberlain, P. (1990). Comparative evaluation of specialized foster care for seriously delinquent youths: A first step. *Community Alternatives: International Journal of Family Care, 2,* 21–36.

Chamberlain, P. (1991). Mediators of male delinquency: A clinical trial. Grant No. R01 MH 47458, Center for Studies of Violent Behavior and Traumatic Stress, NIMH, U.S. PHS.

Chamberlain, P. (1994). *Family connections,* Vol. 5. Eugene, OR: Castalia Publishing.

Chamberlain, P., & Reid, J. B. (1987). Parent observation and report of child symptoms. *Behavioral Assessment, 9,* 169–177.

Chamberlain, P., & Reid, J. B. (1991). Using a specialized foster care community treatment model for children and adolescents leaving the state mental hospital. *Journal of Community Psychology, 19,* 266–276.

Chamberlain, P., & Reid, J. B. (1994). Differences in risk factors and adjustment for male and female delinquents in treatment foster care. *Journal of Child and Family Studies, 3,* 23–39.

Chesney-Lind, M. (1988). Girls in jail. *Crime and Delinquency, 34*(2), 150–168.

Colton, M. (1989a). Attitudes of special foster parents and residential staff towards children. *Children and Society, 3*(1), 3–18.

Colton, M. (1989b). Foster and residential children's perceptions of their social environments. *British Journal of Social Work, 19*(3), 217–233.

Craft, M., Stevenson, G., & Granger, C. (1964). A controlled trial of authoritarian and self-governing regimes with adolescent psychopaths. *American Journal of Orthopsychiatry, 34*(3), 543–554.

Dishion, T. J., Patterson, G. R., Stoolmiller, M., & Skinner, M. L. (1991). Family, school, and behavioral antecedents to early adolescent involvement with antisocial peers. *Developmental Psychology, 2,* 172–180.

Egeland, B., Jacobvitz, D., & Papatola, K. (1987). Intergenerational continuity of parental abuse. In J. Lancaster & R. Gelles (Eds.), *Biosocial aspects of child abuse.* San Francisco: Jossey-Bass.

Elder, G. H., Caspi, A., & Downey, G. (1983). Problem behavior in family relationships: A multigenerational analysis. In A. Sorensen, F. Weinert, & L. Sherrod (Eds.), *Human development: Interdisciplinary perspective* (pp. 92–118). Hillsdale, NJ: Erlbaum Associates.

Elliott, D. S., Huizinga, D., & Ageton, S. S. (1985). *Explaining delinquency and drug use.* Beverly Hills, CA: Sage Publications.

Farrington, D. P. (1978). The family backgrounds of aggressive youths. In L. A. Hersov, M. Berger, & D. Shaffer (Eds.), *Aggression and antisocial behaviour in childhood and adolescence* (pp. 73–93). Oxford: Pergamon Press.

Glueck, S., & Glueck, E. (1950). *Unraveling juvenile delinquency.* Cambridge, MA: Harvard University Press.

Gold, D., & Andres, D. (1978). Developmental comparisons between ten-year-old children with employed and nonemployed mothers. *Child Development, 49,* 75–84.

Henggeler, S. W., Edwards, J., & Borduin, C. M. (1987). The family relations of female juvenile delinquents. *Journal of Abnormal Child Psychology, 15*(2), 199–209.

Herrenkohl, E., Herrenkohl, R., & Toedter, L. (1983). Perspectives on the intergenerational transmission of abuse. In D. Finkelhor, R. Gelles, G. Hotaling, & M. Straus (Eds.), *The dark side of families: Current family violence research* (pp. 305–316). Beverly Hills: Sage Publications.

Huesmann, L. R., Eron, L. D., Lefkowitz, M. M., & Walder, L. O. (1984). Stability of aggression over time and generations. *Developmental Psychology, 20,* 1120–1134.

Hunt, A., Day, D. M., & Levene, K. (1991). *The parent daily report: A manual.* Toronto: Earlscourt Child & Family Centre.

Klein, M. W. (1969). Gang cohesiveness, delinquency, and a street work program. *Journal of Research in Crime and Delinquency, 6,* 135–166.

Klein, M. W. (1971). *Street gangs and street workers.* Englewood Cliffs, NJ: Prentice-Hall.

Laub, J. H., & Sampson, R. J. (1988). Unraveling families and delinquency: A reanalysis of the Gluecks' data. *Criminology, 26*(3), 355–379.

Lewis, D. O., Yeager, C. A., Cobham-Portorreal, C. S., Klein, N., Showalter, C., & Anthony, A. (1991). A follow-up of female delinquents: Maternal contributions to the perpetuation of deviance. *Journal of the American Academy of Child and Adolescent Psychiatry, 30,* 197–201.

McCord, J. (1988). Parental behavior in the cycle of aggression. *Psychiatry, 51,* 14–23.

Meadowcroft, P., Thomlison, B., & Chamberlain, P. (1994). Treatment foster care services: A research agenda for child welfare. *Child Welfare League of America, 23*(5), 565–581.

Merikangas, K. R., & Spiker, D. G. (1982). Assortative mating among inpatients with primary affective disorder. *Psychological Medicine, 12,* 753–764.

Miller, W. B. (1962). The impact of a "total community" delinquency control project. *Social Problems, 10,* 168–191.

Morris, R. (1964). Female delinquency and relational problems. *Social Forces, 43,* 82–89.

Offord, D. R., Boyle, M. C., & Racine, Y. A. (1991). The epidemiology of antisocial behavior in childhood and adolescence. In D. J. Pepler & K. H. Rubin (Eds.), *The development and treatment of childhood aggression* (pp. 31–54). Hillsdale, NJ: Erlbaum Associates.

Pastorelli, T. (1995). Italian and U.S. boys' daily rates of problem behaviors: A comparison across cultures (in press).

Patterson, G. R. (1986). Performance models for antisocial boys. *American Psychologist, 41,* 432–444.

Patterson, G. R., Capaldi, D. M., & Bank, L. (1990). An early starter model for predicting delinquency. In D. Pepler & K. H. Rubin (Eds.), *The development and treatment of childhood aggression* (pp. 139–168). Hillsdale, NJ: Erlbaum Associates.

Patterson, G. R., Chamberlain, P., & Reid, J. B. (1982). A comparative evaluation of a parent-training program. *Behavior Therapy, 13,* 638–650.

Patterson, G. R., & Stouthamer-Loeber, M. (1984). The correlation of family management practices and delinquency. *Child Development, 55,* 1299–1307.

Phillips, E. L., Wolf, M. M., & Fixsen, D. L. (1973). Achievement Place: Development of an elected manager system. *Journal of Applied Behavior Analysis, 6,* 541–563.

Quinton, D., & Rutter, M. (1984). Long-term follow-up of women institutionalized in childhood: Factors promoting good functioning in adult life. *British Journal of Developmental Psychology, 2,* 191–204.

Redl, F., & Wineman, D. (1957). *The aggressive child.* New York: Free Press.

Reese, A. N., & Palmer, F. H. (1970). Factors related to change in mental tests performance. *Developmental Psychology Monograph 3.*

Rivera, V. R., & Kutash, K. (1994). Components of a system of care: What does the research say? Tampa: University of South Florida, Florida Mental Health Institute, Research and Training Center for Children's Mental Health.

Robins, L. N., & Price, R. K. (1991). Adult disorders predicted by childhood conduct problems: Results from the NIMH Epidemiologic Catchment Area Project. *Psychiatry, 54*(2), 116–132.

Rutter, M. (1989). Pathways from childhood to adult life. *Journal of Child Psychology and Psychiatry, 30*(1), 23–51.

Rutter, M., & Giller, H. (1984). *Juvenile delinquency: Trends and perspectives.* New York: Guilford Press.

Simons, R. L., Whitbeck, L. B., Conger, R. D., & Chyi-In, W. (1991). Intergenerational transmission of harsh parenting. *Developmental Psychology, 27*(1), 1–13.

Small, R., Kennedy, K., & Bender, B. (1991). Critical issues for practice in residential treatment: The view from within. *American Journal of Orthopsychiatry, 61*(3), 327–338.

Steinberg, L. (1986). Latchkey children and susceptibility to peer pressure: An ecological analysis. *Developmental Psychology, 22,* 433–439.

Streit, F. (1981). Differences among youthful criminal offenders based on their perceptions of parental behavior. *Adolescence, 16*(62), 409–413.

U.S. General Accounting Office (1994). *Residential care: Some high-risk youth benefit, but more study needed* (Publication No. B-249960). Washington, DC: Author.

Vorrath, H., & Brendtro, L. K. (1985). *Positive peer culture.* Chicago: Aldine.

Warren, M. Q., & Rosenbaum, J. L. (1987). Criminal careers of female offenders. *Criminal Justice and Behavior, 13*(4), 393–418.

Weinrott, M. R., Bauske, B., & Patterson, G. R. (1979). Systematic replication of a social learning approach. In P. O. Sjoden, S. Bates, & W. S. Dockens III (eds.), *Trends in behavior therapy* (pp. 331–352). New York: Academic Press.

Wells, E. L., & Rankin, J. H. (1988). Direct parental controls and delinquency. *Criminology, 26*(2), 263–285.

Wells, K. (1991). Placement of emotionally disturbed children in residential treatment: A review of placement criteria. *American Journal of Orthopsychiatry, 61*(3), 339–347.

Westen, D., Ludolph, P., Misle, B., Ruffins, S., & Block, J. (1990). Physical and sexual abuse in adolescent girls with borderline personality disorder. *American Journal of Orthopsychiatry, 60*(1), 55–66.

Widom, C. S. (1978). Towards an understanding of female criminality. In B. A. Maher (Ed.), *Progress in experimental personality research,* Vol 1 (pp. 247–259). New York: Academic Press.

Widom, C. S. (1989). Child abuse, neglect, and adult behavior: Research design and findings on criminality, violence, and child abuse. *American Journal of Orthopsychiatry, 59*(3), 355–367.

Wilson, H. (1987). Parental supervision re-examined. *British Journal of Criminology, 27*(3), 215–301.

Yesavage, J. A., Becker, J. M., & Werner, P. W. (1983). Family conflict, psychopathology and dangerous behavior by schizophrenics in hospital. *Psychiatry Research, 8,* 271–280.

Yesavage, J. A., & Widrow, L. (1985). Early parental discipline and adult self-destructive acts. *Journal of Nervous and Mental Disease, 173*(2), 74–77.

Zoccolillo, M. (1993). Gender and the development of conduct disorder. *Development and Psychopathology, 5,* 65–78.

Zoccolillo, M., & Rogers, K. (1991). Characteristics and outcome of hospitalized adolescent girls with conduct disorder. *Journal of the American Academy of Child and Adolescent Psychiatry, 30*(6), 973–981.

3

Stress–Coping Model of Adolescent Substance Use

Thomas Ashby Wills and Marnie Filer

1. Introduction

The goal of this chapter is to discuss research on adolescent substance use from the perspective of a stress-coping model. In addition to the long-term health implications of cigarette smoking and alcohol use (e.g., Helzer, 1987; U.S. Department of Health and Human Services, 1988), adolescent substance use is of concern to clinical psychology both because early onset of substance use has prognostic significance for later substance abuse problems (Robins & Przybeck, 1985) and because substance use tends to be correlated with other problem behaviors, including aggressive and depressive symptomatology (e.g., see Cole & Carpentieri, 1990; Loeber, 1988). Thus, research aimed at a better understanding of adolescent substance use has relevance for informing research on other types of child behavior problems.

This chapter presents a program of epidemiological research on adolescent substance use. The approach of epidemiology is to study the distribution of health and illness in the general population (Mausner & Kramer, 1985). Rather than focusing on samples of adolescents in treatment, the epidemiological approach obtains data on reasonably large samples from the general population of adolescents, most of whom are not substance users, and conducts analyses to determine factors associated with higher or lower levels of substance use (termed "risk factors" and "protective factors," respectively). The epidemiological approach is particularly relevant for the study of substance use because the majority of persons with substance abuse problems do not seek treatment, and

Thomas Ashby Wills and Marnie Filer • Ferkauf Graduate School of Psychology and Department of Epidemiology and Social Medicine, Albert Einstein College of Medicine, Yeshiva University, Bronx, New York 10461.

Advances in Clinical Child Psychology, Volume 18, edited by Thomas H. Ollendick and Ronald J. Prinz. Plenum Press, New York, 1996.

different types of selection biases may operate to guide persons into clinical settings [e.g., see Cox (1987) for substance abuse; Weissman (1987) for depression]. Studying predictors of substance use among community residents helps to ensure that variables identified as discriminating users from nonusers are not involved in selection processes.

A second aspect of epidemiological research is prospective designs, in which a sample is followed over time to determine variables that predict onset of substance use. As in other areas of research, cross-sectional data on substance use may have considerable ambiguity. As engaging in substance abuse is likely to create a number of new problems for the abuser, it is difficult for concurrent studies conducted on persons with identified substance abuse problems to differentiate variables that may be consequences of substance abuse from those that are predictors; for example, despite a large volume of research on adult alcoholics, it is still unclear whether depression typically occurs before or after onset of alcohol problems (e.g., see Cox, 1987). Prospective designs, in which predictor variables are measured before the onset of substance use problems, help to resolve this issue. The work discussed in this chapter is based on this approach, studying factors associated with substance use during the age range from 12 years onward, the age range in which initiation of substance use typically occurs (Johnston, O'Malley, & Bachman, 1989).

In this chapter, we present findings derived from a stress–coping model. As in diathesis–stress models of adult mental health problems (Rohde, Lewinsohn, Tilson, & Seeley, 1990; Monroe & Simons, 1991), it is posited that life stress is a general risk factor that predisposes to various kinds of problems. We also posit that coping processes operate to either retard or accelerate the development of problems. We assume that adolescents cope with problems in ways that may be either adaptive or maladaptive and that the individual person's profile of coping shifts the person either toward or away from problem development. A difference from a strict diathesis–stress model is that we consider the role of protective factors such as parental support and children's competence, which may help to reduce the impact of risk factors. Consistent with diathesis–stress models, we consider the possibility that conditions present during early childhood may contribute a risk burden to the developing child (cf. Zucker, 1994). We do find suggestions of early conditions that contribute to risk, and our research has suggested that their effects are partly mediated through stress and coping processes.

In the following sections, we present the tenets of a stress–coping perspective on adolescent substance use and discuss research derived from this perspective. As we proceed in the chapter, we consider theoretical issues that have arisen in the course of this research, leading to some possible modifications of the model. In a final section, we discuss implications for future research, giving attention not only to substance abuse per se but also to questions about conduct disorder among adolescents.

2. Theoretical Models of Adolescent Substance Use

Here, we discuss three theoretical models of adolescent substance use and other problem behaviors, based largely on research from community samples rather than clinical settings. These models have tended to focus either on vulnerability to substance abuse or on resilience—that is, resistance to development of problems in environments that would ordinarily be expected to be conducive to problem development. We give an exposition of the stress–coping model of substance use and then consider models that focus on competence and deviance-prone attitudes, respectively.

2.1. Stress–Coping Model

Stress–coping theory, as originally formulated by Lazarus and Folkman (1984), is a general model of how persons adapt to life challenges. Stress is posited to occur when demands from the environment exceed the resources a person has available to meet those demands. Stress–coping theory posits that in this situation, the person makes an appraisal of the potential seriousness and changeability of the stressor and then chooses a coping mechanism that should be most likely to ameliorate the problem. The transactional formulation of Lazarus and Folkman (1984) posits that following the onset of stress, there ensues a dynamic process whereby persons repeatedly appraise the success of their coping efforts, modify their current coping if necessary, and continue this process until the problem is resolved (e.g., Folkman & Lazarus, 1985).

The original formulation of stress–coping theory posited two general domains of coping. *Problem-focused coping* is defined as encompassing efforts aimed at dealing with the external environment to remove the source of the problem. This type of coping is assumed to involve processes such as getting information, considering alternative courses of action, making a decision about a plan of action, and taking direct action to solve the problem. In contrast, *emotion-focused coping* is defined as comprising efforts aimed at dealing with the person's internal (emotional) environment, in order to manage and reduce psychological distress associated with the problem. This type of coping is assumed to involve processes such as cognitively reframing the problem situation in a more positive way, minimizing the threat associated with the problem, focus-ing on positive aspects of the situation, and considering how things could be worse. The position of the original theory was that problem-focused coping would be employed in situations in which the problem was changeable, whereas emotion-focused coping would be employed in situations in which the problem was not changeable. It was assumed in the original theory that either problem-focused or emotion-focused coping would be effective if appropriately employed (depending on the situation) and hence would lead to successful adaptation to life prob-lems.

Stress–coping theory stimulated a large amount of research in social and clinical psychology and has undergone considerable development over the past ten years (e.g., see Aldwin, 1994; Carpenter, 1992; L. Cohen, 1988; Compas, 1987; Garmezy & Rutter, 1983; Goldberger & Breznitz, 1993; LaGreca, Siegel, Wallander, & Walker, 1992; Wills, 1990c; Zeidner & Endler, 1995). One major shift involves recognition that peoples' actual ways of coping with problems are not always effective ways. This recognition led to methods for assessing potentially mal-adaptive as well as adaptive approaches to coping (e.g., Carver, Scheier, & Weintraub, 1989); these maladaptive approaches include withdrawing from social interaction when troubled (withdrawal), wishing the prob-lem would just go away (wishful thinking), denying that the problem exists (denial), distracting oneself from thinking about the problem (dis-traction), venting negative emotions on other people (variously termed anger, emotional venting, or catharsis), or taking the attitude that one cannot cope and giving up on any attempt to deal with the problem (helplessness). A second major shift was based on data showing a strong correlation between measures of problem- and emotion-focused coping (Stone, Helder, & Schneider, 1988). This finding suggested that the di-mensionality of coping be conceptualized in terms of *approach vs. avoid-ance*, whether the person actively invests effort in trying to approach and deal with the problem (termed "approach coping" or "engagement") or declines to invest any effort in trying to deal with the problem— variously termed "avoidant coping" (Moos & Schaefer, 1993; Rohde et al., 1990) or "disengagement" (Carver et al., 1989).[1] In this chapter, we shall use the terms *active coping* and *avoidant coping* to refer to these two domains.

Two other dimensions of coping should be noted. Recognition that

---

[1] Coping theory does not assume that any given coping mechanism is universally effective or ineffective in all possible situations. For example, coping through distraction is effec-tive for dealing with short-term physical stressors (e.g., see Suls & Fletcher, 1985), though evidence on long-term life stressors suggests that distraction and avoidance may be neutral or ineffective.

coping is inherently a social process as well as an individual process (S. Cohen & Wills, 1985) has led to inclusion of measures for assessing the use of social support as a coping mechanism. Also, the common empirical finding that religion is used as a coping mechanism by persons in the general population (e.g., Park & Cohen, 1992; Timmer, Colten, & Veroff, 1985) has led to incorporation of measures of religious coping in current research. Neither social support nor religious coping fits clearly under the approach–avoidance rubric, and these aspects are often analyzed as separate dimensions of coping.

The stress–coping model of substance use employs these theoretical constructs but involves two additional postulates. First is the proposition that life stress is a risk factor for substance use. There is considerable empirical evidence for this proposition. Measures of negative life events and perceived stress have been shown to be correlated with smoking and alcohol use among adolescents (e.g., Mitic, McGuire, & Neumann, 1985; Wills, 1985) and among adults (e.g., S. Cohen & Williamson, 1988; Cooper, Russell, Skinner, Frone, & Mudar, 1992). Prospective studies with adolescent samples have shown that life stress is related to increase in substance use over time (Newcomb & Harlow, 1986; Wills, 1986), thus indicating that high stress is not simply a consequence of prior substance use. Several studies have shown that life stress is related to use of psychotropic medications (Cafferata, Kasper, & Bernstein, 1983; Mellinger, Balter, Manheimer, Cisin, & Parry, 1978; Timmer et al., 1985) and to illicit drug use (Chaney & Roszell, 1985; Hall, Havassy, & Wasserman, 1991; McKirnan & Peterson, 1988; McMahon & Kouzekanani, 1991). Moreover, it has been shown that stress–coping factors predict relapse to cigarette smoking or alcohol use by those trying to achieve reduction or abstinence (Abrams, Monti, Pinto, Elder, Brown, & Jacobus, 1987; Carey, Kalra, Carey, Halperin, & Richards, 1993; S. Cohen & Lichtenstein, 1990; Shiffman, 1985; Moos, Finney, & Cronkite, 1990). The consistency of stress effects across the different phases of substance use has led to theoretical discussions of life stress as a general predisposing factor for substance use (e.g., see Wills, 1990c).

A second aspect of the stress–coping theoretical model is the proposition that substances themselves have coping functions. Though the physiological mechanisms of drug effects are still under investigation, it is clear that people perceive that tobacco or alcohol use helps calm them down when they are tense or anxious and helps them feel better when they are depressed (see e.g., Hull & Bond, 1986; Marlatt, 1987; Wills & Shiffman, 1985). Similar functions are observed for the use of both tobacco and alcohol, grouped under the domains of *negative-affect reduction* and *positive-affect enhancement* (e.g., Cappell & Greeley, 1987; Wills, 1988), and it is believed that people are able to employ dose-dependent effects to obtain these functions in different situations. Evidence on specific functions also indicates that persons perceive that substance use will help relieve boredom, help them to perform better in some situations, or help distract them from unpleasant self-awareness (e.g., Brown, Goldman, Inn, & Anderson, 1980; Revell, Warburton, & Wesnes, 1985; Steele & Josephs, 1990). While light smokers or drinkers score higher on social motives for substance use (e.g., having a drink at a party), heavy users typically score higher on all perceived coping functions of tobacco or alcohol use (Cooper, Russell, & George, 1988; Wills & Shiffman, 1985), suggesting that coping functions help to motivate and sustain high levels of use. Cessation research has suggested that relapse occurs in stressful situations because negative emotions prime memories about previous coping functions of substance use (Perkins & Grobe, 1992; Shadel & Mermelstein, 1993).

Because using substances for coping with problems is empirically correlated with avoidant-type measures of coping, it is often classified as an avoidant coping mechanism (Khantzian, 1990; Rohde et al., 1990) and sometimes is explicitly included in global indices of avoidant coping (e.g., Moos & Schaefer, 1993).[2] We have measured coping-related motives for substance use as a separate construct. For example, we found in a sample of 10th-grade students that perceived coping functions of stress reduction, mood enhancement, and boredom relief were related to high levels of substance use (Wills & Cleary, 1995b). Thus, coping functions are just as relevant for substance use among adolescents as for such use among adults.

The stress–coping model suggests that the tendency to gravitate toward substance use as a coping mechanism will be increased when a person's fund of active coping resources (e.g., problem solving, cognitive strategies) is reduced or impoverished, and research on relapse to smoking or alcohol use shows that persons are likely to relapse if they make no attempt to cope with problem situations (Shiffman, 1985, 1994). Also, when a young person begins to become involved in substance use rather than in more active and effortful ways of coping, he or she loses the opportunity to practice and develop more adaptive coping mechanisms, so the theoretical prediction is that coping and competence will be further decreased. Thus, the stress–coping model suggests a dynamic perspective in which the exercise of active coping mechanisms decreases the likelihood of substance use and strengthens general coping ability, whereas use of substances as a way of dealing with problems reduces the use of active coping mechanisms and makes substance use

---

[2] This practice does present a potential confound when using standardized measures of avoidant coping to predict substance use (e.g., Cooper et al., 1988). In our research, items pertaining to substance use are not included in the avoidant coping measures.

and other avoidant coping more likely in the future (Wills & Hirky, 1995). Evidence on the operation of these types of cycles with adolescents will be presented in a subsequent section.

2.2. Competence and Resiliency Models

Resiliency models are based on the observation that some children who grow up in situations of adversity (e.g., parents' mental illness) emerge as young adults showing relatively good adaptation, whereas others develop a range of problems such as psychological difficulties, criminal behavior, and drug abuse. In response to such observations, the concept of *resilience* has developed. Masten (1994) defines resilience as a pattern over time characterized by good eventual adaptation despite developmental risks, acute stressors, or chronic adversities. Models of resilience are relevant for this discussion because in essence they are stress-buffering models (S. Cohen & Wills, 1985): They propose that having certain attributes or competencies reduces or eliminates the impact of stressful circumstances (e.g., Garmezy & Masten, 1991; Luthar & Zigler, 1991). The primary difference is that resilience researchers have focused on situations in which the adverse situation is complex and persistent over time (e.g., poverty, parental substance abuse), whereas coping research has generally studied situations in which the stressors are more specific and time-limited. Both types of research, however, have aimed to develop knowledge and theory about what enables persons to cope with challenging circumstances.

Resilience research has usually proceeded by studying a high-risk sample and measuring variables that may discriminate persons who attain relatively good functioning (i.e., the resilient subjects) from those who develop problems. In the best case, the research design is prospective and assesses predictor variables at a relatively early time point so analyses can determine factors that are present before the divergence of good vs. poor functioning. Results from concurrent or retrospective designs, on the other hand, may be ambiguous as to whether putative resilience factors occurred before or after the development of good functioning.

An example of a prospective approach is the longitudinal study by Werner and Smith (1982). This study followed a 1955 birth cohort of 698 children of Polynesian and Asian backgrounds who lived on the Hawaiian island of Kauai. Initial assessment occurred when the child was 1 year old, and the sample was subsequently assessed at 2, 10, and 18 years of age. Data were obtained from interviews with parents and children, from standardized tests administered at home or in school, and from community agency records (e.g., police, family court, or mental health service). A paper by Werner (1986) examined a group of 49 youths selected from the larger sample because one or both parents had serious problems with alcohol abuse during the subject's childhood (between the ages of 2 and 10 years). Most of these children grew up in chronic poverty in addition to having parents who were substance abusers, so the sample can be characterized as having a significant burden of adversity.

The criterion of resilience was determined from data gathered at 18 years of age; at this time, 41% of the high-risk subsample had developed serious mental health or behavior problems, but 59% were classified as not having significant problems (i.e., the resilient group). Analyses performed to discriminate resilient vs. nonresilient subjects indicated that the former had experienced more attention and support from their parent(s) during childhood. Data from the early school years indicated that the resilient children had better academic performance. Data from adolescence indicated that the resilient teenagers had perceptions of more internal control, believing that their actions determined their outcomes. Werner (1986) concluded that resilience was attributable to joint contributions from characteristics of the caretaking environment and competencies of the child, including communication skills and ability to form good social relationships.

A body of research has developed on resilience factors, usually replicating findings of the Werner (1986) study and suggesting some additional factors (e.g., see Masten, 1994; Luthar & Zigler, 1991). Reviewers suggest that constitutional factors including intelligence and certain temperamental characteristics (e.g., approach vs. withdrawal to situations, soothability when upset) may contribute to forming attachment with caregivers. Abilities to plan, take active steps to deal with environmental challenges, and use social problem-solving skills have been suggested as characteristics of resilient children. In addition to parental support as identified by Werner (1986), several studies suggest that a network of social relationships with other adults, such as teachers or ministers, contributes to resilience (e.g., Braithwaite & Gordon, 1992; Lewis & Looney, 1983). Some of the variables may be viewed as factors that contribute to better coping and competence (e.g., intelligence), whereas other variables are close to dimensions of coping that have been studied in other contexts (e.g., planning and problem solving).

2.3. Deviancy Model

Because use of tobacco and alcohol is illegal for adolescents, it is necessary for a comprehensive model to consider processes involved generally in deviant behavior. An adolescent who may be predisposed to try some deviant behavior has several potential barriers to contend with: The behaviors are officially proscribed, they may get one in trouble with parents or teachers, and they run counter to prevailing attitudes among conventional peers. Problem-behavior theory (Jessor & Jessor, 1977) was originally developed as a general model of deviance proneness and provides a perspective similar to the perspectives provided by sociological models of deviance. Because problem-behavior theory has been extensively used in research on adolescent substance use (Donovan & Jessor, 1978; Donovan, Jessor, & Jessor, 1983; Jessor, Chase, & Donovan, 1980) and accounts for the association among a variety of adolescent problem behaviors including heavy drinking, marijuana use, and precocious sexual intercourse (Donovan & Jessor, 1985), we briefly discuss this model.

Problem-behavior theory views involvement in deviant behavior as resulting from a combination of variables ranging from distal to proximal. At the distal level are attitudinal factors conducive to deviance. The theory suggests that placing a high value on personal independence from adults and a low value on the conventional rewarding activity of academic achievement is a risk factor technically termed the "independence–achievement value discrepancy." In this theory, value on religion is also posited as a distal factor predicted to be inversely related to substance use because of an assumed correlation with conventional values. Attitudinal tolerance for deviant actions (e.g., lying, stealing) is also posited as a distal risk factor. In this model, attachment to parents is posited to be a distal protective factor, because of internalization of conventional values. These distal factors are proposed to operate through the proximal factor of associating with deviant peers. If a teen has little attachment to parents and has attitudes tolerant of deviance, he or she is predicted to seek out peers with similarly deviant attitudes. In the experience of initial association with deviant peers, the adolescent gains access to proscribed substances (e.g., cigarettes), gets reinforcement from peers for trying out deviant behavior, and learns how to perform deviant behaviors and avoid negative consequences. Involvement in a deviant peer group is posited to be the proximal factor for initiation and subsequent escalation to a variety of deviant behaviors. It should be noted that from the perspective of the participants, the behaviors involved are fun and exciting and it is the larger society that is deviant, being characterized as boring, punitive, or both (Goldstein, 1990).

An accomplishment of the Jessor and Jessor (1977) model is that it provides a theoretical account for two important facts: (1) various adolescent problem behaviors tend to be intercorrelated (e.g., Donovan & Jessor, 1985) and (2) behaviors as seemingly diverse as smoking, drinking, marijuana use, and sexual intercourse all have similar predictors

(Jessor & Jessor, 1977). This theory accounts for the correlation among problem behaviors as a consequence of their being defined as deviant behaviors by adult authorities; hence, a set of attitudes favorable toward deviance will lead to involvement in all these activities. However, problem-behavior theory has not given much attention to whether deviant attitudes are related to life problems of adolescents and whether substance use itself may provide coping functions (cf. Folkman, Chesney, Pollack, & Phillips, 1992). Through focusing on external controls as the primary avenue for producing conventional behavior, this theory has given less attention to internal controls and coping mechanisms that may help adolescents to obtain competence and adaptation.

In summary, these models of adolescent problems have some common constructs and some divergent predictions. The stress–coping model views substance use and possibly other problem behaviors as deriving from a high level of life stress, a low level of active coping, and a high level of avoidant coping. The resiliency model views adaptation to adversity (i.e., lack of problem behavior in circumstances in which it would otherwise be expected) as partly attributable to having certain competencies during childhood, though it has no specific postulates about how these competencies are developed. The problem-behavior model generally has not recognized a role of life stress in adolescent problem behavior, but rather has focused on the presence of deviance-prone attitudes and values. All three models suggest the importance of parental relationship as a protective factor, but for different reasons: Coping and competence models suggest that parental support is protective because it helps to develop individual competence and ameliorate the effect of stressful circumstances, whereas problem-behavior theory suggests that such support is protective because attachment to parents produces more conventional values. In the following sections, we report research that tested predictions from these models.

3. Overview of Research Methods

In this chapter, we discuss findings from six studies, designed and conducted in a parallel manner to test questions about coping, competence, and deviancy. Some basic methods used in this research are similar across studies. The target subjects are the entire population in public school districts, and we typically survey around 90% of the eligible population. Sample sizes in various studies have ranged from about 500 subjects to approximately 1800 subjects. The samples are multiethnic, typically about 30% African-American, 25% Hispanic, and 40% white. The subjects range in age from 11 years to around 15 years, that is, from late childhood through middle adolescence. The communities in which the families reside are economically diverse and representative of the state population. The modal level of parental education is high school graduate, so the families would be characterized as working class on the average.

In this school-based research, data were obtained primarily through self-report questionnaires administered in school classrooms. The questionnaires are 12–16 pages long and take about 40 minutes to complete. Questionnaires were administered by project staff, who gave instructions to students according to a standardized protocol and circulated in the classroom to answer questions about individual items. The surveys were administered under confidential conditions, the questionnaires being labeled only with a code number and the students instructed not to write their names on the questionnaires. We emphasized to students that their survey responses would not be known by their parents or teachers, and we obtained a Certificate of Confidentiality from the Public Health Service, which provides the best possible legal protection for the privacy of subjects' data. Methodological research has shown that when subjects are assured of confidentiality, their reports of problem behavior have good validity (e.g., Murray & Perry, 1987).

The predictor measures were self-report scales designed for epidemiological research, derived from standardized inventories and from our own previous research. Typically, these scales comprise 6–12 items per scale and have a Likert-type response format, in which subjects indicate the extent (on a 1–4 or 1–5 scale) to which a given statement is true or not true for themselves. These scales have internal consistency reliability (Cronbach alpha) from the upper 60s to the middle 80s. The general intent of these measures is not to obtain clinical judgments or diagnoses, but to produce a continuous score for each scale such that a given score indicates that the subject has a higher or lower level of the construct. For the most part, these measures were normally distributed in the samples of students we surveyed.

In some studies, we obtained independent reports from teachers on the same constructs reported by the students (e.g., academic competence). Teachers were given rating sheets for each student in their classes and made ratings of selected characteristics on the same items responded to by the students, adapted for a third-party format. Teachers made these ratings outside school hours, around the time when the student questionnaires were administered; teachers did not know what students said about themselves on the self-report questionnaire. Consistent with previous research (Achenbach, McConaughy, & Howell, 1987), we found modest convergence between student and teacher data, with correlations ranging from around $r = 0.40$ for more observable characteristics to $r = 0.10$ for less observable characteristics. While the correlation between student and teacher reports is modest, we found that the teacher reports typically had independent predictive value (Wills, Du-Hamel, & Vaccaro, 1995b).

The primary dependent variable in our research was a composite score for substance use. This score was based on questions about the typical frequency of the subject's use of cigarettes, alcohol, and marijuana; responses were usually on a 1–6 scale with scale points Never Used, Tried Once-Twice, Used Four-Five Times, Use a Few Times a Month, Use a Few Times a Week, and Use Every Day. An additional item to index heavy drinking asked whether there was a time in the last month when the subject had three or more drinks on one occasion; response points were No, Happened Once, and Happened Twice or More. These four items were combined into a composite score or latent construct representing overall level of substance use, consistent with previous methodological studies (Hays, Widaman, DiMatteo, & Stacy, 1987; Needle, Su, & Lavee, 1989). Our data showed smoking, alcohol, and marijuana use to be substantially intercorrelated, as is typically found in adolescent research (e.g., Jessor & Jessor, 1977), and frequency of use increased with age, also a typical finding (e.g., see Johnston et al., 1989). In absolute terms, the rate of regular cigarette smoking (defined as a few times a week) in our samples was initially in the low single digits (3–5% of the sample) in the 7th grade, but increased to about 15% by the 9th grade. Rates of heavy alcohol use (more than 2 times in past month) also started low, but could rise to 25–30% by high school. Rates of marijuana use in these samples tended to be low, with around 90% of the sample having little or no experience with marijuana. Only in small subgroups of heavy substance users were substantial rates of regular marijuana use observed.

Statistical analyses used multivariate methods such as multiple regression or structural modeling. The criterion variable typically was a composite score for overall substance use.[3] Analyses entered relevant predictors (e.g., different types of coping) together because predictor variables can be intercorrelated and it is important to demonstrate unique effects, such as the effect of one type of coping on substance use, controlling for effects of other types of coping. Analyses were always replicated with demographic controls, entering indices for gender, ethnicity, family structure, and parental socioeconomic status together with

---

[3] In our samples of younger adolescents, the criterion score for substance use is skewed, because the great majority of subjects have little or no use and only a small proportion of subjects have a greater level of use. We have tested various transformations of the substance use score to deal with the skewness issue and have found that they do not produce any notable change in the results.

the predictor variables. All the findings we report in this chapter were obtained independent of demographics; that is, they are not attributable to a correlation of stress–coping factors with characteristics such as gender or socioeconomic status. At various times, we have tested for simple main effects, moderation effects, or mediation effects (Baron & Kenny, 1986). In moderation or interaction, one variable serves to alter the effect of another variable, as in stress-buffering effects, whereby the impact of negative life events is reduced for persons with a high level of social support. A mediation process, in contrast, is one in which the relationship between one variable and an outcome is transmitted or mediated through another variable; for example, we found that the relation between low socioeconomic status and adolescent substance use was mediated in part through negative life events.

4. Stress and Substance Use

4.1. Convergent Assessments of Stress and Substance Use

The first part of the stress–coping model predicts that life stress will be involved in the initiation of substance use during early adolescence. Our investigation of this question began with a study of junior high school students in the borough of Manhattan (Wills, 1985, 1986; Wills & Warshawsky, 1983). Several midsize samples (600–900 subjects) were studied in a staggered cohort design, in which subjects were followed for a 2-year period over the interval from the beginning of 7th grade to the end of 8th grade. In this design, the subjects were surveyed four times, at 6-month intervals, over the study period.

The aim of this study was to measure the construct of stress in several different ways and test whether a relationship of stress to early substance use could be detected. The results did indicate that stress was related to substance use during this period of adolescence. Convergent results were found for a 14-item scale indexing subjective perceptions of perceived stress during the past week (e.g., anxiety, somatic symptoms), a 12-item scale of daily negative events ("hassles") during the past week, and a 22-item checklist of major life events during the past year, based on previous inventories for adolescents (Johnson & McCutcheon, 1980; Newcomb, Huba, & Bentler, 1981). Subjects with higher stress scores had higher levels of smoking or alcohol use, and this relationship was true for each type of stress measure. Typical effect sizes were standardized regression coefficients in the range from 0.15 to 0.25. Moreover, prospective analyses testing the effect of stress measures at 6-month lags showed that stress was related to increases in substance use over time (Wills, 1986). This study established that life stress in early adolescence is a risk factor for substance use, and prospective findings ruled out the possibility that a high level of stress was simply a consequence of prior substance use.

Questions about stress and substance use were pursued in further research. The replicability of the relationship between stress and substance was tested in a cross-sectional sample of 1289 adolescents, ages 11–13 years, from schools in low-income areas of New York City (Spanish Harlem and the South Bronx). In this sample, the students were largely from minority backgrounds (51% Hispanic and 25% African-American). The relationship between negative life events and substance use was replicated, and the effect size was substantial, representing a standardized regression coefficient of around 0.30 (Wills, Vaccaro, & McNamara, 1992a). Similar effects were found in independent studies in Missouri (Chassin, Mann, & Sher, 1988), New Jersey (Labouvie, 1986), and Los Angeles (Castro, Maddahian, Newcomb, & Bentler, 1987), so it is evident that the relationship between stress and adolescent substance use is not restricted to inner-city populations.

To test whether the impact of negative affect on substance use could be offset by feelings of positive well-being (Diener, 1984), we used 12-item scales of negative and positive affect based on mood dimensions from Zevon and Tellegen (1982). The prediction was confirmed: The relationship between negative affect and substance use was almost eliminated among subjects with high positive affect (Wills et al., 1992). This buffering-type effect (cf. S. Cohen & Wills, 1985; Luthar & Zigler, 1991) indicates that while negative experiences do pose risks for adolescents, these risks may be offset to some extent by having a substantial number of positive experiences.

4.2. Causation of Negative Life Events

We have considered a suggestion from diathesis-stress theory that negative life events could be self-caused, resulting from premorbid psychopathology of the respondent (Depue & Monroe, 1986). In the first study, separate tests were conducted for negative life events that could have been caused by an adolescent subject (e.g., suspension from school) and negative life events that were unlikely to be caused by the adolescent (e.g., parental unemployment). These tests showed that the two sets of events made independent contributions for predicting adolescent substance use (Wills, 1986), but these contributions were not decisive either way. On the one hand, an adolescent's disobedience or aggressiveness could be responsible for bringing on some types of negative events. On the other hand, there was evidence that some life events not logically linked to the adolescent's personality also had a predictive effect. Thus, there is something about living in a stressful environment that makes people more likely to smoke or drink in early adolescence.

Are negative life events simply a proxy for deviancy? To try to resolve this question, we included measures of deviance-prone attitudes together with life stress in analyses predicting substance use. This question was tested in a longitudinal study in which subjects were first surveyed in 7th grade and were followed up with a similar survey at 1-year intervals. The measures of deviance proneness (from Jessor & Jessor, 1977) were values on independence and achievement (4 items each), value on religion (4 items), and a 10-item scale on attitudinal tolerance for deviant behaviors. Prospective analyses were performed in which, for example, substance use at 8th grade was predicted from negative life events at 7th grade with control for deviant attitudes at 7th grade and substance use at 7th grade (i.e., covariate). Results indicated that negative life events were related to increased substance use over time, with control for deviant attitudes (Wills, Vaccaro, McNamara, & Hirky, 1993b). Thus, the relationship between life stress and substance use in early adolescence was not accounted for by deviancy, at least as measured in this study.

4.3. Moderating Effects of Attitudes

Attitudes, however, may act as moderating factors, serving to alter the impact of life events. We tested the interaction of negative life events and attitudinal variables from the Jessor and Jessor (1977) theory and found significant moderation effects. The attitudinal measure of tolerance for deviance showed an exacerbating effect: The relationship between negative life events and adolescents' substance use was stronger among persons who scored high on tolerance for deviance. Value on religion, in contrast, had a buffering effect: The impact of negative life events was reduced among persons who had a high score on religious values (Wills, Vaccaro, McNamara, & Hirky, 1993b). Thus, the effect of life stress must be considered in the context of other factors.

5. Coping and Substance Use

5.1. Assessment of Coping

The second part of the stress–coping model predicts that the way adolescents deal with problem situations will be related to early substance use. In measuring coping in adolescents, we had to deal with a basic issue for coping research. If you assess how subjects cope with one particular problem, then the results from the coping measure may be situation-specific, but if you assess how subjects cope with generally defined problems, the results from this coping measure may be tapping into the subjects' dispositional characteristics (e.g., see Stone, Kennedy-Moore, Newman, Greenberg, & Neale, 1992). We have tried to steer a middle course in this area. We measured how subjects cope with a range of problems, thus placing more emphasis on the generality issue, but we also assessed coping with several different methods, to determine whether findings are method-specific. The response-based method follows from the typical assumptions of psychometric theory (Moos & Schaefer, 1993). The subject is given a general lead-in statement and an inventory with 30–40 items and is asked to indicate, for each item, how much she or he does this when she or he has a problem. Factor analysis is typically employed to determine coping dimensions based on sets of intercorrelated items. In the intention-based method, following from the work of Stone and Neale (1984), subjects are first given definitions of general coping goals (e.g., "Do something to see the problem in a different way," that is, cognitive coping) and are then asked the extent to which they pursue this coping intention for a given type of problem. This approach is assessed across different types of problems (problems with schoolwork, parents, health, and feeling sad or down). The bottom line for this research is that findings are replicated across methods, so assessment method does not seem crucial for the results.

We have assessed two broad domains that would now be characterized theoretically as active coping vs. avoidant coping (Carver et al., 1989; Moos & Schaefer, 1993). Under the first domain, we assessed behavioral coping: the extent to which the subject gets information about a problem, considers alternatives, takes direct action ("I do something to solve the problem"), and uses resourcefulness to reach the goal ("I try different ways to solve the problem"). We also assessed a dimension termed "cognitive coping," the extent to which the person uses various cognitive strategies. We find these two dimensions to be highly correlated (rs of 0.60 or more), which justifies viewing them as reflecting an approach of investing effort in actively dealing with problems (Wills, Vaccaro, McNamara, & DuHamel, 1992b). In one study, we have assessed physical exercise (e.g., going running or bike riding, going to a gym to work out) as a way of dealing with stress; correlations with other measures show that this technique does not fall clearly in either domain.

Under the domain of avoidant coping, we assessed several specific mechanisms, which tend to be intercorrelated at lower levels (rs generally around 0.30). General avoidance is defined as trying to distract oneself from a problem (e.g., "I try to put the problem out of my mind"), social withdrawal (e.g., "I just tell people to leave me alone"), daydreaming ("I daydream about better times"), and wishful thinking ("I just wish the problem would go away"); empirically, these items all appear in one factor for general avoidance (cf. Rohde et al., 1990). Anger coping is defined by items indicating that when a person has a problem he or she takes it out on someone else through getting mad, engaging in verbal aggression (blaming and criticizing other people or "yelling and screaming"), or getting back at others through property damage ("I throw things, break someone's things") or physical aggression ("I hit someone"). Helplessness coping is defined by a scale of disengagement taken from Carver et al. (1989), indicating that when the subject has a problem she or he just says in various ways "I can't deal with it" and gives up trying to solve the problem. A dimension termed Social Entertainment is assessed by items indicating that when the subject has a problem he or she just "hangs out" with other kids, goes to a movie or a party. Several studies have shown that this type of measure is correlated with anger, helplessness, and general avoidance (cf. Sussman, Brannon, Dent, Hansen, Johnson, & Flay, 1993), so it is classified as an avoidant coping mechanism.[4]

For the other dimensions previously discussed, social support and religious coping, assessment has been done with different methods across studies. Social support is assessed in some studies as a coping mechanism with a focus on emotional support ("When I have a problem I talk with my mother/father" or "I talk with a friend I feel close to") and in others with measures indexing whether support is perceived to be available in times of trouble. Similarly, religion is assessed in some instances as a coping mechanism ("When I have a problem, I pray for guidance and strength") and in others as a value dimension indexing identification with religious beliefs. We find that scores from these different methods are correlated and produce similar findings, so again we do not think measurement approach is a decisive factor for the results.

To assess the perception of substance use as a coping mechanism, we have taken several different approaches. With younger subjects for whom rates of substance use are low in absolute terms, we simply ask them whether they engage in any of several substance-related behaviors (smoke a lot, drink alcohol to feel better, smoke marijuana, or take pills to feel better) when they have a problem. With older subjects, we ask direct questions as to whether smoking cigarettes or drinking alcohol provides any of several different coping functions (e.g., calm down

---

[4] In earlier work, the coping measure included an item, adapted from other inventories, about going shopping (see Wills, 1985). This item loaded on the Entertainment dimension, giving some support to the facetious maxim about coping, "When the going gets tough, the tough go shopping."

when tense, cheer up when in a bad mood). Data from a study with
10th-graders indicated that scores from these two methods were correlated about 0.60 with each other (Wills & Cleary, 1995b), so we have
reason to believe that they provide similar information, indexing substance use that is specifically pursued for coping with problems (cf.
Cooper et al., 1988; McKirnan & Peterson, 1988).

5.2. Analysis of Coping–Substance Use Relationships

Tests of the relationship between coping and substance use are
derived from multiple regression analyses with substance use score as
the criterion variable.[5] Findings on the relationship between coping dimensions and adolescents' substance use have been consistent across
methods and studies (Wills, 1986; Wills, McNamara, Vaccaro, & Hirky,
1995d; Wills, Vaccaro, Benson, & Schreibman, 1994c). Active coping
mechanisms are inversely related to substance use. The strongest effects
are found for behavioral coping, with effect sizes around $\beta = -0.15$ and
sometimes greater.[6] Cognitive coping also has an independent, inverse
effect. Thus, there is evidence for the proposition that an active approach to coping is a protective factor with respect to substance use.
Physical exercise has complex effects, typically appearing as a stress-
buffering effect (Wills, 1986) or as a delayed effect (Wills et al., 1995d),
but the effects usually indicate that a higher level of exercise coping is
related to a lower level of substance use. Religious coping has an independent effect, related to a lower level of substance use (Wills, 1985).
Thus, these coping mechanisms are indicated as protective factors.

Coping mechanisms grouped under the domain of avoidant coping
are related to a higher level of substance use. Anger coping always has
the strongest relationship with substance use, with effect sizes of $\beta \geq$
0.20; subjects who cope with problems by getting angry and engaging in
verbal or physical aggression show a higher level of early substance use.
Helplessness also shows substantial correlations with more substance
use. It is highly related to anger, however, and sometimes is nonsignificant in multivariate analyses because of this relationship (Wills et al.,
1992b). Social entertainment and "hanging out" show independent effects, related to higher level of substance use. Finally, the measure of
general avoidant coping generally shows no significant net relationship

---

[5] As the aim in these analyses is to predict overall level of substance use, we exclude the
measure of substance use coping from the predictor set.

[6] While this may not seem like a large effect, it should be noted that it is a unique effect,
obtained net of other coping mechanisms entered and removing any shared variance
with demographic characteristics.

to substance use; though it has a significant zero-order correlation with substance use, the multivariate analyses indicate that anger and helplessness are the coping measures that have significant effects. These findings depart from some current theory on coping. They suggest that although mechanisms grouped under the rubric of avoidant coping are indeed related to substance use, the significant mechanism is not the cognitive aspects of avoidance (e.g., distraction), but the fact that a person feels helpless and *unable to cope* with problems and is able to react only through anger. This is the dimension that is indicated by our research as being the crucial aspect of coping for predicting maladaptive outcomes (Wills & Hirky, 1995).

5.3. Moderation Effects of Active and Avoidant Coping

Does coping interact with life stress? We have examined this question in several studies. With substance use as an outcome, the answer is not exactly what is predicted by the original coping theory of Lazarus and Folkman (1984). For active coping, we do find occasional buffering-type interactions for individual coping mechanisms such as behavioral coping. However, stress–buffer interactions are neither strong nor consistent. In contrast, we consistently find reverse (vulnerability) interactions for avoidant mechanisms of anger, hanging out, and helplessness; for example, a significant Stress × Anger Coping interaction indicates that the effect of life stress on substance use is *increased* among adolescents with a high level of anger coping. Note that this does not mean that there are simply two additive effects; rather, the interaction indicates that avoidant coping makes adolescents disproportionately more vulnerable at a high level of stress. Similar exacerbating effects of avoidant coping have been noted for adult depression (see Rohde et al., 1990), but we find that it is not general avoidance, but rather helplessness and anger, that produce stress-exacerbating effects.

The real buffering effect of active coping seems to be with respect to avoidant coping. We have combined the active coping mechanisms (behavioral, cognitive, and exercise) into a single score and the avoidant coping mechanisms (anger, helplessness, and hanging out) into another single score, and tested the overall interaction of Active Coping × Avoidant Coping. We find that the interaction is strong and consistent, with active coping reducing the impact of avoidant coping on substance use (Wills et al., 1995d). This finding suggests that the real impact of active coping is that, within the individual adolescent's coping repertoire, it helps counteract effects of avoidant coping that otherwise could begin to move the adolescent into a trajectory that could lead to trouble.

5.4. Effects of Coping over Time

Longitudinal analyses suggest a similar conclusion. For example, in two studies, we have been able to test the effects of coping at one time point on increase in substance use over 6- to 12-month intervals. Again, the scales for active coping mechanisms and the scales for avoidant coping mechanisms were all entered simultaneously in multivariate analyses (Wills, 1986; Wills et al., 1995d). Results generally show significant effects for avoidant coping, with anger and hanging out being related to increase in substance use. In contrast, we do not consistently find prospective effects for active coping. The contrast between the concurrent and prospective results suggests a "braking vs. acceleration" model of substance use. Active coping acts, in effect, to restrain an adolescent from moving in the direction of involvement with substance use. However, if an adolescent is beginning to show early experimentation with tobacco and alcohol, then avoidant coping acts as an accelerant that increases the frequency and intensity of substance use. In this sense, active coping is the brake that keeps a teenager from moving in the direction of trouble, whereas having a high level of avoidant coping is like stepping on the accelerator.

How do patterns of coping develop in adolescence? The research addressed this question because coping mechanisms are presumably still being formed at this time. We have analyzed one data set to study whether there are systematic effects of coping at 7th grade on patterns of coping 1 and 2 years later, testing the ability of the set of coping predictors at one time point to predict change in a given type of coping over a defined interval (Wills et al., 1995d). The results indicate the operation of two processes, a "positive cycle" and a "vicious cycle." Early use of active coping resulted in an increase in active coping and a decrease in helplessness; that is, active coping built more active coping (a positive cycle). In contrast, having a higher initial level of anger increased levels of general avoidance, hanging out, and helplessness over time; in turn, a higher initial level of any of these behaviors increased the levels of the others. This, then, is a vicious cycle: Early avoidant coping not only is related initially to worse outcomes, but also tends to shift the person in the direction of more avoidant coping in the future.

5.5. Coping Functions of Substance Use

The last prediction derived from the stress–coping model is that substance use helps provide coping functions for adolescents. We tested this question directly in a recent study with a sample of 10th-graders. We asked subjects who had smoked or drunk alcohol to rate the extent to which they perceived each of 9 different items as a reason for their substance use; parallel items were used for separate ratings of tobacco and alcohol use. There were two distinct factors in these motive data. One factor represents social influence ("I feel pressured to do it, "I feel other students are doing it"). The second factor represents coping motives ("To calm down when I'm feeling tense and nervous," "To cheer up when I'm in a bad mood," "To forget about my worries," "To relax"). The other items represent self-confidence enhancement ("To feel more self-confident and sure of myself"), boredom relief ("Because I feel there's nothing better to do"), and curiosity ("Curious about how they tasted"). Confidence enhancement and boredom relief loaded about equally on the social factor and the coping factor, and curiosity was uncorrelated with either, so each of these constructs was analyzed as a single item.

For statistical analysis, the five motive scores were entered together in multiple regression with the appropriate substance use index (smoking or alcohol) as criterion (Wills & Cleary, 1995b). Results indicated that coping motives had the strongest effect, with $\beta = 0.56$ for smoking and $\beta = 0.45$ for heavy drinking. Boredom showed an independent but smaller contribution, related to higher level of substance use (βs of 0.08 and 0.12, respectively). Social pressure, which is commonly invoked in lay publications as the major reason for adolescent substance use, was nonsignificant in all analyses. Curiosity had a small independent effect, but was inversely related to level of use. Thus, we find evidence that coping functions of substance use are relevant for adolescents and seem to be uniquely related to high-intensity use. There is some qualification to this conclusion because the study was cross-sectional, so the direction of effect could not be established; it is possible that adolescents who engage in regular substance use become more aware of coping functions. Most likely there is reciprocity in the process, with perceptions of coping functions contributing to increases in use and higher levels of use producing more awareness of coping functions.

6. Stress-Buffering Effects of Support and Competence

6.1. Buffering Effects of Parental Support

Our research on family factors in adolescent substance use has been guided by a coping model of social support (Cohen & Wills, 1985; Thoits, 1986). The basic proposition is that parents may contribute to children's adaptation because they provide useful support and assistance when the child has a problem. The functional model of social support suggests several dimensions of supportive relationships that may be involved in support and coping processes (Wills, 1985). With no intention of ruling out the potential importance of other dimensions (Wills, 1990b), our research on adolescents has focused on two dimensions: *emotional support*, the ability to talk with a parent about feelings and problems and to receive sympathy and understanding in this transaction, and *instrumental support*, the ability to go to a parent when there is a practical problem (e.g., with transportation, schoolwork, or money) and receive useful assistance from this transaction. Support has been measured with two different methods. One approach is to measure support as a coping mechanism (Lazarus & Folkman, 1984), with parallel wordings used to obtain measures of emotional support from parents and peers (see Carver et al., 1989; Wills & Vaughan, 1989). The other approach is to assess perceived availability of emotional and instrumental support from parents (e.g., Wills et al., 1992a).

The crucial prediction from the stress–coping model is that parental support will show stress-buffering effects with respect to adolescent substance use. It is known that attachment to parents is related to lower levels of substance use among adolescents (e.g., Brook, Brook, Gordon, Whiteman, & Cohen, 1990; Kandel, Kessler, & Margulies, 1978). Our model suggests, however, that this relationship obtains because parental support reduces the impact of life stressors. Several tests of this prediction have indicated significant Stress × Support interactions for adolescent substance use. There is a strong relationship between stress and substance use among adolescents with low parental support, but this effect is reduced among adolescents with high parental support. Similar findings have been obtained in different samples with coping-type measures of parental support (Wills, 1986) and with functional measures of emotional and instrumental support from parents (Wills et al., 1992a). The evidence thus indicates that parental support serves as a stress-buffering agent, as suggested also in studies of resilient children (see Luthar & Zigler, 1991; Sandler, Miller, Short, & Wolchik, 1989).

In working to understand how parental support operates, we have tested longitudinal data and shown that parental support has inverse prospective effects with respect to adolescents' substance use (Wills, Vaccaro, McNamara, & Hirky, 1993a), so it is clear that parental support is a true protective factor, serving to decrease substance use onset or progression. We showed that parental support is related to higher levels of all other protective factors that we measure and to lower levels of all risk factors that we measure, so it is clear that parental support is a powerful factor for adolescents' coping (Wills, Blechman, & McNamara, 1995a). We found that parental support is strongly correlated with active coping and self-regulation ability and is prospectively related to increased active coping over time (Wills et al., 1995a,b). Thus, it is seen that parental support is an integral part of a stress–coping model because parental support is an important factor for promoting active coping and self-control ability.

How is parental support related to substance use? So far, we have conducted one mediational analysis, from an 8th-grade data set, to determine how the relationship between parental support and adolescents' substance use is mediated. We found that the effect of parental support was mediated through five pathways: (1) reduced use of anger as a coping mechanism, (2) reduced tolerance for deviance, (3) increased self-control of behavior, (4) reduced level of negative life events, and (5) reduced affiliation with deviant peers (Wills & Cleary, 1995a). It is clear from this analysis that the effect of parental support occurs through multiple domains.

6.2. Buffering Effects of Academic and Social Competence

Models of resiliency have posited that certain types of competence are important factors for helping children to be resistant to the impact of stress and adversity (Garmezy & Masten, 1991; Luthar & Zigler, 1991). Clinical research models have also been proposed that construe childhood depression and behavior problems as deriving from low competence (Blechman, McEnroe, & Carella, 1986; Blechman, Tinsley, Carella, & McEnroe, 1985; Blechman, Wills, & Adler, 1992; Cole, 1991). We have investigated questions posed by these models. Various kinds of competence (e.g., academic competence) are usually construed as measurements of performance capability, determined to some extent by the child's intellectual endowment, social environment, and patterns of coping.

For studying competence as a protective factor, we have used measures of perceived competence. These measures are derived from the Harter (1985) Perceived Competence Inventory for Adolescents. The items ask the respondent (or a third party) how he or she perceives the subject's competence in each of several domains. We have studied dimensions regarded as central in the resiliency models: *academic competence,* doing well at schoolwork, and *social competence,* having good social relationships and feeling accepted. For reasons discussed subsequently, we separated social competence into two types: peer competence, the perception of having friends and being popular with peers, and adult competence, the perception of being liked and accepted by adults. We have also examined what Harter (1985) terms *behavioral competence,* the ability to control one's behavior and act the way one is supposed to.

For investigating buffering effects, we have used the same approach employed in social support research, testing the interaction of Stress × Competence in relation to substance use as the outcome variable. We do find that some competence measures serve as stress-buffering agents, as predicted by resiliency models. In one study, for example, we found significant Stress × Competence interactions for self-reported academic competence and adult competence with respect to more serious types of substance use (e.g., heavy drinking or marijuana use); for children with high competence on either of these dimensions, the relationship between life stress and substance use was reduced (Wills et al., 1992a). These stress-buffering interactions were replicated in a subsequent study for both self-reports and teacher ratings (Wills et al., 1995a; Wills, Vaccaro, McNamara, & Spellman, 1991). These results are consistent with prior research on resilience and indicate how these factors protect against the development of problem behavior.

Different results are found for the measure of peer social competence, which contains items such as "I find it easy to make friends with other kids [students]" and "I do a lot of things with other kids." (The term "students" is used after 7th grade.) This competence measure typically shows no significant zero-order correlation with substance use, but is positively related to substance use when entered together in multiple regression with the other competence measures; we have now replicated this finding in several studies (Wills et al., 1991, 1992a). This result is technically known as a *suppression effect*; considering the context of correlations of peer social competence with other measures is construed as suppressing irrelevant variance (Tzelgov & Henik, 1991) and thereby helping to clarify an effect. Similar effects have been found by other investigators (Chassin, Pillow, Curran, Molina, & Barrera, 1993; Fondacaro & Heller, 1983; Kandel et al., 1978); for example, Chassin et al. (1993) noted that sociability had no zero-order correlation with adolescent substance use, but a multivariate model indicated that sociability was related both to more positive mood and to more affiliation with substance-using peers.

Results from other research also point to the double-edged nature of peer social relationships. For example, Wills and Vaughan (1989) found that parental support was inversely related to substance use, whereas peer support was positively related to substance use, particularly for subjects whose social network contained a number of smokers. Larson (1983) found in daily observations of adolescents that those who spent more time with peers had more positive hedonic moods but also had worse academic performance; similarly, Cauce, Felner, and Primavera (1982) found that peer social support was related to more positive self-concept but also to lower academic competence. Wills and Vaughan (1989) found that substance use was disproportionately elevated for adolescents with high peer support and low parental support, similar to findings from Kandel et al. (1978) for a score reflecting the relative balance of adult and peer relationships (cf. Wills, 1990a). Contrasted with the consistent findings of stress-buffering effects for parental support (Burke & Weir, 1978; Greenberg, Siegel & Leitch, 1983; Wills, 1986), these data indicate that peer sociability has complex effects.

We have discussed these findings in some detail because they are apparently contradictory to research on peer rejection, which indicates that subjects who are unpopular with classmates during early childhood are at risk for subsequent adjustment problems (Asher & Coie, 1990; Hymel, Rubin, Rowden, & LeMare, 1990; Morison & Masten, 1991). Is peer social competence, then, overall a protective factor or a risk factor? We think the resolution of this question may derive from considering the role of undercontrol and disinhibition. Tarter (1988) has suggested that what is characterized as sociability, assertiveness, or gregariousness in previous studies (e.g., Loper, Kammeier, & Hoffmann, 1973; Jones, 1968) is really a style of interacting that is active and unrestrained. This style may well be attractive to certain types of peers, particularly those who have high levels of risk taking and sensation seeking (see Wills, Vaccaro, & McNamara, 1994d), and may be correlated with aggressiveness, the most reliable long-term predictor of substance abuse (cf. Kellam, Brown, & Fleming, 1982; Loeber, 1988). Thus, we believe that children who are more aggressive in early grades will tend to be rejected by conventional classmates, but as these children grow older, stronger, and cognitively more sophisticated, they will find their way into networks of more deviant peers who themselves are disinhibited, alienated from family and school, and inclined to risk-taking activities (Patterson, DeBaryshe, & Ramsey, 1989). This does not mean that a high-risk adolescent around 14 years old lacks friends; rather, the issue is that she or he has different types of friends, combined with a low attachment to family, and spends the majority of her or his time with peers rather than engaging in activities (such as schoolwork) that are conventionally rewarding but less hedonically positive.

7. Temperament, Stress, and Coping Patterns

The initial assumption of our research, derived from a strict stress–coping model, was that coping ability emerges during early adolescence in a learning process shaped mostly by environmental demands and environmental feedback (Compas, 1987; Lazarus & Folkman, 1984). Although it would seem plausible that constitutional characteristics such as intelligence might be related to the development of coping ability, available evidence from college samples indicated that characteristics such as problem-solving confidence were not strongly correlated with IQ (Heppner & Petersen, 1982). Thus, it seemed reasonable to pursue the implications of an environmental model and test the relations of stress and coping variables to substance use.

In recent years, however, a body of evidence has been accumulating to suggest that the precursors of risk for substance abuse may occur before 12 years of age. In addition to suggestive findings on early onset from follow-back analyses (Robins & Przybeck, 1985) and from several prospective data sets (Kellam et al., 1982; Lerner & Vicary, 1984; Seltzer & Oechsli, 1985), data from one of our studies indicated that adolescents who showed rapid escalation of substance use during the middle-school period, and hence appeared most vulnerable for substance abuse problems in later adolescence, already showed elevated levels of substance use by 12 years of age (Wills, McNamara, Vaccaro, & Hirky, 1995e; Wills et al., 1994c). Theoretical suggestions from clinical research on alcoholism had also drawn parallels between dimensions of temperament studied by developmental researchers and constructs suggested as risk factors for adult alcoholism in prospective studies (Tarter, 1988; Tarter, Alterman, & Edwards, 1985; Windle, 1990). These various trains of thought bore the implication that stress and coping processes might be influenced by prior dispositional factors.

7.1. Temperament and Stress–Coping Factors

We decided to test this question in a study with teacher ratings of temperament. For a sample of 869 6th-grade students, we obtained teacher ratings that included five constructs from the Revised Dimensions of Temperament Survey (DOTS-R) (Windle & Lerner, 1986); the students completed a self-report questionnaire on their stress–coping processes and substance use. Results showed that temperament dimensions of activity level and mood were significantly related to early cigarette and alcohol sampling by subjects, with high activity and less positive mood being related to more substance use. Further, temperament measures of high activity level and low adaptability were related to recent negative events, negative affect, anger coping, helplessness coping, and low academic competence. Because such dimensions have been shown to be relatively stable from early childhood (Plomin & Dunn, 1986), there were grounds for believing that the temperament dimensions were antecedents of the stress–coping factors and substance use, though this postulate could not be proven from the cross-sectional data. Thus, a linkage of temperament dimensions to stress–coping factors was suggested.

At this time, we were also thinking about self-control as a basic factor in this process. Research on self-control has a significant history in clinical psychology (e.g., Karoly & Kanfer, 1982), and it has been suggested that deficits in self-control are involved in adult alcoholism and other types of substance abuse (Khantzian, 1990; Miller & Brown, 1991) as well as being a factor in the prospective studies (e.g., Block, Block, & Keyes, 1988; Jones, 1968). To pursue questions about self-control and the convergence of other predictors of substance use, we conducted a study with a sample of 457 middle-school students. This study included a measure of generalized self-control adapted from the Self-Control Rating Schedule (Kendall & Wilcox, 1979; Kendall & Williams, 1982) together with measures of stress-coping factors, deviance-prone attitudes (again from Jessor & Jessor, 1977), and sensation seeking [from Cloninger (1987) and Zuckerman (1979)]. Results indicated that, as predicted, poor self-control was substantially correlated with substance use, and the effect size (a standardized regression coefficient of about 0.25) was in the upper range of those usually found for psychosocial predictors.

Somewhat to our surprise, though, self-control was highly correlated with all the other constructs, related to lower achievement orientation, more independence, lower behavioral competence, more anger, more negative life events and negative affect, and greater risk taking and sensation seeking. Though we did not assess coping processes directly in this study, results showed that a measure of good self-control was related to a measure (from Cloninger, 1987) that indexed planning, decision making, and problem solving, virtually identical to what is assessed in a typical behavioral coping measure. The intercorrelations among self-control and other constructs were in the range 0.30–0.60, so these data suggest that self-control is a construct having extensive ramifications to constructs that have been studied as predictors of adolescent substance use. Moreover, we performed a clustering analysis on the predictor variables (excluding substance use) and found that a cluster representing problem youth was characterized by extreme elevations on poor self-control, risk taking, impulsiveness, sensation seeking, anger, value on independence, negative life events, and tolerance for deviance. Independent analyses showed that this cluster of subjects also had markedly elevated scores on substance use. Thus, this study showed that problem youth did not differ on just one dimension; they differed on almost everything. This finding was consistent with findings from our longitudinal analysis of escalation (Wills et al., 1995e), which showed that a subgroup of adolescents vulnerable to escalation was differentiated by extreme scores on stress–coping factors, competence, and deviant attitudes. Clearly, there was some prior process that contributed to these children's being different on all these factors by the 7th grade, and it was not demographic status, because all these analyses were done with demographic controls. Temperament dimensions were plausible candidates.

To follow up on the suggestion that temperament and undercontrol are basic dimensions of risk, we questioned whether the relation of temperament to substance use is mediated through self-control, stress–coping factors, and peer affiliations. This question was tested in a study with a sample of 1826 students in 7th grade; at this time point, a proportion showed significant levels of substance use. Temperament was measured through a self-report version of the DOTS-R; generalized self-control was measured with the scale from Kendall and Wilcox (1979). Results again showed that high activity level and low positive mood were related to more substance use. We found that the relation between the temperament dimension of activity level and adolescents' substance use was mediated through less behavioral coping and self-control, more maladaptive coping (anger and helplessness), and more sensation-seeking attributes (risk taking and novelty seeking). These in turn were related to more affiliation with deviant peers, which was indicated as the proximal factor for initiation of substance use. The findings replicated our previous results on temperament and substance use with a different assessment method and provided some indication of how the relation between temperament and substance use is mediated. The mediational findings were consistent with recent models of temperament and personality development (Tarter, Moss, & Vanyukov, 1995; Rothbart & Ahadi, 1994), which suggest that early temperament dimensions develop into more complex manifestations of self-control ability as children grow older and develop new cognitive and social skills.

7.2. Temperament, Self-Control, and Conduct Disorder

Is temperament, then, a proxy for conduct disorder? So far, we have not used clinical labels, but the previously observed relationship between delinquency and substance use (Loeber, 1988) argues that a test of this question is needed. The proxy argument suggests that previously observed relationships among negative life events, anger, and adolescent substance use are all indicating manifestations of conduct disorder.

To address this question, we are conducting a new study with a sample of 1810 students initially surveyed in 6th grade. In this study, we followed the theoretical distinction of Tarter (1988) between temperament and conduct disorder; temperament (e.g., activity level) describes a dimension of behavior that is relatively stable from early childhood, whereas conduct disorder describes a range of socially defined nonnormative behaviors. Tarter (1988) has argued that concomitant features of high activity level (e.g., restlessness, irritability) may predispose to difficulties in interpersonal relationships and in school settings, factors that may be conducive to alienation from school and affiliation with deviant peers, which have been proposed as proximal variables for antisocial behavior (Loeber, 1988; Patterson et al., 1989). Positing that development of antisocial behavior is driven through deficits in self-control, we included self-report and teacher ratings of temperament, self-control, and stress–coping factors, plus measures of externalizing and internalizing symptomatology from the Child Behavior Checklist (CBCL) (Achenbach, 1991).

Though we have just started analysis of these data, some correlational results are consistent with the theoretical model of self-control development. Temperament dimensions of activity level and negative emotionality are related to higher levels of early substance use, dimensions of good attentional orientation and positive emotionality are inversely related to substance use, and sociability is unrelated to substance use in zero-order correlations [as in Chassin et al. (1993) with a high-risk sample]. The first two ("risky") temperament dimensions are related to less behavioral coping, poor self-control, more maladaptive coping (anger and helplessness), and more negative life events. The converse pattern occurs for the last two (protective) temperament dimensions, which are related to good coping and self-control ability. Finally, activity level and negative emotionality are substantially related to high scores on the Externalizing scale of the CBCL. Thus, there is some evidence that conduct disorder develops from temperament dimensions related to negative emotionality (Wills, Cleary, Filer, Mariani, & Spera, 1995).

8. Current Conclusions and Further Directions

In this research program, we initially set out to test the implications of a stress–coping model for adolescents, having reason to expect that this theory would be relevant for adolescent substance use and would have general implications for adolescent adjustment. Results across the various studies have supported some of our ideas about how stress and coping work, but have also raised new questions about the basis of vulnerability in childhood and adolescence. In this final section, we summarize what we have currently concluded and what questions need further study in research on prevention and treatment.

The specific findings indicate several conclusions consistent with our original beliefs. First, life stress is a risk factor for children and adolescents; it is related over time to onset and escalation of substance use. We do not believe that adolescents' personality is totally uninvolved in causing some of the negative life events, but we have shown in several ways that growing up in a stressful environment has adverse consequences. Second, coping is important for risk and protection. Active coping is shown consistently to be related to low levels of substance use, and avoidant coping is related to higher levels of substance use. Thus, the way in which adolescents cope with problems has significant implications for their adjustment. While patterns of coping may well have roots in earlier development and socialization processes, the results from our longitudinal analyses show that patterns of coping are developing over time in the adolescent population. If you are a 12-year-old, it is important to be motivated and reinforced for dealing with problems through active coping mechanisms, which take more effort but have more long-term payoff. If a teen is using predominantly avoidant coping mechanisms at this age, it sets the stage for a vicious cycle of increasingly avoidant coping over time. Findings from our stress–coping research thus suggest specific coping mechanisms that can be measured and incorporated as target dimensions in clinical research.

The pattern of findings also lends support to the general orientation of coping and competence models. Stress–coping theory and resiliency theory have been the main intellectual currents drawing attention to protective factors and buffering processes, and across the studies discussed here, we consistently find evidence of buffering processes. Buffering effects are found for family support, for several types of competence, and for some aspects of coping. Thus, these models point out factors that contribute to adjustment through helping to mitigate the impact of life stress. Our findings do not show that moderation effects are always beneficial ones, and in fact we think it is important for clinical theory that a number of our findings go the other way, pointing out that deviant attitudes and maladaptive coping worsen the impact of life stress. This result implies that clinical treatments can have an indirect impact on clients' functioning through aiming to reduce the use of maladaptive coping; not only is this reduction a relatively good thing in itself, but also it means that the other current stressors faced by clients will have less effect. This approach is a different concept of protection (i.e., reducing things that make stressors worse), but it can be one with particular implications for clinical patients, who may have ended up in treatment because they have exacerbated their ongoing life stressors instead of resolving their problems.

The research also shows academic competence to be a stress-buffering agent, and though such competence has not been a traditional focus for clinical interventions, its significance as a buffering agent should be recognized. The findings may have implications for clinical research to assess and target academic performance as an outcome goal. We also should note the consistency with which religious participation appears as a buffering agent, both in our own studies and in other research on resiliency. It is difficult to ignore the empirical evidence on buffering effects in both the short and the long term (e.g., Brunswick, Messeri, & Titus, 1992; Park & Cohen, 1992). We do not think this evidence implies that forcing a troublesome adolescent to sit in a church or synagogue for a required number of hours would necessarily produce salubrious effects. It is clear from studies of general populations, however, that affiliation with a religious institution has a protective effect for some portion of the community, and exploring how this effect is relevant for clinical programs may be a worthwhile topic for further research.

Another theoretical issue is that the effect of other factors may be mediated through stress and coping variables. We previously gave an example of how the effects of temperament on substance use are mediated. In other work, we showed that the relationship of low socioeconomic status to adolescent substance use is mediated through lower academic competence and behavioral control and a greater number of negative life events (Wills, McNamara, & Vaccaro, 1995c). We also showed that the impact of parental polysubstance use on adolescents is mediated partly through lower self-control, more tolerance for deviance, perceived coping functions of substance use, and affiliation with deviant peers (Wills, Schreibman, Benson, & Vaccaro, 1994b). We note that socioeconomic status is a factor related to treatment outcome (Wahler, 1990), but a factor that is largely outside the clinician's control. The stress–coping model, however, suggests how the impact of extratreatment factors can be mediated through individual-level coping processes, and this approach may provide an issue for clinical research.

The findings from this research have questioned our initial model in some respects. First, while stress–coping theory has placed considerable emphasis on the role of problem-focused coping for counteracting life stress, we find little evidence of stress-buffering interactions for the coping variables. Rather, buffering effects of active coping are consistently found for reducing the impact of maladaptive coping. This type of buffering process occurs more within the person, so in the language of diathesis–stress models, the source of stress (e.g., tendency to use anger) arises from within the person. Assuming that the source of stress is partly endogenous does not mean that active coping is unimportant, but rather that it helps to counteract the tendency of maladaptive coping to move the person toward a troublesome trajectory. Second, we find that measures of negative life events and coping processes are related to dispositional-type variables that logically must have been operating from an earlier time point. This finding questions the assumption that the origin of stressors is totally external to the person and that coping develops through a classic social learning process based exclusively on modeling or environmental feedback. We have sometimes heard a response to this concept on the order of, "Oh, well, then you're just studying personality." We think this view trivializes the issues. Personality is an abstraction, describing a dimension that can be measured with relative stability. Coping, however, is the means by which this abstraction gets outside the skin; it is the way a person's profile of characteristics shapes the kinds of events he or she experiences and the way he or she responds to these events. Hence, we think that findings that stress and coping processes are related to dispositional variables provide an interesting new direction for clinical personality research.

There are two implications of the findings presented herein that we think are important for further clinical research. First is the role of helplessness. Our findings show that the strongest risk factor for adolescent problem behavior is a complex of coping dimensions (anger, avoidance, and helplessness) that reflect the adolescent's perception that she or he is unable to cope with problems. While the construct of pessimism or hopelessness is not new to clinical psychology in the study of adult depression (cf. Beck, 1986; Rosenbaum, 1990), we think that the roots of adolescent aggression in coping inability have not been fully appreciated. It is beginning to be recognized that there is a substantial component of subjective distress associated with conduct disorder (e.g., Blechman, 1992; Cole & Carpentieri, 1990; Harrington, Fudge, Rutter, Pickles, & Hill, 1991). Though it is not difficult to observe that teenagers with conduct disorder are angry and alienated, the findings discussed herein suggest some directions for research that will help us understand more about why they are angry and alienated. In longitudinal analyses of coping, we have found that there is no simple explanation for the correlation among avoidant types of coping mechanisms, but rather that they all tend to feed on each other over time, so that teens with an unfavorable coping profile feel progressively more helpless and alienated. Moreover, it seems likely that younger adolescents who feel that they cannot do the things that enable them to "fit in" will have the capacity to find persons with similar attitudes to hang out with. Though this approach will provide a source of companionship, it provides a social group that, in addition to encouraging a variety of deviant activities, will enmesh the subject in a closed system that over time builds progressively higher levels of anger, alienation, and disengagement from coping. We think that this kind of process is implicated in the correlations between substance use and adolescent suicide that are beginning to be reported (e.g., see Carter, Anda, Casper, & Escobedo, 1994). This perspective may provide a direction for studying the origins of suicide risk in adolescence.

The second issue we see as important derives from the fact that problem youth do not differ on just one dimension, such as aggressiveness; rather, they differ on just about every dimension we measure, but most particularly on self-control (Wills et al., 1994d). This result ties in to long-standing questions about the correlation among adolescent problem behaviors (Donovan & Jessor, 1985) and the stability of aggression (Huesmann, Eron, Lefkowitz, & Walder, 1984; Olweus, 1979). We think that a direction toward understanding this may come from our findings that link adolescent substance use and externalizing symptomatology to dimensions of temperament and self-control. These temperament dimensions appear to be present from a relatively early age, and a profile of temperament attributes characterized as "difficult temperament" (i.e., high activity level, negative emotionality, poor attentional orientation) may have considerable impact on the child's development of coping patterns and social relationships. This realization leads to thinking about clinical research that would take very seriously the significance of early onset (Christie, Burke, Regier, Rae, Boyd, & Locke, 1988; Robins & Przybeck, 1985) and would study samples of children (possibly high-risk samples rather than clinical patients) from a relatively early age to investigate how early temperamental attributes shape the development of coping and competence (cf. Lerner & Vicary, 1984; Rothbart & Ahadi, 1994). Our current data draw attention to deficits in self-control as a possible early precursor to several types of behavior problems observed in later adolescence, including delinquency and high-intensity drug use and sexual behavior. These findings suggest a theoretical perspective based on the interaction of activation and inhibition systems as an approach to clinical research on the roots of adolescent psychopathology (e.g., see Cloninger, 1987; Loeber, 1988; Tarter et al., 1995).

We would like to discuss as the last point two cross-cutting issues for further research on adolescent behavior problems. We suggest that, like stress and coping factors, adolescent problems are inherently social phenomena, and ignoring the social context of the behaviors may miss an important part of the picture, as some clinical researchers have long been arguing (e.g., Patterson, 1986). First, we note that the nature of an adolescent's peer network is crucial for both understanding and prediction. From the assessment standpoint, the most useful single question one can ask would be about the behaviors of a subject's three best friends. From this standpoint of clinical intervention, the data indicate that a group of like-minded peers provides an important coping function for a troubled adolescent. We do not believe that a deviance-prone adolescent lacks friends. Rather, in a world that has conveyed rejection from several quarters (e.g., school and family), a group of similarly troubled adolescents provides acceptance, a set of shared values that helps provide a coherent world view (e.g., "Teachers are just out to get you,"

"School sucks"), and a social setting that provides fun, excitement, and risk-taking that contrast with conventional routes to achievement, which may be characterized as effortful and boring. To recognize this aspect of adolescent behavior problems is both to recognize a social system that serves to maintain and reinforce antisocial behavior and to recognize the difficulty of asking a troubled adolescent (who may be rejected to some extent by both parents and classmates) to give up a set of people who provide such an important function, the only harbor when a storm starts to blow, but one that will provide refuge.

Finally, one must be struck by the significance in these data of supportive family relationships as a protective factor. We find that family support not only is a buffering agent but also has extensive relationships to coping and competence, less deviant attitudes, and less substance use. While the role of family factors has of course been studied before in research on drug abuse and clinical psychology (e.g., Bry, 1983), we find the extent and magnitude of the effects for parental support to be noteworthy. We also find that the degree of family support may be both a consequence of other factors (e.g., low socioeconomic status) and a predictor of adolescent characteristics such as adaptive coping and academic competence. Thus, the stress–coping model provides a framework for helping to understand how the effects of family support on deviant outcomes occur and suggests dimensions of support that may be amenable to clinical intervention. Both aspects of the model may be useful for further clinical research.

ACKNOWLEDGMENTS

This research was supported by Grant 80A-23 from the Centers for Disease Control, Grants DA-05950 and DA-08880 from the National Institute on Drug Abuse, and Grant S-184A-00035 from the U.S. Department of Education. In this research program, the following graduate students and professional staff have assisted in the work: Gregory Benson, Kate DuHamel, Sean D. Cleary, Edith Friedman, A. Elizabeth Hirky, John Mariani, Grace McNamara, Stephen Ramirez, Angela Riccobono, Dan Schreibman, Mark Spellman, Donna Spitzoff, Donato Vaccaro, Aaron Warshawsky, Jody Wallach, Roger Vaughan, and Caroline Zeoli.

9. References

Abrams, D. B., Monti, P. M., Pinto, R. P., Elder, J. P., Brown, R. A., & Jacobus, S. I. (1987).
    Psychosocial stress and coping in smokers who relapse or quit. *Health Psychology, 6,*
    289–303.

Achenbach, T. M. (1991). *Manual for the Youth Self-Report and 1991 profile.* Burlington: University of Vermont.

Achenbach, T. M., McConaughy, S. H., & Howell, C. T. (1987). Child/adolescent behavioral and emotional problems: Implications of cross-informant correlations for situational specificity. *Psychological Bulletin, 101,* 213–232.

Aldwin, C. M. (1994). *Stress, coping, and development: An integrative perspective.* New York: Guilford Press.

Asher, S. R., & Coie, J. D. (Eds.) (1990). *Peer rejection in childhood.* New York: Cambridge University Press.

Baron, R. M., & Kenny, D. A. (1986). The moderator–mediator distinction in social–psychological research. *Journal of Personality and Social Psychology, 51,* 1173–1182.

Beck, A. T. (1986). *Cognitive therapy and the emotional disorders.* New York: International Universities Press.

Blechman, E. A. (Chair) (1992). *Mechanisms accounting for the covariation between depression and aggression.* Symposium presented at the meeting of the American Psychological Society, San Diego, June 1992.

Blechman, E. A., McEnroe, M. J., & Carella, E. T. (1986). Childhood competence and depression. *Journal of Abnormal Psychology, 95,* 223–227.

Blechman, E. A., Tinsley, B., Carella, E. T., & McEnroe, M. J. (1985). Childhood competence and behavior problems. *Journal of Abnormal Psychology, 94,* 70–77.

Blechman, E. A., Wills, T. A., & Adler, V. (1992). Process measures in interventions for drug-abusing women: From coping to competence. In M. M. Kilbey & K. Asghar (Eds.), *Methodological issues in epidemiological, prevention, and treatment research on drug-exposed women and their children* (pp. 314–343). Rockville, MD: National Institute on Drug Abuse.

Block, J., Block, J., & Keyes, S. (1988). Longitudinally foretelling drug use in adolescence: Early personality and environmental precursors. *Child Development, 59,* 336–355.

Braithwaite, R. L., & Gordon, E. W. (1992). *Success against the odds.* Washington, DC: Howard University Press.

Brook, J. S., Brook, D. W., Gordon, A. S., Whiteman, M., & Cohen, P. (1990). The psychosocial etiology of adolescent drug use: A family interactional approach. *Genetic, Social, and General Psychology Monographs, 116*(2), 111–267.

Brown, S. A., Goldman, M. S., Inn, A., & Anderson, L. R. (1980). Expectations of reinforcement from alcohol. *Journal of Consulting and Clinical Psychology, 48,* 419–426.

Brunswick, A. F., Messeri, P. A., & Titus, S. P. (1992). Predictive factors in adult substance abuse: A prospective study of African-American adolescents. In M. Glantz & R. Pickens (Eds.), *Vulnerability to drug abuse* (pp. 419–472). Washington, DC: American Psychological Association.

Bry, B. H. (1983). Empirical foundations of family-based approaches to adolescent substance abuse. In T. J. Glynn, C. G. Leukefeld, & J. P. Ludford (Eds.), *Preventing adolescent drug abuse* (pp. 154–171). Rockville, MD: National Institute on Drug Abuse.

Burke, R. J., & Weir, T. (1978). Benefits to adolescents of informal helping relationships with their parents and peers. *Psychological Reports, 42,* 1175–1184.

Cafferata, G. L., Kasper, J., & Bernstein, A. (1983). Family roles and stressors in relation to sex differences in obtaining psychotropic drugs. *Journal of Health and Social Behavior, 24,* 132–143.

Cappell, H., & Greeley, J. (1987). Alcohol and tension reduction. In H. T. Blane & K. E. Leonard (Eds.), *Psychological theories of drinking and alcoholism* (pp. 15–54). New York: Guilford Press.

Carey, M. P., Kalra, D. L., Carey, K. B., Halperin, S., & Richards, C. S. (1993). Stress and unaided smoking cessation: Prospective investigation. *Journal of Consulting and Clinical Psychology, 61*, 831–838.

Carpenter, B. N. (Ed.) (1992). *Personal coping: Theory, research, and application.* Westport, CT: Praeger.

Carter, K. E., Anda, R. E., Casper, M. L., & Escobedo, L. G. (1994). Smoking as a risk marker for suicidal behaviors in adolescence. Paper presented at the meeting of the American Psychological Association, Los Angeles, August 1994.

Carver, C. S., Scheier, M. F., & Weintraub, J. K. (1989). Assessing coping strategies. *Journal of Personality and Social Psychology, 56*, 267–283.

Castro, F. G., Maddahian, E., Newcomb, M. D., & Bentler, P. M. (1987). A multivariate model of the determinants of cigarette smoking among adolescents. *Journal of Health and Social Behavior, 28*, 273–289.

Cauce, A. M., Felner, R. D., & Primavera, J. (1982). Social support in high-risk adolescents. *American Journal of Community Psychology, 10*, 417–428.

Chaney, E. F., & Roszell, D. K. (1985). Coping in opiate addicts maintained on methadone. In S. Shiffman & T. A. Wills (Eds.), *Coping and substance use* (pp. 267–293). New York: Academic Press.

Chassin, L. A., Mann, L. M., & Sher, K. J. (1988). Self-awareness theory, family history, and adolescent alcohol involvement. *Journal of Abnormal Psychology, 97*, 206–217.

Chassin, L. A., Pillow, D. R., Curran, P. J., Molina, B., & Barrera, M. (1993). Relation of parental alcoholism to early adolescent substance use: A test of mediating mechanisms. *Journal of Abnormal Psychology, 102*, 3–19.

Christie, K. A., Burke, J. D., Regier, D. A., Rae, D. S., Boyd, J. H., & Locke, B. Z. (1988). Epidemiologic evidence for early onset of mental disorders and higher risk of drug abuse in young adults. *American Journal of Psychiatry, 145*, 971–975.

Cloninger, C. R. (1987). Neurogenetic adaptive mechanisms in alcoholism. *Science, 236*, 410–416.

Cohen, L. (1988) (Ed.). *Life events and psychological functioning: Theoretical and methodological issues.* Newbury Park, CA: Sage Publications.

Cohen, S., & Lichtenstein, E. (1990). Perceived stress, quitting smoking, and smoking relapse. *Health Psychology, 9*, 466–478.

Cohen, S., & Williamson, G. M. (1988). Perceived stress in a probability sample of the United States. In S. Spacapan & S. Oskamp (Eds.), *The social psychology of health* (pp. 31–67). Newbury Park, CA: Sage Publications.

Cohen, S., & Wills, T. A. (1985). Stress, social support, and the buffering hypothesis. *Psychological Bulletin, 98*, 310–357.

Cole, D. A. (1991). Preliminary support for a competence-based model of depression in children. *Journal of Abnormal Psychology, 100*, 181–190.

Cole, D. A., & Carpentieri, S. (1990). Social status and the comorbidity of child depression and conduct disorder. *Journal of Consulting and Clinical Psychology, 58*, 748–757.

Compas, B. E. (1987). Coping with stress during childhood and adolescence. *Psychological Bulletin, 101*, 393–403.

Cooper, M. L., Russell, M., & George, W. H. (1988). Coping, expectancies, and alcohol abuse. *Journal of Abnormal Psychology, 97*, 218–230.

Cooper, M. L., Russell, M., Skinner, J. B., Frone, M. R., & Mudar, P. (1992). Stress and alcohol use: Moderating effects of gender, coping, and alcohol expectancies. *Journal of Abnormal Psychology, 101*, 139–152.

Cox, W. M. (1987). Personality theory and research. In H. T. Blane & K. E. Leonard (Eds.), *Psychological theories of drinking and alcoholism* (pp. 55–89). New York: Guilford Press.

Depue, R. A., & Monroe, S. M. (1986). Conceptualization and measurement of human disorder in life stress research. *Psychological Bulletin, 99*, 36–51.

Diener, E. (1984). Subjective well-being. *Psychological Bulletin, 95,* 542–575.

Donovan, J. E., & Jessor, R. (1978). Adolescent problem drinking: Psychosocial correlates in a national sample study. *Journal of Studies on Alcohol, 39,* 1506–1524.

Donovan, J. E., & Jessor, R. (1985). Structure of problem behavior in adolescence and young adulthood. *Journal of Consulting and Clinical Psychology, 53,* 890–904.

Donovan, J. E., Jessor, R., & Jessor, S. L. (1983). Problem drinking in adolescence and young adulthood: A follow-up study. *Journal of Studies on Alcohol, 44,* 109–137.

Folkman, S., Chesney, M. A., Pollack, L., & Phillips, C. (1992). Stress, coping and high-risk sexual behavior. *Health Psychology, 11,* 218–222.

Folkman, S., & Lazarus, R. S. (1985). If it changes it must be a process: Study of emotion and coping during three stages of a college examination. *Journal of Personality and Social Psychology, 48,* 150–170.

Fondacaro, M. R., & Heller, K. (1983). Social support factors and drinking among college student males. *Journal of Youth and Adolescence, 12,* 285–299.

Garmezy, N., & Masten, A. S. (1991). The protective role of competence indicators in children at risk. In E. M. Cummings, A. L. Greene, & K. H. Karraker (Eds.), *Life span developmental psychology: Perspectives on stress and coping* (pp. 151–174). Hillsdale, NJ: Erlbaum Associates.

Garmezy, N., & Rutter, M. (1983) (Eds.). *Stress, coping and development in children.* New York: McGraw-Hill.

Goldberger, L., & Breznitz, S. (Eds.) (1993). *Handbook of stress: Theoretical and clinical aspects, 2nd ed.* New York: Free Press.

Goldstein, A. P. (1990). *Delinquents on delinquency.* Champaign, IL: Research Press.

Greenberg, M. T., Siegel, J. M., & Leitch, C. J. (1983). The nature and importance of attachment relationships to parents and peers during adolescence. *Journal of Youth and Adolescence, 12,* 373–386.

Hall, S. M., Havassy, B. E., & Wasserman, D. A. (1991). Effects of commitment to abstinence, moods, stress, and coping on relapse to cocaine use. *Journal of Consulting and Clinical Psychology, 59,* 526–532.

Harrington, R., Fudge, H., Rutter, M., Pickles, A., & Hill, J. (1991). Adult outcomes of childhood and adolescent depression: II. Links with antisocial disorders. *Journal of the American Academy of Child and Adolescent Psychiatry, 30,* 434–439.

Harter, S. (1985). *Manual for the self-perception profile for children and adolescents.* Denver: University of Denver.

Hays, R. D., Widaman, K. F., DiMatteo, M. R., & Stacy, A. W. (1987). Structural equation models of current drug use. *Journal of Personality and Social Psychology, 52,* 134–144.

Helzer, J. E. (1987). Epidemiology of alcoholism. *Journal of Consulting and Clinical Psychology, 55,* 284–292.

Heppner, P. P., & Petersen, C. H. (1982). The development and implications of a personal problem-solving inventory. *Journal of Counseling Psychology, 29,* 66–75.

Huesmann, L. R., Eron, L. D., Lefkowitz, M. M., & Walder, L. O. (1984) Stability of aggression over time and generations. *Developmental Psychology, 20,* 1120–1134.

Hull, J. G., & Bond, C. F., Jr. (1986). Social and behavioral consequences of alcohol consumption and expectancy. *Psychological Bulletin, 99,* 347–360.

Hymel, S., Rubin, K. H., Rowden, L., & LeMare, L. (1990). Children's peer relationships: Longitudinal prediction of internalizing and externalizing problems from middle to late childhood. *Child Development, 61,* 2004–2021.

Jessor, R., Chase, J. A., & Donovan, J. E. (1980). Psychosocial correlates of marijuana use and problem drinking in a national sample of adolescents. *American Journal of Public Health, 70,* 604–613.

Jessor, R., & Jessor, S. L. (1977). *Problem behavior and psychosocial development*. New York: Academic Press.

Johnson, J. H., & McCutcheon, S. (1980). Assessing life stress in older children and adolescents. In I. G. Sarason & C. D. Spielberger (Eds.), *Stress and anxiety*, Vol. 7 (pp. 111–125). Washington, DC: Hemisphere.

Johnston, L. D., O'Malley, P. M., & Bachman, J. G. (1989). *Drug use, drinking, and smoking: National survey results from high school, college, and young adult populations 1975–1988*. Rockville, MD: National Institute on Drug Abuse.

Jones, M. C. (1968). Personality correlates and antecedents of drinking patterns in adult males. *Journal of Consulting and Clinical Psychology, 32*, 2–12.

Kandel, D., Kessler, R. C., & Margulies, R. Z. (1978). Antecedents of adolescent initiation into stages of drug use. In D. B. Kandel (Ed.), *Longitudinal research on drug use* (pp. 73–100). New York: John Wiley.

Karoly, P., & Kanfer, F. H. (1982). *Self-management and behavior change*. New York: Pergamon Press.

Kellam, S. G., Brown, C. H., & Fleming, J. P. (1982). Social adaptation to first grade and teenage drug, alcohol and cigarette use. *Journal of School Health, 52*, 301–306.

Kendall, P. C., & Wilcox, L. E. (1979). Self-control in children: Development of a rating scale. *Journal of Consulting and Clinical Psychology, 47*, 1020–1029.

Kendall, P. C., & Williams, C. L. (1982). Assessing the cognitive and behavioral components of children's self-management. In P. Karoly & F. H. Kanfer (Eds.), *Self-management and behavior change* (pp. 240–284). New York: Pergamon Press.

Khantzian, E. J. (1990). Self-regulation and self-medication factors in alcoholism and the addictions. In M. Galanter (Ed.), *Recent developments in alcoholism*, Vol. 8 (pp. 255–271). New York: Plenum Press.

Labouvie, E. W. (1986). Alcohol and marijuana use in relation to adolescent stress. *International Journal of the Addictions, 21*, 333–345.

LaGreca, A. M., Siegel, L. J., Wallander, J. L., & Walker, C. E. (Eds.) (1992). *Advances in pediatric psychology*, Vol. 1, *Stress and coping in child health*. New York: Guilford Press.

Larson, R. W. (1983). Adolescents' daily experience with family and friends: Contrasting opportunity systems. *Journal of Marriage and the Family, 45*, 739–750.

Lazarus, R. S., & Folkman, S. (1984). *Stress, appraisal and coping*. New York: Springer.

Lerner, J. V., & Vicary, J. R. (1984). Difficult temperament and drug use. *Journal of Drug Education, 14*, 1–8.

Lewis, J. M., & Looney, J. G. (1983). *The long struggle: Well-functioning working class black families*. New York: Brunner/Mazel.

Loeber, R. (1988). Natural histories of conduct problems, delinquency, and associated substance use. In B. B. Lahey & A. E. Kazdin (Eds.), *Advances in clinical child psychology*, Vol. 11 (pp. 73–124). New York: Plenum Press.

Loper, R. G., Kammeier, M. L., & Hoffmann, H. (1973). MMPI characteristics of college freshmen who later became alcoholic. *Journal of Abnormal Psychology, 82*, 159–162.

Luthar, S. S., & Zigler, E. (1991). Vulnerability and competence: A review of research on resilience in childhood. *American Journal of Orthopsychiatry, 61*, 6–22.

Marlatt, G. A. (1987). Alcohol, the magic elixir: Stress, expectancy, and the transformation of emotional states. In E. Gottheil, K. Druley, S. Pashdo, & S. Weinstein (Eds.), *Stress and addiction* (pp. 302–322). New York: Brunner/Mazel.

Masten, A. S. (1994). Resilience in individual development: Successful adaptation despite risk and adversity. In M. C. Wang & E. Gordon (Eds.), *Educational resilience in inner-city America* (pp. 3–25). Hillsdale, NJ: Erlbaum Associates.

Mausner, J. S., & Kramer, S. (1985). *Epidemiology: An introductory text*, 2nd ed. Baltimore: W. B. Saunders.

McKirnan, D. J., & Peterson, P. L. (1988). Stress, expectancies, and vulnerability to substance abuse. *Journal of Abnormal Psychology, 97*, 461–466.

McMahon, R. C., & Kouzekanani, K. (1991). Stress, social support, and the buffering hypothesis in the prediction of cocaine abuse relapse. Paper presented at the meeting of the American Psychological Association, San Francisco, August 1991.

Mellinger, G. D., Balter, M. B., Manheimer, D. I., Cisin, I. H., & Parry, H. J. (1978). Psychic distress, life crisis, and use of psychotherapeutic medications. *Archives of General Psychiatry, 35*, 1045–1052.

Miller, W. R., & Brown, J. M. (1991). Self-regulation as a conceptual basis for the prevention of addictive behaviours. In N. Heather, W. Miller, & J. Greeley (Eds.), *Self-control and the addictive behaviors* (pp. 3–79). Sydney: Maxwell Macmillan.

Mitic, W. R., McGuire, D. P., & Neumann, B. (1985). Perceived stress and adolescents' cigarette use. *Psychological Reports, 57*, 1043–1048.

Monroe, S. M., & Simons, A. D. (1991). Diathesis–stress theories in the context of life stress research: Implications for the depressive disorders. *Psychological Bulletin, 110*, 406–425.

Moos, R. H., Finney, J., & Cronkite, R. (1990). *Alcoholism treatment: Context, process, and outcome.* New York: Oxford University Press.

Moos, R. H., & Schaefer, J. A. (1993). Coping resources and processes: Current concepts and measures. In L. Goldberger & S. Breznitz (Eds.), *Handbook of stress*, 2nd ed. (pp. 234–257). New York: Free Press.

Morison, P., & Masten, A. S. (1991). Peer reputation in middle childhood as a predictor of adaptation in adolescence. *Child Development, 62*, 991–1007.

Murray, D. M., & Perry, C. L. (1987). The measurement of substance use among adolescents: When is the "bogus pipeline" method needed? *Addictive Behaviors, 12*, 225–233.

Needle, R., Su, S., & Lavee, Y. (1989). A comparison of the empirical utility of three composite measures of adolescent overall drug involvement. *Addictive Behaviors, 14*, 429–441.

Newcomb, M. D., & Harlow, L. L. (1986). Life events and substance use among adolescents. *Journal of Personality and Social Psychology, 51*, 564–577.

Newcomb, M. D., Huba, G. J., & Bentler, P. M. (1981). Multidimensional assessment of stressful life events among adolescents. *Journal of Health and Social Behavior, 22*, 400–415.

Olweus, D. (1979). Stability of aggressive reaction patterns in males. *Psychological Bulletin, 86*, 852–875.

Park, C. L., & Cohen, L. H. (1992). Religious beliefs and practices and the coping process. In B. N. Carpenter (Ed.), *Personal coping: Theory, research, and application* (pp. 185–198). Westport, CT: Praeger.

Patterson, G. R. (1986). Performance models for antisocial behavior. *American Psychologist, 41*, 432–444.

Patterson, G. R., DeBaryshe, B. D., & Ramsey, E. (1989). A developmental perspective on antisocial behavior. *American Psychologist, 44*, 329–335.

Perkins, K. A., & Grobe, J. E. (1992). Increased desire to smoke during acute stress. *British Journal of Addictions, 87*, 1037–1040.

Plomin, R., & Dunn, J. (Eds.) (1986). *The study of temperament: Changes, continuities, and challenges.* Hillsdale, NJ: Erlbaum Associates.

Revell, A. D., Warburton, D. M., & Wesnes, K. (1985). Smoking as a coping strategy. *Addictive Behaviors, 10*, 209–224.

Robins, L. N., & Przybeck, T. R. (1985). Age of onset of drug use as a factor in drug and other disorders. In C. L. Jones & R. J. Battjes (Eds.), *Etiology of drug abuse* (pp. 178–192). Rockville, MD: National Institute on Drug Abuse.

Rohde, P., Lewinsohn, P. M., Tilson, M., & Seeley, J. R. (1990). Dimensionality of coping and its relation to depression. *Journal of Personality and Social Psychology, 58,* 499–511.

Rosenbaum, M. (1990) (Ed.). *Learned resourcefulness: On coping skills, self-control, and adaptive behavior.* New York: Springer.

Rothbart, M. K., & Ahadi, S. A. (1994). Temperament and the development of personality. *Journal of Abnormal Psychology, 103,* 55–66.

Sandler, I. N., Miller, P., Short, J., & Wolchik, S. A. (1989). Social support as a protective factor for children in stress. In D. Belle (Ed.), *Children's social networks and social supports* (pp. 277–307). New York: John Wiley.

Seltzer, C. C., & Oechsli, F. W. (1985). Psychosocial characteristics of adolescent smokers before they started smoking. *Journal of Chronic Diseases, 38,* 17–26.

Shadel, W. G., & Mermelstein, R. J. (1993). Cigarette smoking under stress: The role of coping expectancies among smokers in a clinic-based smoking cessation program. *Health Psychology, 12,* 443–450.

Shiffman, S. (1985). Coping with temptations to smoke. In S. Shiffman & T. A. Wills (Eds.), *Coping and substance use* (pp. 223–242). Orlando, FL: Academic Press.

Shiffman, S. (1994). Smoking relapse episodes: New methods and findings. Paper presented at the meeting of the American Psychological Association, Los Angeles, August 1994.

Steele, C. M., & Josephs, R. A. (1990). Alcohol myopia: Its prized and dangerous effects. *American Psychologist, 45,* 921–933.

Stone, A. A., Helder, L., & Schneider, M. S. (1988). Coping with stressful events: Coping dimensions and issues. In L. Cohen (Ed.), *Life events and psychological functioning: Theoretical and methodological issues* (pp. 182–210). Newbury Park, CA: Sage Publications.

Stone, A. A., Kennedy-Moore, E., Newman, M. G., Greenberg, M., & Neale, J. M. (1992). Conceptual and methodological issues in current coping assessments. In B. N. Carpenter (Ed.), *Personal coping: Theory, research and application* (pp. 15–29). Westport, CT: Praeger.

Stone, A. A., & Neale, J. M. (1984). A new measure of daily coping. *Journal of Personality and Social Psychology, 46,* 892–906.

Suls, J., & Fletcher, B. (1985). The relative efficacy of avoidant and non-avoidant coping strategies: A meta-analysis. *Health Psychology, 4,* 249–288.

Sussman, S., Brannon, B. R., Dent, C. W., Hansen, W. B., Johnson, C. A., & Flay, B. R. (1993). Relations of coping effort, perceived stress, and cigarette smoking among adolescents. *International Journal of the Addictions, 28,* 599–612.

Tarter, R. E. (1988). Are there inherited behavioral traits that predispose to substance abuse? *Journal of Consulting and Clinical Psychology, 56,* 189–196.

Tarter, R. E., Alterman, A., & Edwards, K. (1985). Vulnerability to alcoholism: A behavior–genetic perspective. *Journal of Studies on Alcohol, 46,* 329–356.

Tarter, R. E., Moss, H. B., & Vanyukov, M. M. (1995). Behavior genetic perspective of alcoholism etiology. In H. Begleiter & B. Kissin (Eds.), *Alcohol and alcoholism,* Vol. 1 (pp. 294–326). New York: Oxford University Press.

Thoits, P. A. (1986). Social support as coping assistance. *Journal of Consulting and Clinical Psychology, 54,* 416–423.

Timmer, S. G., Colten, M. E., & Veroff, J. (1985). Life stress, helplessness, and use of alcohol and drugs to cope. In S. Shiffman & T. A. Wills (Eds.), *Coping and substance use* (pp. 171–198). Orlando, FL: Academic Press.

Tzelgov, J., & Henik, A. (1991). Suppression situations in pschological research: Definitions, implications, and applications. *Psychological Bulletin, 19,* 524–536.

U.S. Department of Health and Human Services (1988). *Surgeon General's report on health consequences of smoking: Nicotine addiction.* Washington, DC: U.S. Government Printing Office.

Wahler, R. G. (1990). Some perceptual functions of social networks in coercive mother–child interactions. *Journal of Social and Clinical Psychology, 9,* 43–53.

Weissman, M. M. (1987). Advances in psychiatric epidemiology: Rates and risks for major depression. *American Journal of Public Health, 77,* 445–451.

Werner, E. E. (1986). Resilient offspring of alcoholics: A longitudinal study from birth to age 18. *Journal of Studies on Alcohol, 47,* 34–40.

Werner, E. E., & Smith, R. S. (1982). *Vulnerable but invincible: A longitudinal study of resilient children and youth.* New York: McGraw-Hill.

Wills, T. A. (1985). Supportive functions of interpersonal relationships. In S. Cohen & S. L. Syme (Eds.), *Social support and health* (pp. 61–82). Orlando, FL: Academic Press.

Wills, T. A. (1986). Stress and coping in early adolescence: Relationships to substance use in urban school samples. *Health Psychology, 5,* 503–529.

Wills, T. A. (1988). Tobacco use, stress, and mood regulation. In *Surgeon General's report on health consequences of smoking: Nicotine addiction* (pp. 394–413). Washington, DC: U.S. Government Printing Office.

Wills, T. A. (1990a). Multiple networks and substance use. *Journal of Social and Clinical Psychology, 9,* 78–90.

Wills, T. A. (1990b). Social support and the family. In E. Blechman (Ed.), *Emotions and the family* (pp. 75–98). Hillsdale, NJ: Erlbaum Associates.

Wills, T. A. (1990c). Stress and coping factors in the epidemiology of substance use. In L. T. Kozlowski et al. (Eds.), *Research advances in alcohol and drug problems,* Vol. 10 (pp. 215–250). New York: Plenum Press.

Wills, T. A., Blechman, E. A., & McNamara, G. (1995a). Family support, coping and competence. In E. M. Hetherington (Ed.), *Stress, coping, and resiliency in children and the family.* Hillsdale, NJ: Erlbaum Associates (in press).

Wills, T. A., & Cleary, S. D. (1995a). How are social support effects mediated: A test for parental support and adolescent substance use. Manuscript submitted for publication.

Wills, T. A., & Cleary, S. D. (1995b). Stress-coping model for alcohol/tobacco interactions in adolescence. In J. Fertig & J. Allen (Eds.), *Alcohol and tobacco: From basic science to policy* (pp. 107–128). NIAAA Research Monograph.

Wills, T. A., Cleary, S. D., Filer, M., Mariani, J., & Spera, K. (1995). Temperament and early-onset substance use: A test of two theoretical models. Manuscript submitted for publication.

Wills, T. A., DuHamel, K., & Vaccaro, D. (1995b). Activity and mood temperament as predictors of adolescent substance use: Test of a self-regulation mediational model. *Journal of Personality and Social Psychology, 68,* 901–916.

Wills, T. A., & Hirky, A. E. (1995). Coping and substance abuse. In M. Zeidner & N. S. Endler (Eds.), *Handbook of coping: Theory, research, and applications.* New York: John Wiley.

Wills, T. A., McNamara, G., & Vaccaro, D. (1995c). Parental education related to adolescent stress–coping and substance use. *Health Psychology, 14,* 464–478.

Wills, T. A., McNamara, G., Vaccaro, D., & Hirky, A. E. (1995d). Coping and substance use: Relationships over time in a community sample of adolescents (submitted).

Wills, T. A., McNamara, G., Vaccaro, D., & Hirky, A. E. (1995e). Escalated substance use: A longitudinal grouping analysis in early adolescence. *Journal of Abnormal Psychology* (in press).

Wills, T. A., Schreibman, D., Benson, G., & Vaccaro, D. (1994b). The impact of parental substance use on adolescents: A test of a mediational model. *Journal of Pediatric Psychology, 19,* 537–555.

Wills, T. A., & Shiffman, S. (1985). Coping and substance use: A conceptual framework. In
S. Shiffman & T. A. Wills (Eds.), *Coping and substance use* (pp. 3–24). Orlando, FL:
Academic Press.

Wills, T. A., Vaccaro, D., Benson, G., & Schreibman, D. (1994). Psychosocial predictors of
early-onset substance use. Paper presented at the meeting of the Society of Behavioral
Medicine, Boston, April 1995.

Wills, T. A., Vaccaro, D., & McNamara, G. (1992a). The role of life events, family support,
and competence in adolescent substance use: A test of vulnerability and protective
factors. *American Journal of Community Psychology, 20,* 349–374.

Wills, T. A., Vaccaro, D., & McNamara, G. (1994d). Novelty seeking, risk taking, and
related constructs as predictors of adolescent substance use: An application of
Cloninger's theory. *Journal of Substance Abuse, 6,* 1–20.

Wills, T. A., Vaccaro, D., McNamara, G., & DuHamel, K. (1992b). Coping and substance
use among urban adolescents. Paper presented at the meeting of the American Psychological Association, Washington, DC, August 1992.

Wills, T. A., Vaccaro, D., McNamara, G., & Hirky, A. E. (1993a). Family support prospectively related to adolescents' competence and substance use. Paper presented at the
meeting of the American Psychological Association, Toronto, August 1993.

Wills, T. A., Vaccaro, D., McNamara, G., & Hirky, A. E. (1993b). Life stress predicts
adolescent substance use net of deviancy. Paper presented at the meeting of the
Society of Behavioral Medicine, San Francisco, March 1993.

Wills, T. A., Vaccaro, D., McNamara, G., & Spellman, M. (1991). Three competence domains relate to adolescent substance use. Paper presented at the meeting of the
American Psychological Association, San Francisco, August 1991.

Wills, T. A., & Vaughan, R. (1989). Social support and substance use in early adolescence.
Journal of Behavioral Medicine, 12, 321–339.

Wills, T. A., & Warshawsky, A. (1983). Stressful events and substance use in early adolescence. In S. Shiffman (Chair), *Stress and smoking.* Symposium presented at the meeting
of the American Psychological Association, Anaheim, California, August 1983.

Windle, M. (1990). Temperament and personality attributes of children of alcoholics. In M.
Windle & J. S. Searles (Eds.), *Children of alcoholics: Critical perspectives* (pp. 129–167).
New York: Guilford Press.

Windle, M., & Lerner, R. M. (1986). Reassessing the dimensions of temperamental individuality across the life span: The Revised Dimensions of Temperament Survey. *Journal of
Adolescent Research, 1,* 213–229.

Zeidner, M., & Endler, N. S. (Eds.) (1995). *Handbook of coping: Theory, research, and applications.* New York: John Wiley.

Zevon, M. A., & Tellegen, A. (1982). The structure of mood change. *Journal of Personality
and Social Psychology, 43,* 111–122.

Zucker, R. A. (1994). Pathways to alcohol problems and alcoholism: A developmental
account of the evidence for multiple alcoholisms and contextual contributions to risk.
In R. A. Zucker, J. Howard, & G. M. Boyd (Eds.), *The development of alcohol problems*
(pp. 255–289). Rockville, MD: National Institute on Alcohol Abuse and Alcoholism.

Zuckerman, M. (1979). *Sensation seeking: Beyond the optimal level of arousal.* Hillsdale, NJ:
Erlbaum Associates.

4

Race, Ethnicity, and Children's Peer Relations

SHARON L. FOSTER, CHARLES R. MARTINEZ, JR., AND ANDREA M. KULBERG

1. Introduction

Problematic peer relations or social skills difficulties are associated with a variety of childhood disorders, including autism (Schreibman & Charlop, 1989), attention deficit–hyperactivity disorder (Whalen, 1989), conduct disorders (Kazdin, 1989), learning disabilities (Stone & LaGreca, 1990), and childhood depression (Helsel & Matson, 1984). Perhaps as a result, clinicians have developed and evaluated numerous social skills programs for alleviating problems that children have in interacting with peers (for reviews, see Dodge, 1989; Schneider, 1992).

With the widespread use of social skills training comes the need for attention to individual–difference variables that could influence the curricula, the format, or the outcome of social skills training programs. Individual–difference factors include gender, age, presence of comorbid difficulties, and the specific nature of the child's peer relationship difficulties. This chapter focuses on another such variable, ethnicity, and examines in particular how ethnicity may relate to peer acceptance and rejection processes.

Several factors argue for the need to examine the extent to which peer interactions and acceptance differ as a function of a child's ethnic group. First, designing an effective social skills training curriculum requires knowledge of skills that promote peer acceptance within a child's social milieu. If distinct ethnically related socialization patterns produce varying definitions of desirable and undesirable behavior or social val-

SHARON L. FOSTER, CHARLES R. MARTINEZ, JR., AND ANDREA M. KULBERG • California School of Professional Psychology, San Diego, California 92121.

Advances in Clinical Child Psychology, Volume 18, edited by Thomas H. Ollendick and Ronald J. Prinz. Plenum Press, New York, 1996.

ues (Aboud, 1987), then somewhat different skills may be required to interact successfully depending upon the ethnic composition of the peer group. Second, culturally distinct social values are particularly likely to develop to the extent that (1) children are socialized within their own ethnic group and (2) the group transmits culturally specific values and shapes, reinforces, and punishes behavior considered to be desirable and undesirable within the group. Both conditions are likely to obtain: Children's behavior with peers correlates with parental socialization practices (Putallaz & Heflin, 1990), and parents and children typically are members of the same ethnic group. Furthermore, children interact largely within groups of same-race/ethnicity peers (e.g., Finkelstein & Haskins, 1983; Sagar, Schofield, & Snyder, 1983), providing further opportunities for within-group influence and socialization.

In addition, peer acceptance and rejection relate both to children's social performance and to peers' judgments of them. Such judgments can be affected by the race/ethnicity of both the peer evaluator and the child being judged. For example, on the basis of qualitative data from a long-term observational study of 6th- and 7th-graders at a desegregated school that was 50% black and 50% white, Schofield (1981) suggested that black children may value toughness because of their socioeconomic status and the history of subordination and exploitation of blacks in the United States. Black children who play with white peers in a manner that they perceive as playful but is "rough" by white standards may often be seen by whites as aggressors. Such differences in interpretation or perception might lead to interethnic conflict or confusion among children in diverse school settings as a result of misperceptions about what types of behavior have an aggressive function in another culture. These different perceptions in turn may lead to peer relationship difficulties for children whose behavior may be adaptive or appropriate among same-race/ethnicity peers but is labeled or interpreted in a pejorative fashion by peers from different backgrounds.

This chapter surveys literature related to the question of whether and how race and ethnicity relate to peer acceptance and rejection processes. Specifically, we address: (1) race/ethnicity-related differences in valued and normative social interactional styles; (2) differences in how peers and adults evaluate children's social performance as a function of the race/ethnicity of both the evaluator and the child being evaluated; (3) patterns of cross- and within-race/ethnicity interaction; and (4) correlates of peer acceptance and rejection within different racial and ethnic groups. Although we focus primarily on data from racial and ethnic groups residing in the United States, we also cite cross-cultural comparisons when appropriate. First, however, we briefly examine conceptual and methodological issues in defining "ethnicity."

2. Defining and Measuring Ethnicity

The terms "ethnicity," "culture," and "race" have lacked consistent definitions in the psychological literature and are often used interchangeably to describe varying groups of people (Betancourt & López, 1993; Foster & Martinez, 1995; Zukerman, 1990). The distinction between these terms is important, however, because they organize people in different ways. "Culture," the broadest of these terms, can be defined as an identified group of people who share a common physical (e.g., buildings, tools, artifacts) and subjective environment (Triandis et al., 1980). Psychologists studying culture and its transmission have largely concerned themselves with the "subjective" aspects of culture, such as social norms, familial roles, shared values and belief systems, and methods and outcomes of socializing its members. Although cultural categorization has most often involved national or regional origin, other ways of designating particular "subjective" cultures are also possible (e.g., gender, religion).

Culture provides the human elements that bind ethnic groups together. "Ethnicity" defines a group of people who share any or all of common cultural backgrounds, national origins, languages, values, and practices (Betancourt & López, 1993; Ocampo, Bernal, & Knight, 1993); many use the term synonymously with "culture." Race is defined as a grouping of people based on genetic similarity and common physical features (e.g., skin color, stature, facial features) (Zukerman, 1990). Terms like "black" and "Asian" have been applied to groups of people on the basis of distinctions involving race or ethnicity. However, considerable evidence supports heterogeneity in values and behaviors among people commonly collapsed into these groups (Betancourt & López, 1993). In addition, investigators sometimes mix terminology (as in a study of "'white" vs. "Asian" children) and frequently fail to specify how they determined the ethnicity or race of research participants.

In this chapter, we use racial terminology when we see a phenomenon as primarily tied to race, ethnicity when we believe it is tied to culture, and race/ethnicity when it is not clear which is more closely implicated in the topic under discussion. As such, we use "white" and "black" to refer to racial groups, and all other terminology (i.e., "European-" or "Anglo-American," "African-American," "Hispanic," "Asian-American") to apply to ethnic groupings.

Using appropriate terminology in discussion of relevant literature is particularly troublesome because (1) writers often use racial and ethnicity labels interchangeably, even though they refer to different constructs, and (2) investigators frequently fail to specify the bases on which they categorize research participants, making it impossible to know with certainty whether they address race or ethnicity. Because of the latter problem, we elected to use researchers' own terminology to describe the populations they investigated. We recognize, however, that this practice may implicitly promote continued imprecision.

An additional difficulty in examining ethnic differences in social behavior lies in the fact that researchers typically operationalize "race" and "'ethnicity" as static variables. This practice masks substantial heterogeneity in cultural beliefs, behaviors, and experiences. Acculturation (Marín & Marín, 1991), ethnic identity (Phinney, 1992), socioeconomic status (Foster & Martinez, 1995), and racial socialization (Thornton, Chatters, Taylor, & Allen, 1990) have all been proposed as important variables to assess or control for when using ethnicity as an independent variable.

"Acculturation" commonly refers to changes in thoughts, feelings, and behaviors as a result of contact with the dominant culture (Dana, 1993; Phinney, 1990). "Ethnic identity," a related construct, refers to that aspect of a person's social identity that derives from the person's knowledge about membership in an ethnic group and the person's sense of belonging to that group (Bernal, Knight, Ocampo, Garza, & Cota, 1993; Phinney, 1992). A similar term, "racial identity," has been used almost synonymously to refer to "the quality of a person's commitment to his or her socially ascribed racial group" (Helms & Carter, 1991, p. 446). In contrast to concepts that focus on identification with the culture of origin, biculturalism explicitly highlights exposure to and skills in meeting the demands of both majority and minority cultures (LaFramboise, Coleman, & Gerton, 1993; Rotheram-Borus, 1993). Unfortunately, despite distinct conceptual similarities and differences among these terms, researchers differ considerably on how they define and operationalize each. This imprecision has led to overlap in the content of measures that allegedly assess different constructs and differences in measures that purport to assess similar constructs.

Developmental issues are particularly important in understanding and measuring these constructs with children and adolescents. For example, Bernal, Knight, Ocampo, Garza, and Cota (1990, 1993) defined five components of ethnic identity in children: (1) ethnic self-identification (categorization of oneself as a member of a particular group); (2) ethnic constancy (knowledge that one's ethnic self-identification remains fixed); (3) degree to which one engages in ethnic role behaviors (e.g., customs, language); (4) knowledge of behaviors relevant to one's ethnic group; and (5) feelings and preferences related to aspects of one's ethnic knowledge (e.g., ethnic pride). Phinney (1992) outlines similar components of ethnic identity, adding that an ethnic identity also includes a sense of belonging to one's identified ethnic group. Bernal et al. (1993) found with Hispanic children that correct ethnic identification of self and others, ethnic constancy, ethnic knowledge, and ethnic preferences all correlated positively and significantly with age. Reviewers concur that children can recognize black and white individuals accurately by the age of 5; correct identification of other minorities emerges later (by about age 7) (Brand, Ruiz, & Padilla, 1974; Aboud, 1987). Components of ethnic identity that require decision making, abstract thought, and cognitive exploration are believed to emerge and solidify during adolescence or adulthood (Phinney, 1992). Thus, the salience and importance of different aspects of ethnic identity are likely to be linked closely to cognitive capacity and development.

A final issue in defining ethnicity relates to the meaning that investigators ascribe to ethnic or racial differences. Researchers typically assume that such differences result from different cultural practices, values, or socialization. Because of the heterogeneity within cultures, however, investigators who wish to attribute race/ethnicity-related differences to cultural values and socialization practices should explicitly assess those values and practices rather than assuming their invariant prevalence in the culture, causal status, or explanatory power (Betancourt & López, 1993).

3. Ethnicity-Related Social Values and Practices

Limited research examines behavioral patterns among different ethnic groups, and research in this area is often constrained by its methods. Much of this research has employed self-report methodology with instruments validated only for white samples. Fewer studies have explored research questions with observational techniques, and many studies employ analog tasks with uncertain external validity. Researchers rarely distinguish between ethnicity and race and often fail to specify how a child's race or ethnicity was determined.

In addition, socioeconomic status is often ignored or poorly controlled. Explicit consideration of socioeconomic status is important not only because it is sometimes confounded with race/ethnicity, but also because its effects intersect with those of culture. Havighurst (1976) maintains, for example, that ethnicity-related differences are likely to be greater at lower than at higher ends of the socioeconomic continuum and that the relative effects of social class and ethnicity differ depending upon one's specific class and cultural background. This interdependence in turn implies that different culturally specific patterns may exist at different socioeconomic levels.

Several additional factors make conclusions about culturally sanctioned or normative interaction styles within each ethnic group tentative. First, heterogeneity within ethnic groups leads some investigators to question the wisdom of providing profiles of commonalities and making cross-ethnic comparisons, fearing that such investigations may promote ethnic stereotypes and supplant studies of functional relationships among variables within ethnic groups (cf. McLoyd, 1990). Second, many assertions about norms and values of different ethnic groups come from ethnographic research and experts' opinions rather than from more systematically collected observational data. Finally, much writing has focused on adults, with limited explicit attention to children in general and to peer interactions in particular.

Despite these caveats, tentative pictures of common racial/ethnic interaction styles emerge from the literature. Here, we describe patterns and values associated with Hispanic, African-American, Asian-American, and Anglo cultures, the four largest ethnic groups in the United States. We use the framework of Rotheram and Phinney (1987) to organize our description of ethnicity-related differences in children's social behavior. Specifically, these authors proposed examining ethnic differences in terms of four dimensions of behavior: (1) orientation toward the group and interdependence vs. the individual and competition; (2) attitudes toward authority; (3) expressive vs. restrained communication styles; and (4) active, outcome-oriented vs. passive, accepting coping styles.

3.1. Hispanic Children

Social scientists commonly use the label "Hispanic" to refer to people whose family origins are in Mexico, Central or South America, Spain, or the Spanish-speaking Caribbean. Because these groups differ historically and culturally, broad-band generalizations should be used cautiously. Nonetheless, Hispanic culture has been generally characterized as emphasizing affiliation, cooperation, and interpersonal relationships (Marín & Marín, 1991; Rotheram & Phinney, 1987). Marín and Marín (1991) use the term "allocentrism" or "collectivism" to describe this cultural value. The research of Knight and Kagan (1977b) and Kagan and Madsen (1972) supports this group orientation and value. Knight and Kagan (1977b) employed an experimental game situation to examine competitive and cooperative behavior in children. The task in this study involved having children make decisions on a game board that affected the number of toys they and a peer would receive. Knight and Kagan found that Mexican-American children displayed more cooperative behavior than Anglo-American children and that the effect increased with age. Kagan and Madsen (1972) reported similar patterns of differences between Anglo-American and Mexican-American children.

Acculturation processes also relate to ethnic group behavioral norms among Hispanic children. Knight and Kagan (1977a) used a behavioral choice card to allow Anglo-American, third-generation Mexican-American, and second-generation Mexican-American children in the 4th, 5th, and 6th grades to make decisions about the amount of rewards they and a peer would receive. The choices a subject could make ranged from altruism/group enhancement to chooser superiority/rivalry. A generally linear pattern of results indicated that second-generation Mexican-American children made more altruistic and equality choices and fewer superiority/rivalry choices than did third-generation Mexican-American children, who made more altruistic and fewer superiority choices than Anglo-American children. Thus, greater acculturation was associated with behavioral patterns that became increasingly similar to those of the majority culture, supporting the contention that acculturation processes diminish differences in the normative behavior of ethnic groups.

Rotheram-Borus and Phinney (1990) studied racial differences along the four dimensions of behavior described previously among black and Mexican-American 3rd- and 6th-grade children. They proposed that social expectations reflect specific norms regarding appropriate behavior and feelings in specific situations. The researchers developed video-taped vignettes of social behavior that assessed responses to situations involving group vs. individual orientation, attitudes toward authority, emotionality, and coping styles. Children self-reported what they would do and how they would feel following each of the vignettes. Results from this study supported the group orientation of Mexican-American children. In two vignettes depicting a peer making a request, Mexican-American children reported more sharing than did black students, and this effect increased with age.

Hispanic children are also described as showing great deference to authority. Hofstede (1980) suggests that "power distance," which describes the interpersonal power or influence present between two people, is a cultural value that distinguishes groups. Marín and Marín (1991) suggest that Hispanic culture emphasizes high power-distance relationships. As such, Hispanics are proposed to value authority, conformity, and authoritarian attitudes from those in charge. The findings of Rotheram-Borus and Phinney (1990) supported these contentions: In a vignette that depicted a teacher scolding a child by expressing disappointment, Mexican-American children were more likely to report feeling bad than were their black peers. In addition, Mexican-American children were more likely to report relying on authority figures to resolve disputes than were black children.

Marín and Marín (1991) describe a Hispanic cultural value known as *simpatía*. Simpatía emphasizes the need for individual members of the culture to behave in ways that promote positive and smooth social interaction. Operationally, Marín and Marín (1991, p. 12) describe simpatía as "a general tendency toward avoiding interpersonal conflict, emphasizing positive behaviors in agreeable situations, and de-emphasizing negative behaviors in conflictive circumstances." Thus, Mexican-Americans are theorized to be more accepting in their orientation than are African-Americans or whites (Rotheram & Phinney, 1987).

In support of this contention, Rotheram-Borus and Phinney (1990) found that Mexican-American children generally verbalized more passive coping styles and less expressive emotionality than their black peers. Specifically, Mexican-American children were more likely to report not getting involved in a fight between peers, more likely to feel bad and less likely to take action when a child was corrected by a peer, and more likely to sit and wait when a peer needed to use a crayon. Similarly, Khorram (1994) found that Mexican-American children reported using avoidance as a conflict resolution strategy more than Anglo children.

Despite considerable within-group heterogeneity, the interactional style profile that emerges for Hispanic children describes them as generally group-oriented, deferent to authority, and accepting in their coping style. With regard to emotionality, the literature suggests that Hispanic children are somewhat constrained in their expression of emotions that are confrontational. It does not necessarily follow from this suggestion, however, that the same pattern would hold for more positive emotional expression.

3.2. African-American Children

African-American culture emphasizes a "we" concept that focuses on interdependence and the survival of the group, contrasting sharply with the individualism of Anglos (Baldwin, 1991; M. K. Ho, 1992). Also due to their collective focus, African-Americans are known to highly value achievements of the group (Hayles, 1991). Like Mexican-Americans, African-Americans place special importance on relationships with extended family members and male–female bonds (Hayles, 1991). Observational findings that black children initiate more peer interactions, particularly cross-race interactions, than white children (Sagar et al., 1983) support the social orientation of African-American children.

Rotheram-Borus and Phinney (1990) found that black children report considerable deference to authority. In response to vignettes depicting a teacher scolding, black children more often reported apologizing than did Mexican-American children, who reported that they would feel bad more often than did black children. These results suggest that both

Mexican-American children and black children defer to authority, but that they express their deference in different ways. The investigators point out that Mexican-American children were more likely than black children to appeal to an authority in resolving a conflict and that they were also more likely to seek information from the teacher when corrected by a peer than were black children. The observational data of Singleton and Asher (1977), however, indicated that black and white children interact equally frequently with teachers.

Kochman (1987) has asserted that black culture is a "high intensity society in which both positive and negative feelings are expressed openly." Rotheram-Borus and Phinney (1990) evaluated the social expectations of children in regard to this expressiveness by asking black and Mexican-American children to respond to vignettes depicting a target boy being corrected by a peer. Mexican-American children were more likely to do nothing or feel bad, while black children were significantly more likely to react actively by accepting the correction and saying "thanks" or feeling angry.

Directness and disagreement in social discussions are a part of the intense language display that is positively valued in African-American culture as an expression of sincerity (Ting-Toomey, 1986). However, Ting-Toomey (1986) noted that members of other ethnic groups (e.g., Anglos) can perceive African-American expressiveness as verbally aggressive or hostile.

Another behavior that non-African-Americans may interpret as aggression is a form of verbal dueling (sometimes called "basing") that occurs among black males starting in childhood (Kochman, 1987). Like a form of rough-and tumble play, this process involves trading increasingly demeaning insults, with the goal of both parties remaining playful about the interaction. The activity becomes aggressive only when one party begins to take the other seriously, thereby ending, and losing, the game for himself or herself. An incident involving a student of the first author illustrated how others can misconstrue this behavior as aggression. The student conducted social skills training in which black and white children lost points in a token economy for verbal aggression on the playground. She initially took away points for black males' verbal dueling, only to be told by the study participants that those exchanges did not involve "real" teasing or insults and that no one minded them.

The importance of direct expression among African-Americans and the potential for Anglos to interpret such expression as aggression is important for understanding findings that on the surface portray African-American children as more overtly aggressive than their Anglo peers. For example, observational data indicate that black preschool and kindergarten children display more aggressive (Weigel, 1985) or negative behavior (Finkelstein & Haskins, 1983), or both, than do white children. As Weigel (1985) notes, however, the definitions of "aggression" and "negative behavior" in these investigations might have included forms of emotionally expressive or boisterous behavior (e.g., rough-and-tumble play, loud or rough talk) that inflated scores of black children. Similarly, Coie, Dodge, and Coppotelli [1982 (Study II)] reported that black 3rd-, 5th-, and 8th-graders received more peer nominations for "disrupts" and "fights" than did white children. The majority of their sample (68%) were white, however, leading to questions about the extent to which the findings reflected mismatches in racial tolerance for expressiveness and assertiveness vs. actual racial/ethnic differences in aggression or disruptiveness. Clearly, investigators should in the future differentiate among subtypes of behavior commonly grouped together as "aggressive" and "disruptive."

In accord with the value placed on expressing strong emotions, African-American children are also described as active in their coping style. Rotheram-Borus and Phinney (1990) found that black children were more likely than Mexican-American children to report stopping the fight in response to a videotaped vignette that depicted two peers fighting. Similarly, Weigel (1985) found that black preschoolers used assertive behaviors such as telling others to start or stop doing something, or to be quiet, more often than peers.

For African-American children, the general interactional profile that emerges describes their normative pattern of behavior as being group-oriented, and deferent to authority, although not particularly dependent on authority. They also appear to express themselves openly, and to use active coping styles, particularly in assertiveness situations.

3.3. Asian-American Children

The ethnic label "Asian-American" has been used widely to describe people of diverse ethnic heritages (e.g., Chinese, Japanese, Filipino, Korean) (Dana, 1993). Any broad-based categorization of these diverse groups can be inappropriate, and thus generalizations of research findings across national origins should be tentative. Nonetheless, Dana (1993) reports that Chinese culture was historically a prominent influence on the core cultures of Japan, Vietnam, and Korea. Thus, it may be possible to induce at least a subset of common cultural values for these groups.

Asian-Americans have been described as highly oriented toward the group and the family. Lin and Liu (1993) state that the cultural value called *hsiao* ("filial piety") has a centuries-long tradition in Chinese families. Chinese families stress attachment and obligations to the family, respect for elders, and strong group identification (Chiu, 1987). In addition, Rotheram and Phinney (1987) characterize Asian cultures as emphasizing affiliation, cooperation, and interpersonal relationships.

The strong emphasis on respect for family also is tied to great respect for defined role relationships within a cohesive, well-organized patriarchal hierarchy (Harrison, Wilson, Pine, Chan, & Buriel, 1990). Thus, Asian-American children have been widely characterized as more obedient, respectful, and accepting of authority than white American children (M. K. Ho, 1987, 1992; Rotheram & Phinney, 1987).

Asian-American children have also been described as minimally expressive in their emotionality and more passive than peers in their coping style. Sue (1973) and M. K. Ho (1987) state that Asian cultural values emphasize restraint of strong feelings. This restraint may be particularly applicable to anger and aggression: Sollenberger (1968) indicated that the majority of Chinese parents reported completely prohibiting aggressive behavior in their offspring. D. Y. F. Ho and Kang (1984) similarly reported both strong prohibitions against aggression and strong emphases on self-control.

The findings of Kobayashi-Winata and Power (1989) also support hypotheses of restrained emotionality and more accepting coping styles among Asian-American than among Anglo-American children. Parents in middle- to upper-middle-class Japanese families who had been temporarily living in the United States rated their children as less verbally assertive than did parents of American children. Teacher ratings mirrored these findings.

Acculturation processes also play a role in the behavior of Asian-American children. For example, some Asian cultures have been described as valuing high academic achievement (e.g., Chiu, 1987; Dana, 1993). Rong and Grant (1992), in a study of educational attainment, found that generation level was an important predictor of educational attainment for Asians, with number of years of schooling increasing from the immigrant to the child-of-immigrant generations, then remaining stable. Acculturation also relates to the conflicts between Asian-American children and their parents. Yau and Smetana (1993) report that conflicts between Chinese-American parents and their adolescent children often concern the differences between Chinese and American cultural values.

Much of the literature concerning the normative pattern of behavior in Asian-American children is qualitative or ethnographic, with very little observational research to substantiate the behavioral norms hypothesized here. Cultural values are potentially predictive of behavior, but their specific relations to children's behavior patterns have yet to be determined. Nevertheless, available literature predicts that Asian-

American children are generally group-oriented, highly deferential to authority, less expressive with their emotions than other groups, and more passive in their coping. More research is needed to determine the accuracy of these predictions among Asian-American children.

3.4. Anglo-American Children

Anglo-American children are of European descent. Like the labels "Asian" and "Hispanic," however, this category subsumes children from very different subcultures with distinct historical and cultural practices (e.g., Italian, German, French, English). Despite this heterogeneity, Anglo culture is generally characterized as valuing individual accomplishment, achievement, and independence from the group (Harrison et al., 1990). Thus, Anglo-American children tend to be significantly more task-oriented in classroom settings than their black counterparts (Sagar et al., 1983), and their self-reported conflicts tend to end in win–lose outcomes significantly more often than do those of Mexican-American children (Khorram, 1994).

Unlike the African-American and Mexican-American focus on social stimuli and relatedness, Anglo children have been reported to focus on objective tasks, cognitive styles, and property, and to use active coping styles (Rotheram & Phinney, 1987). Such a focus supports the valuing of assertive behaviors such as verbally disagreeing or saying no to unreasonable requests (Cotler & Guerra, 1976). The findings of Khorram (1994) supported this portrayal: Anglo-American children reported greater use of assertiveness than Mexican-Americans in conflict situations with peers. Knowledgeable peers also reported how participants were likely to respond to conflict, and these data produced comparable findings.

Anglo verbal expressiveness has limits, however, and must not become too emotional or contain gestures or comments personal enough to infringe upon the privacy of others (Rotheram & Phinney, 1987). According to Ting-Toomey (1986), the Anglo style of communication used during conflict may be interpreted as overly solicitous or friendly by groups with more intense and direct communication styles such as African-Americans. To African-Americans, the Anglo use of this "avoidance" communication style during confrontations can represent hypocrisy and weakness (Ting-Toomey, 1986). In addition, African-Americans may be more interested in the emotional experience of the argumentative situation, while Anglos are more interested in "good taste" and a solution.

Thus, available information portrays Anglo-American culture as promoting individual orientation and moderate emotional expressiveness. Children would also be predicted to show active coping styles and less deferential attitudes toward authority than those found in other ethnic groups.

The behavioral patterns and values described in this section are limited by a paucity of observational research with children. Such investigations could serve to specify more clearly how children of different ethnic groups handle important social situations and which behaviors each culture emphasizes as desirable. In addition, the limited observational data on children only occasionally take into account the ethnicity of the child's interactional partner(s). Yet children interact differently at least to some extent with members of other ethnic groups. Although Finkelstein and Haskins (1983) found that children directed similar proportions of talk, negative behavior, and commands to same- and cross-race peers, Singleton and Asher (1977) indicated that black (but not white) boys interacted more positively with cross-race than with same-race peers.

Despite the need for more research, existing evidence suggests that different cultures may support different behavioral norms in children's peer interactions. The findings of Wright, Giammarino, and Parad (1986) underscore the importance of cultural norms for peer acceptance and rejection. In a study of behavior-problem boys (average age: 10) in a summer camp setting, adult and peer reports of aggression correlated positively with peer rejection among low-aggression groups, but not among high-aggression groups. The reverse was true for withdrawal, presumably because withdrawal was a more normative response in low-aggression than in high-aggression groups. This finding implies that adjusting one's behavior to the behavioral norms of the peer group may be an important determinant of acceptance by those peers.

4. Social Cognition and Perceptions of Peers

Acceptance in the peer group depends not only on children's performance, but also on peers' evaluation of that performance. Children's evaluations of peers from different racial/ethnic groups are affected by how they process information from the environment, most often referred to as their "social cognition" (for a review, see Taylor & Fiske, 1981). The Triandis (1972) theory of subjective culture posits that separate ethnic groups perceive social environments differently in relation to their unique values, beliefs, and expectations. Thus, children's perceptions of peers may vary on the basis of their sociocultural and ethnic background.

Spencer and Markstrom-Adams (1990) state that by age 10–12, children have gained the cognitive skills necessary for a knowledge of their reference group, with a greater preference toward and identification with their own ethnic group. Despite suggestions regarding the potentially important influence of the ethnic and cultural reference group, empirical evidence for the way in which perceptions of peer behavior vary dependent upon the reference group of the observing child is relatively sparse. In addition, many factors confound or complicate the measurement of children's unique values, beliefs, and expectations, including socioeconomic status, social stereotypes, physical features, and language differences (Lawrence, 1991; Sagar & Schofield, 1980; Spencer & Markstrom-Adams, 1990; Zebrowitz, Montepare, & Lee, 1993), ethnic and cultural identity formation (Phinney, 1990), and developmental processes underlying children's social cognition (Aboud, 1987; Ramsey, 1987).

Ethnicity-specific social cognition may take several forms. First, children may form different attributions about the same behaviors performed by children from different racial or other groups. Second, children may form expectations of others on the basis of social stereotypes and ethnic attitudes. Third, children may judge peers' behavior differently as a function of their own or the peers' race or ethnicity.

4.1. Attributions

Attributions about the causes of others' behavior affect children's reactions to their peers (Zadney & Gerard, 1974; Dodge, 1980). It has been postulated that much interpersonal misunderstanding in diverse school settings is the result of children's making different causal attributions for the same behavior (Triandis, 1972). Studies examining causal attributions and race support this hypothesis.

The study by Sagar and Schofield (1980) of black and white 6th-grade males demonstrated that both black and white males considered ambiguous hypothetical acts by black males to be more threatening than the same behaviors by white males. Although the investigators noted that the tendency of males to read more meanness and threat into blacks' ambiguous behavior may have been based upon the "black-violent" stereotype prevalent in American society, they also found evidence for more generic cultural differences in interpretation of behavior. Specifically, white subjects attributed more meanness and less friendliness than black subjects to stimulus characters (regardless of race) in behavioral scenarios in which no physical contact was involved, but in which one person was attempting to obtain a material good from another. Sagar and Schofield hypothesized that the black cultural value of considering property a collective asset would make this behavior acceptable, in contrast to white cultural valuing of personal ownership, which may make this act seem inappropriate to them.

Attributional information such as that discussed above is particularly important in multiethnic settings in which children interact with peers from cultures with different value structures and rules for appropriate ways of behaving in various contexts. Such situations are inherently ambiguous and require interpretation of social cues in both peer and adult–child interactions. In the case of ambiguously aggressive behavior, for example, children who attribute hostile intentions to hypothetical peers are more likely to report that they would retaliate aggressively toward those peers (Dodge, 1980; Graham, Hudley, & Williams, 1992). Aggression in turn may provoke negative reactions (including rejection) from the peers who experience it.

Because of the importance of attributions in the ambiguous context, interventions to change them have been attempted. Because aggressive males tend to attribute hostile intent to peers following ambiguous peer provocations, Hudley and Graham (1993) assigned aggressive African-American elementary school boys to either an attribution intervention group, an attention training program, or a no-treatment control group. Boys in the 12-session cognitive intervention, which trained them not to infer hostile peer intent in negative social encounters of ambiguous origin, were less likely to infer hostile intent by peers in hypothetical or simulated provocations after treatment than they were prior to treatment. In addition, relative to boys in the other two conditions, boys in the intervention condition engaged in fewer verbally hostile behaviors in an analog situation after treatment. Teachers also rated boys in the intervention condition as significantly less aggressive after the treatment than before. Such interventions hold considerable promise for increasing children's social competence in multicultural school settings in the future.

4.2. Stereotypes, Biases, and Intergroup Attitudes

Racial and ethnic stereotypes are prevalent in our society, are established at very early ages, and can affect perceptions of behavior performed by members of a child's own or another racial/ethnic group. As a type of social cognition, stereotypes are usually trait- or category-based and can affect inferences that are made about others in the absence of relevant information (Kleinpenning & Hagendoorn, 1991). Ethnic stereotypes are often equated with prejudices (Kleinpenning & Hagendoorn, 1991) or with incorrect, negative overgeneralizations (Schofield, 1981). Schofield (1981) points out, however, that social stereotypes need not be negative, inaccurate, or prejudicial, and can at times be based on a "kernel of truth."

Stereotypes vary dependent on the presence, absence, and salience of cues that provide information about membership in social groups or categories (Zarate & Smith, 1990). Stereotypes can also vary within groups, depending on the context of interethnic evaluation (Kleinpenning & Hagendoorn, 1991). Social expectations and stereotypes are probably multidetermined: Investigators believe that they emerge out of interaction with persons from different cultural groups (Schofield, 1981), media portrayals (Spencer, 1983), and labeling and instruction by parents, teachers, and peers (Patchen, 1982; Spencer, 1983).

Related to stereotypes is the concept of ethnic attitudes, which Aboud (1987, p. 41) defines as an "organized predisposition to respond in a favorable or unfavorable manner toward people from different ethnic groups." This predisposition is evaluative in nature, elicited by a person's ethnicity, and stable over time and across situations. Children's ethnic attitudes are believed to be less well organized than those of adults and to change with age and experience (Ramsey, 1987).

Aboud (1987) reviewed studies examining racial/ethnic attitudes with children and reached several conclusions. First, children express positive attitudes toward their own group as early as age 3 or 4. Second, whites show a stronger preference for their own group than do black, Amerindian, Chicano, or Chinese children. Third, findings regarding black children's own-group attitudes vary, with some studies finding own-race preference, others white preference, and others no discernible preference.

Fourth, findings from other (nonblack) minority groups also vary, but show pro-white attitudes and the absence of same-race preference more frequently than do studies of black children. These groups maintain a predominantly white preference into the preadolescent years, but without the development of concomitant positive attitudes toward their own groups.

Fifth, studies of children's racial/ethnic attitudes frequently use methodologies that force children to choose which of two pictures (or dolls) they prefer in answer to questions such as "Which is nicer?" This forced-choice paradigm confounds own-group positive attitudes with negative attitudes toward others. In studies in which children use rating scales to evaluate other-race peers, white children show moderately negative attitudes toward children from other groups. Some black children show anti-white attitudes as well.

Sixth, some evidence suggests that white children's negative attitudes may decline somewhat after age 7, perhaps due to exposure to other groups, sensitivity to prejudice and social issues with increasing age, or increasingly socially desirable response styles. The pattern is not as clear for black children, who sometimes develop more favorable and sometimes less favorable attitudes toward their white peers as they age.

Seventh, Aboud cites several methodological issues that characterize this literature, including questionable convergent validity of the measures, frequent focus on only two ethnic groups (with the perhaps mistaken assumption that rejection of one group implies rejection of all), and lack of attention to possible social desirability biases. In addition, the studies Aboud (1987) describes typically present the child with same-race and different-race stimuli and ask children to select among or rate the stimuli. This paradigm would be expected to generalize best to first-impression situations. It may be less generalizable, however, to more everyday social interactions in which children experience both the visible racial characteristics and the behavior of their peers.

A few studies have examined how racial/ethnic attitudes may operate in the context of social interactions using analog situations. In these studies, children typically view videotapes or pictures of other children who display identical behavior. Experimenters typically vary the race of the participants, the race of the stimulus child or children, and sometimes types of behavior as well. Main effects involving the race of the perceiver (subject) indicate different social perceptions among groups. Main effects having to do with the race of the stimulus child imply biased evaluations or stereotyping of the stimulus child. Interactions between the race of the perceiver and the race of the stimulus child may indicate that one group of raters and not another shows a particular bias or that different groups judge stimulus children of different races differently. Interactions with types of behavior indicate that judgments may be context- or behavior-specific.

A study by Lawrence (1991) using this paradigm supported the notion that social stereotyping strongly influences children's perceptions of peers. Children ages 6–9 interpreted drawings of ambiguous behavior differently on the basis of their own race, the race of the stimulus child, and the race of the experimenter. Specifically, white children interpreted the behavior of white cartoon characters as more positive than that of black characters when with a white experimenter and when viewing those scenes rated by adults as highest in aggressive content. These differences did not occur, however, when the white children were shown drawings by a black experimenter. Black children showed no race-of-character or race-of-experimenter bias.

Steinberg and Hall (1981) studied 128 kindergarten and 1st-grade black and white males of varying socioeconomic status groups. Subjects rated how much they liked six unknown videotaped target male children (half black, half white) who displayed either positive, negative, or neutral behavior. White and black males rated positive behavior targets equally, but rated black neutral and negative targets lower than white neutral and negative targets. It is not clear, however, whether this result was a function of particular devaluing of negative behaviors when performed by black children or of differences between the stimuli depicting black and white children.

Adults as well may judge children's social behavior differently on the basis of race or ethnicity. Lethermon, Williamson, Moody, and Wozniak (1986) found that even after training, adult white raters accorded white children higher global skills ratings than black children in role plays of social situations. Black raters did not differ in how they rated the black and white children. In addition, regardless of the race of the child being rated, black raters rated children higher than white raters on appropriate assertion, effective assertion, response latency, and smiles. Similarly, Lethermon, Williamson, Moody, Granberry, Lemanek, and Bodiford (1984) found that untrained black adult raters rated videotaped black girls' performance more highly on various dimensions of social skill than did white raters, particularly when the videotaped girl's performance had previously been characterized as "unskilled" on the basis of a systematic coding scheme. Taken together, the results of these experiments suggest that whites overvalue white children's performance or devalue blacks', or both. Black adults and children less frequently show this differentiation, but when they do, they too evaluate black children more negatively than white children.

A few additional studies have examined ethnic interpersonal attitudes using children's or adolescents' self-reports about their beliefs and behaviors about same- and other-race/ethnicity peers. Phinney and Cobb (1993) found that Hispanic and Anglo adolescents with more positive attitudes toward other ethnic groups were more likely to say that another person should not be excluded from a club of other-ethnicity adolescents. Anglo males, more than Hispanic males and Anglo females, had less favorable attitudes toward other ethnic groups and were more likely to mention the rights of club members as a reason for exclusion.

Patchen (1982) gathered questionnaire data from over 3000 black and white high school students, and also interviewed a subset of the students. Questionnaire and interview data showed that many students of each race saw students of the other race as being "stuck-up" and "not friendly" toward the opposite race. Convergent with the qualitative data of Schofield (1981), whites held a stereotype of blacks that included toughness, physical violence, and being noisy and disruptive. Black students saw whites as less tough than blacks, inclined to act superior, and academically motivated.

Patchen (1982) also indicated that students' attitudes toward other-race classmates varied considerably. Positive attitudes among both blacks and whites correlated positively with self-reported cross-race friendships and friendly contacts ($rs = 0.25$ to 0.37) and negatively with reported unfriendly contact and avoidance ($rs = -0.31$ to -0.56). Overall, interracial attitudes improved as the percentage of black students in classes increased. This was true of black students' attitudes toward whites, however, only when their white classmates endorsed fewer ethnocentric (white superiority) beliefs. Interestingly, black teens' interracial attitudes were unrelated to proximity of white students in their classes. Among white students, however, sitting next to black students in more classes related positively to more positive attitudes toward blacks. Of course, these correlational data cannot speak to the question of whether friendly contact improves attitudes or whether more positive attitudes lead to friendlier contact.

Ethnic attitudes also related to academic achievement among Patchen's sample of black and white high school students. Patchen suggests that academic competition may affect the pleasantness of interracial contact, making students who perform less well resentful of those who do better and affecting overall reactions of children toward their peers. His data indicated that, for black students, as intelligence increased, more positive attitudes existed toward white schoolmates. In contrast, high-IQ whites reported slightly less positive attitudes toward black peers, although behaviorally, high-IQ whites also reported the most interracial friendliness. Patchen (1982, p. 135) speculated that this result was due to the "strong commitment to school among high-IQ whites and a consequent disapproval of the nonconventional school behavior which white students perceived among some blacks."

Patchen's data also speak to possible sources of children's ethnic attitudes. He argues that important others in children's lives (family, peers, teachers) have a large impact on multiethnic attitudes and behavior. This impact could occur via direct teaching, modeling particular interpretations of behavior, and reinforcing or punishing interracial interaction. Patchen's data support these potential sources of influence: High school students' own interracial behavior and attitudes were consistent with both the actual and the perceived racial attitudes of peers of their same race. Among both white and black students, reports of parents' and peers' attitudes toward the other race contributed significantly in predicting the students' own attitudes. Among whites, perceived teacher attitudes also contributed to predictions of positive attitudes, but not among blacks. Rather, black students' perceptions of favoritism toward whites on the part of school personnel related negatively to their attitudes toward whites.

The data of Spencer (1983) similarly highlighted the role of the family in establishing racial attitudes and preferences with much younger children. Specifically, she found that values transmitted by parents predicted children's racial attitudes and preferences. Eurocentrism was common for both black and white preschool children, but Afrocentrism was more likely among black children by age 9 if their parents reported specific teaching concerning black history, civil rights, discrimination, and racial climate.

In sum, racial/ethnic social cognition can take various forms, including attributions for and judgments of behavior, stereotyping, and general positive or negative attitudes toward different-race/ethnicity peers. These phenomena can appear in the form of different groups appraising the same situation differently, as well as differential reactions to the actions of others as a function of the other's race or ethnicity. The literature to date has focused primarily on black and white children, and generalizability of the findings to other groups remains to be established. Nonetheless, this work has highlighted the importance of cognitive variables in children's interpretation of ambiguous behavior, particularly when the behavior might be perceived as aggressive. Furthermore, the exact nature and occurrence of biased or differential judgment appears to depend upon the context (including the race of the experimenter) and the nature of the cognition or judgment being assessed. Clearly, however, more research is needed to understand when and how children make racially or ethnically based judgments in their daily lives and how these judgments affect their relationships with peers.

5. Friendship, Peer Acceptance, and Ethnicity

Investigators commonly assess children's peer acceptance, rejection, and friendship using sociometric measures. Perhaps the most common of these measures are peer nominations, in which children select from a roster or set of pictures of their peers according to some criterion, such as those they like best and those they like least. From these selections, children can be categorized as popular or accepted (liked by many, disliked by few), rejected (liked by few, disliked by many), neglected (liked by few, disliked by few), controversial (liked by many, disliked by many), and average (e.g., Coie et al., 1982). Peer ratings provide an alternative sociometric measure in which children rate how much they like each classmate on a Likert scale. Sociometric measures can also be used to determine children's friendships by, for example, asking children to nominate their best friends or examining whether two children mutually nominate each other or rate each other highly or both (Bukowski & Hoza, 1989).

To what extent do differences in culturally normative behavior and social cognition translate into different processes of peer acceptance, rejection, and friendship formation in different ethnic groups? Two lines of research examine whether different processes may operate in children's peer relations. The first lies in studies of cross-race peer preference and interactions. The second, a less well developed literature, examines whether correlates of peer acceptance and rejection vary among children from different ethnic groups.

5.1. Cross- and Same-Race Friendship and Interactional Preferences

Despite the sociopolitical movement toward school desegregation, considerable evidence supports the view that black and white children show same-race preferences in their sociometric choices. Black and white children from kindergarten through 7th grade consistently give higher liking ratings and friendship nominations to same-race than to other-race peers (Finkelstein & Haskins, 1983; Hallinan & Smith, 1985; Sagar et al., 1983; Singleton & Asher, 1977, 1979; St. John & Lewis, 1975).

Gender differences in racial cleavage are less consistent than findings of racial cleavage per se. Sagar et al. (1983) found that 6th-grade boys chose more same-race friends than did girls, but Hallinan and Teixeira (1987) found this to be true only for white 4th- to 7th-graders, with black girls selecting more cross-race friends than black males. Similarly, Sagar et al. (1983) found that white girls were particularly likely to indicate preferences for spending time with same-race females. Interestingly, Hallinan and Smith (1985), Sagar et al. (1983), and Singleton and Asher (1979) found that black children showed less same-gender preference than white children in liking ratings and friendship, although gender is consistently a more potent predictor of friendship and liking than race in both black and white samples (e.g., Sagar et al., 1983; Singleton & Asher, 1979).

Racial cleavage is evident in observed interaction patterns as well as sociometric choices. Studies document that black and white children interact in classroom and play settings a higher percentage of the time with same-race peers than with children of another race (Finkelstein & Haskins, 1983; Sagar et al., 1983), although Singleton and Asher (1977) found this difference only for girls. Furthermore, Finkelstein and Haskins (1983) found that kindergarten children's groups were more racially homogeneous at the end of the school year than at the beginning, implying that mere exposure to others does not guarantee increased multiracial interactions.

Despite consistent data that children like and interact with same-race peers more than with different-race peers, it is important to note several additional findings. First, most researchers in this area agree that aggregation along racial lines is less pronounced than gender cleavage (Singleton & Asher, 1977; St. John & Lewis, 1975). Second, many black and white children report having friends of the other race. Hallinan and Teixeira (1987) reported that 18% of black 4th- to 7th-grade children's best-friend choices were white classmates; 13% of whites' nominations were black. DuBois and Hirsch (1990) reported that 31.3% of white and 23.9% of black 7th- to 9th-grade students reported a close other-race friend at school, and 80% of both races reported at least one friend from a different racial group. Among a more racially and ethnically diverse group of kindergartners and 3rd-graders, Howes and Wu (1990) found that 28–34% of European-American children's reciprocated friendships were with members of other ethnic groups; rates were higher for other ethnic groups (37–38% for Spanish-Americans, 36–40% for African-Americans, and 43–50% for Asian-Americans). Furthermore, although children direct the majority of their interaction toward same-race peers, they still interact with other-race peers (Finkelstein & Haskins, 1983; Singleton & Asher, 1977).

In addition, although children give higher liking ratings to same-race peers than to others, this preference does not appear to result in disproportionately greater representation of particular racial groups among rejected children, at least in racial or ethnically heterogeneous populations. Patterson, Kupersmidt, and Vaden (1990) and Wentzel (1991) found that race and social status were not related in samples of predominantly black and white children. Bichard, Alden, Walker, and McMahon (1988) reported similar findings in a mixed Caucasian/East Indian/Oriental Canadian sample, as did Howes and Wu (1990) with an ethnically mixed group of Asian-American, African-American, Euro-American, and Spanish-American kindergarten and 3rd-grade children. Coie et al. (1982) likewise found no relationship between race and re-jected status. They did, however, find blacks to be overrepresented among controversial children and underrepresented among popular children, which they point out may have been a function of blacks' minority status in their sample.

Several social or psychological factors could account for or contrib-ute to racial cleavage in childhood. Opportunity for interracial interac-tion is one explanation. Both Patchen (1982) and DuBois and Hirsch (1990) found that black and white adolescents' reports of neighborhood cross-race friendship were more likely if they also reported large num-bers of cross-race children living in their neighborhood.

Classroom findings related to opportunities for interaction have been more mixed. Hallinan and Smith (1985) examined whether oppor-tunities for classroom interaction correlated with cross-race peer friend-ship nomination measures with black and white 5th- through 7th-graders. As the proportion of one racial group in a classroom increased, the other racial group nominated more cross-race friends. Patchen (1982) reported similar findings for black and white high school students: As the reports of the number of classes in which an other-race student sat nearby increased, so did reports of cross-race friendly contact. In addition, Hallinan and Teixeira (1987) found that grouping children by perceived academic ability related to interracial sociability in students in the 4th through 7th grades. Specifically, groupings that were generally homogeneous with regard to race were related to the same-race friendship choices of the students in the sample.

On the other hand, Patchen found curvilinear relationships between the percentage of adolescents' classes that were black and indicators of racial cleavage and discord. For both races, interracial attitudes generally deteriorated and reports of interracial avoidance and unfriendly contact increased as the percentage of blacks in classes increased from none to 30–60%. This attrition did not occur among black students, however, if they reported friendly contact with whites prior to high school. As blacks became an increasing majority in students' classrooms, reports of interracial attitudes and behavior improved considerably—unless black students were surrounded by white classmates with Eurocentric views. Thus, the relationship between opportunities for interaction and increased classroom interaction is most consistent among white students. For black students, the relationship is more complex and appears to depend upon other contextual factors, such as their history with white peers and the nature of those peers' views.

Racial cleavage may occur for numerous additional reasons, including modeling, adult or peer encouragement to interact with same-race peers, or prejudice-based majority-group exclusion of minority members. Alternatively, children may select others as friends on the basis of similarity, which has long been known to contribute to friendship choice (Epstein, 1989). Similarity can be based on any or all of physical (e.g., having the same skin color, appearance, gender), interest (e.g., liking the same activities), and behavioral characteristics (e.g., having similar interactional styles).

Similarity is an important component of ingroup and outgroup processes, which may also play a role in promoting and maintaining racial cleavage (Brislin, 1981). The distinction between ingroup and outgroup behavior has been examined as a component of social identity formation (Brewer & Kramer, 1985; Tajfel, 1982). "Social identity" refers to that component of a person's self-concept that derives from membership in a particular social group, as well as the value and emotional significance of that membership (Tajfel, 1982). Accordingly, ingroup members attempt to differentiate themselves from outgroups and are motivated to maintain group distinctiveness, which serves to enhance a positive social identity for ingroup members (Tajfel, 1982). Further, people perceive ingroup members as similar to each other in order to maintain positive group identity. They view members of outgroups as homogeneous and attribute negative qualities to outgroup members to maintain ingroup self-esteem, thus giving rise to stereotypes and prejudice (Brewer, 1991). Children as young as 3 can distinguish their own group from another and show ingroup favoritism in their evaluations (Yee & Brown, 1992). Vaughan, Tajfel, and Williams (1981), in an analog study, found that 7- and 11-year-old children showed distinct ingroup preference: Children made choices that minimized ingroup rewards, but favored the ingroup over the outgroup.

Another basis for racial cleavage may lie in the nature of the interactions a child has with other-race/ethnicity peers. Children may avoid others if their interactions with those peers are particularly negative. Patchen (1982) indicated that 49–72% of both black and white students reported at least occasional cross-race arguments and name-calling. Although even higher percentages reported within-race arguments and name-calling, the relatively low rates of cross-race interaction may make these cross-race negative exchanges particularly salient. Furthermore, students' reports of avoiding other-race peers correlated .38–.43 with their reports of unfriendly contact with other-race classmates.

Finally, children's preferences for same-race peers may be tied to their social values—that is, they may prefer certain interaction styles among their peers as a function of their own background. Successful peer interaction in multiethnic groups probably depends at least in part upon performance of behaviors appropriate for that context and avoidance of inappropriate response styles. Differing implicit norms for what constitutes "appropriate" behavior could therefore increase the likelihood of misunderstanding and mutual rejection. Such differing behavioral norms would be reflected in different patterns of behavior associated with acceptance and rejection in different ethnic groups, the topic to which we turn next.

5.2. Correlates of Peer Acceptance and Rejection

Reviews of literature examining behavioral correlates of peer acceptance and rejection generally concur that rejected children display a behavioral profile characterized by aggression, disruption, rule violation, and withdrawal. Popular children, in contrast, display more sociable and prosocial styles. Neglected children are nonaggressive and interact relatively infrequently with peers (e.g., Coie, Dodge, & Kupersmidt, 1990; Newcomb, Bukowski, & Pattee, 1993).

Unfortunately, reviews to date have ignored ethnicity as a possible mediator of the relationship between peer status and behavior. A number of studies, however, have examined either primarily white or primarily black samples, and comparisons of their findings indicate some congruence in findings. Specifically, rejection is related to physical and verbal aggression and disruptive/inappropriate behavior among predominantly[1] white [e.g., Coie et al., 1982 (Study I); Pope, Bierman, & Mumma, 1991] and black (e.g., Coie & Dodge, 1988; Coie & Kupersmidt, 1983; Dodge, Coie, Pettit, & Price, 1990) samples of elementary schoolchildren. Furthermore, aggression is associated with hostile interpretations of ambiguous provocations in mixed black/white (Dodge, 1980) and Latino/African-American samples (Graham et al., 1992) and in black (Coie & Dodge, 1987) and white (Feldman & Dodge, 1987) samples. Similarly, findings that popular children display high rates of cooperation, leadership, and norm-setting characterize predominantly black (Coie & Kupersmidt, 1983; Dodge et al., 1990) and white samples [Coie et al., 1982 (Study I)].

This research supports the comparability of the behavioral and cognitive correlates of social status, as least at a very general level. Several factors nonetheless suggest caution in overgeneralizing from this work. First, although the literature on correlates of peer status is voluminous, a considerable number of authors fail to report the racial/ethnic composition of their samples. Those who do focus primarily on black and white samples, and few studies address other racial/ethnic groups, gender, or the interaction of race/ethnicity and gender.

Findings must be interpreted very carefully when they are based on racially or ethnically mixed samples in which one group forms the majority. Findings in the sample as a whole may or may not generalize to the ethnic groups of which it is composed (e.g., Kupersmidt & Coie, 1990). One common solution is to test for racial/ethnic differences before analyzing the data. Investigators who do so, however, must have a large enough sample to ensure sufficient power to detect both interaction and main effects involving race or ethnicity. If race/ethnicity is disregarded in analyses, different patterns among ethnic groups will contribute error variance to analyses of data from a mixed-ethnicity group, possibly obscuring or attenuating the findings. Investigators may also make potentially inappropriate generalizations across ethnic groups on the basis of results dominated by data from the majority group included in the study (Foster & Martinez, 1995). Furthermore, even if the sample size is suffi-

---

[1] In this overview, we consider a sample to be "predominantly" of one racial or ethnic group if that group comprised at least 60% of the sample. We use the term "mixed sample" if no more than 60% of the participants came from a single race or ethnic group.

cient to examine race or ethnicity as a variable in the investigation, it is often impossible to tease apart the frequently confounded relationship between race and minority status.

Other factors complicate the assessment of acceptance and rejection in multiethnic groups as well. Researchers studying sociometric status commonly categorize children on the basis of nominations from all participating peers. Because children award same-race classmates higher liking ratings and more friendship nominations, minority children who are popular are more likely to be cross-racially/ethnically acceptable than are popular children from the majority group.[2] Similarly, majority-group rejected children are likely to be disliked across racial/ethnic groups. Children who are liked within their own group but not accepted in another will fall into average or controversial classifications using the Coie et al. (1982) system. Identifying and studying these children may be particularly important for determining racially or ethnically unique behaviors that contribute to acceptance and rejection. Furthermore, findings of racial cleavage indicate that children interact largely with same-race peers and therefore have much greater acquaintance with those peers' interaction styles. Thus, in samples with more than one ethnic/racial group, it is important to disentangle within-race/ethnicity acceptance and behavior from cross-race/ethnicity acceptance and behavior.

A handful of studies have addressed whether correlates of acceptance and friendship differ as a function of ethnicity. Although these studies indicate some similarities, they also point to subtle differences. Coie et al. (1982) reported that peers viewed popular white but not black children as displaying high levels of leadership, whereas they viewed controversial black children as displaying particularly high levels of disruptiveness and starting fights, relative to controversial white children (who also showed greater levels of these behaviors than popular children). Because of the focus of the investigation, Coie et al. (1982) did not specifically compare peers' evaluations of black vs. white rejected children on these items. For both black and white children, peer nominations for cooperation were highest for popular children. Similarly, shyness was highest among neglected children and help-seeking was highest among rejected children, regardless of race. Unfortunately, Coie et al. (1982) considered only the race of the children who were nominated, and not that of the nominating peers.

---

[2] This cross-acceptability will not always obtain, however: Membership in particular status groups will depend upon the percentage of children in each racial/ethnic group in the classroom as well as upon the particular pattern of cross-ethnicity nominations or ratings or both within the nominating group. Among equal samples of two different ethnic groups who choose only children from their own group as liked and disliked, each social status group will be composed of equal numbers from each of the two ethnic groups.

The findings of St. John and Lewis (1975) underscore the importance of disentangling same- and cross-race patterns. Predictors of same- and cross-race friendship nominations among black and white 6th-graders differed. For white children, academic achievement and skill correlated with friendship nominations by both white and black peers. For black children, academic skill was associated with friendship nominations by whites, but only minimally with nominations by blacks. Similarly, white children's friendship nominations of both white and black peers correlated positively with the peers' socioeconomic status, but socioeconomic status was unrelated to the friendship choices black students made. Gerard and Miller (1975) reported similar findings that high-achievement minority children were more likely than low-achievement minority children to receive positive sociometric choices from the majority children.

Chen, Rubin, and Sun (1992) correlated 2nd-grade children's peer nominations of peers who fit behavioral descriptors with positive, negative, and friendship nominations in the People's Republic of China and in Canada. Peer nominations on items assessing aggression and disruption correlated highly ($rs > .70$) with negative liking nominations in both cultures. Sociability–leadership nominations correlated positively with positive liking and friendship nominations in both groups. Interestingly, shyness–sensitivity nominations correlated positively with positive and friendship nominations in China, but negatively in Canada, a finding that Chen et al. (1992) attribute to the positive value the Chinese culture places on self-restraint. It is an open question, however, whether these findings would hold among Chinese-American samples (particularly highly acculturated samples).

In addition to correlational studies, a few experimental studies have presented children of differing backgrounds with identical behavioral stimuli (written or videotaped vignettes) and asked the children how much they would like the target child depicted in each vignette. Foster, Kulberg, Sullivan, Bologlu, Maloney, and Chang (1994) asked Latina and Anglo 5th-grade girls to rate how much they liked other girls depicted in written behavioral scenarios (ethnicity not mentioned) and videotaped interactions of Anglo girls. Although both groups indicated that they disliked aggressive peers, results showed that Latina liking ratings were significantly less reactive to physical aggression, verbal aggression, and exclusion than Anglos. This difference held for the videotaped stimuli, but not for questionnaire responses.

Although it is possible that significantly higher liking ratings of these types of aggressive behaviors may relate, for example, to the Latina cultural valuing of exclusion behavior over direct expressions of aggression (Marín & Marín, 1991; Rotheram & Phinney, 1987; Rotheram-Borus & Phinney, 1990; Khorram, 1994), methodological confounds in the study suggest caution in interpreting the results. Confounds included both the absence of Latina girls from the videotaped vignette stimuli and the lack of corroboration of the results of the questionnaires (which were arguably less culturally biased because ethnicity was not mentioned in the written scenarios). It is interesting, however, that despite the aforementioned confounds, Latina and Anglo girls did not differ with regard to three positive categories of behavior—(1) giving, loaning, and sharing; (2) including others; and (3) saying "yes" to a request—a finding that supported the social validity of these behaviors in both Anglo and Latina girls' peer groups.

Steinberg and Hall (1981) found similar results in their study (described earlier) of black and white males who rated black or white videotaped children displaying either positive (compliment, invitation), negative (property violation), or neutral (parallel play) behavior. Regardless of age, socioeconomic status, and race, behavior accounted for 50% of the variance in likability. White males gave lower liking ratings than blacks to the negative target. This result was consistent with findings that black children generally rate peers as more likable and make more friendship choices than whites (Hallinan & Teixeira, 1987; Hallinan & Smith, 1985; Singleton & Asher, 1977). Both blacks and whites, however, judged negative black stimulus children more harshly than white stimulus children.

Even if behaviors associated with rejection and acceptance are similar for different ethnic groups, their developmental significance may differ. Numerous investigations indicate that both aggression and peer rejection predict later academic and adjustment difficulties (e.g., Ollendick, Weist, Borden, & Greene, 1992; for reviews, see Kupersmidt, Coie, & Dodge, 1990; Parker & Asher, 1987). Kupersmidt and Coie (1990) examined whether social status and aggression assessed in 112 5th-graders predicted school adjustment and court contacts 7 years later. Social status was unrelated to negative outcomes in the sample as a whole, but was a significant predictor when only the white subsample was analyzed. Unfortunately, Kupersmidt and Coie lacked sufficient black subjects to examine this group separately. In addition, although their study was limited to low- to middle-income children, they did not explicitly control for socioeconomic status, which is often confounded with ethnicity. Roff, Sells, and Golden (1972) found that in a largely white sample, the significant relationship between peer rejection and delinquency found for most socioeconomic levels did not hold for the lowest socioeconomic group.

The findings of Kupersmidt and Coie and Roff and colleagues highlight the importance of within-ethnicity examinations of predictors of childhood and adult adjustment, as well as the importance of controlling for socioeconomic status. When Coie, Lochman, Terry, and Hyman (1992) examined predictors of adjustment to middle school with an all-black sample from predominantly black schools, both aggression and peer rejection assessed in 3rd grade emerged as significant predictors of parent ratings of externalizing behavior on the Child Behavior Checklist, self-ratings of internalizing problems, and teacher ratings of adjustment in the 6th grade. Only peer acceptance predicted parent-rated internalizing problems, while only aggression predicted children's self-rated internalizing difficulties. The discrepancy between the results of Coie et al. (1992) and those of Kupersmidt and Coie (1990) may be due to assessment of different outcomes, the longer follow-up interval in Kupersmidt and Coie's sample, and the different ages of their groups. Coie et al. (1992) offer the more intriguing hypothesis that predictors may be less valid in mixed-race samples (as in the Kupersmidt and Coie sample) than in same-race groups. Alternatively, rejection and aggression may have different consequences for peer socialization in same- and mixed-race groups, particularly if different ethnic groups define different behaviors as "harmful" or "aggressive" and react differently to these behaviors.

Like studies of peer status, investigations of friendship and social support indicate that subtly different processes may underlie friendship processes in different ethnic groups. Among predominantly white samples, for example, girls report more intimate disclosure in friendships than boys, a gender difference observed from late elementary school through adolescence (e.g., Buhrmester & Furman, 1987). DuBois and Hirsch (1990) found similar differences for whites, but found no gender differences among blacks in junior high school students' reports of frequency of talking to friends about problems and relying on one's best friend for help. Similarly, Jones, Costin, and Ricard (1994) report that African-American 6th- and 9th-grade males and females did not differ in reports of intimate disclosure with best friends, although European-Americans did. A small sample of Mexican-American boys and girls did not differ in reports of intimacy, but a replication with a larger sample revealed patterns comparable to that of the European-American sample. Interestingly, African-American students reported higher levels of conflict with their best friends than did Mexican-American and European-American students. If these findings are not the result of socioeconomic status (which was not explicitly controlled in this study of largely lower- to middle-class children), they imply that African-American males may rely more than European-American males on reciprocal self-disclosure of problems in forming friendships, and conflict (as defined by the instrument used in this investigation) may have different significance in African-American teens' close friendships than in those of Mexican- and European-American adolescents.

In sum, the literature on racial and ethnic differences in correlates of peer status and friendship, although sparse, points to subtle differences in acceptable or desirable behavior that are associated with race/culture. Different cultural norms, in turn, may lead children to choose peers as desired playmates and friends when these peers behave according to the implicit behavioral norms promoted by the culture.

Further research on both single-race/ethnicity and multiethnic groups will be needed to determine the extent to which different norms exist and are tied to children's social values. Studying samples predominantly comprised of nonwhite children will be important both to study peer acceptance and friendship within different groups and to avoid the many aforediscussed methodological issues that are involved in studying acceptance in multirace/ethnicity settings.

Studies of children within peer groups composed largely of same-race/ethnicity peers may also illuminate stronger findings than studies of multiethnic peer groups. Children's social values—that is, the positive or negative valences they place on certain interpersonal qualities (Aboud, 1987)—probably emerge through their socialization histories with parents and other family members, teachers, and peers. The behaviors they value in others are likely to match those endorsed by their culture to the extent that children (1) come in contact in the larger society with values and norms that match those of the culture of their family and (2) interact largely with peers who come from similar racial/ethnic backgrounds. Ethnicity-specific social values and norms of minority cultures would therefore be expected to be moderated to some extent by the amount of contact children have with socializing agents of the dominant culture—the premise that underlies the concept of acculturation.

Despite its difficulties, study of the relationships among same- and cross-race/ethnicity behavior, acceptance, and overall indicators of behavioral, emotional, and academic adjustment will also be important to understanding peer relations in multicultural settings. As we have seen, different groups can view the same behavior differently, leading to different interpretations and judgments. Furthermore, children may behave differently in same-race vs. different-race interactions (Singleton & Asher, 1977). What skills are tied to effective performance in racially different groups? What is the developmental significance of these skills? And to what extent is multicultural social skill (i.e., the ability to alter one's behavior to fit the norms and rules of different groups and contexts) important for psychological adjustment? To what extent do ethnicity-specific findings hold for both boys and girls? Answers to all these questions will require more direct focus on issues related to race and ethnicity and will expand the knowledge base regarding the behavioral and cognitive processes that underlie effective social performance in different groups.

6. Conclusions, Implications, and Future Directions

This chapter raises a number of issues and implications for clinicians and researchers interested in promoting children's social competence. First, it challenges the notion that socially competent behavior can be defined independently of the context in which the child interacts—in this case, the racial and ethnic context. Instead, the literature suggests that different cultures may have different behavioral preferences and values and that these differences may relate to the behaviors that children value in their peers.

Knowing how different cultures are alike in what they value and how they differ will be crucial for social skills assessment. One goal of social skills assessment ordinarily involves judging effective and ineffective components of a child's social repertoire. Existing instruments and approaches such as teacher rating scales and observational systems can assist in this process. Because the bulk of these instruments have been created and validated with mostly white samples, assessors of children from nonwhite groups would be well-advised to appraise their assessment tools and judgments for Eurocentric biases in implicit assumptions about what constitutes "effective" behavior, to collect social validity data on the appropriateness of social skills targets from members of the child's ethnic group, to assess the child's social behavior within its cultural context, and to determine the implicit and explicit norms in that context. Accomplishing these ends may entail assessing the child's effectiveness in both same-ethnicity and mixed-ethnicity peer groups.

In addition, the research of Lethermon et al. (1984, 1986) on appraisal of social skills based on role-play assessment indicates that global judgments may vary dependent on the race of both the rater and the child being assessed. Even after training, white raters differentially evaluated black and white children's global social skill, whereas black raters did not. These findings imply that the race of raters must be carefully controlled when using assessment systems that require global evaluations of performance. In addition, a few studies have indicated that black raters sometimes afford higher ratings generally than white raters (e.g., Lethermon et al., 1986; Singleton & Asher, 1979) and that black children make more friendship choices than white children when they are allowed to nominate as many peers as they wish (Hallinan & Smith, 1985; Hallinan & Teixeira, 1987). These results may require standardizing ratings or nominations within race or rater if cross-race comparisons of subjects are likely to be confounded by these evaluator differences. Finally, exploring the reasons behind rater differences in global ratings may yield important information about the implicit bases or cues that persons from different backgrounds use in evaluating social behavior.

Social skills training programs could also benefit from explicit attention to whether the curriculum being trained matches the culture in which children will use the skills they acquire. Teaching a child a response that many in his or her culture find unacceptable or odd would not be expected to enhance peer acceptance. Furthermore, cultural agents in the natural environment are unlikely to reinforce the behavior, leading to problems with generalization, maintenance, and treatment credibility. Considering the "cultural fit" of the content of social skills training is particularly crucial in multicultural settings in which professionals provide a single, set curriculum to a diverse group of students. In these cases, it may be wise to discuss and train a variety of responses to deal with different social situations and to discuss the consequences and acceptability of the responses within different cultural milieus.

Contemporary writing points to a few behaviors that are particularly likely to manifest cultural differences. One is aggression. Ethnic groups may differ in how their members define aggression, what forms they tolerate vs. discourage, situations in which it occurs (e.g., conflict, rough play, competition), and their interpretations of others who engage in ambiguous and possibly aggressive behavior. Aggression is particularly important because (1) various forms of aggression are associated with peer rejection in both black and white samples, (2) black and white adolescents report perceived aggression as a frequent component of unfriendly other-race contact (Patchen, 1982), and (3) both black and white males read disproportionately more aggressive intentionality into the ambiguous behavior of black male children than into that of white male children (Sagar & Schofield, 1980). Efforts to study aggression in different ethnic groups should recognize, however, that the psychological literature has typically defined aggression from an implicitly Anglo male perspective and that behaviors commonly accepted as "aggressive" among this group may not be viewed in the same way by others.

Material reviewed in this chapter also suggests other behaviors that may be subject to varying cultural sanctions. Many writers maintain that Hispanic, African-American, Asian-American, and Anglo cultures promote differences in expressiveness and coping styles. These differences have clear implications for the acceptability of different forms of assertiveness in children, particularly with authority figures: Asian-American and Hispanic groups in particular might be expected to view assertion more negatively than Anglo and African-American groups. In addition, different cultural emphases on cooperation and competition imply that achievement-oriented behavior may be valued differently, particularly when the achievement benefits the individual child and not a group or family.

Understanding children's social values from a multicultural perspective could also assist educators and mental health professionals interested in promoting positive multicultural relationships. Investigators frequently promote the "opportunity" hypothesis—namely, that opportunities to interact will promote greater multicultural understanding and friendship. While some data support this hypothesis (e.g., Hallinan & Smith, 1985), other data (Patchen, 1982) and the analysis in this chapter suggest that the nature of that contact may be crucial. Specifically, we propose that contact will be beneficial to the extent that children (1) share the same social values regarding desirable and undesirable behavior in the particular situation, (2) interact in situations that elicit behaviors consonant with those common values, and (3) lack prejudices or biases that would lead to negative interpretations of the behavior of a child from the other ethnic group(s) involved in the interactions. In situations in which these conditions are not present, increased opportunities to interact may in fact promote *poorer* multicultural peer relations when children behave in ways they find acceptable but their peers do not. In situations in which social values conflict, adults may need to help children understand and accept their differences in the context of rules of conduct they agree upon, also correcting any attributional biases that may occur.

As researchers increasingly address ethnicity-related issues in peer relations, it will be important to consider several important methodological features. Specifically, in cross-ethnic comparisons, ethnic and racial terms must be clearly operationalized and assessed. In addition, investigators should clearly determine whether their variables are more likely to be related to racial chacteristics of the child (e.g., appearance) or to aspects of cultural socialization and identification (e.g., ethnicity) and assess participants accordingly. Measures must have adequate evidence of reliability and validity (particularly content and construct validity) within each of the groups under investigation. In addition to assessing ethnicity-related differences, investigators should examine the hypothesized cultural mechanisms that underlie the proposed differences (Betancourt & López, 1993). These mechanisms should consider explanations that relate to being a member of a majority or minority group (e.g., the experience of exclusion or discrimination based on skin color or national origin) as well as ethnicity-related socialization practices. In addition, it is crucial to control for factors commonly confounded with ethnicity, such as socioeconomic status. Furthermore, it will also be important to examine within-ethnicity acceptance and rejection separately from acceptance and rejection within the entire peer group.

Investigators are likely to encounter considerable variability within ethnicity groups as well as between them. Understanding this variation will require greater understanding of mechanisms that promote differences among members of the same cultural group. These mechanisms include acculturation, degree of involvement and affiliation with the dominant culture as well as with one's culture of origin, and diversity in socialization practices within the culture. Each of these mechanisms may operate differently depending upon the developmental level and gender of the child as well.

Examining ethnicity-related issues in children's peer relations poses a number of methodological and conceptual challenges to researchers and clinicians. Such examinations are crucial from a practical perspective as clinicians increasingly deal with children from diverse backgrounds and must find culturally compatible as well as effective interventions. They are also crucial from a conceptual perspective, as examinations of ethnicity force us to examine the often-unchallenged implicit assumptions underlying conceptualizations of competent functioning and to explore the generalizability of our knowledge base, assessment techniques, and intervention strategies. Such explorations can ultimately enrich our understanding of both social interaction processes in general and children's problems in social adaptation in particular.

ACKNOWLEDGMENT

The authors express their appreciation to Dr. Anita L. Greene for her insightful comments and suggestions on an earlier version of this chapter.

7. References

Aboud, F. E. (1987). The development of ethnic self-identification and attitudes. In J. S. Phinney & M. J. Rotheram (Eds.), *Children's ethnic socialization: Pluralism and development* (pp. 32–55). Newbury Park, CA: Sage Publications.

Baldwin, J. A. (1991). African (black) psychology: Issues and synthesis. In R. L. Jones (Ed.), *Black psychology*, 3rd ed. (pp. 125–135). New York: Harper & Row.

Bernal, M. E., Knight, G. P., Ocampo, K. A., Garza, C. A., & Cota, M. K. (1990). Development of ethnic identity in Mexican-American children. *Hispanic Journal of Behavioral Sciences, 12,* 3–24.

Bernal, M. E., Knight, G. P., Ocampo, K. A., Garza, C. A., & Cota, M. K. (1993). Development of Mexican American identity. In M. E. Bernal & G. P. Knight (Eds.), *Ethnic identity: Formation and transmission among Hispanic and other minorities* (pp. 31–46). Albany: State University of New York Press.

Betancourt, H., & López, S. R. (1993). The study of culture, ethnicity, and race in American psychology. *American Psychologist, 48,* 629–637.

Bichard, S. L., Alden, L., Walker, L. J., & McMahon, R. J. (1988). Friendship understanding in socially accepted, rejected, and neglected children. *Merrill-Palmer Quarterly, 34,* 33–46.

Brand, E. S., Ruiz, R. A., & Padilla, A. M. (1974). Ethnic identification and preference: A review. *Psychological Bulletin, 81,* 860–890.

Brewer, M. B. (1991). The social self: On being the same and different at the same time. *Personality and Social Psychology Bulletin, 17,* 475–482.

Brewer, M. B., & Kramer, R. M. (1985). The psychology of intergroup attitudes and behavior. *Annual Review of Psychology, 36,* 219–243.

Brislin, R. W. (1981). *Cross-cultural interactions: Face-to-face interaction.* New York: Pergamon Press.

Buhrmester, D., & Furman, W. (1987). The development of companionship and intimacy. *Child Development, 58,* 1101–1113.

Bukowski, W. M., & Hoza, B. (1989). Popularity and friendship: Issues in theory, measurement, and outcome. In T. J. Berndt & G. W. Ladd (Eds.), *Peer relationships in child development* (pp. 15–45). New York: John Wiley.

Chen, X., Rubin, K. H., & Sun, Y. (1992). Social reputation and peer relationships in Chinese and Canadian children: A cross-cultural study. *Child Development, 63,* 1336–1343.

Chiu, L.-H. (1987). Child-rearing attitudes of Chinese, Chinese-American, and Anglo-American mothers. *International Journal of Psychology, 22,* 409–419.

Coie, J. D., & Dodge, K. A. (1987). Social-information-processing factors in reactive and proactive aggression in children's peer groups. *Journal of Personality and Social Psychology, 53,* 1146–1158.

Coie, J. D., & Dodge, K. A. (1988). Multiple sources of data on social behavior and social status in the school: A cross-age comparison. *Child Development, 59,* 815–829.

Coie, J. D., Dodge, K. A., & Coppotelli, H. (1982). Dimensions and types of social status: A cross-age perspective. *Developmental Psychology, 18,* 557–570.

Coie, J. D., Dodge, K. A., & Kupersmidt, J. B. (1990). Peer group behavior and social status. In S. R. Asher & J. D. Coie (Eds.), *Peer rejection in childhood* (pp. 17–59). Cambridge: Cambridge University Press.

Coie, J. D., & Kupersmidt, J. B. (1983). A behavioral analysis of emerging social status in boys' groups. *Child Development, 54,* 1400–1416.

Coie, J. D., Lochman, J. E., Terry, R., & Hyman, C. (1992). Predicting early adolescent disorder from childhood aggression and peer rejection. *Journal of Consulting and Clinical Psychology, 60,* 783–792.

Cotler, S. B., & Guerra, J. J. (1976). *Assertion training.* Champaign, IL: Research Press.

Dana, R. H. (1993). *Multicultural assessment perspectives for professional psychology.* Needham Heights, MA: Allyn & Bacon.

Dodge, K. A. (1980). Social cognition and children's aggressive behavior. *Child Development, 51,* 162–170.

Dodge, K. A. (1989). Problems in social relationships. In E. J. Mash & R. A. Barkley (Eds.), *Treatment of childhood disorders* (pp. 222–244). New York: Guilford Press.

Dodge, K. A., Coie, J. D., Pettit, G. S., & Price, J. M. (1990). Peer status and aggression in boys' groups: Developmental and contextual analyses. *Child Development, 61,* 1289–1309.

DuBois, D. L., & Hirsch, B. J. (1990). School and neighborhood friendship patterns of blacks and whites in early adolescence. *Child Development, 90,* 524–536.

Epstein, J. L. (1989). Selection of friends: Changes across the grades and in different school environments. In T. J. Berndt & G. W. Ladd (Eds.), *Peer relationships in child development* (pp. 158–187). New York: John Wiley.

Feldman, E., & Dodge, K. A. (1987). Social information processing and sociometric status: Sex, age, and situational effects. *Journal of Abnormal Child Psychology, 15*, 211–227.

Finkelstein, N. W., & Haskins, R. (1983). Kindergarten children prefer same-color peers. *Child Development, 54*, 502–508.

Foster, S. L., Kulberg, A. M., Sullivan, N., Bologlu, L., Maloney, T., & Chang, M. K. (1994). *Latina and Anglo girls' evaluations of positive and negative peer behavior.* Paper presented at the meeting of the Association for Advancement of Behavior Therapy, San Diego, November 1994.

Foster, S. L., & Martinez, C. R., Jr. (1995). Ethnicity: Conceptual and methodological issues in child clinical research. *Journal of Clinical Child Psychology, 24*, 214–226.

Gerard, H., & Miller, N. (1975). *School desegregation.* New York: Plenum Press.

Graham, S., Hudley, C., & Williams, E. (1992). Attributional and emotional determinants of aggression among African-American and Latino young adolescents. *Developmental Psychology, 28*, 731–740.

Hallinan, M. T., & Smith, S. S. (1985). The effects of classroom racial composition on students' interracial friendliness. *Social Psychology Quarterly, 48*, 3–16.

Hallinan, M. T., & Teixeira, R. A. (1987). Opportunities and constraints: Black–white differences in the formation of interracial friendships. *Child Development, 58*, 1358–1371.

Harrison, A. O., Wilson, M. N., Pine, C. J., Chan, S. A., & Buriel, R. (1990). Family ecologies of ethnic minority children. *Child Development, 61*, 347–362.

Havighurst, R. J. (1976). The relative importance of social class and ethnicity in human development. *Human Development, 19*, 56–64.

Hayles, V. R., Jr. (1991). African American strengths: A survey of empirical findings. In R. L. Jones (Ed.), *Black psychology,* 3rd ed. (pp. 379–400). New York: Harper & Row.

Helms, J. E., & Carter, R. T. (1991). Relationships of white and black racial attitudes and demographic similarity to counselor preferences. *Journal of Counseling Psychology, 38*, 446–457.

Helsel, W. J., & Matson, J. L. (1984). The assessment of depression in children: The internal structure of the Child Depression Inventory (CDI). *Behaviour Research and Therapy, 22*, 289–298.

Ho, D. Y. F., & Kang, T. K. (1984). Intergenerational comparisons of child-rearing attitudes and practices in Hong Kong. *Developmental Psychology, 20*, 1004–1016.

Ho, M. K. (1987). *Family therapy with ethnic minorities.* Newbury Park, CA: Sage Publications.

Ho, M. K. (1992). *Minority children and adolescents in therapy.* Newbury Park, CA: Sage Publications.

Hofstede, G. (1980). *Culture's consequences.* Beverly Hills: Sage Publications.

Howes, C., & Wu, F. (1990). Peer interactions and friendships in an ethnically diverse school setting. *Child Development, 61*, 537–541.

Hudley, C. & Graham, S. (1993). An attributional intervention to reduce peer-directed aggression among African-American boys. *Child Development, 64*, 124–128.

Jones, D. C., Costin, S. E., & Ricard, R. J. (1994). *Ethnic and sex differences in best friendship characteristics among African-American, Mexican-American, and European-American adolescents.* Paper presented at the meeting of the Society for Research on Adolescence, San Diego, February 1994.

Kagan, S., & Madsen, M. C. (1972). Experimental analyses of cooperation and competition of Anglo-American and Mexican children. *Developmental Psychology, 6*, 49–59.

Kazdin, A. E. (1989). Hospitalization of antisocial children: Clinical course, follow-up status, and predictors of outcome. *Advances in Behaviour Research and Therapy, 11,* 1–67.

Khorram, A. (1994). *A comparative study of conflict resolution among Mexican-American and Anglo-American children.* Unpublished doctoral dissertation. California School of Professional Psychology—San Diego.

Kleinpenning, G., & Hagendoorn, L. (1991). Contextual aspects of ethnic stereotypes and interethnic evaluations. *European Journal of Social Psychology, 21,* 331–348.

Knight, G. P., & Kagan, S. (1977a). Acculturation of prosocial and competitive behaviors among second- and third-generation Mexican-American children. *Journal of Cross-Cultural Psychology, 8,* 273–284.

Knight, G. P., & Kagan, S. (1977b). Development of prosocial and competitive behaviors in Anglo-American and Mexican-American children. *Child Development, 48,* 1385–1394.

Kobayashi-Winata, H., & Power, T. G. (1989). Child rearing and compliance: Japanese and American families in Houston. *Journal of Cross-Cultural Psychology, 20,* 33–356.

Kochman, T. (1987). The ethnic component in black language and culture. In J. S. Phinney & M. J. Rotheram (Eds.), *Children's ethnic socialization: Pluralism and development* (pp. 219–238). Newbury Park, CA: Sage Publications.

Kupersmidt, J. B., & Coie, J. D. (1990). Preadolescent peer status, aggression and school adjustment as predictors of externalizing problems in adolescence. *Child Development, 61,* 1350–1367.

Kupersmidt, J. B., Coie, J. D., & Dodge, K. A. (1990). The role of poor peer relationships in the development of disorder. In S. R. Asher & J. D. Coie (Eds.), *Peer rejection in childhood* (pp. 274–305). Cambridge: Cambridge University Press.

LaFramboise, T., Coleman, H. L. K., & Gerton, J. (1993). Psychological impact of biculturalism: Evidence and theory. *Psychological Bulletin, 114,* 395–412.

Lawrence, V. W. (1991). Effect of socially ambiguous information on white and black children's behavioral and trait perceptions. *Merrill-Palmer Quarterly, 37,* 619–630.

Lethermon, V. R., Williamson, D. A., Moody, S. C., Granberry, S. W., Lemanek, K. L., & Bodiford, C. (1984). Factors affecting the social validity of a role-play test of children's social skills. *Journal of Behavioral Assessment, 6,* 231–245.

Lethermon, V. R., Williamson, D. A., Moody, S. C., & Wozniak, P. (1986). Racial bias in behavioral assessment of children's social skills. *Journal of Psychopathology and Behavioral Assessment, 8,* 329–337.

Lin, C., & Liu, W. T. (1993). Intergenerational relationships among Chinese immigrant families from Taiwan. In H. P. McAdoo (Ed.), *Family ethnicity* (pp. 271–286). Newbury Park, CA: Sage Publications.

Marín, G., & Marín, B. V. (1991). *Research with Hispanic populations.* Newbury Park, CA: Sage Publications.

McLoyd, V. C. (1990). Minority children: Introduction to the special issue. *Child Development, 61,* 263–266.

Newcomb, A. F., Bukowski, W. M., & Pattee, L. (1993). Children's peer relations: A meta-analytic review of popular, rejected, neglected, controversial, and average sociometric status. *Psychological Bulletin, 113,* 99–128.

Ocampo, K. A., Bernal, M. E., & Knight, G. P. (1993). Gender, race and ethnicity: The sequencing of social constancies. In M. E. Bernal & G. P. Knight (Eds.), *Ethnic identity: Formation and transmission among Hispanic and other minorities* (pp. 11–30). Albany: State University of New York Press.

Ollendick, T. H., Weist, M. D., Borden, M. C., & Greene, R. W. (1992). Sociometric status and academic, behavioral, and psychological adjustment: A five-year longitudinal study. *Journal of Consulting and Clinical Psychology, 60,* 80–87.

Parker, J. G., & Asher, S. R. (1987). Peer relations and later personal adjustment: Are low-accepted children at risk? *Psychological Bulletin, 102,* 357–389.

Patchen, M. (1982). *Black–white contact in schools: Its social and academic effects.* West Lafayette, IN: Purdue University Press.

Patterson, C. J., Kupersmidt, J. B., & Vaden, N. A. (1990). Income level, gender, ethnicity, and household composition as predictors of children's school-based competence. *Child Development, 61,* 485–494.

Phinney, J. S. (1990). Ethnic identity in adolescents and adults: Review of research. *Psychological Bulletin, 108,* 499–514.

Phinney, J. S. (1992). The multigroup ethnic identity measure. *Journal of Adolescent Research, 7,* 156–176.

Phinney, J. S., & Cobb, N. J. (1993). *Adolescents' reasoning about discrimination: Ethnic and attitudinal predictors.* Paper presented at the Biennial Meeting of the Society for Research in Child Development, New Orleans, March 1993.

Pope, A. W., Bierman, K. L., & Mumma, G. H. (1991). Aggression, hyperactivity, and inattention–immaturity: Behavior dimensions associated with peer rejection in elementary school boys. *Developmental Psychology, 27,* 663–671.

Putallaz, M., & Heflin, A. H. (1990). Parent–child interaction. In S. R. Asher & J. D. Coie (Eds.), *Peer rejection in childhood* (pp. 189–216). Cambridge: Cambridge University Press.

Ramsey, P. G. (1987). Young children's thinking about ethnic differences. In J. S. Phinney & M. J. Rotheram (Eds.), *Children's ethnic socialization: Pluralism and development* (pp. 56–72). Newbury Park, CA: Sage Publications.

Roff, M., Sells, S. B., & Golden, M. M. (1972). *Social adjustment and personality development in children.* Minneapolis: University of Minnesota Press.

Rong, X. L, & Grant, L. (1992). Ethnicity, generation, and school attainment of Asians, Hispanics, and non-Hispanic whites. *Sociology Quarterly, 33,* 625–636.

Rotheram, M. J., & Phinney, J. S. (1987). Ethnic behavior patterns as an aspect of identity. In J. S. Phinney & M. J. Rotheram (Eds.), *Children's ethnic socialization: Pluralism and development* (pp. 201–218). Newbury Park, CA: Sage Publications.

Rotheram-Borus, M. J. (1993). Biculturalism among adolescents. In M. E. Bernal & G. P. Knight (Eds.), *Ethnic identity: Formation and transmission among Hispanics and other minorities* (pp. 81–102). Albany: State University of New York Press.

Rotheram-Borus, M. J., & Phinney, J. S. (1990). Patterns of social expectations among black and Mexican-American children. *Child Development, 61,* 542–556.

Sagar, H. A., & Schofield, J. W. (1980). Racial and behavioral cues in black and white children's perceptions of ambiguously aggressive acts. *Journal of Personality and Social Psychology, 39,* 590–598.

Sagar, H. A., Schofield, J. W., & Snyder, H. N. (1983). Race and gender barriers: Preadolescent peer behavior in academic classrooms. *Child Development, 54,* 1032–1040.

Schneider, B. H. (1992). Didactic methods for enhancing children's peer relations: A review. *Clinical Psychology Review, 12,* 363–382.

Schofield, J. W. (1981). Complementary and conflicting identities: Images and interaction in an interracial school. In S. R. Asher & J. M. Gottman (Eds.), *The development of children's friendships* (pp. 53–90). New York: Cambridge University Press.

Schreibman, L., & Charlop, M. H. (1989). Infantile autism. In T. H. Ollendick & M. Hersen (Eds.), *Handbook of child psychopathology,* 2nd ed. (pp. 105–129). New York: Plenum Press.

Singleton, L. C., & Asher, S. R. (1977). Peer preferences and social interaction among third-grade children in an integrated school district. *Journal of Educational Psychology, 69,* 330–336.

Singleton, L. C., & Asher, S. R. (1979). Racial integration and children's peer preference: An investigation of developmental and cohort differences. *Child Development, 50,* 936–941.

Sollenberger, R. (1968). Chinese American child-rearing practices and juvenile delinquency. *Journal of Social Psychology, 74,* 13–23.

Spencer, M. B. (1983). Children's cultural values and parental child rearing strategies. *Developmental Review, 4,* 351–370.

Spencer, M. B., & Markstrom-Adams, C. (1990). Identity processes among racial and ethnic minority children in America. *Child Development, 61,* 290–310.

Steinberg, J., & Hall, V. (1981). Effects of social behavior on interracial acceptance. *Journal of Educational Psychology, 73,* 51–56.

St. John, N. H., & Lewis, R. G. (1975). Race and the social structure of the elementary classroom. *Sociology of Education, 48,* 346–368.

Stone, W. L., & LaGreca, A. M. (1990). The social status of children with learning disabilities: A reexamination. *Journal of Learning Disabilities, 23,* 32–37.

Sue, D. W. (1973). Ethnic identity: The impact of two cultures on the psychological development of Asians in America. In S. Sue & N. N. Wagner (Eds.), *Asian-Americans: Psychological perspectives* (pp. 140–149). Palo Alto, CA: Science & Behavior Books.

Tajfel, H. (1982). Social psychology of intergroup relations. *Annual Review of Psychology, 33,* 1–39.

Taylor, S. E., & Fiske, S. T. (1981). Getting inside the head: Methodologies for process analyses in attribution and social cognition. In J. H. Harvey, W. Ickes, & R. F. Kidd (Eds.), *New directions in attribution research,* 3rd ed. (pp. 459–524). Hillsdale, NJ: Erlbaum Associates.

Thornton, M. C., Chatters, L. M., Taylor, R. J., & Allen, W. R. (1990). Sociodemographic and environmental correlates of racial socialization by black parents. *Child Development, 61,* 401–409.

Ting-Toomey, S. (1986). Conflict communication styles in black and white subjective cultures. In Y. Kim (Ed.), *Interethnic communication: Current research* (pp. 75–87). Newbury Park, CA: Sage Publications.

Triandis, H. (1972). *The analysis of subjective culture.* New York: John Wiley.

Triandis, H., Lambert, W., Berry, J., Lonner, W., Heron, A., Brislin, R., & Draguns, J. (Eds.). (1980). *Handbook of cross-cultural psychology,* Vols. 1–6. Boston: Allyn & Bacon.

Vaughan, G. M., Tajfel, H., & Williams, J. (1981). Bias in reward allocation in an intergroup and an interpersonal context. *Social Psychology Quarterly, 44,* 37–42.

Weigel, R. M. (1985). Demographic factors affecting assertive and defensive behavior in preschool children: An ethnological study. *Aggressive Behavior,* 27–40.

Wentzel, K. R. (1991). Relations between social competence and academic achievement in early adolescence. *Child Development, 62,* 1066–1078.

Whalen, C. K. (1989). Attention deficit and hyperactivity disorders. In T. H. Ollendick & M. Hersen (Eds.), *Handbook of child psychopathology,* 2nd ed. (pp. 131–169). New York: Plenum Press.

Wright, J. C., Giammarino, M., & Parad, H. W. (1986). Social status in small groups: Individual–group similarity and the social "misfit." *Journal of Personality and Social Psychology, 50,* 523–536.

Yau, J., & Smetana, J. G. (1993). Chinese-American adolescents' reasoning about cultural conflicts. *Journal of Adolescent Research, 8,* 419–438.

Yee, M. D., & Brown, R. (1992). Self-evaluations and intergroup attitudes in children aged three to nine. *Child Development, 63,* 619–629.

Zadney, J., & Gerard, H. B. (1974). Attributed intentions and informational selectivity. *Journal of Experimental Social Psychology, 10,* 34–52.

Zarate, M. A., & Smith, E. R. (1990). Person categorization and stereotyping. *Social Cognition, 8,* 161–185.

Zebrowitz, L. A., Montepare, J. M., & Lee, H. K. (1993). They don't all look alike: Individuated impressions of other racial groups. *Journal of Personality and Social Psychology, 65,* 85–101.

Zukerman, M. (1990). Some dubious premises in research and theory on racial differences: Scientific, social, and ethical issues. *American Psychologist, 45,* 1297–1303.

5

Childhood Neuromotor Soft Signs, Behavior Problems, and Adult Psychopathology

CRAIG S. NEUMANN AND ELAINE F. WALKER

1. Introduction

Research on the childhood precursors of mental disorders is important for two reasons. First, knowledge of precursors will ultimately be required in order to identify persons who may benefit from preventive intervention. In the case of the major mental disorders, however, particularly schizophrenia, preventive intervention is currently viewed as a long-term goal. A second and more immediate goal concerns the origins of mental illness; information on the nature and timing of precursors can be critical for generating tenable hypotheses about etiology. It is the latter goal that has played a primary role in longitudinal research on childhood precursors of psychopathology.

As the empirical literature on the precursors of mental illness has accumulated, it has become apparent that there is both continuity and discontinuity in the development of psychopathology. Evidence for continuity includes the relation between childhood anxiety/dysphoria and adult depression (Hammen, Burge, & Stansbury, 1990; Zahn, Nurnberger, Berrettini, & Robinson, 1991) and between childhood thought abnormalities and later schizophrenia (Neumann, Grimes, Walker, & Baum, 1994; Walker, 1991).

Even more extensive, however, is the evidence for discontinuity. Dysfunction in a broad range of childhood behavioral domains has been found to precede the onset of most major mental illnesses in adulthood.

CRAIG S. NEUMANN AND ELAINE F. WALKER • Department of Psychology, Emory University, Atlanta, Georgia 30322.

Advances in Clinical Child Psychology, Volume 18, edited by Thomas H. Ollendick and Ronald J. Prinz. Plenum Press, New York, 1996.

For example, deficits in cognitive and socioemotional functions occur at a higher rate in children who later develop affective disorders (Cicchetti & Aber, 1986; Orvaschel, Walsh-Allis, & Ye, 1988) and schizophrenia (Walker, 1991). More recently, there is increasing evidence that soft signs of neuromotor dysfunction precede the onset of a variety of mental disorders (Brumback, 1993; Fish, Marcus, Hans, Auerbach, & Perdue, 1992; Hans & Marcus, 1991; Walker, Savoie, & Davis, 1994).

The presence of neuromotor deficits in children who subsequently develop major mental disorders is consistent with the assumption that a biological vulnerability is involved in these illnesses. Moreover,, these deficits may have potential for shedding light on the nature of the underlying vulnerability. As Meehl (1989) has pointed out, neuromotor signs would be expected to be more direct manifestations of biological vulnerability than are cognitive and socioemotional factors. In this chapter, we address three general issues: (1) the nature and temporal course of soft signs of neuromotor dysfunction in children, (2) the relation between neuromotor dysfunction and adjustment problems in children, and (3) the implications of these findings for theories of the neurodevelopment of behavioral problems and mental disorder.

We begin by examining past research findings on neuromotor soft signs in children. The findings suggest that these signs are present in nonclinical samples of children and that developmental factors influence their expression. It also appears that these signs are linked with subsequent cognitive and behavioral problems. We then present some findings from our archival research program on the precursors of mental illness (Walker & Lewine, 1990). Specifically, we address the relation of childhood neuromotor functions with specific childhood behavioral problems, as well as adult psychiatric outcome. On the basis of these findings, and past research, we offer some hypotheses about the neural processes that mediate the links between neuromotor functions and psychiatric symptoms.

2. Soft Signs of Neuromotor Dysfunction in Children

It is well established that some children manifest "soft signs" of neurological impairment (e.g., perceptual–motor dysfunction, abnormal movements, motor coordination problems). While such soft signs often suggest problems in neurological functioning, by definition they cannot be linked to "hard" (i.e., localized) signs of neurological abnormality; thus, they usually do not constitute a diagnosable neurological condition (e.g., cerebral palsy). Nonetheless, it appears that neurological soft signs may have considerable prognostic value for later behavioral, cognitive, and academic functioning; this being the case, they suggest problems in brain functioning.

Soft signs are predominantly indexed by the observation of motor functions and include abnormalities in movement and deficits in motor skills. Thus, the terms "neurological soft signs" and "neuromotor soft signs" are often used interchangeably. A surge of research in this area originated in the 1960s. In 1962, Prechtl and Stemmer (1962) coined the term "choreiform syndrome" to describe the chorea-like twitchings of the extremities and head of hyperactive children who had been referred for school problems. The authors claimed that the syndrome was a form of minimal brain damage, and this viewpoint generated an active area of research (Ingram, 1963). While the validity of a *syndrome* of minimal brain damage has been questioned, neuromotor dysfunction and its relationship to behavior and cognition remain important areas of study (Rutter, 1990).

Recent estimates of the proportion of children who show soft signs range from approximately 7% to 28% (e.g., Hynd & Hooper, 1992; Rubin & Barlow, 1980; Soorani-Lunsing, Hadders-Algra, Huisjes, & Touwen, 1993a). In a large-scale prospective project, Rubin and Barlow (1980) conducted three neurological examinations of 1132 infants in their first year of life and found that about 16% showed suspect neurological exams. Taylor and colleagues (Szatmari & Taylor, 1984; Taylor, Powell, Cherland, & Vaughan, 1988) report that about 8% of 7- to 10-year-old boys and girls manifest significant motor overflow movements (i.e., superfluous, unintended movements) on a modified version of the Fog Test (Fog & Fog, 1963). Shaffer, O'Connor, Shaffer, and Prupis (1983) (see also Shaffer et al., 1985) identified a group compromising about 28% of 7-year-old children who displayed abnormalities of motor coordination (e.g., irregular performance of finger-to-finger opposition and rapid alternating movements). The Gillbergs and their colleagues (e.g., C. Gillberg, 1983; I. C. Gillberg, 1985; I. C. Gillberg & C. Gillberg, 1989; I. C. Gillberg, Gillberg, & Groth, 1989; C. Gillberg & Rasmussen, 1982a,b; C. R. Gillberg, Carlstrom, Svenson, & Waldenstrom, 1982) have been involved in a population screening study and ongoing longitudinal research project with children. In their initial sample of 6- to 7-year-old children, they found that 7.1% showed neurological soft signs.

There is also evidence of "syndromes" of neuromotor dysfunction in children. Investigators working in the Groningen Perinatal Project (e.g., Hadders-Algra, Huisjes, & Touwen, 1989; Soorani-Lunsing et al., 1993a; Soorani-Lunsing, Hadders-Algra, Olinga, Huisjes, & Touwen, 1993b) selected a group of 160 neurologically abnormal neonates and followed them up at the age of 9 years. They then selected children at 9 years who displayed "minor neurological dysfunction" (MND) for follow-up at ages 12 and 14. Comparing these older children to a matched control group, the investigators were able to identify and differentiate MND into the following categories: fine manipulative disability, choreiform dyskinesia, hypotonia, and coordination problems.

The research cited above represents only a few of the more recent and well-controlled studies in this area. The neurological assessments are often conducted by neurologists or pediatricians, and measurement reliability is good. Taken together, the findings of these and other studies indicate that soft signs of neuromotor functioning can be reliably rated and are apparent in a subgroup of randomly selected children. Further, because central nervous system (CNS) damage can produce neuromotor symptoms, researchers generally assume that soft signs are an indication of abnormal or immature brain functioning.

2.1. Determinants of Soft Signs

Not surprisingly, researchers have found that childhood neurological soft signs are associated with prenatal complications (Goodman, 1990), prematurity (e.g., Gorga, Stern, Ross, & Nagler, 1991), very low birthweight (e.g., Khadilkar, Tudehope, Burns, O'Callaghan, & Mohay, 1993; Marlow, Roberts, & Cooke, 1993), and perinatal complications (e.g., Soorani-Lunsing et al., 1993a), as well as with some postnatal variables [e.g., malnutrition (Agarwal, Das, Agarwal, Upadhyay, & Mishra, 1989), socioeconomic status (SES) (Hadders-Algra et al., 1989; Soorani-Lunsing et al., 1993a)]. Given that multiple births are associated with more prenatal complications, it is not surprising that twins display more neurological abnormalities than nontwins (Kragt, Huisjes, & Touwen, 1985; Torrey, Bowler, Taylor, & Gottesman, 1994). The literature on the heritability of neurological soft signs is rather limited. Nonetheless, there is some research that suggests that there is a genetic contribution to the acquisition and performance of a gross motor skill (Bulayeva, 1981; Williams & Gross, 1980).

It is of interest to note that the same etiological factors have been implicated in psychopathology. The genetic contribution to mental illness is well documented (Gottesman, 1991), and there is a rapidly accumulating body of literature indicating that obstetrical complications, such as prolonged labor, fetal distress, or use of forceps, are associated with major mental disorder in adulthood, including schizophrenia and major affective disorder (McNeil, 1987). Obstetrical complications have also been found to be associated with childhood schizoid and schizotypal traits (Foerster, Lewis, Owen, & Murray, 1991).

2.2. Developmental Changes in Soft Signs

There is substantial evidence for discontinuity in neurological soft signs; they typically "fade" with development. Soorani-Lunsing et al. (1993a) found that among a group of children who showed MND at 9 years, 55% were normal at 14 years. For the remaining 45% of this group, MND signs were still present, but in a less severe form. Because the children who had clearly entered puberty (evidencing three or more signs) tended to have fewer MND signs, as opposed to children who were simply older, the authors suggested that puberty played a role in the decrease in MND.

Other findings indicate, however, that the developmental decrease in soft signs is apparent long before the onset of puberty. Several researchers have noted a significant reduction in soft signs after 2 years of age, and this reduction has been attributed to the fact that the first 2 years are critical for consolidation of motor skills (Fish et al., 1992; Walker et al., 1994). I. C. Gillberg et al. (1989) reported that perceptual–motor problems subsided in 45% of cases from 7 to 10 years and that there was disappearance of such problems in 70% of cases between 10 and 13 years. Similarly, Wolf, Gunnoe, and Cohen (1983) found that motor overflow decreased significantly with age (i.e., from 5 to 10 years). Thus, the rate and severity of neuromotor soft signs decline across childhood.

It is important to note, however, that subtle indicators of motor dysfunction are apparent after more overt soft signs have faded. I. C. Gillberg et al. (1989) found that a complex-reaction time measure administered at age 13 was able to discriminate between the groups with and without early neurological soft signs, even though the more overt soft signs had faded with development. Rubin and Barlow (1980) found that neurological soft signs in infancy were linked with motor skills deficits at 12 years. In sum, it appears that the maturation of the CNS, and the concomitant consolidation of fine and gross motor skills, results in a diminution of observable neuromotor soft signs in children. Nevertheless, more subtle motor performance deficits may persist.

3. The Relation between Childhood Neuromotor Functions and Behavior Problems

The literature on childhood neurological soft signs has also shown that they are associated with concurrent and later problems in academic functioning, cognition, and behavior. In the domains of academic functioning and cognition, Marlow et al. (1993) reported that in very-low-birthweight infants, the presence of motor problems at 6 years was the best predictor of school problems at 8 years. In the prospective study by Rubin and Barlow (1980), the authors found that infants who were identified as neurologically suspect or abnormal on more than one examination during the first year of life performed significantly below the comparison group on measures of intelligence, language development, and school achievement at 12 years. Interestingly, problems in these areas of functioning were also noted for 12-year-old children who had been neurologically suspect or abnormal on just one infant examination. These findings are strengthened by the fact that the relationships held when birthweight and SES were controlled.

In addition to academic performance deficits, neuromotor soft signs are also linked with behavior problems at school. Taylor and colleagues (Szatmari & Taylor, 1984; Taylor et al., 1988) have found that children aged 7–10 who display high levels of motor overflow movements also manifest behavior problems at school and are judged poor scholastically. Noteworthy is that among those with motor overflow, the percentage of girls with school behavior problems (12%) was comparatively less than that of boys (28%). Moreover, the authors note that compared to their respective control groups, boys who show overflow seem to display more problems, both cognitive and motoric, than do girls who demonstrate overflow.

In their longitudinal project, the Gillbergs and their colleagues (e.g., C. Gillberg, 1983; I. C. Gillberg, 1985; I. C. Gillberg & C. Gillberg, 1989; I. C. Gillberg et al., 1989; C. Gillberg & Rasmussen, 1982a,b; C. R. Gillberg et al., 1982) have documented that early (age 7) deficits in attention, motor functioning, and perception (referred to as "DAMP" by the authors) are associated with later (age 10–13) problems in behavior and school achievement. For example, at 10 years, 80% of the DAMP children had behavior problems, compared to 20% of those without DAMP. The corresponding figures for school achievement problems were 76% and 16%, respectively. At 13 years, 60% of the DAMP group still had behavior problems (25% for controls), and 65% still had school achievement problems (8% for controls).

Finally, Soorani-Lunsing et al. (1993b) found certain profiles of cognitive and behavioral problems in children at 12 years who had displayed MND at 9 years. For instance, fine manipulative disability was related to both problems of cognition and behavior problems, whereas coordination deficits were related to cognitive problems, and hypotonia and choreiform dyskinesia were related to behavioral problems. These findings are interesting because they suggest that certain types of neurological soft signs may be related in some specific way to later problems in behavior or cognition or both.

In sum, children who show neurological soft signs at a young age may display fewer or no soft signs as they mature. However, they are more likely to show behavioral and cognitive problems later in their development. Moreover, subtle signs of motor impairment may persist in the older child, and certain types of soft signs may be related to specific patterns of cognitive and behavioral problems. Finally, the child's sex may play a role in the expression of soft signs and other problems.

3.1. Childhood Neuromotor Soft Signs and Clinical Psychopathology

Given the findings that childhood neurological soft signs are associated with cognitive and behavioral problems, it is not surprising that they are also related to concurrent and adult psychopathology. Cross-sectional studies have shown that children with overt brain damage have a heightened incidence of psychiatric illness. For instance, compared with healthy children, those with congenital brain dysfunction (e.g., Breslau, 1990; Rutter, 1990) and those with acquired brain damage (e.g., Chadwick, Rutter, Brown, Shaffer, & Traub, 1981) manifest higher rates of psychiatric disorder. Conversely, children with psychiatric conditions have been shown to manifest an elevated rate of neurological soft signs. Brumback and Weinberg (1990) have reported that clinically depressed adolescents often manifest left-sided motor dysfunction (e.g., tremor, hyperflexia, and hypotonia), whereas manic adolescents show similar findings on the right side. Adolescents with obsessive–compulsive disorder have been found to demonstrate left hemibody neurological abnormalities (Behar et al., 1984). Further, children with psychiatric conditions have also been found to display neuropsychological performance deficits (Tramontana & Sherrets, 1985).

Only a few longitudinal studies of early neuromotor functions have resulted in reliable data on adult outcome. Among these studies, however, the findings are consistent in showing an association with adult psychiatric outcome as well. In our research on the precursors of mental illness, we examined childhood home movies and found an elevated rate of motor skills deficits and neuromotor abnormalities in young children (birth to 2 years) who later develop adult-onset schizophrenia (Walker et al., 1994). Fish et al. (1992) have reported similar findings. Neurological soft signs (e.g., mirror movements, dysdiadochokinesis, poor coordination) have also been observed in children (aged 7) who subsequently manifest anxiety and affective symptoms as adolescents and adults (Hollander, DeCaria, Aronowitz, Klein, Liebowitz, & Shaffer, 1991).

As previously mentioned, more subtle signs of neuromotor dysfunction often persist in children who showed early soft signs. Thus, it is not surprising that adult psychiatric patients manifest neuromotor dysfunction. Investigators have found that adult patients with schizophrenia (Woods, Kinney, & Yurgelun-Todd, 1986), affective disorders (Hollander et al., 1991), and obsessive–compulsive disorder (Hollander et al., 1990) show more neurological soft signs than healthy comparison subjects. Finally, monozygotic twins who are discordant for adult-onset schizophrenia have been shown to both display neurological soft signs at a higher rate compared to healthy controls, though the twin with schizophrenia displays more neurological abnormalities than the non-schizophrenic twin (Torrey et al., 1994). Thus, it appears that factors that can affect CNS functioning are not only related to neurological abnormalities, but also linked with adult psychiatric outcomes.

4. The Emory Study of Precursors of Adult Psychopathology

Despite the extensive evidence that neuromotor dysfunction is associated with concurrent psychopathology in both adults and children, data on the relation of very early childhood neuromotor function with later behavior problems or adult psychiatric status have been limited. This sparseness is largely due to the complexity of conducting longitudinal research that spans broad periods in the life course.

In our laboratory at Emory University, we have been studying the childhood precursors of schizophrenia and major affective disorders. Using an archival–observational approach (see Walker & Lewine, 1990) that involves the use of childhood home movies, in conjunction with parental reports, we have been able to study the neuromotor, affective, and behavioral aspects of childhood development in subjects with known adult psychiatric outcomes.

As previously mentioned, we have found that preschizophrenic children display an elevated rate of motor skills deficits and neuromotor abnormalities in childhood films during the birth to 2-year age period (Walker et al., 1994). Interestingly, the preschizophrenic children did not show more neuromotor abnormalities than their siblings, or than patients with affective disorders, after the first 2 years of life. Moreover, neuromotor abnormalities declined with development for all groups; this trend generally fits with the data, presented above, which suggest a diminution of neuromotor soft signs with age.

Our studies of the childhood films also revealed that preschizophrenic children display less positive and more negative affective expressions than their healthy siblings (Walker, Grimes, Davis, & Smith, 1993). Walker and coworkers found that there were significantly lower proportions of positive expressions among the total expressions of the preschizophrenic female subjects, compared to their same-sex healthy siblings. This difference extended from infancy through adolescence. However, both the preschizophrenic male and female subjects showed greater negative expressions than the same-sex comparison group across all age periods. And retrospective parental reports on these subjects indicate that preschizophrenic children show a differential pattern of behavioral problems throughout development, compared to their siblings (Neumann et al., 1994). The Neumann et al. (1994) study revealed that the preschizophrenic subjects had a variety of childhood behavior problems, including both internalized and externalized problems, when compared to their healthy siblings. Also, the types of problems differed in their developmental course, although the modal trend was toward increasing problems with age.

In this chapter, we present data on the relationship of childhood neuromotor abnormalities with specific dimensions of childhood adjustment and emotional expressions. We use our data base to address two questions. First, what is the relation between childhood neuromotor function and various dimensions of behavior? In particular, are neuromotor deficits associated with specific behavior problems, or is the relation generalized across behavioral dimensions? Second, is there evidence of a temporal sequence, such that signs of neuromotor dysfunction precede the onset of behavioral problems, or is the association concurrent, as well as longitudinal? The former pattern, a temporal sequence, would be consistent with the notion that maturational factors are moderating the expression of the underlying CNS impairment (Walker, 1994).

4.1. Subjects

The patient sample from whom the present data were obtained is comprised of 49 patients who received a diagnosis of schizophrenia ($N = 30$) or major affective disorder ($N = 19$) in adolescence/early adulthood. Diagnoses were confirmed through a structured interview (Schedule for Affective Disorders and Schizophrenia) (Endicott & Spitzer, 1978). The majority of the affective patients ($N = 16$) were diagnosed with bipolar disorder, and the remainder suffered from major depressive illness. None of the subjects in this study was ever evaluated or treated for a neurological disorder. All are currently over 25 years of age.

Data were also collected on samples of healthy siblings of the patients. The nearest-in-age, same-sex healthy sibling of each patient was selected as a comparison subject. In the event that a same-sex sibling was unavailable, the nearest-in-age opposite-sex sibling served as a control. The sibling control groups were comprised of 30 subjects and 18 siblings, respectively, from the schizophrenia and affective patients' families. All siblings have no history of referral or treatment for a neurological or psychiatric disorder.

Finally, data were collected on a comparison sample of 21 subjects from families with no mental illness in first-degree relatives. Further information on the subjects of this study is provided in Walker et al. (1994).

4.2. Procedures and Measures

Retrospective data on the childhood behavior of 29 of the pre-schizophrenic children (6 females and 23 males) and 28 of their healthy siblings (15 males and 13 females) were provided by parents. Unfortunately, it was not possible to obtain ratings of childhood behavior for a sufficient number of the affective patients and siblings to permit analysis. However, data on neuromotor and affective functions were obtained for all subjects through observational coding of childhood home movies. These data are described in detail in earlier reports as part of this ongoing project (Walker et al., 1993, 1994).

4.2.1. Parental Ratings of Childhood Behavior

The behavioral rating scale used in this study consists of 104 items from the Child Behavior Checklist (CBCL) (Achenbach, 1991). The items yield scores for the following behavior-problem dimensions: Withdrawn, Anxious/Depressed, Social Problems, Thought Problems, Attention Problems, Delinquent Behavior, and Aggressive Behavior. For use in our study, CBCL questions were modified for retrospective application. Parents of the schizophrenia patients rated all their offspring. Parents responded to each item, within four age periods (birth–4 years, 4–8 years, 8–12 years, and 12–16 years).

4.2.2. Observational Coding of Childhood Affect and Neuromotor Functions

The procedures for obtaining the home movies used for rating facial emotion and neuromotor functions are described in detail in Walker et al. (1993). In brief, participating family members provided all available home movies of the patient and sibling control made from birth through 15 years of age. Films were then transferred in chronological order onto standard VHS videotapes, and a digital display of elapsed time was inscribed on the tapes in tenths of a second. At each age level, there were instances of missing data (i.e., no film) for some subjects, so that the number of subjects varies by age. The average duration of total footage on subjects was 80 minutes (SD = 73.37). A preliminary study found no evidence of diagnostic group differences in the amount of footage of schizophrenic patients and their siblings or in the nature of the interpersonal contexts and events in which they appeared (Litter & Walker, 1993).

Coding of facial expressions was conducted using the AFFEX facial coding scheme (Izard, Dougherty, & Hembree, 1983). Proportional scores were derived for positive ("joy") and negative emotion at the same four age periods, as for parental CBCL scoring: birth–4 years, 4–8 years, 8–12 years, and 12–16 years. To derive the emotion score, the total duration of the positive or negative emotion expressed during the age period was divided by the total duration of coded facial expressions for that period (for further details on the emotion coding, see Walker et al., 1993).

The Neuromotor Rating Scale used in this study was designed to assess the presence of neuromotor abnormalities and to document the quality of the subject's motor development (see the Appendix). It comprises two subscales: Neuromotor Abnormalities (NA) and Motor Skills (MS). The NA scale focuses on "soft signs" of neurological dysfunction, including abnormalities of movement. The MS scale rates the general quality of movement and proficiency of motor skills. The inclusion of items for both scales was constrained by the necessity that they all be ratable through observation of the subjects' spontaneous activity.

Each item in the NA subscale is rated as present or absent. The age of occurrence of each abnormality, as well as the side (right, left, or both) of occurrence of limb abnormalities, are recorded. The MS subscale items are rated on a numerical scale ranging from below average (1) to above average (5).

The neuromotor coding was done by two raters. Both had formal training in normal and abnormal motor development and clinical experience in the assessment of motor functions in children. The raters were blind to the diagnostic outcome of the subjects. The raters viewed all the videotape on each of the subjects they rated. They were provided with a chronological index for each videotape. The index listed the subject's age (in months for the first 2 years, then by year up to age 15) and was keyed to the elapsed time inscribed on the videotape. [For more detailed information on the NA and MS scales, see Walker et al. (1994).]

It should be noted that the majority of the neuromotor abnormalities and the motor skills deficits that were observed in our previous study occurred in the first 2 years of life (Walker et al., 1994). Thus, although the NA and MS scales were applied across the entire childhood period, they primarily indexed abnormalities and skills deficits in early childhood. Further, the NA and MS scores are only modestly interrelated (-0.38, $p < 0.01$, one-tailed), indicating that the two scales are measuring partially independent factors. Thus, neuromotor abnormalities can occur in the absence of motor skills deficits and vice versa.

4.3. Findings

4.3.1. Neuromotor Functions and Childhood Behavior

First, the preschizophrenic subjects and their healthy siblings were combined, and correlations were derived between the NA and MS scores and the CBCL behavioral dimensions correlations (Table 1). (It should be noted that higher NA scores indicate more neuromotor abnormalities, whereas higher MS scores indicate better motor skills.)

The results listed in Table 1 indicate that the relations of the NA and

TABLE 1
Correlations of Neuromotor Abnormality and Motor Skills Scores
with Child Behavior Checklist Behavior Dimensions: All Subjects

Correlation variables	Age periods			
	Birth–4 yr	4–8 yr	8–12 yr	12–16 yr
Withdrawn				
NA	0.026	−0.008	0.281[a]	0.296[a]
MS	0.025	0.059	−0.159	−0.154
Social Problems				
NA	0.264[a]	0.407[b]	0.424[b]	0.404[b]
MS	−0.130	−0.351[b]	−0.398[b]	−0.231[a]
Anxious/Depressed				
NA	0.185	0.190	0.443[b]	0.416[b]
MS	−0.115	0.020	−0.090	−0.029
Attention Problems				
NA	0.414[b]	0.296[a]	0.292[a]	0.282[a]
MS	−0.407[b]	−0.273[a]	−0.228[a]	−0.058
Thought Problems				
NA	−0.121	−0.072	0.173	0.270[a]
MS	−0.068	−0.144	−0.186	−0.024
Delinquency				
NA	−0.1220	−0.2027	−0.1741	−0.0377
MS	−0.0200	0.0104	0.1671	0.0681
Aggression				
NA	−0.2011	0.0283	0.0419	0.0990
MS	−0.2007	−0.2068	−0.0082	0.0844

[a,b]One-tailed tests: [a]$p < 0.05$; [b]$p < 0.01$.

MS scores with the CBCL behavioral dimensions are not generalized. Instead, the significant correlations are restricted to those behaviors that are typically classified as "internalized" behavior problems. Across the age periods, the "externalized" problems, Delinquency and Aggression, are not significantly associated with the NA or MS scores.

Also of interest in Table 1 is the difference between the NA and MS scores in the extent of their association with the behavior ratings. The NA score is significantly related with five of the seven behavior factors, whereas the MS score is correlated with only two of the seven factors. This observation suggests that neuromotor abnormalities are more predictive of behavioral problems than are motor skills deficits.

Further, the general pattern for the Withdrawn, Social Problems, Anxious/Depressed, and Thought Problems dimensions is an increased association with NA over time. Thus, the greater the NA score, the more behavior problems in these dimensions at later age periods. In contrast, Attention Problems are more highly correlated with NA at the birth to 4-year age period, and there is somewhat of a decreased association with NA over time. The same time pattern emerges between Attention Problems and the MS score. In this case, a decrease in MS is most strongly associated with Attention Problems at the birth to 4-year age period. (Note also that lower MS scores are somewhat associated with increased Social Problems over time, at least from 4 to 12 years.)

When the total sample is split into the preschizophrenic subjects and their healthy siblings, the differences in correlations of NA and MS with the behavior dimensions are quite dramatic (see Tables 2 and 3).

Of course, statistical power is substantially reduced by halving the total sample, but for the preschizophrenic subjects, the same general temporal pattern found in Table 1 appears to hold. Clearly, for the Social Problems and Anxious/Depressed dimensions, there is an increased association with NA over time. Lower MS scores are still associated with increases in Social Problems from 4 to 12 years. Similarly, NA and MS are more strongly associated with Attention Problems at the birth to 4-year age period than at later age periods. Though there is a trend for NA to show an increase in association with the Withdrawn and Thought Problems dimensions at later age periods, these correlations failed to reach statistical significance.

In contrast to the findings for the combined sample, there are significant relations with externalized behavior problems for the preschizophrenic sample. Noteworthy are the correlations between NA and MS and Delinquency and Aggression. Higher MS scores are associated with *more* delinquent (at 8 to 12 years) and aggressive (at 12 to 16 years) behavior. Finally, an increase in NA is linked with *less* delinquent behavior at the 4- to 8-year age period. For the preschizophrenic subjects,

TABLE 2

Correlations of Neuromotor Abnormality and Motor Skills Scores with Child Behavior
Checklist Behavior Dimensions: Preschizophrenic Group

Correlation variables	Age periods			
	Birth–4 yr	4–8 yr	8–12 yr	12–16 yr
Withdrawn				
NA	−0.022	−0.110	0.265	0.298
MS	0.091	0.157	−0.087	−0.063
Social Problems				
NA	0.236	0.357[a]	0.397[a]	0.407[a]
MS	−0.080	−0.374[a]	−0.436[a]	−0.206
Anxious/Depressed				
NA	0.127	0.043	0.422[a]	0.389[a]
MS	−0.194	0.123	−0.042	0.070
Attention Problems				
NA	0.483[b]	0.266	0.264	0.264
MS	−0.454[b]	−0.192	−0.119	0.096
Thought Problems				
NA	−0.213	−0.242	0.141	0.222
MS	−0.016	−0.067	−0.131	0.134
Delinquency				
NA	−0.230	−0.321[a]	−0.278	−0.123
MS	0.157	0.154	0.325[a]	0.192
Aggression				
NA	−0.244	0.025	−0.043	0.019
MS	−0.183	−0.075	0.216	0.337[a]

[a,b]One-tailed tests: [a]$p < 0.05$; [b]$p < 0.01$.

therefore, greater neuromotor abnormalities and poorer motor skills are associated with *higher* scores for some of the internalized problems (Social Problems, Anxious/Depressed, Attention Problems), but *lower* scores for the externalized problems (Delinquency and Aggression).

In striking contrast to the preschizophrenic subjects, the healthy siblings' NA and MS scores show very little relationship with the behavior-problem dimensions. The only coefficient that reaches significance is the one relating NA and Social Problems; an increase in NA is associated with more Social Problems at the 4- to 8-year age period. Also, there is no apparent trend for NA to increase in association with the behavior dimensions over time. It is important, however, to interpret these findings with caution. The sibling comparison group is, by intention, comprised solely of subjects who have *no* lifetime history of psychiatric referral or treatment. Thus, they represent the upper end of

TABLE 3
Correlations of Neuromotor Abnormality and Motor Skills Scores with Child Behavior
Checklist Behavior Dimensions: Sibling Comparison Group

	Age periods			
Correlation variables	Birth–4 yr	4–8 yr	8–12 yr	12–16 yr
Withdrawn				
NA	0.047	−0.029	0.051	0.015
MS	−0.068	0.056	−0.035	−0.052
Social Problems				
NA	0.137	0.351[a]	0.306	0.153
MS	−0.050	−0.139	−0.084	0.020
Anxious/Depressed				
NA	0.132	0.173	0.206	0.140
MS	0.207	0.136	0.273	0.232
Attention Problems				
NA	−0.008	−0.025	0.010	0.020
MS	−0.027	−0.091	−0.138	−0.070
Thought Problems				
NA	−0.149	−0.149	−0.120	−0.135
MS	−0.058	−0.058	−0.055	0.052
Delinquency				
NA	−0.076	−0.198	−0.140	−0.102
MS	−0.284	−0.181	0.046	0.063
Aggression				
NA	−0.259	−0.252	−0.034	−0.003
MS	−0.228	−0.322	−0.253	−0.192

[a]One-tailed tests: $p < 0.05$.

the distribution with respect to psychological adjustment, and the consequent restriction in variability would be expected to limit the magnitude of the correlations.

4.3.2. Summary

The findings presented above provide further evidence of the association between neuromotor soft signs and adjustment problems in children. They suggest that the CNS impairment that is expressed in the form of neuromotor dysfunction is also expressed in multiple dimensions of behavior. However, the relation is not generalized; only behavior problems typically classified as "internalized" increase as a function of poorer NA and MS scores. In addition, the findings support the notion of a temporal sequence in the expression of dysfunction. The relation of early neuromotor abnormalities with behavior problems tends to become stronger with age (this strengthening being not readily attributable to statistical artifact, which would more likely result in higher correlations among concurrent measures). It is likely that the maturation of the CNS plays a role in this developmental pattern. In previous papers (Walker, 1994; Walker et al., 1994; Neumann et al., 1994), we have discussed the process through which CNS maturation might alter the behavioral expression of congenital CNS impairment. We address this issue in greater detail in Section 5.

4.3.3. Prospective Data

The behavioral data discussed above are retrospective in nature, a circumstance that could produce an artifactual pattern of results due to bias or recency effects in recall. The stronger relations we observe between NA and later behavior problems may reflect greater reliability for the more recent ratings (i.e., 12 to 16 years). One way of confirming the validity of observed developmental trends is to replicate them with alternative methods.

It is therefore useful to compare the findings presented above with prospective data on the relationship between motor functioning and behavior problems. In a prospective study of biological offspring of normal and psychiatrically disturbed parents, we collected behavioral data on children at two time points (for a detailed description of the study, see Walker, Downey, & Bergman, 1989). At the first assessment, the Bruininks–Oseresky Test of Motor Proficiency (Bruininks, 1978) was administered to the children, and a parent completed the CBCL. At the second assessment, 1 year later, the CBCL was again completed by a parent. The Bruininks Test measures the child's proficiency in fine and gross motor coordination. It is most comparable to the MS scale from our retrospective study. Because the same child behavior rating scale, the Achenbach CBCL (Achenbach, 1991; Achenbach & Edelbrock, 1981), was used in both the prospective and the retrospective study, the patterns of results can be readily compared.

At the first assessment, the subjects averaged 9.70 (SD = 2.35) years of age. The second assessment was conducted 1 year later. We focused on this preadolescent developmental period because it is a critical one with respect to the prodromal signs of psychopathology. The age period covered in this prospective study is narrow, however, and thus limits the comparisons with the findings from our retrospective data.

There were 107 subjects with data at both assessments: 22 offspring of schizophrenic parents (14 males and 8 females), 31 offspring of parents with depression (17 males and 14 females), and 54 subjects from families with no mental illness (27 males and 27 females). The families of the high-risk subjects were of low–average SES (most parents were either unemployed or in blue-collar positions), and the normal comparison group was selected to be comparable with respect to demographic factors. This demography is in contrast to that of the subjects from the archival study, who are predominantly from middle-class families (Walker et al., 1991).

Table 4 presents correlations between the Bruininks Motor Proficiency (MP) total score and the CBCL behavior dimensions. At the first assessment, five of the seven behavior dimensions are significantly related with the MP score. At the second assessment, six of the seven coefficients reach significance. Further, the magnitude of the correlation coefficients is higher at the second assessment for all but one of the behavior dimensions. Again, the pattern suggests stronger relations between motor functions and behavior problems with age.

Comparing Table 1 (8- to 12-year age period) with Table 4 reveals that some of the correlations observed in the previous findings with the MS scale also pertain to the prospective data with the MP test. For instance, both fail to show a relationship between motor scores and the

TABLE 4

Correlations between Bruininks Motor Proficiency
Scores and Child Behavior Checklist
Behavior Dimensions

Correlation variables	Mean age	
	10 years	11 years
Withdrawn		
MP	−0.082	−0.176
Social Problems		
MP	−0.377[b]	−0.424[b]
Anxious/Depressed		
MP	−0.254[a]	−0.269[a]
Attention Problems		
MP	−0.240[a]	−0.301[b]
Thought Problems		
MP	−0.299[b]	−0.218[a]
Delinquency		
MP	−0.121	−0.219[a]
Aggression		
MP	−0.286[b]	−0.319[b]

[a,b]One-tailed tests: [a]$p < 0.05$; [b]$p < 0.01$.

Withdrawn dimension. Similarly, both indicate that motor functioning is inversely related to the Social Problems and Attention Problems dimensions. Thus, in both data sets, low level of motor skills is linked with increased problems in attention and social functioning.

There are some differences, however, between these two sets of findings. In contrast to the correlations in Table 1, the data in Table 4 indicate that MP is inversely correlated with the Anxious/Depressed dimension. This finding is unique, in that the previous data (Tables 1, 2, and 3) do not suggest such a relationship.

Another discrepancy between the two sets of findings is the direction of the relation between motor scores (MS and MP) and externalized behavior problems. In the prospective sample, there are inverse relationships between MP and Delinquency and Aggression (see Table 4). In contrast, for the preschizophrenic subjects in the archival study sample (Table 2), there are positive relationships between MS and Delinquency and Aggression. Recall that the preschizophrenic group is composed mainly of males (23 vs. 6 females), whereas the prospective study sample has a more balanced sex ratio. In order to determine whether sex is influencing these relations, we conducted further analyses. When derived separately for each sex, the correlations between MS and Delinquency and MS and Aggression are as follows: for females, -0.648, $p = 0.08$, and -0.248, $p = .31$; for males, 0.317, $p = 0.07$, and 0.244, $p = 0.13$. Although these correlations do not reach conventional levels of significance, there is a trend that suggests that the relationship between motor functioning and externalized behavior problems is positive for males and negative for females. Partial support for these findings is provided by the prospective data. For the female subjects, MP is significantly negatively correlated with the Delinquency and Aggression dimensions (e.g., $r = -0.375$, $p = 0.02$, and $r = -0.441$, $p = 0.007$, respectively). There is no significant relationship, however, between motor functioning and Delinquency and Aggression for the male subjects in the prospective sample ($r = -0.160$, $p = 0.15$, and $r = -0.175$, $p = 0.13$, respectively). Although these correlations must be interpreted cautiously, they do suggest some interesting hypotheses regarding motor functioning and externalized behavior problems as moderated by sex. The patterns of correlations suggest that, for males, motor skills are unrelated to externalized behavior problems; for females, however, better motor skills are associated with lower rates of externalized behavior problems.

One limitation of prospective research on childhood precursors is the time required to obtain data on adult psychiatric outcome. We do not yet have such data on the subjects of our prospective study, so we cannot conduct diagnostic group comparisons like those from our retrospective study. Although there is reason to expect a higher rate of psychopathology in the offspring of the psychiatrically disturbed parents (Gottesman, 1991), even the majority of these children will be free of mental disorder in adulthood.

4.3.4. Summary

Apart from the unique relationship between MP and the Anxious/Depressed dimension in the prospective data, the patterns of relationships between motor functions and behavior problems within the two data sets are similar. Our confidence in the findings is strengthened by the fact that although the data sets were obtained with different methods, each of which has unique limitations that could influence the reliability/validity of the results (Walker, Davis, & Gottlieb, 1991), the patterns of intercorrelations in the retrospective data presented above are partially cross-validated by the prospective data. Thus, convergent validity is obtained for the patterns of findings.

4.3.5. Neuromotor Functions and Childhood Affect

Both the prospective and the retrospective data on the behavioral problems presented above are based on parental reports. Ideally, it would be desirable to explore the relation between neuromotor functioning and behavioral adjustment as measured through direct observation. We do not have access to observational data on behavioral problems for either sample. As previously described, however, we did obtain observational data on emotional expressions from the childhood home movies used in our study of precursors of mental illness.

Next, we will briefly present some data concerning the relationship between neuromotor functioning and affective expressions. In this case, data were available on all subjects: the preschizophrenic subjects and their healthy siblings, the pre–affective disorder subjects and their healthy siblings, and control subjects from families with no mental illness. As noted previously, when the NA items were coded from the childhood films, the rater recorded the side of occurrence (right, left, or both) of each abnormality. In our analyses, we also examined these separate NA scores. Doing so allowed us to determine whether there was evidence to support hypotheses proposed by Brumback (1993) about lateralization of neuromotor dysfunction and signs of depression in children—specifically, that left-side abnormalities are linked with depression. Table 5 presents the correlations between positive and negative affective expressions and MS scores and NA scores (total and left, right, or both sides of the body) for all subjects.

Compared to the data on behavioral problems, there are fewer sig-

TABLE 5

Correlations of Neuromotor Abnormalities and Motor Skills
with Affective Expressions: All Subjects

Correlation variables	Age periods			
	Birth–4 yr	4–8 yr	8–12 yr	12–16 yr
Neuromotor/negative affect				
NA Total	0.078	0.075	0.120	0.353[b]
Left	0.139	0.089	0.174	0.495[b]
Right	0.016	−0.038	−0.036	−0.110
Both	−0.157	−0.113	−0.028	0.229[a]
MS	0.021	−0.074	−0.102	−0.215[a]
Neuromotor/positive affect				
NA Total	−0.200[a]	0.011	−0.055	0.114
Left	−0.119	−0.078	−0.138	0.055
Right	0.087	0.154	−0.044	0.206[a]
Both	−0.205[a]	0.053	0.051	0.038
MS	0.036	0.022	0.069	0.058

[a,b]One-tailed tests: [a]$p < 0.05$; [b]$p < 0.01$.

nificant correlations between the emotional scores and the neuromotor variables. Nonetheless, the NA and the MS variables are associated with the expression of negative affect in the 12- to 16-year age period. For the NA score, greater total, left-sided, and both-sided abnormalities are related to increases in negative affect expressions. Conversely, lower MS scores are associated with higher rates of negative expressions in the 12- to 16-year age period. With respect to the positive affective expressions, the total NA score and NA on both sides are associated with decreases in positive affect in the birth to 4-year age period. Finally, right-sided NA scores are positively correlated with positive expressions in the 12- to 16-year age period. This finding may reflect the increase in later positive emotion expressions by preschizophrenic males reported in Walker et al. (1993). These authors suggested that the increase may be indicative of inappropriate affect.

There are some interesting parallels between the findings from the analyses of the emotion scores and the behavior-problem ratings. The association between NA and negative expressions at the 12- to 16-year age period is consistent with the association of NA with the Withdrawn and Anxious/Depressed behavior dimensions at the 12- to 16-year period. Also, the NA score is inversely related with positive affective expressions in the birth to 4-year age period, the same period in which there is an association between NA and Social and Attention Problems.

Because the numbers of subjects for whom films were available varied among the age periods, the emotion data are limited in terms of how much information can be derived by dividing them into diagnostic subgroups (e.g., preschizophrenic, preaffective, sibling, and control). Nonetheless, if the following results are considered cautiously, they may be helpful in generating hypotheses for future research.

Among the preschizophrenic subjects, an increase in the NA score on both sides is associated with decreases in positive ($= -0.437$, $p <$ 0.05) *and* negative ($r = -0.404$, $p < 0.05$) affective expressions at the birth to 4-year age period. Left-sided NA scores are positively correlated (0.439, $p < 0.05$) with negative affect at the 12- to 16-year age period, and right-sided NA scores are positively correlated (0.416, $p < 0.05$) with positive affect at the 12- to 16-year age period. Notice that these data fit with the ideas of Brumback (1993). He has suggested that mania (positive affect) is associated with right-sided soft signs and that depression (negative affect) is related to left-sided findings.

With respect to the pre–affective disorder subjects, we find that an increase in the right-sided NA score is positively correlated (0.450, $p <$ 0.05) with an increase in positive affective expressions at the birth to 4-year age period. A decrease in MS is linked (-0.440, $p < 0.05$) with increases in negative expressions at the 4- to 8-year age period. Notably, this last finding somewhat matches the "high-risk" data presented above, which showed that a decrease in MS was associated with an increase in the Anxious/Depressed behavior dimension at age 10.

Finally, we combined the data from the healthy siblings of the patient groups and the controls to form a "no mental illness" (NMI) group. In contrast to the two patient groups, right-sided NA scores are positively correlated (0.361, $p < 0.01$) with negative affective expressions (at the 8- to 12-year age period). Increases in NA are positively associated (0.238, $p < 0.05$) with increases in negative expressions in the NMI group (at the 4- to 8-year age period). Similar to the pre–affective disorder group, the NMI group showed a negative correlation (-0.336, $p < 0.01$) between MS and negative expressions at the 4- to 8-year age period.

5. Conclusions

As research findings on the origins of psychopathology have accumulated, it has become increasingly apparent that there are multiple determinants of virtually all classes of psychiatric disorder. No single etiological agent has emerged as the causal factor for any diagnostic category. It is now clear that genetic factors, biological insults to the CNS, and psychosocial stressors all play a role, to varying degrees, in the etiology of psychopathology.

In this chapter, we have focused on childhood neuromotor soft signs as indicators of the integrity of CNS function. Like many other investigators, we assume that neuromotor dysfunction is an indication of CNS impairment that has been either acquired (e.g., through exposure to obstetrical complications) or inherited. The net result is biological vulnerability to cognitive dysfunction and behavioral maladjustment. However, there is no simple, direct causal pathway between neuromotor dysfunction and behavioral maladjustment.

It is important to note that neuromotor signs are limited with respect to their sensitivity and specificity as risk markers for behavioral disorder. The magnitude of the correlations presented in this chapter suggests a moderate relation. Normal children may also show soft signs without ever developing behavioral, cognitive, or psychiatric problems (Hynd & Hooper, 1992). Conversely, some severely disturbed, chronic schizophrenic patients in our study showed above-average motor skills and no soft signs as children. To some extent, the modest sensitivity and specificity of neuromotor soft signs must be assumed to reflect the limits of our measures; there is error in the measurement of both motor functions and behavioral characteristics. It is also likely, however, that the magnitude of the association between these two variables is partially determined by other variables that serve as moderators. More specifically, other factors are moderating the relation between neuromotor abnormalities and behavioral maladjustment.

It appears that one important moderating influence is CNS maturation. Taken together, the findings from our research and from previous investigations indicate that the maturation of the CNS plays a critical role in the expression of neuromotor dysfunction, behavioral maladjustment, and clinical psychopathology. As we have shown, there is extensive evidence that childhood neuromotor abnormalities and motor skills deficits decrease dramatically with age. Further, our research indicates that this developmental trend holds for children with adult psychiatric outcomes, such as schizophrenia, as well as for children with healthy adult outcomes (Walker et al., 1994). In striking contrast, the incidence of behavioral maladjustment, especially clinical symptoms of psychiatric disorder, increases with age and peaks in young adulthood (Neumann et al., 1994). Thus, the modal developmental trajectories for the manifestation of dysfunction in the neuromotor and behavioral domains are essentially reversed—each presumably affected in different ways by CNS maturation.

Further, the evidence suggests that the stage of CNS maturation can influence the strength of the observed relation between neuromotor functions and behavioral adjustment. Findings from both our archival and prospective studies suggest that the strength of the relation between childhood neuromotor functioning and adjustment is greatest for behavioral problems measured in the preadolescent/adolescent period. The findings presented in Tables 1, 2, and 3 indicate a striking absence of significant links between the NA and MS scores and behavior problems in the period between birth and 4 years of age. One notable exception to the general findings, however, is that there is an early relationship between NA and MS and Attention Problems.

The apparent influence of developmental level on the magnitude of the intercorrelations has noteworthy implications for researchers. To some extent, the controversy in the literature surrounding the strength of the association between neuromotor soft signs and cognitive and behavior problems may be due to differences among studies in the ages of the subjects when they are assessed. This possibility points to the importance of a developmental approach to research in this area.

Another conclusion that can be tentatively drawn from the findings is that there are subtypes or subsyndromes of motor dysfunction. Several investigators have emphasized the distinction between abnormalities in movement and delays in motor skills or proficiency. We attempted to capture this distinction in our NA and MS scales. Our findings indicate that abnormalities in movement may have greater relevance for subsequent behavioral problems than do motor skills deficits. This result is consistent with the assumption that abnormalities are more often a reflection of CNS dysfunction, whereas skill level is largely influenced by normative individual differences in maturational rate, which are both environmentally and biologically determined. Clearly, however, the subtyping of motor dysfunction is an area that is in need of further research.

Finally, a central goal of this chapter was to explore the specificity of the association between neuromotor dysfunction and behavior problems. The results of our analyses indicate that behavioral problems of the "internalized" type show a relatively stronger association with motor dysfunction, particularly neuromotor abnormalities. Externalizing problems, in contrast, show a less consistent relation with NA and MS scores. It appears that motor skills deficits may be associated with externalized problems only among females.

5.1. Neurodevelopmental Processes

Developmental changes in the expression of motoric, cognitive, and behavioral dysfunction, and their interrelations across time, pose a formidable challenge as we attempt to generate plausible models about the origins of psychopathology. The correlations that we and others have observed between early neuromotor abnormalities and childhood behavior problems, particularly in adolescence, suggest that a specific brain impairment can have manifestations in multiple functional domains. This assumption receives strong support from studies of neurological disorders such as Sydenham's chorea (Wilcox & Nasrallah, 1988) and Rett's syndrome (Nomura & Segawa, 1992). Both of these disorders involve severe motor symptoms, as well as cognitive deficits and psychiatric symptoms that change over time. Further, both are believed to be caused by damage to a specific subcortical brain region—the basal ganglia.

Assuming, then, that damage to a circumscribed brain region can influence diverse aspects of human behavior, what produces the sometimes dramatic changes in the expression of dysfunction over time? In a recent paper, Walker (1994) has speculated on how normative differences in the rate of maturation of various cortical regions might play a role in these developmental changes.

Specifically, there is evidence that the motor cortex is the most mature and metabolically active region of the cortex in infancy (Konner, 1991; Gibson, 1991; Chugani, 1994). The frontal and limbic regions of the cortex mature at a slower rate, but then exceed the motor cortex in functional activation by late childhood. Further, the development of the frontal and association cortex extends into early adulthood (Thatcher, 1994), as does the development of the limbic cortex (Benes, 1994).

The protracted periods of maturation that characterize certain brain regions provide a neurodevelopmental basis for explaining developmental changes in motor, cognitive, and behavioral phenomena. This basis for explanation holds for both normative phenomena and signs of dysfunction. The motor cortex, which appears to be the most activated cortical region early in life, subserves the execution and control of movement. The frontal region is assumed to play a major role in complex cognitive processes and behavioral inhibition and organization (Dawson & Fischer, 1994; Diamond, Werker, & Lalonde, 1994; Fischer & Rose, 1994). The limbic cortex (anterior cingulate cortex) is critical to the acquisition of complex emotional behaviors; the maturation of its interconnections with frontal regions, which extends into early adulthood, may play a critical role in the integration of cognition with emotion (Benes, 1994).

Each of these functionally specialized regions of the cortex shows a relative increase in activation, and physical maturation, during the developmental periods when the capacities it subserves are in ascendance. These developmental periods span the time from the acquisition of motor skills in the first 2 years of life to the emergence of the most sophisticated abstract capacities in early adulthood. However, although these regions are functionally and physically differentiated at the cortical level, it is believed that they are each linked with subcortical areas via "parallel" circuits (Alexander, Crutcher, & DeLong, 1990). These functionally segregated circuits converge on subregions of the basal ganglia.

Given the evidence that the various regions of the cortex mature at different rates, it is likely that these circuits are also characterized by a temporal sequence of maturation.

The pattern of regional maturation of cortical circuitry is consistent with the temporal sequence of manifest dysfunction observed in research on the precursors of psychopathology. Specifically, Walker (1994) describes how subtle damage in the basal ganglia might result in a malfunction of the motor circuit that is expressed in early neuromotor signs. But the neuromotor abnormalities become less pronounced as the CNS matures and other cortical regions become activated. Then, with the activation of other regions and their circuitry, dysfunction is manifested in other domains. Thus, subcortical damage may gradually be expressed in the behavioral domains influenced by the frontal circuit, particularly behavioral inhibition. These deficits in behavioral control (i.e., externalized behavior problems) may increase with age, whereas motor dysfunction becomes less pronounced. As the limbic circuit matures, deficits may also be expressed in the socioemotional domain, so that there is an increase in internalized behavior problems in adolescence. Ultimately, depending on the nature and extent of the brain impairment, psychiatric symptoms may emerge in adulthood.

The finding of age-related increases in the magnitude of the correlation between early neuromotor scores and behavior problems is consistent with the neurodevelopmental framework. It suggests how a relatively circumscribed brain abnormality can be expressed in different forms as a function of CNS maturation. In other words, because of the changes produced by CNS maturation, the resultant behavioral expressions are not isomorphic across time. Early childhood neuromotor dysfunction is therefore more predictive of adolescent behavior problems than it is of concurrent behavior problems. Our data do suggest, however, that childhood neuromotor dysfunction is related to concurrent attentional problems. In support of this latter finding, Stanger, Achenbach, and McConaughy (1993) found that attentional problems were predictive of behavioral disturbance 3 years later.

5.2. Directions for Future Research

As mentioned above, neuromotor soft signs do not appear to be specific to children with subsequent behavior problems. A critical question for future research concerns the factors that determine the relationship between motor and behavioral functions. It is well established that various clinical movement disorders (e.g., Parkinson's disease, Huntington's chorea), which involve different syndromes of motor dysfunction, are due to different impairments in the basal ganglia. It is likely that there are also various syndromes of neuromotor soft signs that are due to different brain impairments. Moreover, there is suggestive evidence that these syndromes are associated with different kinds of behavioral problems or cognitive dysfunctions, or both, later in childhood (Soorani-Lunsing et al., 1993b). Further research may help elucidate these syndromes and their behavioral correlates. Clearly, the findings of such research will hold promise for enhancing our understanding of brain–behavior relations and the neural origins of psychopathology.

Another important issue for future research concerns the role of the psychosocial environment in determining the behavioral and psychiatric outcomes for children with soft signs of neuromotor dysfunction. There is reason to believe that psychological stress exacerbates neuromotor dysfunction (Bhattacharya, Tripathi, & Kashyap, 1989; Gurvits et al., 1993). There is also evidence that the quality of the familial rearing environment partially determines the behavioral outcome of the children who have experienced obstetrical complications and postnatal brain trauma (Breslau, 1990). The interplay between psychosocial stressors and biological vulnerabilities is undoubtedly highly complex, yet research aimed at elucidating it is of critical importance.

In summary, the ideas and research findings we have presented in this chapter reflect the growing interest of researchers in the developmental origins of maladjustment. Like many others in the burgeoning field of developmental psychopathology, we assume that the maturation of the CNS plays a central role in determining the nature and temporal course of behavioral signs of dysfunction. Our findings and those of other investigators suggest that early neuromotor abnormalities may hold important clues about the subsequent developmental course, as well as the integrity of the CNS. We believe future research in this area is a high priority.

ACKNOWLEDGMENTS

Support for this work was provided by a National Institute of Mental Health Research Grant (MH46496) and a Research Scientist Development Award (MH00876). The National Alliance for Research on Schizophrenia and Depression also provided support.

6. Appendix: Neuromotor Rating Scale

Neuromotor Abnormalities (NA)

Abnormal hand posture
Abnormal oral/facial movements
Associated reactions

Bradykinesia
Choreoathetoid movements
Dysmetria
Dysmorphic features
Hypertonicity
Hypotonicity
Intention tremors
Mirror movements
Musculoskeletal abnormalities
Postural abnormality of trunk or legs
Repetitive movements
Rest tremors
Retained primitive reflexes
Spastic movements
Tics

Motor Skills (MS)

Alignment
Dissociation of movement
Gait
Protective extension
Righting reactions
Shoulder and pelvic stability
Smoothness of transitional movement
Standing posture
Weight shift

7. References

Achenbach, T. M. (1991). *Manual for the Child Behavior Checklist/4–18 and 1991 Profile*. Burlington: Department of Psychiatry, University of Vermont.

Achenbach, T. M., & Edelbrock, C. S. (1981). Behavioral problems and competencies reported by parents of normal and disturbed children aged four through sixteen. *Monographs of the Society for Research in Child Development, 46*(1), 1–82.

Agarwal, K. N., Das, D., Agarwal, D. K., Upadhyay, S. K., & Mishra, S. (1989). Soft neurological signs and EEG pattern in rural malnourished children. *Acta Paediatrica Scandinavica, 78*(6), 873–878.

Alexander, G. E., Crutcher, M. D., & DeLong, M. R. (1990). Basal ganglia–thalamocortical circuits: Parallel substrates for motor, oculomotor, "prefrontal" and "limbic" functions. *Progress in Brain Research, 85*, 119–145.

Behar, D., Rapoport, J. L., Berg, C. J., Denckla, M. B., Mann, L., Cox, C., Fedio, P., Zahn, T., & Wolfman, M. G. (1984). Computerized tomography and neuropsychological test measures in adolescents with obsessive–compulsive disorder. *American Journal of Psychiatry, 141*(3), 363–369.

Benes, F. (1994). Development of the cortical limbic system. In G. Dawson & K. W. Fischer (Eds.), *Human behavior and the developing brain* (pp. 176–206). New York: Guilford Press.

Bhattacharya, S. K., Tripathi, S. R., & Kashyap, S. K. (1989). The combined effects of noise and illumination on the performance efficiency of visual search and neuromotor task components. *Journal of Human Ergology, 18*(1), 41–51.

Breslau, N. (1990). Does brain dysfunction increase children's vulnerability to environmental stress? *Archives of General Psychiatry, 47,* 15–20.

Bruininks, R. H. (1978). *Bruininks–Oseretsky Test of Motor Proficiency.* Circle Pines: American Guidance Service.

Brumback, R. A. (1993). Is depression a neurologic disease? *Behavioral Neurology, 11*(1), 79–104.

Brumback, R. A., & Weinberg, W. A. (1990). Pediatric behavioral neurology: An update on the neurologic aspects of depression, hyperactivity, and learning disabilities. *Neurological Clinics, 8,* 677–703.

Bulayeva, K. B. (1981). Population–genetic analysis of some neurodynamic parameters of man. *Behavior Genetics, 11*(4), 303–308.

Chadwick, O., Rutter, M., Brown, G., Shaffer, D., & Traub, M. U. (1981). A prospective study of children with head injuries. II. Cognitive sequelae. *Psychological Medicine, 11*(1), 49–61.

Chugani, H. (1994). Development of regional brain glucose metabolism in relation to behavior and plasticity. In G. Dawson & K. W. Fischer (Eds.), *Human behavior and the developing brain* (pp. 153–175). New York: Guilford Press.

Cicchetti, D., & Aber, J. L. (1986). Early precursors of later depression: An organizational perspective. *Advances in Infancy Research, 4,* 87–137.

Dawson, G., & Fischer, K. W., (Eds.) (1944). *Human behavior and the developing brain.* New York: Guilford Press.

Diamond, A., Werker, J. F., & Lalonde, C. (1994). Toward understanding commonalities in the development of object search, detour navigation, categorization and speech perception. In G. Dawson & K. W. Fischer (Eds.), *Human behavior and the developing brain* (pp. 380–426). New York: Guilford Press.

Endicott, J., & Spitzer, R. L. (1978). A diagnostic interview: The Schedule for Affective Disorders and Schizophrenia. *Archives of General Psychiatry, 35*(7), 87–44.

Fischer, K. W., & Rose, S. P. (1994). Dynamic development of coordination of components in brain and behavior. In G. Dawson & K. W. Fischer (Eds.), *Human behavior and the developing brain* (pp. 3–65). New York: Guilford Press.

Fish, B., Marcus, J., Hans, S. L., Auerbach, J. G., & Perdue, S. (1992). Infants at risk for schizophrenia: Sequelae of genetic neurointegrative defect. *Archives of General Psychiatry, 49,* 221–235.

Foerster, A., Lewis, S. W., Owen, M. J., & Murray, R. M. (1991). Low birth weight and a family history of schizophrenia predict poor premorbid functioning in psychosis. *Schizophrenia Research, 5*(1), 13–20.

Fog, E., & Fog, M. (Eds.) (1963). *Cerebral inhibition examined by associated movements.* London: S.I.M.P. with Heinemann Medical.

Gibson, K. (Ed.). (1991). *Myelination and behavioral development.* New York: Aldine De Gruyter.

Gillberg, C. (1983). Three year follow-up at age 10 of children with minor neurodevelopmental disorders. I. Behavioural problems. *Developmental Medicine and Child Neurology, 25,* 438–449.

Gillberg, C. R., Carlstrom, G., Svenson, B., & Waldenstrom, E. (1982). Perceptual, motor and attentional deficits in seven-year-old children: Epidemiological aspects. *Journal of Child Psychology and Psychiatry, 23,* 131–144.

Gillberg, C., & Rasmussen, P. (1982a). Perceptual, motor and attentional deficits in seven-year-old children: Screening procedure in pre-school. *Acta Paediatrica Scandinavica, 71,* 121–129.

Gillberg, C., & Rasmussen, P. (1982b). Perceptual, motor and attentional deficits in seven-year-old children: Background factors. *Developmental Medicine and Child Neurology, 24,* 752–770.

Gillberg, I. C. (1985). Children with minor neurodevelopmental disorders. III. Neurological and neurodevelopmental problems at age 10. *Developmental Medicine and Child Neurology, 27,* 3–16.

Gillberg, I. C., & Gillberg, C. (1989). Children with preschool minor neurological disorders. IV. Behavior and school achievement at age 13. *Developmental Medicine and Child Neurology, 31,* 3–13.

Gillberg, I. C., Gillberg, C., & Groth, J. (1989). Children with preschool minor neurodevelopmental disorders. V. Neurodevelopmental profiles at age 13. *Developmental Medicine and Child Neurology, 31,* 14–24.

Goodman, R. (1990). Technical note: Are perinatal complications causes or consequences of autism? *Journal of Child Psychology and Psychiatry, 31,* 809–812.

Gorga, D., Stern, F. M., Ross, G., & Nagler, W. (1991). The neuromotor behavior of preterm and full-term children by three years of age: Quality of movement and variability. *Journal of Developmental and Behavioral Pediatrics, 12*(2), 102–107.

Gottesman, I. (1991). *Schizophrenia genesis.* New York: W. H. Freeman.

Gurvits, T. V., Lasko, N. B., Schachter, S. C., Kuhne, A. A., Orr, S. P., & Pitman, R. K. (1993). Neurological status of Vietnam veterans with chronic posttraumatic stress disorder. *Journal of Neuropsychiatry and Clinical Neurosciences, 5*(2), 183–188.

Hadders-Algra, M., Huisjes, H. J., & Touwen, B. C. (1989). Ante and perinatal factors and behavior and functional disorders in 6 to 9 year old children. *Tijdschrift voor Kindergeneeskunde, 57*(3), 77–81.

Hammen, C., Burge, D. & Stansbury, K. (1990). *Developmental Psychology, 26*(1), 24–30.

Hans, S., & Marcus, J. (1991). Neurobehavioral development of infants at risk for schizophrenia. In E. F. Walker (Ed.), *Schizophrenia: A life-course developmental perspective* (pp. 35–53). New York: Academic Press.

Hollander, E., DeCaria, C. M., Aronowitz, B., Klein, D. F., Liebowitz, M. R., & Shaffer, D. (1991). A pilot follow-up study of childhood soft signs and the development of adult psychopathology. *Clinical and Research Reports, 3*(2), 186–189.

Hollander, E., Shiffman, E., Cohen, B., Rivera-Stein, M. A., Rosen, W., Gorman, J. M., Fyer, A. J., Papp, L., & Liebowitz, M. R. (1990). Signs of central nervous system dysfunction in obsessive–compulsive disorder. *Archives of General Psychiatry, 47,* 27–32.

Hynd, G. W., & Hooper, S. R. (1992). *Neurological basis of childhood psychopathology.* Newbury Park, CA: Sage Publications.

Ingram, T. T. S. (1963). Chronic brain syndromes in childhood other than cerebral palsy, epilepsy and mental defect. In *Minimal cerebral dysfunction.* London: Spastics Society Heinemann.

Izard, C. E., Dougherty, L. M., & Hembree, E. A. (1983). *A system for identifying affect expressions by holistic judgments (AFFEX).* Newark: Instructional Resources Center, University of Delaware.

Khadilkar, V., Tudehope, D., Burns, Y., O'Callaghan, M., & Mohay, H. (1993). The long-term neurodevelopmental outcome for very low birthweight (VLBW) infants with "dystonic" signs at 4 months of age. *Journal of Paediatric Child Health, 29,* 415–417.

Konner, M. (Ed.) (1991). *Universals of behavioral development in relation to brain myelination.* New York: Aldine De Gruyter.

Kragt, H., Huisjes, H. J., & Touwen, B. C. (1985). Neurological morbidity in newborn twins. *European Journal of Obstetrics, Gynecology, and Reproductive Biology, 19*(2), 75–79.

Litter, J., & Walker, E. (1993). Interpersonal behavior of preschizophrenia children. *Child Psychiatry and Human Development, 23,* 283–295.

Marlow, N., Roberts, L., & Cooke, R. (1993). Outcomes at 8 years for children with birth weights of 1250g or less. *Archives of Disease in Childhood, 68*(3), 286–290.

McNeil, T. (1987). Perinatal influences in the development of schizophrenia. In H. Helmchen & F. A. Henn (Eds.), *Biological perspectives of schizophrenia* (pp. 125–138). New York: John Wiley.

Meehl, P. (1989). Schizotaxia revisited. *Archives of General Psychiatry, 46,* 935–944.

Neumann, C. S., Grimes, K., Walker, E. F., & Baum, K. (1994). Developmental pathways to schizophrenia: Behavioral subtypes. Unpublished manuscript.

Nomura, Y., & Segawa, M. (1992). Motor symptoms of the Rett syndrome: Abnormal muscle tone, posture, locomotion and stereotyped movement. *Brain and Development, 14*(Suppl.), S21–S28.

Orvaschel, H., Walsh-Allis, G., & Ye, W. (1988). Psychopathology in children of parents with recurrent depression. *Journal of Abnormal Child Psychology, 16*(1), 17–28.

Prechtl, H. F. R., & Stemmer, C. H. (1962). The choreiform syndrome in children. *Developmental Medical Child Neurology, 4,* 119–127.

Rubin, R. A., & Barlow, B. (1980). Infant neurological abnormalities as indicators of cognitive impairment. *Developmental Medical Child Neurology, 22,* 336–343.

Rutter, M. (1990). Isle of Wight revisited: Twenty-five years of child psychiatric epidemiology. *Annual Progress in Child Psychiatry and Development,* 131–179.

Shaffer, D., O'Connor, P. A., Shaffer, S. Q., & Prupis, S. (1983). Neurological "soft signs": Their origins and significance for behavior. In M. Rutter (Ed.), *Developmental neuropsychology* (pp. 144–163). New York: Guilford Press.

Shaffer, D., Schonfeld, I., O'Connor, P. A., Stokman, C., Trautman, P., Shafer, S., & Ng, S. (1985). Neurological soft signs and their relationship to psychiatric disorder and intelligence in childhood and adolescence. *Archives of General Psychiatry, 42,* 343–351.

Soorani-Lunsing, R. J., Hadders-Algra, M., Huisjes, H. J., & Touwen, B. C. L. (1993a). Minor neurological dysfunction after the onset of puberty: Association with perinatal events. *Early Human Development, 33,* 71–80.

Soorani-Lunsing, R. J., Hadders-Algra, M., Olinga, A. A., Huisjes, H. J., & Touwen, B. C. L. (1993b). Is minor neurological dysfunction at 12 years related to behavior and cognition? *Developmental Medicine and Child Neurology, 35*(4), 321–330.

Stanger, C., Achenbach, T. M., & McConaughy, S. H. (1993). Three year course of behavioral/emotional problems in a national sample of 4- to 16-year-olds. 3. Predictors of signs of disturbance. *Journal of Consulting and Clinical Psychology, 61*(5), 839–848.

Szatmari, P., & Taylor, D. C. (1984). Overflow movements and behavior problems: Scoring and using a modification of Fogs' test. *Developmental Medicine and Child Neurology, 26,* 297–310.

Taylor, D. C., Powell, R. P., Cherland, E. E., & Vaughan, C. M. (1988). Overflow movements and cognitive motor and behavioral disturbance: A normative study of girls. *Developmental Medicine and Child Neurology, 30,* 759–768.

Thatcher, R. W. (1994). Cyclic cortical reorganization: Origins of human cognitive development. In G. Dawson & K. W. Fischer (Eds.), *Human behavior and the developing brain* (pp. 323–267). New York: Guilford Press.

Torrey, E. F., Bowler, A. E., Taylor, E. H., & Gottesman, I. I. (1994). *Schizophrenia and manic–depressive disorder.* New York: Basic Books.

Tramontana, M. G., & Sherrets, S. D. (1985). Brain impairment in child psychiatric disorders: Correspondences between neuropsychological and CT scan results. *Journal of the American Academy of Child Psychiatry, 24*(5), 590–596.

Walker, E. (Ed.) (1991). *Schizophrenia: A life-course developmental perspective.* New York: Academic Press.

Walker, E. (1994). Developmentally moderated expressions of the neuropathology underlying schizophrenia. *Schizophrenia Bulletin, 20*(3), 453–480.

Walker, E., Davis, D., & Gottlieb, L. (1991). Charting the developmental trajectories leading to psychopathology. In D. Cicchetti & S. Tith (Eds.), *Developmental psychopathology,* Vol. 3 (pp. 185–205). Rochester, NY: Rochester University Press.

Walker, E., Downey, G., & Bergman, A. (1989). The effects of parenatal psychopathology and maltreatment on child behavior: A test of the diathesis–stress model. *Child Development, 60*(1), 15–24.

Walker, E., Grimes, K., Davis, D., & Smith, A. (1993). Childhood precursors of schizophrenia: Facial expressions of emotion. *American Journal of Psychiatry, 150,* 1654–1660.

Walker, E., & Lewine, R. J. (1990). Prediction of adult-onset schizophrenia from childhood home-movies of the patients. *American Journal of Psychiatry, 147,* 1052–1056.

Walker, E., Savoie, T., & Davis, D. (1994). Neuromotor precursors of schizophrenia. *Schizophrenia Bulletin, 20*(3), 441–451.

Wilcox, J. A., & Nasrallah, H. (1988). Sydenham's chorea and psychopathology. *Neuropsychobiology, 19*(1), 6–8.

Williams, L. R., & Gross, J. B. (1980). Heritability of motor skills. *Acta Geneticae Medicae et Gemellologiae, 29*(2), 127–136.

Wolf, P. H., Gunnoe, C. E., & Cohen, C. (1983). Associated movements as a measure of developmental age. *Developmental Medicine and Child Neurology, 25,* 417–425.

Woods, B. T., Kinney, D. K., & Yurgelun-Todd, D. (1986). Neurologic abnormalities in schizophrenic patients and their families. *Archives of General Psychiatry, 43,* 657–668.

Zahn, T. P., Nurnberger, J. I., Berrettini, W. H., & Robinson, T. N. (1991). Concordance between anxiety and autonomic nervous system activity in subjects at genetic risk for affective disorder. *Psychiatry Research, 36*(1), 99–110.

6

Students with Attention-Deficit Hyperactivity Disorder and Their Teachers

Implications of a Goodness-of-Fit Perspective

Ross W. Greene

1. Introduction

The past three decades have witnessed heightened levels of awareness and study of what has come to be known as attention-deficit hyperactivity disorder (ADHD). Children diagnosed with ADHD exhibit a constellation of "developmentally deviant" behaviors represented diagnostically by the broad categories of "inattentiveness" or "hyperactivity/impulsivity," or both, as specified in the fourth edition of the *Diagnostic and Statistical Manual of Mental Disorders* (DSM-IV) (American Psychiatric Association, 1994). The style of behaving associated with ADHD places these children at heightened risk for behavioral, academic, and social difficulties, as well as for a variety of comorbid diagnoses (e.g., Abikoff & Klein, 1992; Biederman, Faraone, Keenan, & Tsuang, 1991; Cantwell & Baker, 1992; Jensen, Shervette, Xenakis, & Richters, 1993; Mannuzza, Klein, Bessler, Malloy, & LaPadula, 1993).

Coinciding with but rarely overlapping this intensified interest in

Ross W. Greene • Pediatric Psychopharmacology Unit, Massachusetts General Hospital and Harvard Medical School, Boston, Massachusetts 02114.

Advances in Clinical Child Psychology, Volume 18, edited by Thomas H. Ollendick and Ronald J. Prinz. Plenum Press, New York, 1996.

ADHD has been the emergence of theories emphasizing the transactional (or reciprocal) influence of environment and biology/constitution on a child's development (e.g., Sameroff & Chandler, 1975; Sameroff & Seifer, 1983). Transactional theory includes the following assumptions: (1) characteristics of both children *and* their environment(s) must be considered simultaneously in understanding developmental outcome; (2) development is best understood as being discontinuous and dynamic rather than as a linear chain of efficient causes and invariant effects; and (3) interactions between children and adults are organized at different levels of complexity (e.g., individual, family, classroom, cultural), and a thorough understanding of the phenomena that affect individuals requires examination at all these organizational levels. Closely related to transactional theory is the concept of "goodness-of-fit," which represents the notion that a fundamental aspect of interactions between children and adults is the degree of "compatibility" between the capacities, motivations, and style of behaving of a child and the expectations and demands of an adult (Bell & Harper, 1977; Seifer, 1988; Thomas & Chess, 1980; Thomas, Chess, & Birch, 1968; Thomas, Chess, Birch, Hertzig, & Korn, 1963).

That the conceptual elegance of transactional/goodness-of-fit thinking has rarely converged with the burgeoning literature on ADHD is both surprising and regrettable. This lack of overlap is perhaps most conspicuous in research on children with ADHD in educational settings. ADHD, perhaps more than any other psychiatric diagnosis, can be characterized as a *situation-specific* style of behaving in that ADHD-related behaviors are presumed to be more or less pronounced depending on certain contextual factors (e.g., Keogh & Barkett, 1980; Whalen & Henker, 1980). That is, aspects of the school environment such as the teacher, classroom climate, and specific tasks are believed to contribute to positive and negative variations in the behavior of students with ADHD. The constructs of situational specificity and goodness-of-fit are obviously congruent in that both accentuate the notion that ADHD-related behavior cannot be conceptualized separately from the contexts in which it occurs. Unfortunately, such constructs have yet to be incorporated into most research designs related to students with ADHD.

Indeed, with a few notable exceptions, the study of children with ADHD in school classrooms has tended toward examination of more linear, unidirectional issues (e.g., whether behavior modification procedures improve the classroom behavior of students with ADHD). The equivocal resolution of these issues is undoubtedly due in part to the disparate research methodology that has been applied to their exploration (for a comprehensive review, see Fiore, Becker, & Nero, 1993). We must also consider, however, the possibility that the issues we have been examining have not been conceptualized broadly enough to do justice to their true complexity. Progressing beyond our current understanding of the difficulties of students with ADHD in school environments will require examination of issues that are more broadly conceived, centering on characteristics both of students with ADHD and of aspects of their school environments. The transactional/goodness-of-fit perspective (for ease of exposition, referred to hereinafter as "goodness-of-fit") provides a useful conceptual base from which to consider these broader issues.

It may be useful to begin contemplating these premises by describing the various compatibility issues that will be explored in later sections.

2. Compatibility Equations

School-based research on students with ADHD has been dominated by treatment outcome studies. In most cases, these studies are designed to answer linear questions regarding the impact of various interventions on the behavior and academic functioning of students with ADHD. The tendency in such studies is to invoke characteristics of either the treatment or the student (most commonly the former) in explanations of positive and negative variations in treatment response. From a goodness-of-fit perspective, these variations are more accurately viewed as a reflection of the match or compatibility between student characteristics and intervention ingredients. Conceptually, this mix of student characteristics and intervention ingredients represents a compatibility equation, or what could be referred to as *student–treatment compatibility* (Greene, 1995). Viewed as such, "treatment" can be defined as the process of searching for the optimal match between treatment ingredients/potencies and the specific needs and characteristics of a particular child, rather than as the application of a standard treatment approach to all children carrying the same ADHD diagnosis (Abramowitz, Eckstrand, O'Leary, & Dulcan, 1992; Hoza, Pelham, Sams, & Carlson, 1992; Swanson, Cantwell, Lerner, McBurnett, & Hanna, 1991). A later section explores in greater depth the manner in which a goodness-of-fit perspective might serve to broaden our understanding of treatment response.

To what degree are commonly recommended school-based interventions for students with ADHD compatible with the motivations, capacities, and style of behaving of the teacher responsible for their implementation? This question, which has received very limited research attention, points toward a second compatibility equation: *teacher–*

treatment compatibility (Greene, 1995). Intuitively, it seems clear that teachers' ability and willingness to implement recommended treatment ingredients would greatly influence treatment outcome (e.g., Pelham & Murphy, 1986), yet treatment outcome research has rarely incorporated variables related to teacher–treatment compatibility. This issue is also discussed in greater detail in a later section.

Treatment is undoubtedly sought not merely because a student carries a diagnosis of ADHD, but because of the tension created by ADHD-related behaviors in interactions between the student and his or her teacher. From a goodness-of-fit perspective, it would be erroneous to view this tension as emanating solely from either student or teacher. More accurately, the tension is indicative of a lack of compatibility between the capacities, motivations, and style of behaving of the student with ADHD and the expectations and demands of her or his teacher. Conceptualized as such, student and teacher characteristics operate in combination to produce what may be referred to as *student–teacher compatibility* (Greene, 1995). The literature has been fairly explicit about the characteristics of students with ADHD that may contribute to tension in interactions with teachers, but we have little or no understanding of teacher characteristics that may also contribute to student–teacher compatibility. Teacher characteristics, and their potential influence on student–teacher compatibility, are discussed at length below.

While these three issues of compatibility are the focus of the ensuing discussion, it must be noted that it may be important to include additional compatibility equations in considerations of contextual factors impacting upon students with ADHD. Two such equations are teacher–setting compatibility (the match between characteristics of the teacher and characteristics of the teaching setting) and child–setting compatibility (the match between characteristics of the child and characteristics of the learning setting). The latter area has already been the focus of several studies. For example, extra- and intratask novelty stimulation have been found to reduce activity and improve performance for students with ADHD, especially on easy, repetitive tasks (e.g., Zentall & Meyer, 1987), and factors such as a high level of noise have been shown to have detrimental effects on the behavior of these students (e.g., Whalen, Henker, Collins, Finck, & Dotemoto, 1979). Nonetheless, our understanding of the child–setting compatibility issue must be characterized as incomplete; other setting variables (e.g., size of class, ratio of "special needs" children, seating arrangements, and open vs. closed classes) are worthy of additional exploration (Pfiffner & O'Leary, 1993). With regard to teacher–setting compatibility, issues such as teaching gratification, job satisfaction, student population preference, grade preference, and general school environment are possible areas of further inquiry. Borrowing phraseology from Carlson and Lahey (1988), our ability to "engineer settings that optimize adaptation" for students with ADHD, and our concepts of interactions between students with ADHD and their teachers, will remain incomplete until these additional person–environment compatibility issues are more closely examined.

2.1. Student–Teacher Compatibility

The notion that school outcome for students with ADHD may be related to student–teacher compatibility has been suggested previously by several writers (Brooks, 1984; Conners & Wells, 1986; Shaywitz & Shaywitz, 1988; for a comprehensive discussion of the "social ecology" of ADHD, see Whalen & Henker, 1980). The goodness-of-fit concept has also been discussed in relation to interactions between teachers and generically defined "emotionally or behaviorally challenging" students (e.g., Kauffman & Wong, 1991; Landrum, 1992), with theorists suggesting that the difficulties of such students are often due in part to incompatibilities between pupils and teachers and mismatches in their behavioral styles, perceptions, or expectations (e.g., Wong, Kauffman, & Lloyd, 1991). Yet there has been little systematic study of teacher characteristics and their impact on interactions with students with ADHD (or other "difficult" student populations).

Although goodness-of-fit has conceptual appeal, it has nonetheless been difficult to operationalize. Goodness-of-fit can be conceived as consisting of objective and subjective components (Siefer, 1993). It is *objective* in the sense that specific behaviors can be examined in the context of the specific expectations or preferences of interaction partners. Objectively defined goodness-of-fit can include (1) objective behavior matching (a process of comparing characteristics of a child and an adult for degree of fit) and (2) objective expectation–behavior matching (a process of comparing adult expectations and child characteristics for degree of fit). Goodness-of-fit is *subjective* in the sense that persons may experience the "objective" degree of fit very differently, both cognitively (i.e., how is a behavior interpreted?) and affectively (i.e., how do the interpretations feel?). Subjectively defined goodness-of-fit can include analyses of the degree to which a child's behavior is experienced as stressful by an adult, the adult's cognitive and affective appraisal of these stressors, and the social supports available to aid in adaptively coping with the experienced stress (e.g., Cutrona & Troutman, 1986; Hammen, 1992).

With goodness-of-fit thusly defined, a connection can be made between goodness-of-fit and the existing literature regarding teachers and behaviorally challenging students. Teacher expectations, an important aspect of objectively defined goodness-of-fit, have been the focus of a considerable number of studies, although the preponderance of such studies has explored the self-fulfilling role of these expectations (for a comprehensive review of this literature, see Good & Brophy, 1991). More recent studies have examined teachers' behavioral expectations of their students, and these studies seem more directly related to the goodness-of-fit issue. For example, researchers have shown that most classroom teachers have similar expectations regarding successful student adjustment. Such adjustment is characterized by a behavioral repertoire that (1) facilitates academic performance (e.g., listening to the teacher, following instructions and directions, working on assigned tasks, complying with teacher requests) and (b) is marked by the absence of disruptive or unusual behaviors that the teacher has difficulty coping with or finds objectionable or that challenge the teacher's authority and disrupt the classroom atmosphere (Hersh & Walker, 1983; Kerr & Zigmond, 1986). Students with ADHD clearly do not fit this description of the model behavioral profile. By definition, therefore, their style of behaving is likely to heighten tension in their interactions with teachers.

Yet the issue of teacher expectations is probably not so simple; there is, in fact, little evidence to support the belief that this disparity between teachers' behavioral expectations and the behavior of students with ADHD leads to circumscribed outcomes. Indeed, if there is modest variability in teachers' behavioral expectations, then these expectations would actually serve as a poor predictor of student–teacher compatibility. Are there related, but more variable, aspects of teacher expectations that might prove to be more potent contributors to objectively defined goodness-of-fit? Greater variability has been found in teachers' views regarding the degree to which various adaptive behaviors are *critical* to a student's success in their classrooms (Lloyd, Kauffman, Landrum, & Roe, 1991), and this finding suggests that *flexibility* of teacher expectations may be a more variable (and predictive) construct. If a teacher expects "3rd-graders to act like 3rd-graders," and there is little flexibility in this expectation, then one might anticipate greater tension in that teacher's interactions with a student with ADHD who is likely to be lagging developmentally in some critical areas (e.g., attention span, self-regulation, and social maturity). If a teacher's expectation that 3rd-graders will act like 3rd-graders is flexible and allows for variations based on each student's developmental status, one might predict less tension. (Interestingly, teachers typically do not have first-hand exposure to their new students prior to each school year; thus, flexibility of teacher expectations may be constricted by a reference point based heavily on grade norms rather than a reference point that would allow for greater variability in children's development.) Knowledge of ADHD and experience in teaching students so diagnosed may be important predictors of flexibility of teacher expectations. These hypotheses await exploration.

As regards subjectively defined goodness-of-fit, some researchers have suggested that "person-perception processes," in the way of teachers' interpretations of, reactions to, and tolerances for the behavior of students with ADHD, might contribute further to student–teacher compatibility (e.g., Whalen, 1989). For example, a variety of interpretations may be applied to the behaviors associated with ADHD. Such behaviors may be perceived, for example, as willful, attention-seeking, beyond the student's control, or the result of poor parenting. These interpretations/attributions may be a defining aspect of the compatibility that exists between a student with ADHD and the teacher (Brooks, 1984). Presumably, teachers react to and tolerate ADHD-related behaviors in diverse ways as well, and these reactions and tolerances may be different for the core behaviors of ADHD than for behaviors that may coincide with ADHD (e.g., oppositional defiance). These issues of subjectively defined goodness-of-fit remain relatively unexplored.

Greene and Abidin (1995) have proposed that subjectively experienced teacher stress may be one useful indicator of student–teacher compatibility, in the same manner that subjectively experienced parenting stress may be conceptualized as a gauge of parent–child compatibility. Although measures of teacher stress exist (e.g., Fimian, 1988; Moracco, Danford, & D'Arienzo, 1982), these instruments are intended to assess *global* teacher stress. A newer instrument, called the Index of Teaching Stress (ITS) (Greene & Abidin, 1995), was developed to measure the stress experienced by a teacher in interactions with a specific student, which relates more directly to the goodness-of-fit issue. Factor analytical studies on the ITS have documented four factors related to teacher self-efficacy and perceptions of student–teacher interactions. Subscales include (1) self-doubt/needs support (in working with a specific student), (2) low satisfaction (in teaching the student), (3) frustration working with the student, and (4) frustration working with the student's parents.

Might other teacher characteristics be related to student–teacher compatibility? Good and Brophy (1991) have suggested that a teacher's behavior management practices may also contribute to the nature of interactions between students and teachers. There is certainly ample evidence from the parenting literature to suggest that behavior management practices may influence the nature of child–parent interactions and the degree to which a child's behavior is viewed as deviant and stressful (e.g., Brody & Forehand, 1986; Webster-Stratton, 1988). For example, researchers have examined differences in parent–child interactions between "hyperactive" and "normal" children and found that hyperactive children are more negative and less compliant in interchanges with their mothers than are normal children and that the mothers of hyperactive children are more negative and commanding than are mothers of normal children (e.g., Campbell, Breaux, Ewing, Szumowski, & Pierce, 1986; Cohen, Sullivan, Minde, Novak, & Keene, 1983). In a comprehensive review, Kendziora and O'Leary (1993) identified various parent characteristics that contribute to "dysfunctional" interactions between parent and child. The parent characteristics include (1) lack of involvement and responding to the child with insufficient warmth and stimulation, (2) being overly harsh and controlling, (3) an inability to establish reasonable expectations and limits for the child, (4) inadvertently attending to inappropriate behavior, (5) being vague or attacking in communicating with the child, (6) inconsistency and ineptitude in handling situations that call for discipline, and (7) being too gentle, lengthy, or delayed in dealing with misbehavior. Many of these characteristics have possible application to interactions between teachers and children with ADHD, but exploration of this possibility has been limited to a select few studies (e.g., Whalen, Henker, & Dotemoto, 1980). The parenting literature is also fairly definitive regarding the negative impact of parental psychopathology (e.g., maternal depression) on parent–child interactions (e.g., Lahey, Piacentini, McBurnett, Stone, Hartdagen, & Hynd, 1988). Although it is probably safe to assume a narrower range of psychopathology in teachers, teacher personality variables should not be ignored in analyses of student–teacher compatibility.

Good and Brophy (1991) have also suggested that the manner in which a teacher goes about instructing students, and the classroom climate that emanates from these teaching practices, may impact upon student–teacher compatibility. What teaching practices may be relevant? A recent study involving a nationwide panel of experts representing general and special education identified and validated 96 teaching practices as being essential to the "effective" teaching of students with "mild handicaps" in regular classrooms (Cannon, Idol, & West, 1992). These practices include the broad areas of assessment and diagnosis (i.e., of student learning needs and patterns), instructional content, instructional practices, planning and managing the teaching and learning environment, and monitoring and evaluation procedures (i.e., for gauging student progress). Included among the 96 teaching practices were the following: assessment of the teacher/learning environment for students with academic or behavioral problems, or both; adjustment and modification of curriculum materials to meet individual student needs; teaching appropriate social skills and providing ample opportunities for practice; providing content to students through student–teacher interaction rather than relying on curricular materials to convey information; minimizing student errors by choosing tasks that students can handle without frustration and monitoring performance to provide immediate help and corrective feedback when needed; establishing positive, interactive communication with students to prevent problems and manage problems as they arise; creating a classroom climate that is warm, supportive, and convivial and that provides equal learning opportunities, but is also outcome-oriented; and maintaining a positive emotional climate through programs that increase self-esteem and acceptance of physical, ethnic, and intellectual differences among students. While these practices were identified as essential to the teaching of mildly handicapped students, they may also have relevance for the teaching of students with ADHD. As yet, however, there are no studies directly examining the extent to which the presence (or absence) of these or other specific teaching practices influences student–teacher compatibility of students with ADHD.

Presumably, other teacher characteristics may contribute to student–teacher compatibility. The foregoing survey of possibilities is by no means exhaustive, but is instead intended to serve as a heuristic for additional hypotheses and investigations.

One additional question remains before we move to a different compatibility issue: What are the implications of student–teacher compatibility for the manner in which ADHD is diagnosed? Because none of the direct measures developed to quantify difficulties with attention span, impulse control, and vigilance has thus far proven to have unequivocal diagnostic utility (e.g., DuPaul, Anastopoulos, Shelton, Guevremont, & Metevia, 1992), a diagnosis of ADHD is frequently based on a child's standing (relative to the norm) on objective behavior checklists (Costello, Loeber, & Stouthamer-Loeber, 1991). On such checklists, teachers (and parents) rate the degree to which various behaviors are present or problematic, and these ratings are thought to provide the most objective data regarding the degree to which a child's behavior meets the criterion of developmental deviance central to the diagnosis of ADHD.

The limitations of behavior checklists are fairly well documented (e.g., Schaughency & Rothlind, 1991; Stanger & Lewis, 1993) and include inaccurate reporter recall regarding certain behaviors, reporter bias (in which the rater over- or underestimates the occurrence of particular behaviors), and reporter misinterpretation of checklist items. Checklist ratings also may be influenced by various characteristics of informants, including their intelligence, education, and emotional status at the time ratings are completed (Barkley, 1990). Thus, there is some suggestion that a teacher's ratings of a particular child are influenced by characteristics of both teacher *and* child and may be conceptualized as a reflection of student–teacher *compatibility* rather than as a definitive account of the child's behavior.

From a goodness-of-fit perspective, behavior ratings are better understood as an index of *this* child's *interactions* with *this* teacher in *this* classroom environment (Greene, 1995), a view that acknowledges the potential variability in teachers' tolerances, perceptions, and responses. Sparse attention has been paid to interteacher variability in rating the presence and severity of ADHD behavior and the possible explanatory mechanisms of this variability. Given the potential ramifications of an ADHD diagnosis, this variability would appear to be an important area of inquiry. Possible variability in teachers' tolerances, perceptions, and responses also suggests that comprehensive and accurate diagnostic processes should include assessment not only of the child but also of the teacher, a point expanded upon in a later section.

2.2. Teacher–Treatment Compatibility

As noted above, treatment outcome may be strongly influenced by the degree to which recommended intervention procedures are compatible with the motivations, capacities, and style of behaving of the teachers responsible for their implementation. Thus, from a goodness-of-fit perspective, treatment outcome should include consideration of teacher–treatment compatibility.

Classroom-based behavior modification procedures represent the most commonly recommended teacher-implemented intervention for students with ADHD, and they typically involve a combination of token reinforcement and mild punishment strategies, as described in detail by numerous authors (e.g., Abramowitz, 1994; Pfiffner & O'Leary, 1993). Others have provided comprehensive overviews of recommended teaching strategies and classroom modifications thought to minimize the difficulties exhibited by students with ADHD (e.g., Algozzine & Ysseldyke, 1992; McCarney, 1989).

A portion of the research literature examining the efficacy of school-based behavioral procedures for students with ADHD has centered on identification of the precise behavioral treatment ingredients that are most effective for this population. Studies examining this issue have tended toward rather small sample sizes (for reviews, see Carlson & Lahey, 1988; Pfiffner & O'Leary, 1993). Nonetheless, this body of research suggests that while the combination of praising appropriate behavior and ignoring inappropriate behavior is successful in improving academic productivity, task attention, and social behavior in non-ADHD populations, children with ADHD seem to benefit most from more powerful or frequent incentives such as tangible rewards and token economies, and also seem to require judicious reprimands augmented by privilege loss or time out for egregious behavior (Pfiffner & O'Leary, 1993).

Are these behavior management procedures compatible with the expectations, capacities, motivations, and behavioral styles of teachers responsible for their implementation? The literature on treatment acceptability suggests a variety of factors, related to characteristics of both teachers and treatments, that may be relevant to this question. Factors such as perceived severity of a child's problem, nature of treatment, perceived effectiveness of a treatment, time demands involved in implementing a treatment, and teacher background variables have been found (with varying degrees of certainty) to influence teacher acceptability of behavioral programs (for a review of these factors, see Elliott, 1988).

For example, research has suggested that (1) greater knowledge of and familiarity with behavioral procedures increase treatment acceptability among teachers (Elliott, 1988); (2) teachers tend to prefer behavioral treatments that are more time-efficient (e.g., Witt, Martens, & Elliott, 1984); and (3) teachers' acceptability ratings are higher for positive behavioral treatments (e.g., praise, token economies) than for reductive treatments (e.g., time out, response cost) (Elliott, Witt, Galvin, & Peterson, 1984; Witt et al., 1984). More recently, replication of the latter finding has occurred as specifically related to interventions for students with ADHD (Power, Hess, & Bennett, 1993). In addition, while clinicians and consultants may be inclined to focus on individual outcomes, teachers may be more concerned with group outcomes (Fantuzzo & Atkins, 1992), and this concern may help explain teachers' relative lack of enthusiasm for individually administered contingencies and preference for behavioral interventions that employ group contingencies. Recent findings also suggest that teachers view combined behavioral and pharmacological interventions as more acceptable and effective for students with ADHD than medication alone (Power et al., 1993).

There would appear to be dissonance between the behavioral procedures viewed as optimal for students with ADHD (i.e., powerful, frequent incentives and prudent reprimands accompanied by privilege loss or time out) and teachers' preferences for procedures that are time efficient, positive, and group-oriented. Thus, the notion of treatment potency—referred to earlier as the practice of applying variable intensities of specific treatment components depending on the individual needs of a given child with ADHD—must be considered as it relates to the needs and characteristics of the *teacher* responsible for implementation. The characteristics and potency of behavior management programs deemed compatible for a child may be incompatible for a teacher whose capacities, motivations, style of behaving, and teaching demands have not been taken into account (Greene, 1995). Such programs would be expected to have low compliance, effectiveness, and maintenance (for a model of treatment acceptability incorporating this perspective, see Reimers, Wacker, & Koeppl, 1987).

2.3. Student–Treatment Compatibility

As defined above, student–treatment compatibility refers to the match between student characteristics and treatment ingredients. School-based interventions for students with ADHD can be grouped into three categories: cognitive–behavioral therapy (CBT), behavior therapy, and medication (Abikoff & Klein, 1992). How might a goodness-of-fit perspective broaden our conceptualizations regarding each of these interventions and potentially enhance their effectiveness?

CBT was initially viewed as a promising treatment for children with ADHD because of its focus on self-guidance and strategic problem-solving (Whalen, Henker, & Hinshaw, 1985). These treatment components had appeal because they directly targeted for change the perceived skills deficits associated with the style of behaving of children diagnosed with ADHD, most notably poor persistence of effort, difficulty sustaining attention, and disinhibition. Evidence that the effects of both pharmacotherapy and traditional behavioral treatment persist only as long as treatment is active contributed further to hopes that CBT would durably transfer across behavior and contexts in ways that medication and behavioral treatment did not (Whalen et al., 1985). CBT procedures include self-instructional training, anger control training, self-monitoring, self-reinforcement, cognitive modeling, and cognitive and interpersonal problem solving. Researchers have examined the utility of these procedures in addressing multiple behaviors in children diagnosed with ADHD, including academic performance, social competence, anger management, and impulse control. Diverse CBT programs and research designs have yielded disparate findings (see Fiore et al., 1993). The emerging general consensus, however, is that there is a relative lack of empirical support for the efficacy of such procedures (e.g., Abikoff, 1987, 1991; Hinshaw & Erhardt, 1991).

Issues of student–treatment compatibility may help clarify these disappointing findings and provide future direction for CBT outcome research. Some researchers have asserted that the underlying model providing the rationale for applying CBT procedures to students with ADHD may have been misguided (e.g., Hinshaw & Erhardt, 1991). Recent conceptualizations of ADHD as a performance deficit rather than a skills deficit lend credibility to this assertion. Specifically, many children with ADHD may actually possess the skills and knowledge needed to exhibit certain target behaviors; the principal effect of their ADHD is to constrain the performance of such behaviors at the instant they are required (e.g., Greene & Barkley, 1995a). If one accepts the performance deficit explanation, then it becomes apparent that the skills training model of intervention typifying most cognitive–behavioral programs has been incompatible with the actual needs of students with ADHD and the mechanisms that underlie their behavior. Hinshaw and Erhardt (1991) have suggested that more compatible goals for CBT procedures might be to (1) increase initial motivation for participation and persistence in behavioral programs; (2) fade the external reinforcers of behavioral programs via self-evaluation procedures; (3) help to program for refractory domains, such as anger management or development of prosocial behavior; and (4) enhance optimal attributions for successful outcomes.

The application of CBT procedures may have been misguided in other ways as well. For example, in most studies, the training of such procedures occurred *outside* the settings in which performance was most critical. The performance deficit view of ADHD suggests that continuous training in the setting(s) in which behavior is to be performed would be more compatible for students with ADHD. Indeed, theorists have posited that the further removed in time and space a treatment for ADHD is from the points of performance of a behavior, the less beneficial the treatment will be in assisting a child with the identified problem (e.g., Ingersoll & Goldstein, 1993).

Moreover, as with other treatment modalities for ADHD, it can probably be assumed that CBT procedures have the potential to benefit some students more than others (Hinshaw, 1992). Do certain student characteristics mitigate the effects of CBT procedures? If the developmental course of ADHD and its treatment are viewed as evolutionary and highly individualized, are there certain points at which CBT procedures may be more compatible with the needs and capabilities of some students? (Many of the treatment strategies described in the emerging literature on ADHD in adults are derived from cognitive–behavioral procedures.) Do intelligence, pretreatment motivation, severity and nature of ADHD-related behaviors, and family factors influence student–treatment compatibility? Can adjustments be made in CBT procedures in response to these student characteristics to improve student–treatment compatibility? Are there cognitions, such as those related to self-concept, self-esteem, and medication compliance, that are responsive to CBT procedures even if immediate effects on overt behavior are less impressive? These are compatibility questions that have received significantly less attention from researchers. Answers to these questions may ultimately improve our ability to match CBT procedures to the needs of students.

Finally, while many ADHD-related behaviors are probably reflective of a performance deficit, some behavioral patterns in some students with ADHD may reflect an actual skills deficit for which skills training would be indicated. This possibility obliges assessment of the degree to which a skills or performance deficit (or both) is most descriptive and explanatory in planning for the optimal match between student and treatment.

Pharmacotherapy is a second and more extensively studied intervention aimed at altering a child's style of behaving for the purpose of increasing compatibility with the classroom environment. Although opinions vary regarding precise neurological or biochemical mechanisms, there seems to be a growing consensus that the style of behaving of children diagnosed with ADHD has a physiological basis (e.g., Greene & Barkley, 1995a; Whalen, 1989). This physiological state and corresponding style of behaving may predispose such children to various secondary characteristics, including oppositional defiance, "cognitive inflexibility," poor academic performance, disorganization, and problematic social functioning (Abikoff & Klein, 1992), all of which may have negative implications for a child's long-term development and outcome. There is general agreement that stimulant medication provides temporary improvement in various aspects of the style of behaving of children with ADHD (e.g., overactivity, inattention, and impulsivity) and some associated features (e.g., noncompliance, aggression, negative social interactions, and academic productivity), but provides no significant improvement in short- or long-term academic achievement or long-term adjustment (Abikoff & Klein, 1992; Pelham & Hinshaw, 1992; Swanson et al., 1993). These conclusions notwithstanding, a certain percentage of children, the percentage being still debated but significant, do not evince a positive response to stimulant medication (e.g., Hunt, Lau, & Ryu, 1991).

Commendably, some researchers have examined medication effects from a transactional perspective. For example, studies have shown that teachers come to interact with and view students with ADHD more positively after the children are medicated (e.g., Whalen et al., 1980). As with CBT procedures, however, the majority of pharmacotherapy research has examined linear treatment outcome questions. How might a goodness-of-fit perspective expand our knowledge and change our perspective on medication effects? To begin with, it is rare for child characteristics (age, intelligence, comorbid conditions, family factors) to be taken into account in studies evaluating the efficacy of pharmacotherapy. Thus, we have little knowledge of possible "markers" that may predict poor response to stimulants. Additional secondary characteristics that often typify the style of behaving of a student with ADHD, such as explosiveness, irritability, sleep disturbance, and cognitive inflexibility, may not be satisfactorily ameliorated with stimulants. Further, some student characteristics (e.g., internalizing behaviors) may increase the likelihood of an adverse response to stimulants (e.g., DuPaul, Barkley, & McMurray, 1994). What medications, in combination with or in place of stimulants, enhance student–treatment compatibility in these instances? (For a discussion of this question, see Hunt et al., 1991.) To what degree is the impetus for medicating a student driven by other compatibility issues (e.g., student–teacher and teacher–treatment compatibility) that might also require intervention?

Behavioral procedures represent the third intervention commonly implemented for students with ADHD in school settings. In addition to identifying optimal treatment ingredients and potencies (discussed earlier), researchers have examined the degree to which behavioral "treatment packages" (combinations of behavioral procedures) are efficacious when applied on a larger scale. Although a clear test of the treatment package approach has yet to be undertaken, there seems to be a general consensus that behavioral treatment (1) improves various aspects of the style of behaving of children diagnosed with ADHD, but does not "normalize" the behavior of these children; (2) does not improve behavior to the same degree as medication when both treatments are implemented separately; and (3) does not produce significant improvement in behavior above and beyond that provided by medication (e.g., Abikoff & Gittelman, 1984; Abikoff & Klein, 1992; Gittelman, Abikoff, Pollack, Klein, Katz, & Mattes, 1980; Pelham, Carlson, Sams, Vallano, Dixon, & Hoza, 1993).

Can a goodness-of-fit perspective clarify these somewhat disappointing findings? Conceptually, at least, behavioral procedures differ from CBT and pharmacotherapy in that they are intended to help make the classroom environment more "user-friendly" for (or compatible with) the student with ADHD (rather than to make the student with ADHD more compatible with the classroom environment). This perspective regarding the role of behavioral procedures is not universally accepted; in many instances, such procedures are conceived in the same manner as pharmacotherapy (i.e., as an agent for fixing the child), rather than as part of a broad effort to engineer a prosthetic environment that optimizes adaptation for students with ADHD. If the true goal of behavioral procedures is to create a classroom environment that is more compatible with the style of behaving of a student with ADHD, then "normalization" of ADHD-related behaviors may be a misguided goal and reference point. In fact, expecting behavioral procedures to normalize the behavior of students with ADHD may actually lead to *increased* levels of frustration and tension in both teacher and student (which may, in turn, negatively impact upon teacher–treatment compatibility and broader issues of student–teacher compatibility). By contrast, if one expects that such procedures will help create an environment in which students with ADHD can more easily reduce the incidence of certain behaviors and more readily perform others, then behavioral programs should perhaps be more accurately conceptualized as one of numerous contextual factors that contribute to student–*setting* compatibility. We should not expect to see the rapid changes in student behavior resulting from changing the existing environment that we would expect in response to pharmacotherapy. Indeed, we may ultimately find that environmental factors unrelated to behavioral programs, such as the presence of an aide or paraprofessional in the classroom, characteristics of the classroom climate, or specific teaching and learning conditions, are actually more powerful contributors to student–setting compatibility over the duration of a school year.

3. Implications for School-Based Assessment and Intervention

As noted earlier, the goodness-of-fit perspective has additional implications for the manner in which ADHD is assessed. The complex array of factors that must be considered in the assessment of ADHD (e.g., Barkley, 1990; Greene & Barkley, 1995b) and other childhood behaviors (e.g., Mash & Terdal, 1988; Ollendick & Greene, 1990) have been reviewed elsewhere. Although these reviews have underscored the necessity of assessing the contexts in which behaviors occur, they have provided little detail about how to assess teacher characteristics that may represent a major aspect of such contexts. How can the assessment process be expanded to include teacher characteristics and other contextual variables? The following points, adapted from the various references cited above, and elucidated earlier by Greene (1995), have been proposed as critical to assessment of, and interventions for, students with ADHD in school settings:

1. Because ADHD-related behavior may not be consistent across time and settings, assessments must be systems-oriented and must incorporate the possibility of situational influences on behavior. Thus, school-based assessments for ADHD should be broad enough to include not only the child but also the multiple adults (e.g., parents and teachers) who interact (and have previously interacted) with the child in multiple settings (e.g., various contexts within the school and home). Diagnostic conclusions will be more definitive if there is stability in the child's behavior across time and contexts. In instances of inconsistency across situations, such as when a child's ADHD-related behavior is more frequent and intense in interactions with a particular classroom environ-

ment, the evaluation process must focus on finer compatibility issues that may account for the inconsistency. As discussed above, this expanded assessment process must by definition include examination of teacher characteristics that may be impacting upon a child's behavior. Such a process should increase understanding of the complex, reciprocal factors that affect child and teacher behaviors and facilitate appropriate interventions in the specific contexts in which incompatibility exists. Targets for intervention may subsequently encompass specific characteristics of the child, teacher, learning context, classroom environment, and tasks.

2. Assessments must be multimodal, involving different informants and methods. These assessments should include naturalistic observation (e.g., direct observation of the child in different contexts), rating scales completed by multiple sources, interviews with multiple sources, and review of other relevant information (e.g., psychoeducational testing). Although the necessity of naturalistic observation has been questioned, it is difficult to imagine circumstances under which a comprehensive understanding of ADHD-related behavior can be achieved in the absence of such observation. Inconsistency among sources would once again compel focus on finer issues of incompatibility, as described above, thereby allowing appropriate interventions in the specific situations (and with the specific individuals) in which (and with whom) incompatibility is evident.

3. A diagnosis should be viewed as merely descriptive, not explanatory. Thus, assessments must focus less on assigning a child to a category and more on obtaining information that is directly relevant to treatment. The qualification "relevant to treatment" refers to the usefulness of information in pinpointing treatment goals, the selection of targets for intervention, the design and implementation of interventions, and the evaluation of intervention outcomes. By itself, a conclusion that a child "has ADHD" provides no useful information about the contexts in which the disorder is most problematic. Pinpointing situations in which ADHD-related behavior is exacerbated (e.g., transitions between classes or activities, group discussions, standing in line for lunch, playing softball, interacting with certain teachers) helps identify the compatibility issues that should be targeted for intervention and thereby allows more educated and fine-tuned selection of intervention options. Furthermore, assessment should be viewed as an ongoing, fluid process, especially in school settings in which contexts can change dramatically from class to class and year to year.

4. Assessments must be conducted by persons who have the training and expertise in ADHD to execute them in an educated fashion and take into consideration the complex compatibility issues discussed

above. Such persons must have the skills to analyze, organize, integrate, and communicate the vast array of information gathered in the assessment process for the purposes of (a) arriving at a comprehensive understanding of a child's interactions with his or her environment(s); (b) requiring that additional information be collected when such an understanding has not been achieved; (c) making accurate judgments regarding the developmental deviance of a child's behavior; (d) determining the most appropriate persons and behaviors to be targeted for change and the interventions most likely to produce these desired changes; and (e) maintaining contact over the long term with the various adults who continue to interact with the child, are responsible for implementation of interventions, and/or are targets of intervention to monitor and maintain the ongoing assessment process and facilitate reformulation of "the problem" as necessary.

5. Interventions should be guided not only by consideration of the needs of the student with ADHD, but also by the degree to which recommended procedures are compatible with the teachers charged with implementation. Selection of intervention procedures should be viewed as a separate assessment process; teachers should be assessed along the various dimensions discussed above prior to design of an intervention program and should be active participants in the design process. Assessment should continue after intervention has been initiated to determine responses of both child and teacher. Finally, intervention should include not only traditional child-targeted strategies such as medication and CBT, but also teacher-targeted strategies such as education and training.

4. Implications for Applied Research

The preceding discussion directly and indirectly suggests a fairly extensive research agenda. As regards student–teacher compatibility, a wide range of teacher characteristics were hypothesized as contributing to objective and subjective fit with students with ADHD, including expectations, flexibility, tolerance thresholds, perceptions, attributions, knowledge of ADHD, level of stress, and behavior management and teaching practices. It would be desirable to enter these teacher factors into predictive equations of school outcome for students with ADHD. It would also be important to manipulate such factors to examine their causal influence. Additional investigations might include examination of the differential effects of medication or behavioral treatment, or both, on children with ADHD, depending on characteristics of the teacher, and longitudinal evaluation of the differential impact of various teachers on a child's outcome in the elementary or middle school years. While there are existing measures of teacher characteristics with acceptable psychometric properties, there is a clear need for additional valid and reliable instruments to be developed.

The discussions of student–treatment and teacher–treatment compatibility presented above suggest additional avenues of research. Our knowledge of the degree to which teachers implement behavioral programs as instructed remains quite limited. Also lacking is knowledge regarding the amount of training required for successful implementation, the points during actual implementation at which teachers begin to abandon the use of such procedures, and the teacher characteristics (e.g., expectations, flexibility, and stress) that are associated with successful or unsuccessful implementation and teachers' willingness to initiate and maintain the use of such procedures. Much of the recent research in this area has been conducted in experimental settings (e.g., summer camps), and it is unclear that results from such settings generalize to typical schoolrooms and teachers. Thus, it is important that such research extend into settings that are more representative of environments in which teachers function. The treatment-acceptability research has provided important information regarding the limits of behavioral interventions in school classrooms and the teacher characteristics that may impact upon acceptability. Nonetheless, because much of the information in this area has been obtained via analog methodology, data should be gathered during actual training and implementation.

The limited discussion of student–setting compatibility suggests additional issues that are germane to analyses of interactions between students with ADHD and their school environment(s). Are formal behavior management programs the most important contributor to student–setting compatibility, or are other climate issues (e.g., ratio of special needs students in the class, presence of an aide or paraprofessional) more influential? Teacher–setting compatibility may also be important to consider. Presumably, teacher factors such as job satisfaction, teaching gratification, grade preference, student population preference, and general school environment account for a portion of the variance related to interactions between a teacher and a student with ADHD.

There exist some noteworthy examples of previous attempts to apply a goodness-of-fit perspective to school-based studies of at-risk student populations. For example, a "template-matching" approach (Bem & Funder, 1978; Cone, 1980; Cone & Hoier, 1986) has been employed in analyses of conditions that impact upon educational transitions for such students. Template matching is a methodology by which behavior profiles of individual students are compared with behavior profiles of environments in which these students are expected to perform. In one study, templates of regular classrooms were compared with profiles of "behavior-disordered" students for the purposes of identifying (1) differences among classrooms and (2) potential interdependencies between students and teachers that must be considered when programming for more compatible transitions from one classroom to another (Hoier, McConnell, & Pallay, 1987).

In a second set of studies, Jacqueline Lerner, Richard Lerner, and colleagues compared the self-rated temperaments of children and the demands (expectations) of some or all of teachers, classmates, and parents with outcome measures including quality of peer relations, academic competence and adjustment, grades, self-esteem, behavior problems, and achievement test scores. It is important to note that only infrequently has the outcome variance accounted for by the goodness-of-fit model been greater than the variance accounted for by temperament scores alone (Lerner, 1984). This result has been due, in part, to modest variability in the expectations of others (Lerner, Lerner, Windle, Hooker, Lenerz, & East, 1986) and to the fact that these expectations have been the only factor considered in goodness-of-fit equations. Nonetheless, this method of testing goodness-of-fit holds promise for the numerous compatibility factors discussed above.

5. Implications for Teacher Training

One of the conclusions that might be drawn from the preceding discussion is that the match between a student with ADHD and her or his teacher is a critical consideration in planning for successful outcomes, and a natural extension of this conclusion is that teachers of students with ADHD must be carefully selected. At this juncture, however, we have (at best) a vague sense as to the teacher characteristics that might optimize compatibility for a given student with ADHD. Indeed, it is not always clear that a child's ADHD diagnosis should be the dominant factor dictating teacher selection. While the current practice of identifying teachers who are an optimal match for students with ADHD is unavoidable, even greater emphasis should be placed on providing all teachers with the knowledge and training necessary to be responsive to the needs of students with ADHD for the purpose of facilitating successful interactions between these students and critical aspects of their school environments. The notion of providing such knowledge and training only to select teachers is impractical; in the real world, there is a student with ADHD in every classroom. Many of the current programs geared toward providing such knowledge and training focus primarily on educating teachers regarding the characteristics of students with

ADHD and implementation of behavior management procedures. Once again, it is not clear that these training components are the most critical aspects of such programs. It is hoped that the research agenda described above will help identify the most essential teacher training ingredients.

6. Summary

The dominant focus of research on children with ADHD in school settings has been the effectiveness of various interventions—medication, behavioral procedures, and cognitive–behavioral therapy—on student behavior and academic performance. In this chapter, it has been asserted that while our understanding of the effects of these interventions is best classified as "incomplete," our understanding of other factors that influence outcome—especially characteristics of teachers and other aspects of classroom environments—may best be described as "embryonic." A transactional/goodness-of-fit perspective was proposed as a useful framework for incorporating these contextual factors into conceptualizations about, and interventions for, students with ADHD.

More specifically, it has been maintained that student–teacher, teacher–treatment, and student–treatment compatibility equations should guide future research related to students with ADHD, assessment and intervention practices, and teacher training programs. While such research efforts may meet resistance due to sensitivity on the part of teachers and school systems regarding the examination of these issues, the limit of what can be learned by merely examining student–treatment compatibility may have been reached (Greene, 1995). Many further important points may not be attainable unless we begin to examine the aforenamed compatibility issues more closely. As noted years ago by two leading ADHD researchers (Henker & Whalen, 1980), as one moves from the molecular level of research to more macrolevels of analysis, the phenomena under study require more qualitative methodologies and more speculative inferential processes. Initially, ethnographic studies may be critical to the identification of relevant variables and possible relationships among them. As researchers develop a more refined set of variables, hypotheses can be tested using quantitative, multivariate methods of research design.

7. References

Abikoff, H. (1987). An evaluation of cognitive behavior therapy for hyperactive children. In B. B. Lahey & A. E. Kazdin (Eds.), *Advances in clinical child psychology,* Vol. 10 (pp. 171–216). New York: Plenum Press.

Abikoff, H. (1991). Cognitive training in ADHD children: Less to it than meets the eye. *Journal of Learning Disabilities, 24,* 205–209.

Abikoff, H., & Gittelman, R. (1984). Does behavior therapy normalize the classroom behavior of hyperactive children? *Archives of General Psychiatry, 41,* 449–454.

Abikoff, H., & Klein, R. G. (1992). Attention-deficit hyperactivity and conduct disorder: Comorbidity and implications for treatment. *Journal of Consulting and Clinical Psychology, 60,* 881–892.

Abramowitz, A. J. (1994). Classroom interventions for disruptive behavior disorders. *Psychiatric Clinics of North America, 3,* 343–360.

Abramowitz, A. J., Eckstrand, D., O'Leary, S. G., & Dulcan, M. K. (1992). ADHD children's responses to stimulant medication and two intensities of a behavioral intervention. *Behavior Modification, 16,* 193–203.

Algozzine, B., & Ysseldyke, J. E. (1992). *Strategies and tactics for effective instruction.* Longmont, CO: Sopris West.

American Psychiatric Association (1994). *Diagnosis and statistical manual of mental disorders,* 4th ed. Washington, DC: American Psychiatric Association.

Barkley, R. A. (1990). *Attention deficit hyperactivity disorder: A handbook for diagnosis and treatment.* New York: Guilford Press.

Bell, R., & Harper, H. (1977). *Child effects on adults.* Hillsdale, NJ: Erlbaum Associates.

Bem, D. J., & Funder, D. C. (1978). Predicting more of the people more of the time: Assessing the personality of situations. *Psychological Review, 85,* 485–501.

Biederman, J., Faraone, S. V., Keenan, K., & Tsuang, M. T. (1991). Evidence of familial association between attention-deficit disorder and major affective disorders. *Archives of General Psychiatry, 48,* 633–642.

Brody, G. H., & Forehand, R. (1986). Maternal perceptions of child maladjustment as a function of the combined influence of child behavior and maternal depression. *Journal of Consulting and Clinical Psychology, 54,* 237–240.

Brooks, R. B. (1984). Success and failure in middle childhood: An interactionist perspective. In M. Levine & P. Satz (Eds.), *Middle childhood: Development and dysfunction* (pp. 87–128). Baltimore: University Park Press.

Campbell, S. B., Breaux, A. M., Ewing, L. J., Szumowski, E. K., & Pierce, E. W. (1986). Parent-identified problem preschoolers: Mother–child interaction during play at intake and 1 year followup. *Journal of Abnormal Child Psychology, 14,* 425–440.

Cannon, G. S., Idol, L., & West, J. F. (1992). Educating students with mild handicaps in general classrooms: Essential teaching practices for general and special educators. *Journal of Learning Disabilities, 25,* 300–317.

Cantwell, D. P., & Baker, L. (1992). Attention deficit disorder with and without hyperactivity: A review and comparison of matched groups. *Journal of the American Academy of Child and Adolescent Psychiatry, 31,* 432–438.

Carlson, C. L., & Lahey, B. B. (1988). Conduct and attention-deficit disorders. In J. C. Witt, S. N. Elliott, & F. Gresham (Eds.), *The handbook of behavior therapy in education,* (pp. 653–678). New York: Plenum Press.

Cohen, N. J., Sullivan, J., Minde, K., Novak, C., & Keene, S. (1983). Mother–child interaction in hyperactive and normal kindergarten-aged children and the effect of treatment. *Child Psychiatry and Human Development, 13,* 312–224.

Cone, J. D. (1980). Template matching procedures for idiographic behavioral assessment. Paper presented at the meeting of the Association for the Advancement of Behavior Therapy, New York.

Cone, J. D., & Hoier, T. S. (1986). Assessing children: The radical behavioral perspective. In R. Prinz (Ed.), *Advances in behavioral assessment of children and families,* Vol. 2. New York: JAI Press.

Conners, C. K., & Wells, K. C. (1986). *Hyperkinetic children: A neuropsychosocial approach.* Beverly Hills: Sage Publications.

Costello, E. J., Loeber, R., & Stouthamer-Loeber, M. (1991). Pervasive and situational hyperactivity—confounding effect of informant: A research note. *Journal of Child Psychology and Psychiatry, 32,* 367–376.

Cutrona, C. E., & Troutman, C. R. (1986). Social support, infant temperament, and parenting self-efficacy: A mediational model of postpartum depression. *Child Development, 57,* 1507–1518.

DuPaul, G. J., Anastopoulos, A. D., Shelton, T. L., Guevremont, D. C., & Metevia, L. (1992). Multimethod assessment of attention-deficit hyperactivity disorder: The diagnostic utility of clinic-based tests. *Journal of Clinical Child Psychology, 21,* 394–402.

DuPaul, G. J., Barkley, R. A., & McMurray, M. B. (1994). Response of children with ADHD to methylphenidate: Interaction with internalizing symptoms. *Journal of the American Academy of Child and Adolescent Psychiatry, 33,* 894–903.

Elliott, S. N. (1988). Acceptability of behavioral treatments: Review of variables that influence treatment selection. *Professional Psychology: Research and Practice, 19,* 68–80.

Elliott, S. N., Witt, J. C., Galvin, G., & Peterson, R. (1984). Acceptability of positive and reductive interventions: Factors that influence teachers' decisions. *Journal of School Psychology, 22,* 353–360.

Fantuzzo, J., & Atkins, M. (1992). Applied behavior analysis for educators: Teacher centered and classroom based. *Journal of Applied Behavior Analysis, 25,* 37–42.

Fimian, M. J. (1988). *Teacher Stress Inventory.* Brandon, VT: Clinical Psychology Publishing Co.

Fiore, T. A., Becker, E. A., & Nero, R. C. (1993). *Research synthesis on education interventions for students with ADD.* Research triangle Park, NC: Research Triangle Institute, Center for Research in Education.

Gittelman, R., Abikoff, H., Pollack, E., Klein, D. F., Katz, S., & Mattes, J. (1980). A controlled trial of behavior modification and methylphenidate in hyperactive children. In C. K. Whalen & B. Henker (Eds.), *Hyperactive children: The social ecology of identification and treatment* (pp. 221–243). New York: Academic Press.

Good, T. L., & Brophy, J. E. (1991). *Looking in classrooms,* 5th ed. New York: HarperCollins.

Greene, R. W. (1995). Students with ADHD in school classrooms: Teacher factors related to compatibility, assessment, and intervention. *School Psychology Review, 24*(1), 81–93.

Greene, R. W., & Abidin, R. A. (1995). *The Index of Teaching Stress: A new measure of student–teacher compatibility.* Paper presented at the 27th Annual Meeting of the National Association of School Psychologists, Chicago, IL.

Greene, R. W., & Barkley, R. A. (1995a). Attention deficit hyperactivity disorder: Diagnostic, developmental, and conceptual issues. In M. Breen & C. Fiedler (Eds.), *Behavioral approach to the assessment of emotionally disturbed youth: A handbook for school-based practitioners.* Austin, TX: Pro-Ed (in press).

Greene, R. W., & Barkley, R. A. (1995b). Clinic-based assessment of attention deficit hyperactivity disorder. *Journal of Psychoeducational Assessment* (in press).

Hammen, C. (1992). Cognitive, life stress, and interpersonal approaches to a developmental psychopathology model of depression. *Development and Psychopathology, 4,* 189–206.

Henker, B., & Whalen, C. K. (1980). The changing faces of hyperactivity: Retrospect and prospect. In C. K. Whalen & B. Henker (Eds.), *Hyperactive children: The social ecology of identification and treatment* (pp. 321–364). New York: Academic Press.

Hersh, R. H., & Walker, H. M. (1983). Great expectations: Making schools effective for all students. *Policy Studies Review, 2,* 147–188.

Hinshaw, S. P. (1992). Intervention for social competence and social skill. *Child and Adolescent Psychiatric Clinics of North America, 1,* 539–552.

Hinshaw, S. P., & Erhardt, D. E. (1991). Attention-deficit hyperactivity disorder. In P. C. Kendall (Ed.), *Child and adolescent therapy: Cognitive–behavioral procedures* (pp. 98–130). New York: Guilford Press.

Hoier, T. S., McConnell, S., & Pallay, A. G. (1987). Observational assessment for planning and evaluating educational transitions: An initial analysis of template matching. *Behavioral Assessment, 9,* 5–19.

Hoza, B., Pelham, W. E., Sams, S. E., & Carlson, C. (1992). An examination of the "dosage" effects of both behavior therapy and methylphenidate on the classroom performance of two ADHD children. *Behavior Modification, 16,* 164–192.

Hunt, R. D., Lau, S., and Ryu, J. (1991). Alternative therapies for ADHD. In L. L. Greenhill & B. B. Osman (Eds.), *Ritalin: Theory and patient management,* (pp. 75–95). New York: Mary Ann Liebert.

Ingersoll, B. & Goldstein, S. (1993). *Attention-deficit disorder and learning disabilities.* New York: Doubleday.

Jensen, P. S., Shervett, R. E., III, Xenakis, S. N., & Richters, J. (1993). Anxiety and depressive disorders in attention deficit disorder with hyperactivity: New findings. *American Journal of Psychiatry, 150*(8), 1203–1209.

Kauffman, J. M., & Wong, K. L. H. (1991). Effective teachers of students with behavioral disorders: Are generic teaching skills enough? *Behavioral Disorders, 16,* 225–237.

Kendziora, K. T., & O'Leary, S. G. (1993). Dysfunctional parenting as a focus for prevention and treatment of child behavior problems. In T. H. Ollendick & R. J. Prinz(Eds.), *Advances in clinical child psychology,* Vol. 15, (pp. 175–206). New York: Plenum Press.

Keogh, B. K., & Barkett, C. J. (1980). An educational analysis of hyperactive children's achievement problems. In C. K. Whalen & B. Henker (Eds.), *Hyperactive children: The social ecology of identification and treatment.* New York: Academic Press.

Kerr, M. M., & Zigmond, N. (1986). What do high school teachers want? A study of expectations and standards. *Education and Treatment of Children, 9,* 239–249.

Lahey, B. B., Piacentini, J. C., McBurnett, K., Stone, P., Hartdagen, S., & Hynd, G. (1988). Psychopathology in the parents of children with conduct disorder and hyperactivity. *Journal of the American Academy of Child and Adolescent Psychiatry, 27,* 163–170.

Landrum, T. J. (1992). Teachers as victims: An interactional analysis of the teacher's role in educating atypical learners. *Behavioral Disorders, 17,* 135–144.

Lerner, R. M. (1984). *On the nature of human plasticity.* New York: Cambridge University Press.

Lerner, R. M., Lerner, J. V., Windle, M., Hooker, K., Lenerz, K., & East, P. L. (1986). Children and adolescents in their contexts: Tests of a goodness-of-fit model. In R. Plomin & J. Dunn (Eds.), *The study of temperament: Changes, continuities, challenges* (pp. 99–114). Hillsdale, NJ: Erlbaum Associates.

Lloyd, J. W., Kauffman, J. M., Landrum, T. J., & Roe, D. L. (1991). Why do teachers refer pupils for special education? An analysis of referral records. *Exceptionality, 2,* 115–126.

Mannuzza, W., Klein, R. G., Bessler, A., Malloy, P., & LaPadula, M. (1993). Adult outcome of hyperactive boys: Educational achievement, occupational rank, and psychiatric status. *Archives of General Psychiatry, 50,* 565–576.

Mash, E. J., & Terdal, L. G. (1988). Behavioral assessment of child and family disturbance. In E. J. Mash & L. G. Terdal (Eds.), *Behavioral assessment of childhood disorders,* 2nd ed. (pp. 3–65). New York: Guilford Press.

McCarney, S. B. (1989). *Attention deficit disorders intervention manual.* Columbia, MO: Hawthorne Educational Services.

Moracco, J., Danford, D., & D'Arienzo, R. V. (1982). The factorial validity of the Teacher Occupational Stress Factor Questionnaire. *Educational and Psychological Measurement, 42*, 275–283.

Ollendick, T. H., & Greene, R. (1990). Behavioral assessment of children. In G. Goldstein & M. Hersen (Eds.), *Handbook of psychological assessment*, 2nd ed., (pp. 403–422). Elmsford, NY: Pergamon Press.

Pelham, W. E., Carlson, C. Sams, S. E., Vallano, G., Dixon, M. J., & Hoza, B. (1993). Separate and combined effects of methylphenidate and behavior modification on boys with attention-deficit hyperactivity disorder in the classroom. *Journal of Consulting and Clinical Psychology, 61*, 506–515.

Pelham, W. E., & Hinshaw, S. (1992). Behavioral intervention for attention deficit disorder. In S. M. Turner, K. S. Calhoun, & H. E. Adams (Eds.), *Handbook of clinical behavior therapy*, Vol. 2 (pp. 259–283). New York: John Wiley.

Pelham, W. E., & Murphy, H. A. (1986). Behavioral and pharmacological treatment of attention deficit and conduct disorders. In M. Hersen (Ed.), *Pharmacological and behavioral treatment: An integrative approach* (pp. 108–148). New York: John Wiley.

Pfiffner, L. J., & O'Leary, S. G. (1993). School-based psychological treatments. In J. L. Matson (Ed.), *Handbook of hyperactivity in children* (pp. 234–255). Boston: Allyn & Bacon.

Power, T. J., Hess, L. E., & Bennett, D. S. (1993). The acceptability of interventions for ADHD among elementary and middle school teachers. Paper presented at the annual convention of the American Psychological Association.

Reimers, T. M., Wacker, D. P., & Koeppl, G. (1987). Acceptability of behavioral treatments: A review of the literature. *School Psychology Review, 16*, 212–227.

Sameroff, A. J., & Chandler, M. J. (1975). Reproductive risk and the continuum of caretaking casualty. In F. B. Horowitz (Ed.), *Review of child development research*, Vol. 4, (pp. 187–244). Chicago: University of Chicago Press.

Sameroff, A. J., & Seifer, R. (1983). Familial risk and child competence. *Child Development, 54*, 1254–1268.

Schaughency, E. A., & Rothlind, J. (1991). Assessment and classification of attention-deficit hyperactive disorders. *School Psychology Review, 20*, 187–202.

Seifer, R. (1988). Assessment of children's temperament. In P. Karoly (Ed.), *Handbook of child health assessment: Biopsychosocial perspectives* (pp. 105–127). New York: John Wiley.

Seifer, R. (1993). Temperament fit, attachment, and depressed mothers. Unpublished manuscript. Providence: Department of Psychiatry and Human Behavior, Brown University School of Medicine.

Shaywitz, S. E., & Shaywitz, B. A. (1988). Attention deficit disorder: Current perspectives. In J. F. Kavanagh & T. J. Truss, Jr. (Eds.), *Learning disabilities: Proceedings of the national conference* (pp. 369–567). Parkton, MD: York Press.

Stanger, C., & Lewis, M. (1993). Agreement among parents, teachers, and children on internalizing and externalizing behavior problems. *Journal of Clinical Child Psychology, 22*, 107–115.

Swanson, J. M., Cantwell, D., Lerner, M., McBurnett, K., & Hanna, G. (1991). Effects of stimulant medication on learning in children with ADHD. *Journal of Learning Disabilities, 24*, 219–230.

Swanson, J. M., McBurnett, K., Wigal, T., Pfiffner, L. J., Lerner, M. A., Williams, L., Christian, D. L., Tamm, L., Willcutt, E., Crowley, K., Clevenger, W., Khouzam, N., Woo, C., Crinella, F. M., & Fisher, T. D. (1993). Effect of stimulant medication on children with attention deficit disorder: A "review of reviews." *Exceptional Children, 60*, 154–162.

Thomas, A., & Chess, S. (1980). *The dynamics of psychological development*. New York: Brunner/Mazel.

Thomas, A., Chess, S., & Birch, H. G. (1968). *Temperament and behavior disorders in children.* New York: New York University Press.

Thomas, A., Chess, S., Birch, H. G., Hertzig, M. E., & Korn, S. (1963). *Behavioral individuality in early childhood.* New York: New York University Press.

Webster-Stratton, C. (1988). Mothers' and fathers' perceptions of child deviance: Roles of parent and child behaviors and parent adjustment. *Journal of Consulting and Clinical Psychology, 56,* 909–915.

Whalen, C. K. (1989). Attention deficit and hyperactivity disorders. In T. H. Ollendick & M. Hersen, *Handbook of child psychopathology,* 2nd ed. (pp. 131–169). New York: Plenum Press.

Whalen, C. K., & Henker, B. (1980). The social ecology of psychostimulant treatment: A model for conceptual and empirical analysis. In C. K. Whalen & B. Henker (Eds.), *Hyperactive children: The social ecology of identification and treatment* (pp. 3–51). New York: Academic Press.

Whalen, C. K., Henker, B., Collins, B. E., Finck, D., & Dotemoto, S. (1979). A social ecology of hyperactive boys: Medication effects in systematically structured classroom environments. *Journal of Applied Behavioral Analysis, 12,* 65–81.

Whalen, C. K., Henker, B., & Dotemoto, S. (1980). Methylphenidate and hyperactivity: Effects on teacher behaviors. *Science, 208,* 1280–1282.

Whalen, C. K., Henker, B., & Hinshaw, S. P. (1985). Cognitive–behavioral therapies for hyperactive children: Premises, problems, and prospects. *Journal of Abnormal Child Psychology, 13,* 391–410.

Witt, J. C., Martens, B. K., & Elliott, S. N. (1984). Factors affecting teachers' judgments of the acceptability of behavioral interventions: Time involvement, behavior problem severity, and type of intervention. *Behavior Therapy, 15,* 204–209.

Wong, K. L. H., Kauffman, J. M., & Lloyd, J. W. (1991). Choices for integration: Selecting teachers for mainstreamed students with emotional or behavioral disorders. *Intervention in School and Clinic, 27,* 108–115.

Zentall, S. S., & Meyer, M. J. (1987). Self-regulation of stimulation for ADDH children during reading and vigilance task performance. *Journal of Abnormal Child Psychology, 15,* 519–536.

7

A Psychosocial Model of Children's Health Status

MELANIE J. BONNER AND JACK W. FINNEY

1. Background and Objectives

1.1. Overview of Children's Health Status

As a result of increasingly sophisticated medical advances, the prognosis for pediatric conditions once considered terminal has improved measurably. Moreover, with appropriate preventive health practices (e.g., immunization), the risk of contracting many acute and infectious diseases has been reduced substantially. Recently, however, the health status of American children has shown signs of deterioration and consequently has become a primary concern among health care professionals. This development is paradoxical inasmuch as, relative to other developmental periods, childhood is generally considered a time in which health should be optimal (Tinsley, 1992). In addition, the childhood and adolescent years should be regarded as a particularly efficacious period to begin preventive health practices, thereby deterring known antecedents to adult disease (e.g., cardiovascular disease). Moreover, these years are even more important in that health habits developed during this period are likely to endure throughout adulthood (Lau, Quadrel, & Hartman, 1990; Maddux, Roberts, Sledden, & Wright, 1986).

Often, researchers and health professionals cite global or static factors or both to account for the apparent demise in children's health status (e.g., poor educational programs, demographic factors). While important, these variables are limited in treatment utility, since they are largely descriptive in nature. Therefore, Tinsley (1992) has suggested that it is necessary to identify variables that are explanatory and can be

MELANIE J. BONNER AND JACK W. FINNEY • Department of Psychology, Virginia Polytechnic Institute and State University, Blacksburg, Virginia 24061.

Advances in Clinical Child Psychology, Volume 18, edited by Thomas H. Ollendick and Ronald J. Prinz. Plenum Press, New York, 1996.

modified with intervention. To accomplish this end, it is necessary to go beyond the biomedical model that has characterized much of the health literature to date. Instead, psychological, social, and behavioral dimensions need to be considered when attempting to assess and predict health outcomes (Kaplan, 1990). Until recently, however, little attention has been granted to these factors, despite the evidence suggesting that they play important roles in illness symptomatology (Mechanic, 1992). Additionally, assessment of these health status variables has generally been limited in scope and characterized by methodological problems.

Currently, health status in children is defined and measured with any or some combination of symptom checklists, illness histories, standardized questionnaires, and medical assessment/diagnosis. In addition, health status has been inferred from health-related behaviors, including the rate of primary care utilization, absenteeism, and bed disability (Watson & Pennebaker, 1989). Unfortunately, nonmedical problems (e.g., psychosocial deficits) are rarely assessed during visits to the pediatrician, with the result that potentially useful evidence for related diagnoses is disregarded. This neglect is compounded by the fact that assessment of child health status (regardless of measure used) is largely dependent on parental perception, interpretation, and report (Tessler, Mechanic, & Diamond, 1976). While the parent is a logical and informed source of such information, individual differences in symptom appraisal make somatic symptomatology subject to a variety of interpretations. These differences are complicated by the diversity of behavioral reactions that children may display in response to relatively similar symptoms. While some children "ignore" somatic sensations, others interpret such sensations as evidence of a serious problem. Regarding this latter group, however, there is often a lack of correspondence between the medical severity of the "illness" and the behavioral manifestations of pain. Such children typically present with subjective "symptoms" of illness, defined as indeterminate complaints that are diagnosed largely on the basis of self-report (e.g., headaches, stomachaches, back pain). In contrast to symptoms, objective "signs" are subject to medical verification (e.g., presence of pathogen) (Leventhal, Meyer, & Nerenz, 1980).

Children and adolescents who repeatedly present with symptom complaints have become an encumbrance to health care professionals, as these patients significantly overuse primary health care resources, and this overuse in turn may have significant health and economic implications (Whitehead, Busch, Heller, & Costa, 1986). However, because mental health is now considered an integral component of health status, the psychological status of such patients warrants investigation. In fact, according to Mechanic (1992), although these patients are generally considered a nuisance to the health system, their subjective symptom complaints may be the best predictor of subsequent morbidity and mortality and hence cannot be ignored.

Health status, then, is a multifactorial construct with variance attributable to more than the presence of identifiable pathogens. Current models need to be revised to reflect additional determinants and sources of variance in health status. Specifically, the socialization of health behaviors can be described as a dynamic process that involves a series of important interactions and transactions between the child and his or her social environment. The social context that appears to be paramount for investigating these transactions is that of the family.

1.2. Objectives

An understanding of the processes by which families transmit concepts of health and illness requires recognition of individual difference characteristics among family members that contribute to the patterns of interactions. Specifically, several child and parental characteristics that have been identified as important for the acquisition of health behaviors will be discussed. These variables were selected on the basis of supporting research evidence. However, while some of these variables are supported by considerable empirical data, others reflect the status of hypotheses that await investigation. Initially, the constructs are discussed separately to enhance clarity. Further important discussion, however, will illustrate that these variables do not function independently within a child, but covary with other developmental processes. After the multiple variables (child, parent, and family) that contribute to the variance in the construct of children's health status are explored, the significant role of the family context (particularly maternal negative affect) will be discussed in relation to socialization of health and illness behaviors in children. In the final section, nonorganic recurrent abdominal pain will be used as an example to illustrate how psychological processes result in learned illness behavior, thereby accounting for variation in medical care utilization.

2. Primary Child Variables Associated with Health Status

Four primary variables that appear to be important to the health status of a child are perceptions of control, coping repertoire, child psychopathology, and the pattern of medical utilization. A brief discussion of these primary variables follows.

2.1. Perceptions of Control

Individual differences in perceptions of control over stimuli have been found to vary with health status. More specifically, the locus of these control perceptions (e.g., internal or external to the organism) has emerged as an important construct for the prediction of health outcomes. Consistently, findings in the health literature have suggested that persons who perceive stimuli to be controllable maintain an internal locus, while the opposite pattern has been found for those who perceive stimuli to be uncontrollable (J. H. Johnson & Sarason, 1978; Lau & Hartman, 1983). For example, in adult populations, it has been found that healthy persons maintain an internal locus of control, while chronically unhealthy patients have an external locus of control (beliefs in powerful others or chance outcomes) (Wallston, Wallston, & DeVellis, 1978). The latter group often responds behaviorally with helplessness and avoidance of the stressful stimuli (LaMontagne, 1984). These findings suggest that perceptions of control may be one factor that moderates the impact of stress of health status (Lau, 1988).

It has also been proposed that the more internal the locus, the more knowledgeable the child is regarding health (Tinsley, 1992; Wallston & Wallston, 1981). Furthermore, there appears to be a progression with development from a primary reliance on external factors to reliance on internal factors (Parcel & Meyer, 1978; Wolfe, Sklov, Hunter, & Berenson, 1982). Thus, the degree to which children assume responsibility for their own health behaviors (including preventive behaviors) is thought to be positively related to the degree of internality in locus of control (Strickland, 1978). This degree is restricted, of course, by the level of independence expected of or tolerated in the child by her or his parent(s).

In an observation related to the transfer of responsibility for health care practices from parent to child, Pratt (1973) found that developmental methods of child rearing (defined as the use of reason and information, rewards, and encouragement of autonomy) were related significantly and positively to child health behaviors. The encouragement of autonomy accounted for the largest proportion of variance (11%) when compared to other indices (reason and rewards) and hence was considered to be the most influential on child health practices. Pratt also proposed that child-rearing practices that foster independence result in the development of positive coping strategies that consequently lead to healthy behavioral patterns in children. The psychological resources with which a child approaches stressful stimuli and illness symptoms will therefore be important for positive health status as well.

2.2. Coping and Stress

Coping has typically been conceptualized as a learned cognitive or behavioral strategy, or both, employed in response to stressful situations (Compas, 1987a; Lazarus & Folkman, 1984). Given the documented relationship between stress and disease, the child's ability to handle such stimuli is paramount to his or her health status. The interpretation of the stress–disease relationship requires investigation of both the child's coping repertoire and the resources provided by the child's social environment (F. Cohen & Lazarus, 1983; Compas, 1987a; Garmezy & Rutter, 1983). Regarding the latter, it is necessary to study contextual factors in the child's environment that reciprocally determine the outcome of a stressful encounter, particularly when symptomatology is temporally associated with the event (see Meyer & Haggerty, 1962).

Relevant empirical questions therefore include: What factors contribute to the development of a child's coping repertoire and what factors interact with the child's coping mechanisms to facilitate or hinder adaptation to a stressor? These are important questions when it is considered that stress experienced early in life can influence subsequent development (Compas, 1987b; Rutter, 1981). That is, early stressful events may initiate a series of transactions that have an enduring and significant impact on later transactions, particularly since it is during the childhood years that coping and adaptation skills undergo rapid development (Compas, 1987a,b). Unfortunately, there is little empirical research on children's coping behaviors in general, and even less in relation to health and illness.

The studies that have been conducted generally lack methodological rigor. For example, most employ scales that ask children to report how they *expect* they would respond if faced with a predetermined list of stressors, which may be quite different from how they actually do respond (Lazarus & Folkman, 1984). Therefore, an open-ended format, whereby the child describes how she or he responded to recent, self-identified stressful events might provide a more efficacious analysis of coping (Compas, 1987a; Compas, Malcarne, & Fondacaro, 1988). Furthermore, several scales have been developed to assess stressful events in childhood, but they generally rely on parental perceptions and reports. In addition to failing to assess the *child's* appraisal of a potential stressor, these scales assess only a limited number of developmentally relevant domains of stress that might arise during the childhood and adolescent periods. Moreover, they tend to focus predominantly on major life events (e.g., divorce) instead of daily stressors that have been found to be more predictive of illness behavior. To illustrate the limitations of such scales, a survey was conducted with 600 adolescents who identified over 200 nonredundant potential stressors (Compas, Davis, Forsythe, & Wagner, 1987). This finding suggests that current coping measures of stress do not adequately represent the range of stressors that may be encountered by children and adolescents. Consequently, these measures may underestimate the relationship between stress and coping at various developmental levels.

Recently, Ryan (1989) developed a taxonomy of coping behaviors in school-age children that revealed a pattern of increased coping strategies across development. For example, 8-year-old children endorsed only a few coping strategies that were primarily in the domain of social support (particularly support from the parent). This observation is consistent with the fact that with children of this age, parents may assume the responsibility for many or most aspects of their child's development including health behaviors. The 12-year-old children, however, identified coping strategies across several domains, including cognitive, relaxation, habitual, and distracting behaviors. This finding suggests that in addition to the increasing number of available coping strategies, the repertoire also becomes more diverse with development.

Regarding this developmental progression, Compas, Banez, Malcarne, and Worsham (1991a) reviewed studies that demonstrated that *emotion-focused* coping strategies (e.g., cognitive strategies employed to regulate the negative emotions that accompany stressful events) (Lazarus & Folkman, 1984) increase with development. This finding has been documented across diverse stressors, including medical (Band, 1990) and familial (Compas & Worsham, 1991) stressors. Although the development of *problem-focused* coping strategies (e.g., behavioral attempts to change stressful aspects of one's environment) (Lazarus & Folkman, 1984) occurs earlier than that of emotion-focused strategies, equivocal results have been found regarding specific developmental patterns.

While these data reveal some normative patterns in coping development, they do not tell us why some children fail to develop more diverse coping skills and how this failure may result in negative health implications. For example, while young children may initiate social contact with a caregiver when symptoms are experienced, it is expected that with increasing age, these children will mobilize other more independent coping mechanisms (e.g., self-care routines). To the extent that this independence is hindered by a poorly developed coping repertoire, subsequent experiences may have deleterious consequences for health status. Unfortunately, most physicians focus on a child's "disease" without acknowledging the coping repertoire that may have adversely contributed to the child's health status (Parmelee, 1986).

While this child characteristic does not account for all, or even a majority of, the variability in children's responses to stressful events, it is clearly an important one that begins to explain some of the differences in a child's vulnerability to illness (Mechanic, 1977). Still, other individual child factors and contextual variables that influence coping strategies that are mobilized in the face of challenges may reveal why some children manifest negative health consequences, and others do not, despite similar risk status. It is perhaps during the childhood period that coping skills should be the target of intervention as a means of quelling the potential impact of stressors likely to be encountered across development. One consequence of a poorly developed coping repertoire may be the development of psychopathology in children.

2.3. Child Psychopathology

As indicated in the definition of health status in the introduction, mental health is an important feature. The influence of mental health factors on health status is generally inferred from the rate of utilization of primary care by psychiatric samples (E. J. Costello, Edelbrock, Costello, Dulcan, Burns, & Brent, 1988b; Finney, Riley, & Cataldo, 1991; Jacobson, Goldberg, & Burns, 1980). Evidence of psychopathology, however, is frequently ignored or misdiagnosed by primary care physicians and has therefore been referred to as the "new hidden morbidity" (E. J. Costello et al., 1988b).

This issue was highlighted in a study that compared physician diagnoses of psychopathology with those based on structured interviews of children and their parent(s) (E. J. Costello et al., 1988b) Physicians completed a brief checklist that assessed their judgments about the presence and nature of emotional or behavioral problems or both in 300 children following the patients' medical appointments. Simultaneously, the families of these children were interviewed using the Diagnostic Interview Schedule for Children (DISC) and the Parent version (A. J. Costello, Edelbrock, Dulcan, Kalas, & Klaric, 1984). The results showed that the pediatricians recognized psychiatric disorders in 5.6% of the sample as compared to 11.8% identified on the basis of the DISC. Interestingly, the largest discrepancy emerged for the anxiety disorders (e.g., an approximate ratio of 1:5 for pediatrician/DISC), which include somatic complaints as part of the diagnostic criteria. Moreover, on the basis of the DISC, children with medical diagnoses in the category of "signs, symptoms, and ill-defined conditions" received the greatest frequency of psychiatric diagnoses. This result provides some evidence of underlying psychopathology for children who present with diffuse and subjective somatic complaints that are not amenable to verifiable medical diagnosis. Overall, while physicians were adequate in identifying healthy children, it was estimated that they failed to identify 83% of the "distressed" children. The authors were appropriately cautious when interpreting these results in light of evidence that structured interviews like the DISC tend to overestimate psychopathology.

Furthermore, structured interviews that comprehensively assess for psychopathology are often time-consuming and costly to administer and hence may not represent a viable tool for physicians. Efforts now need to be made to efficiently screen children so that the frequency of undetected mental health problems can be reduced and treated. This screening is particularly crucial given that primary care physicians are often regarded as the "gatekeepers" of health (E. J. Costello, Burns, Costello, Edelbrock, Dulcan, & Brent, 1988a).

Additional evidence of the "hidden morbidity" can be inferred from psychological intervention studies conducted in primary care facilities. Finney et al. (1991) evaluated the effects of brief targeted therapy in a sample of 93 referred children (ages 1–15) and evaluated the effects of treatment on children's medical care utilization. A sample of 93 nonreferred children (untreated group) were selected for comparison and were matched with the treatment group on the variables of sex, age, HMO membership, and completion of a pediatric primary encounter. Children in the treatment group presented with various behavioral and school problems as well as toileting and psychosomatic problems for which therapy was delivered by a psychological consultation service operating in a pediatrics outpatient clinic. The results showed that the treatment group evidenced improvement in psychological functioning and significantly reduced medical encounters (e.g., for acute illnesses and nonmorbidity) to the level of the comparison group. Reductions in utilization were attributed primarily to the decrease in services used by the behavior problem and toileting groups. Interestingly, the psychosomatic group, which had the highest pre-study utilization rate, evidenced a nonsignificant *increase* in medical services. Perhaps with this sample, it is necessary to identify other treatment targets (e.g., coping skills, perceptions of control, parent variables) that contribute to the maintenance of somatic complaints that ostensibly require medical care.

The results of these studies illustrate what has been referred to as the "offset effect" or the reduction in medical care use subsequent to mental health treatment. Finney et al. (1991) proposed that when other factors are present (e.g., psychosocial problems), acute or minor illnesses result in additional stress that is potentially reduced through medical care utilization. The "offset" occurs when there is an increase in mental health services for the treatment of psychosocial problems and a concomitant decrease in medical care services.

These data suggest, then, that primary care utilization may be one consequence of psychopathology. Given that such utilization is perhaps the most obvious behavioral index of health status, factors that contribute to it need to be studied carefully (Tinsley & Holtgrave, 1989).

2.4. Child Health Care Utilization

It has been estimated that infants contract an average of eight minor illnesses during their first few years (Haskins, Hirschibiel, Collier, Sanyal, & Finkelstein, 1981) and approximately four to six yearly between the ages of 4 and 10 (Parmelee, 1986). Many of these illnesses are acute problems that are largely manageable at home. A small but significant sample of children, however, will present repeatedly in primary care facilities, accounting for a disproportionately large number of medical visits (Finney et al., 1991). Utilization of health care, then, is considered a primary health behavior and should be considered in any discussion of health status (Tinsley & Holtgrave, 1989). Not surprisingly, a child's physical health status (typically indexed by symptom reports) consistently emerges as one of the most significant predictors of utilization (Newacheck & Halfon, 1986; Wolinsky, 1978). Interestingly, however, some empirical studies have found that actual health *need* accounts for less than one sixth of the variance in primary care use (Levy, 1980; Riley et al., 1993).

Therefore, while utilization rates generally decrease across development for normal samples, some children will continue to seek services for seemingly minor and medically untreatable conditions. The task, then, is to determine what besides the medical pathology is contributing to negative health status and accounting for variance in utilization. A discussion of child health care utilization, however, is limited in that children predominantly rely on their parent(s) to initiate primary health care services. In fact, most young children rely on their parents to interpret or tell them when they are sick (Palmer & Lewis, 1976). Few studies actually assess a child's report of symptoms.

In one provocative study, researchers designed an "adult-free system" in an elementary school whereby children were allowed to seek health services without the permission of the teacher (C. E. Lewis, Lewis, Lorimer, & Palmer, 1977). The findings revealed that 12% of the sample made over 50% of the visits to the school nurse. Furthermore, these children generally presented with vague or diffuse complaints of stomachaches and headaches. Interestingly, a disproportionate number of these children reportedly had behavioral and social problems, but an absence of any documented history of medical conditions that would explain their repeated visits. In fact, upon being asked about the etiology of their symptoms, many of these high users attributed the somatic sensations to a "math headache" or some other nonmedical, potentially stress-laden condition.

These findings emphasize that while some children might recognize that their "illness" is associated with a stressful event (e.g., tests), they still continue to seek *medical* services for relief. These results also suggest that such children may have learned to manifest their stress in somatic complaints.

Early reports by Mechanic (1964) indicated that maternal distress may be a significant predictor of when a mother will take her child to the doctor even when the child manifests relatively benign symptoms. Maternal psychological distress symptoms become masked in more "acceptable" symptoms for both the mother and the child (Mechanic, 1983). Therefore, we need to consider both parents' own utilization patterns and those on behalf of their children when investigating children's health status. Specifically, the shared variance between a mother's distress and her appraisal, interpretation, and subsequent reporting of her child's symptoms should be explored.

In summary, the four primary constructs discussed above (perceptions of control, coping, psychopathology, and utilization) are hypothesized to be child-related characteristics important to health status. These variables are likely to interact to determine—in part—children's health status. Research to identify these interactions/transactions is important to better understand how children's health status is determined and modifiable.

Additional factors that perhaps have less clear empirical precedents on which to base hypotheses about health status are considered secondary variables. In general, these variables are related to the child's cognitive development, particularly appraisal of signs and symptoms as well as conceptions of health and illness.

3. Secondary Variables Associated with Health Status

3.1. Symptom Appraisal, Interpretation, and Labeling

Most children learn at a relatively young age how to categorize symptoms, attach meaning to them, and treat them accordingly (Mechanic, 1983). Across development, the acquisition of new knowledge about health and illness occurs against this backdrop of existing health beliefs. Therefore, the knowledge acquired during this early socialization period has important implications for subsequent illness experiences and health status.

According to Mechanic (1983, 1992), the illness behavior process begins with symptom perception and appraisal. These appraisals appear to be a function of several variables including prior learning and previous experience (e.g., illness experience), "intuitive" models of body functioning, and cultural definitions of symptoms. Symptom labeling can therefore be highly subjective and idiosyncratic depending upon one's learning history.

Symptom evaluation is also influenced by the context in which it occurs. For example, when symptoms are ambiguous, the child typically relies on external cues (including the reaction of others) to give meaning to the physical sensations. The child will particularly tend to do so if she or he has not had previous experience with a particular symptom. Therefore, the label that symptom is ultimately given will depend in part on the interpretation provided by the parent(s). To explain this process, Leventhal et al. (1980) proposed a self-regulatory model whereby persons search for consistent information between their symptom experience and the label chosen to describe it. This cognitive process contributes to the construction of a framework for subsequent identification and labeling of an illness experience (Mechanic, 1972, 1992).

In addition to contextual influences, child's cognitive factors contribute to the appraisal process. Specifically, choosing accurate labels that guide illness interpretations and subsequent treatment behaviors requires a certain level of knowledge of health and illness Such knowledge is particularly important, since somatic sensations commonly associated with illness are similar to symptoms associated with emotional distress (e.g., stomach upset). A conceptually unsophisticated child may have considerable difficulty differentiating these seemingly identical symptoms (Parmelee, 1986). Through its effects on the appraisal process, a child's cognitive status may have important implications.

3.2. Concepts of Health and Illness

Several studies regarding children's concepts of illness have demonstrated the importance of cognitive processes for health status. Burbach and Peterson (1986) summarized data that illustrated that one's knowledge and understanding of illness and its causes may influence the onset, course, and recovery of illness. Specifically, Piagetian theory (Piaget, 1929) of cognitive and moral development has been adapted to explain how a child's understanding of health-related concepts follows a relatively predictable sequence.

Perhaps the most comprehensive description of this stage theory has been presented by Bibace and Walsh (1980). They demonstrated that children in the preoperational stage are considered the least sophisticated and conceive of illness as a concrete phenomenon, caused by magical processes. Conversely, children in the formal operational stage conceptualize illness as having both physiological and psychological parameters. While the existing research has been criticized for methodological problems (i.e., inadequate description of samples, instruments, and procedures used to assess developmental status; observer bias and expectancy effects; validity of assessment techniques; and lack of interrater reliability data), evidence of developmental patterns has consistently been reported (Brewster, 1982; Campbell, 1975; Lau & Klepper, 1988; Natapoff, 1982; Perrin & Gerrity, 1981; Simeonsson, Buckley, & Monson, 1979).

While the results of these studies are suggestive, only moderate relations have been found between children's health knowledge/concepts and *actual* health behavior (Radius, Dillman, Becker, Rosenstock, & Horvath, 1980; Tinsley, 1992). It is important to consider that a child's concepts are also formed by relevant experiences that can contribute positively or negatively to health behavior. Furthermore, the conceptual level of disease understanding that will result in adaptive functioning is unknown. In some cases, having a sound and accurate understanding of health and illness does not always predict health status even in cognitively sophisticated adults. For example, many adults understand the etiology (or at least the associated risk factors) of heart disease, and yet their behaviors disregard this knowledge.

Perhaps the most important implication of the cognitive research is its usefulness in the development of interventions or health curricula (Natapoff, 1982). That is, health interventions that fail to consider whether a child is cognitively capable of comprehending and processing the information may not be beneficial. Few health promotion or preventive programs aimed at children have been successful, and such cognitive incapacity may be one explanation for this apparent failure (Natapoff, 1982).

In summary, because cognitive status does not necessarily correspond with functional status, it is important to consider the relationship among the child characteristics (both cognitive and behavioral) that have been discussed in order to obtain a more comprehensive understanding of how a child's behavior contributes to his or her health status. These relations are briefly discussed below to illustrate how, together, these variables may account for a more significant portion of the variance in health status than any one variable alone. Following this discussion, the important contribution of parental characteristics is discussed as another potentially significant contribution to the variance, primarily through its influence on the child's socialization experiences.

3.3. Relationships among Primary and Secondary Variables

In healthy samples, there appears to be a developmental progression among most of the constructs described above (e.g., external to internal, less responsibility for health care to more, concrete to abstract concepts, limited coping strategies to more diverse strategies, frequent to less frequent utilization). Therefore, in the developing organism, the relationships among these variables may influence patterns of growth positively or negatively. More specifically, deficits in one domain may have consequences for other domains because of the hypothesized reciprocal nature of these developmental processes.

As summarized in the previous section, several studies have illustrated the role of a child's cognitive status as particularly pertinent to the appraisal and interpretation of somatic symptoms. In general, children appear to acquire health and illness concepts and knowledge in a relatively predictable sequence, with appraisal abilities becoming more sophisticated with development. A child's level of cognitive sophistication will therefore determine, in part, her or his ability to assume responsibility for health behaviors (Maddux et al., 1986). Cognitive status has been found to be associated with greater acceptance of responsibility for medical care and compliance with regimens (Strickland, 1978), as well as with health outcome (Wallston & Wallston, 1981). Older and more cognitively mature children would be expected to assume a primary role in health care practices, including preventive ones. Furthermore, it has been reported that in most samples, utilization rate decrease with age, perhaps in correspondence with personal increases in responsibility for health behaviors with age. Certainly, if a child's conceptual level is limited, he or she would be expected to assume less responsibility for illness prevention or treatment efforts.

Similarly, cognitive status is related to perceptions of control over symptoms. Having knowledge of the etiology of an illness may inform the child as to what factors are amenable to personal control vs. those that require external intervention. Children with relatively unsophisticated concepts and knowledge perceive less control and attribute it to external sources. That is, they do not understand that their own behaviors might have implications for the development and course of their illness and therefore rely on others (e.g., parents, doctors) to treat their symptoms. Conversely, children who have a better-developed understanding of health and illness concepts are likely to perceive that they have some internal control over the outcome (e.g., via practicing self-care). For example, Shagena, Sandler, and Perrin (1988) found that health locus of control mediated that relationship between illness experiences and concepts of illness in samples of chronically ill and healthy

children. Children with an internal locus demonstrated a more sophisticated understanding of the cause, treatment, and prevention of illness.

The label a child chooses for these symptoms (i.e., psychological or
somatic) will depend in part on the child's cognitive status and perceptions of control over the symptoms. If an external locus is assumed,
purely somatic labels may be chosen. Conversely, a cognitively sophisticated child will select appropriate labels that reflect the influence of
psychological processes on physiology and will enact self-care (internal
locus).

Finally, in a reciprocal manner, a child's conceptualization of an
illness will in part determine, and be determined by, available coping
strategies (Baumann, Cameron, Zimmerman, & Leventhal, 1989). That
is, as children become more cognitively sophisticated in their understanding of health and illness, so too do their coping strategies. Specifically, children evolve from having a coping repertoire consisting primarily of limited behavioral strategies to one that is more expansive,
providing them with a range of both cognitive and behavioral strategies
to employ in response to stressors (Ryan, 1989). Without some level of
cognitive sophistication, the efficacy of these more cognitive strategies
would likely to go unrealized and underutilized (Natapoff, 1982).

Accurate assessment of control of a stressor is also important to the
particular coping strategy that is employed (Compas, 1987a; Compas et
al., 1991a; Lazarus and Folkman, 1984). Although both problem- and
emotion-focused coping strategies are typically employed to some degree simultaneously, when a person's appraisal suggests that a problem
is within her or his control (e.g., internal locus), a problem-focused
coping strategy generally apppears to be most efficacious. Conversely,
emotion-focused strategies are typically more effective for persons with
perceptions of less control and an external locus orientation.

The relationship between coping and control factors will also have
implications for the amount of responsibility assumed. For example,
children with a limited repertoire of coping skills (both problem-focused
and emotion-focused) will likely perceive less control and will consequently place the responsibility of treatment in the hands of an external
agent. A study that explored the differences in coping styles employed
by persons in general medical contexts demonstrated this important
point (Miller, Brody, & Summerton, 1988). Two groups of patients in a
primary care setting who differed in terms of their symptom monitoring
(high vs. low) were studied. With the use of data from physician and
patient evaluations regarding medical and psychological problems as
well as responses on a coping style measure, differences between the
groups emerged. Specifically, physician evaluations revealed that patients who engaged in high monitoring had less severe medical prob-

lems and slower recovery than those who manifested low monitoring. Furthermore, the high monitorers reported less improvement in stress-related/psychological problems. Interestingly, even though the high monitorers had less severe diagnoses, they demanded more tests and requested more information from the doctors, yet they desired less active involvement in their care than the low monitorers. Therefore, they sought more information, but failed to use is instrumentally. In fact, the high monitorers indicated that they preferred to play a "passive" role in their care. Therefore, while high monitorers complain more about less severe illnesses, they assume no responsibility for self-care but instead rely upon external sources of control. While this study was conducted with adults, when it is considered that it is the mother who often makes medical decisions on behalf of her child, this behavioral pattern may be important to the socialization of health behaviors. The authors also point out that these findings have important implications for medical utilization. In particular, overreliance on external sources of control (e.g., physicians) suggests that high monitorers may overutilize medical services as a means of coping with their psychological distress.

3.4. Summary

In summary, children with unsophisticated concepts of illness may incorrectly interpret symptoms somatically and as more severe because they have fewer mechanisms to cope with the pain/illness. The availability of fewer coping mechanisms fosters an external locus of control and reliance on others to assume responsibility for taking care of their illnesses. When perceptions of control are low and external, and symptoms are appraised as exceeding one's coping resources, psychopathology may be the result. Hence, utilization of primary care may be the consequence, even for relatively minor ailments, thereby maintaining an external orientation and somatic labeling.

These variables are not only reciprocal in nature, but also subject to experiential influence. That is, while these constructs appear to follow a relatively consistent developmental progression in most normal children, a child's socialization experiences may alter the development of these processes. For example, a child could be functioning in the formal operational stage (as indexed by Piagetian tasks), but because of his or her socialization experience surrounding health and illness behaviors and attitudes, a sophisticated understanding of this domain would be inhibited. Therefore, each of these developmental variables is considered only one component of the child's complex behavioral system. It is important to consider the interaction among these variables and how this complex system is shaped through the process of social learning.

The available empirical literature suggests that parents play a preeminent role in this socialization process. Therefore, characteristics of parental health behaviors as well as factors that influence their own health status should be considered in any discussion of child health status. It is particularly important to consider these parent factors, since it is typically the parent who serves as the vehicle for treatment for childhood illnesses (e.g., the parent decides when to administer over-the-counter medication or when to consult a physician). Therefore, parental health beliefs and attitudes, family functioning, psychological status, and utilization patterns will be discussed briefly. This discussion will set the stage to demonstrate what the parent and child bring to their bidirectional interactions in the socialization context to influence and shape health behaviors either positively or negatively.

4. Parental Factors That Influence Children's Health Status

4.1. Health Beliefs and Behaviors

The majority of studies that have assessed the impact of parental health beliefs have been limited to investigations of sociodemographic differences (Dielman, Leech, Becker, Rosenstock, Horvath, & Radius, 1982). For example, socioeconomic status is consistently highly correlated with beliefs regarding the importances of preventive health practices by mothers on behalf of their children (Green, 1979). While these sociodemographic factors are important, as with child health status factors, it is necessary to identify parental behaviors that are more amenable to behavior change as well.

Tinsley and Holtgrave (1989) examined the relationship between mothers' beliefs about their control over their children's health and utilization of childhood preventive health behaviors. Results indicated that a high perception of internal control was significantly and positively associated with preventive health examinations and immunizations. It is further significant that these results were obtained even when socioeconomic status was controlled. Furthermore, these results were related to child health status as assessed by the Pediatric Complications Scale (an index of postnatal events that has been demonstrated to be related to health status) (Littmann & Parmelee, 1978). This study suggests that an internal locus may be crucial to the practice of preventive health care.

Further evidence of the importance of parental health behaviors was obtained by Dielman et al. (1982). These researchers demonstrated that in addition to demographic variables, parental health behaviors (e.g., nutrition, smoking, drinking, preventive visits to physician) were significant predictors of several child health behaviors. Although they found parental health *beliefs* to be important, they illustrated that this variable was operative through its indirect effects on parental behavior as opposed to directly influencing child health behaviors.

Similarly, the influence of beliefs on behaviors was illustrated in a study in which maternal health beliefs were positively related to the mother's willingness to give nonprescription medication to her child during illness episodes (Maiman, Becker, & Katlic, 1985). Specifically, the mother's attitude regarding her child's susceptibility to illness as well as her beliefs about the effectiveness of medication predicted her medication behavior on behalf of her child.

The importance of this research is underscored when the primary role that parents play in the development of their child's health status is considered. Moreover, it is generally assumed that the health status behaviors of adults have their origins in childhood. Although prospective and longitudinal data pertaining to this issue are limited, it is reasonable to assume that what is learned during the developmental years is integral to the development of a foundation on which adult health behaviors will be formed (Gochman & Parcel, 1982).

4.2. Family Functioning

Dysfunction has been found in families of children with poor health status (Riley et al., 1993; Schor, 1986). For example, using the Family Adaptability and Cohesion Evaluation Scale II (Olson, Portner, & Bell, 1986), Phipps (1991) found a significant negative relationship between family level of adaptability and acceptance of the sick role. Moreover, it has been suggested that stressful life events and maladaptive family contexts are implicated in the etiology or maintenance, or both, of acute (for a review see S. Cohen & Williamson, 1991), chronic (Sklar & Anisman, 1981), and psychosomatic illnesses (Minuchin, Baker, Rosman, Liebman, Milman, & Todd, 1975). For example, Mechanic (1964) found that mothers who report life stress and family dissatisfaction also report more illness in themselves and their children.

It is important to note that stress is not inherent in an illness situation, but is a product of the interaction between the situation and the family's capacity to deal with it. A stressful family environment may not have the resources or capacity to effectively handle the additional stress that might be created by an illness experience. Conversely, illness symptoms may be interpreted differently depending on the level of stress the family is enduring at the time.

One must consider therefore the impact of the family on a child's illness symptoms, as well as the reciprocal influence of the symptoms on the family environment (Eiser, 1990). Interventions directed toward altering maladaptive sequences of interactions between family members may be critical in producing adaptive changes both in family functioning and in the child's health conditions, since it is in this context that health behaviors are learned (Fiese & Sameroff, 1989). Evidence of the potential positive effects of targeting such family variables comes from intervention studies in which health promotion efforts have resulted in positive behavior change and maintenance when a systems approach was employed (C. C. Johnson, Nicklas, Arbeit, Franklin, & Berenson, 1988; Patterson et al., 1989). One intervention target in particular that may have implications for both family dysfunction and health status is parental psychopathology.

4.3. Parental Psychopathology

A number of studies have implicated parental distress as playing a role in health status. In an early study using four samples diverse with respect to age, education, and background characteristics, Tessler and Mechanic (1978) found a statistically significant relationship between several indices of psychological distress and perceived health status. Similar findings have been found in other community samples (Cockerham, Kunz, & Lueschen, 1988). Consistent with many investigations of health, however, the data collected by Tessler and Mechanic revealed that *physical* health status still accounted for the largest proportion of variance in overall health status. It should be noted, however, that these studies generally employed measures of physical health status that rely on the respondents' self-evaluation (e.g., via symptom reports). The subjectivity of such reports, together with data that suggest that symptom endorsement is not independent of psychological status (Watson & Pennebaker, 1989), calls into question the validity of such indices as proxies for physical health status.

The importance of this potential source of bias has been highlighted in more recent analyses of the relationship between physical and psychological health. One construct in particular that has emerged as a significant contributor to the variance in health status is negative affect (NA) (defined as anxiety, depression, hostility, and other negative emotional states). Specifically, health status variables that are difficult to verify medically (e.g., stomachaches, headaches, nausea) are significantly correlated with indices of NA. This correlation is not surprising, given that such ambiguous somatic complaints mimic symptoms experienced and endorsed by persons characterized by NA and are considered part of the diagnostic criteria for depression and anxiety disorders (American Psychiatric Association, 1987).

In an analysis of measures of health status (including symptom checklists and reports), Watson and Pennebaker (1989) found that many of these measures have a strong NA component. Their findings revealed that NA represented a distinct and significant source of variance in health status that they referred to an "somatopsychic distress." They suggested, then, that the items endorsed may represent subjective interpretations of visceral sensations that are significantly influenced by mood or emotional status (see also Croyle & Uretsky, 1987; Salovey & Birnbaum, 1989). Moreover, they revealed that the higher the level of NA, the greater the symptom scores, with correlations ranging from 0.30 to 0.50. These findings were interpreted as particularly robust, given that they were obtained across a variety of symptom measures that were similar conceptually but different in terms of content and form (e.g., response format, time frame, number of items).

The current data do not allow us to determine the direction of causality, and many would argue that the association between psychological distress and physical health status is reciprocal (Tessler & Mechanic, 1978). Watson and Pennebaker (1989) suggest, however, that it is not that psychological distress causes poor health status (historically referred to as the "psychosomatic theory") or that poor health status leads to psychological distress (termed the "disability hypothesis"); instead, it is the person's appraisal, interpretation, and subsequent labeling of symptoms that is influenced by psychological distress (termed the "symptom perception hypothesis").

Evidence against the *psychosomatic* theory comes from numerous studies in which NA has been found to be unrelated or related only indirectly to *objective* indices of health status (e.g., medical verification). Specifically, the causal relations frequently hypothesized are attributed to the shared variance found when one uses a measure of NA to predict health status as indexed by a health perception scale. For example, NA is moderately associated with chest pain (e.g., angina, which is subjective), which in turn is related to cardiac pathology (objective index). There is no direct relationship, however, between NA and the diagnosable cardiac problems. Additional evidence is found in blood pressure studies that revealed the opposite relationship from what is predicted by the psychosomatic hypothesis (Pennebaker & Watson, 1988). Specifically, high NA was found to be associated with *lower* blood pressure (both systolic and diastolic).

While these results are suggestive, other data are less conclusive. For example, in a review of the relationship between stress and infectious diseases, a moderate relationship was found between stress and the onset of upper respiratory infections, herpesvirus, and bacterial infections (S. Cohen & Williamson, 1991). Interestingly, however, a stronger association was found between stress and *illness behavior.* Therefore, NA may indeed represent a third variable that is operative in the relationship commonly found between measures of stress and illness. Precisely how NA influences this relationship remains inconclusive.

Regarding the *disability hypothesis,* it is intuitive that poor health might result in increased levels of *NA;* particularly in the face of chronic conditions involving pain and physical disability. However, in college samples, normal adults, and patient populations, little empirical evidence has supported a causal link. In none of these samples was Watson (1988) able to demonstrate increased levels of NA following the diagnosis of an illness. Furthermore, NA was found to be unrelated to the severity of medical diagnosis.

The data summarized above led to the development of the *symptom perception hypothesis* (Watson & Pennebaker, 1989). Broadly defined, this hypothesis proposes that persons characterized by NA attend to and complain about somatic sensations more readily because their heightened emotional status interferes with the interpretation of symptoms. Specifically, high-NA persons become more vigilant and aware of internal bodily sensations that otherwise might not be noticed. For example, Watson and Clark (1984) found that high-NA subjects appraised ambiguous stimuli as negative or threatening. Evidence from social–psychological studies is consistent with this hypothesis (see Croyle & Uretsky, 1987; Salovey & Birnbaum, 1989).

To summarize, neither the psychosomatic not the disability hypothesis can fully account for the association between NA and health status. Instead, it appears that one's subjective appraisal of somatic sensations is critical in defining health status. Regardless of the prevailing theory, it should be acknowledged that health status has at least two sources of variance, one objective and the other subjective. Many symptom checklists have established reliability and validity and correlate significantly with objective indices of health status. However, the significant subjective source of variance cannot be ignored. Another index of health status in which the influence of NA has been implicated and in which the appraisal of symptoms is important is in the decision to seek physician care. In particular, interactions between parental psychopathology and other health-relevant behaviors may be involved in the maintenance of patterns of high rates of utilization.

4.4. Parental Health Care Utilization Patterns

As reviewed earlier with regard to child health characteristics, the utilization of medical care is an important health behavior. Utilization patterns are generally found to be characterized by family aggregation, wherein the similarity within a family is greater than that between families. Recently, Quadrel and Lau (1990) conducted a multivariate analysis of adolescents' orientations toward physician use. Using structural equations models, these authors revealed strong associations between parental and adolescent utilization patterns across three types of symptoms including flu (e.g., sore throat, vomiting), fatigue (e.g., poor appetite, overtiredness), and serious illness (e.g., blood in urine, lump in abdomen). This effect increased in strength with increasing chronological age of the adolescent.

Moreover, several studies have revealed that it is maternal health care utilization that is the most significant predictor of child use of primary care facilities (Riley et al., 1993). Mechanic (1964) reported moderate correlations between a mother's propensity to seek primary health care and her tendency to take her child for services. Similarly, Schor, Starfield, Stidley, and Hankin (1987) found that family membership accounted for nearly one third of the variance in health care utilization patterns, with the influence of the mother being 2.3 times that of the father (correlations = 0.40 and 0.27, respectively).

As explicated in Section 4.3, NA has been found to result in misinterpretation or overinterpretation of somatic sensations. As a consequence, such persons repeatedly present in the physician's office with diffuse and ambiguous complaints that are not amenable to a verifiable medical diagnosis. For example, in an early prospective study, Tessler et al. (1976) reported that measures of distress were significantly related to both subjective and objective reports of utilization by enrollees in a prepaid group practice. These results were obtained even when level of illness and attitude toward physician were controlled. In fact, although the distressed sample did not evidence higher levels of illness, they presented more often with medical complaints when compared to the nondistressed sample. When distress was entered into a regression equation, it accounted for 16% of the variance in patient-initiated utilization.

More recently, Manning and Wells (1992) investigated medical care utilization by 4829 enrollees in a fee for service insurance plan. Results revealed that increased psychological distress (operationalized as negative affective states including depression, anxiety, and loss of emotional and behavioral control) was associated with increased use of medical services. While this finding was diminished somewhat when perceptions of physical health status were controlled (via symptom checklists), the association was not eliminated. Because objective indices of health status were not taken, however, the potential confound of distress on health perception cannot be ignored.

The studies summarized here point to the robust findings of the relationship between distress and primary care utilization. This behavioral pattern is complicated by the fact that medically treatable conditions are rarely found and psychological problems are misdiagnosed in such patients. For example, Katon (1984) reported that although depression occurred in 12–25% of patients presenting in primary care settings, it was misdiagnosed or treated improperly, or both, in numerous cases. Similarly, Nielson and Williams (1980) revealed that primary care physicians misdiagnosed depression in as many as 50% of the cases in their study.

Therefore, while *perceptions* of health status are frequently used as predictors of utilization (dependent variable), its validity as a predictor may be contaminated by the influence of NA, particularly when utilization rates are high. Moreover, given that a mother's utilization patterns are significantly associated with those of her child, this issue becomes directly relevant to child health status.

The child and parental variables discussed in the previous sections appear to have significant effects on the child's acquisition of health beliefs and behaviors. However, they do not function independently of one another. Rather, the socialization of health behaviors appears to be a product of a continuous and reciprocal interaction between the developing child and her or his constantly evolving social and familial environment. In attempting to understand how health behaviors are socialized, then, one must consider several contexts, in particular the family context.

5. Socialization of Health Behaviors

At the macro level, prescriptions of the child's culture regarding health standards and practices are important in definitions of health status. For example, differences in health practices dependent upon industrialization and other economic factors have been noted (Susser, Hopper, & Richman, 1983). On a smaller scale, other systems including the child's school and community play a role in the development of health behaviors and attitudes. The family context, however, has been recognized as one of the most fundamental contexts in which children's health behaviors and attitudes are socialized.

5.1. Family Context

As children progress in the rapid development of abilities to think, understand, reason, and subsequently make informed decisions about their behavior, various family contextual factors impinge upon this development positively or negatively. As with the attainment of other developmental milestones (e.g., social, motor, and emotional), the development of health and illness attitudes and behaviors cannot be separated from the context in which they occur.

Socialization experiences are likely to have an effect on subsequent experiences with somatic sensations as well as utilization of health care facilities (Maddux et al., 1986; Melamed & Bush, 1985). In addition to being a discriminative stimulus for symptom reporting, the parent has substantial authority to sanction the sick role. According to Walker and Zeman (1992), mothers are most likely to assume this position than fathers. At a minimum, then, this circumstance suggests that it is important to consider maternal variables when assessing and treating illness behavior in children. In fact, Maddux et al. (1986, p. 31) asserted that "the most important advances in child health in the past century have been accomplished primarily through efforts at changing the behavior of adults." Moreover, the socialization process that begins early in the life of a child appears to have long-term consequences, influencing adult patterns of health and illness behavior (Lau et al., 1990; Tinsley, 1992).

Using structural equations (latent variables analysis), Lau et al. (1990) provided evidence that behaviors and health beliefs acquired during childhood and adolescence remain consistent. Using a longitudinal data set of 532 subjects and one caretaker (the mother in 80% percent of the cases), the influence of parental health beliefs and behaviors on children's health beliefs and behaviors was explored. Data were collected from subjects and parents during the adolescent years and once yearly during college. The longitudinal multivariate model that was developed revealed a significant and powerful influence of parents as socializers of both healthy and unhealthy behaviors. Moreover, this influence endured, even after the child left the family context for college. While definitive cause-and-effect statements cannot be made with this type of analysis, the most powerful paths appeared to go from parent to child. The authors noted, however, that bidirectional influences should be explored.

What, then, is the process by which health behaviors are socialized? Social learning theory provides perhaps the most applicable theoretical framework for interpreting this socialization process. In particular, observation of parent health behaviors appears to be one mechanism by which children learn to practice both positive and negative health behaviors.

6. Social Learning Processes: Reinforcement and Modeling

6.1. Reinforcement of Illness Behaviors

In addition to being a discriminative stimulus for symptom reporting, symptom complaints may be for some children the only or the primary means by which they elicit reinforcement from a parent. Specifically, symptom complaints may come under control of external contingencies via reinforcement of the child's pain expression directly (e.g., sympathy, provision of medication) or indirectly (e.g., by allowing the child to avoid undesirable activities), or in both ways.

One example of reinforcement of pain in females comes from Whitehead et al. (1986), who proposed that the monthly menstrual cycle provides repeated occasions to experience pain and subsequent reinforcement by a parent (particularly the mother). In a study of 351 menarcheal females, the researchers found that their retrospective reports of how their mothers treated them when menstrual symptoms were experienced during adolescence were significantly related to the number of menstrual symptoms, clinic visits, and disability days for these same symptoms during adulthood. Information regarding encouragement of sick-role behavior was also independently collected from the mothers of the sample in order to avoid the potential confound of current attitudes and behaviors as well as demand characteristics. The results demonstrated specificity between the types of symptoms that were encouraged (e.g., menstrual pain vs. cold symptoms) and the symptoms later exhibited with consistency in adulthood. Whitehead interpreted these results from a social learning perspective. Whitehead's results also provide further support for the powerful and enduring effects of early socialization.

Certainly it appears necessary for the person to have a learning history that rewards such illness behaviors, and while reinforcement and secondary gains are probable consequences, their etiological role in pediatric pain has been challenged by some. For example, Liebman, Honig, and Berger (1976) reported an equivocal relationship between pain complaints and school avoidance. Additionally, Ross and Ross (1984) reported that only 35% of 740 children reported using pain for secondary gains when specifically queried about the issue. Therefore, unverified pediatric pain may be maintained by additional factors. In other words, reinforcement for somatic complaints may not be sufficient to initiate and maintain illness behavior for some children. Instead, direct modeling of health behaviors may be another important socialization mechanism.

6.2. Direct Modeling of Health Behaviors

According to Bandura (1977), factors that help determine whether social modeling will occur include the model's salience and credibility and the consequences of the model's behavior in question. Given the numerous interactions that take place between a parent and a child, parents exert considerable power in shaping child behaviors through modeling.

Patterns of health behaviors and attitudes modeled by parents significantly impact the child's subsequent health status (Tinsley, 1992). In particular, family members model specific behaviors that may serve as antecedents to health behaviors or that may influence the consequences of particular health behaviors (Sallis & Nader, 1988). For example, Dielman et al. (1982) illustrated that specific parental health behaviors (e.g., smoking, drinking, nutrition, exercise) predicted the practice of similar child health behaviors. Although no one behavior was found to be a consistent predictor, the results demonstrated the direct influence of parental health practices.

Lau et al. (1990) investigated the effects of social modeling, communication of beliefs, and explicit training as three potential mechanisms to explain parental influence on child health status. Using structural equations (described in Section 5.1), they found that while all three mechanisms appear to be important, the most significant support comes from direct modeling of health and illness behavior. Specifically, parental modeling emerged as the most significant influence on their children's baseline behaviors.

Additionally, Rickard (1988) found that compared to diabetic and healthy children, those experiencing chronic lower back pain demonstrated behaviors similar to those of the parent who experienced pain in the same area. Rickard attributed this apparent mimicking of pain symptoms to parental modeling during interactions between the parent and child.

Further evidence of parental modeling comes from Osborne, Hatcher, and Richtsmeier (1989), who examined the role of social modeling in pediatric patients with unexplained pain (UP) and explained pain (EP). Patients in the UP group included children who presented in a primary care facility for recurrent abdominal or chest pain. The EP group included children with sickle cell anemia. Data regarding current and historical familial pain experiences were collected independently from the parent and child, including pain location, intensity, and frequency, as well as consequences for illness behavior during health visits. The hypothesis that patients in the UP group would identify a model of pain/illness in the family environment significantly more than those in the EP group was supported. Significant associations were found between the child and the model in the domains of location, intensity, and frequency when child reports were examined, although differences were found in terms of location when parental reports were examined. Interestingly, however, parents who reported having *current* unexplained abdominal pain themselves also reported similar pain experiences in their children significantly more than those parents without current abdominal pain.

Finally, regarding consequences of pain, only 30% of the children perceived similar consequences for their own and the model's pain. Furthermore, group differences in the types of consequences that were provided were evident. When consequences were identified, the UP group typically reported positive or neutral responses, while the EP group generally reported negative consequences for their pain. Hence, it appears that other mechanisms (e.g., the presence of a pain model) were more important in the etiology and maintenance of the unexplained pain than was reinforcement. Consistent with Ross and Ross (1984), positive reinforcement and secondary gain may be important but may be ancillary to other social learning processes. Because pain is expected in sickle cell anemia patients, it perhaps was not as important or necessary for them to adopt additional pain behaviors from models.

Of particular relevance to the current position, when the children in the Osborne study were asked to describe the most salient feature of the identified model's illness behavior, only 44% identified pain as most remarkable. This finding suggests that other characteristics associated with the model's behavior are important to the child's illness behavior. Empirical evidence therefore supports the assertion that health and illness behaviors can be influenced by reinforcement and secondary gains or as a result of *direct* parental modeling of *health* behaviors (e.g., vicarious learning). These social learning mechanisms, however, do not account for all the variance in child health status.

Additional characteristics that are modeled and shaped by parents during the childhood socialization period that account for individual difference in health status need to be explored. This analysis requires going beyond investigating the direct transmission of *health* behaviors to exploring characteristics that make a child more or less susceptible to stress and illness. Lau et al. (1990) proposed a model termed *windows of vulnerability* to account for the enduring and pervasive influence of parents' beliefs and behaviors on their child's health status and at the same time acknowledged the influence of other socialization factors. Specifically, the model illustrated that parental influence has a strong and significant impact on children's health beliefs and behaviors unless the child is exposed to another powerful, nonfamilial agent (e.g., peers) during "vulnerable" periods (e.g., during the transition to college). During such periods, the child's behavior may come under the control of other variables. These data suggest that one must consider socialization and developmental processes that make a person more or less vulnerable to risk factors. Furthermore, this model places the learning of health behaviors in the broader context of socialization and development of other important child characteristics that have been demonstrated to influence health status (e.g., coping, control perceptions, parental factors).

Particularly germane to the current discussion is that parents may model *coping* skills and thereby teach their child to respond to stressors (including an illness experience) in particular ways. That is, the shaping of particular strategies prior to an illness experience will be crucial to the appraisal of stressors, and subsequent interpretation and labeling of somatic sensations and the family context may be the most important determinant of the child's capacity to cope with stress and illness. It follows that children whose learning context is insufficient for the development of effective coping behaviors may manifest recurrent and non-verifiable somatic complaints.

In particular, parents may model behaviors that demonstrate ineffective coping with stress and consequently lead their child to label sensations of distress somatically, so that the sensations function as a learned response to stressors. Given that hassles and stressors are an inevitable part of most persons' lives, inadequate methods of dealing with them could contribute to dysfunction and maladaptive development. Therefore, the coping resources available to family members may account for the differences in responses to such stressors and may explain why some children overutilize medical services for ambiguous somatic complaints. It is this lack of independent coping skills in a child's repertoire that Maccoby (1983) suggests leaves the children particularly vulnerable to the negative effects of stress.

Empirical and clinical research surrounding social modeling of coping mechanisms will be described in the next section to illustrate that it is within the family context that children do indeed learn how to cope with stressors. Additionally, the discussion will review data that illustrate that ineffective coping with stress is associated with negative health outcomes (e.g., infectious diseases, immune system dysfunction, and nonorganic illness).

6.3. Social Learning and Coping Responses

While it has been argued that coping includes instinctive/reflexive responses (Silver & Wortman, 1980), coping reactions generally refer to *learned* responses to stressful stimuli (Compas, 1987a; Lazarus & Folkman, 1984). Characteristics of a child (cognitive, social, behavioral, and developmental status) will play a role in determining what is experienced as stressful as well as what strategies will be employed to manage the stress (Maccoby, 1983). Moreover, given that the mother is the primary socialization agent, a child's coping skills cannot be fully understood without consideration of the mother's own ability to cope with stress, her affective status, and her expectations regarding her child's ability to cope (Melamed & Bush, 1985). Coping can best be conceptualized as a process that exists in the relationship between the child and the resources provided by his or her context (Compas, 1987a). If a child's strategies for controlling stress are ineffective, developmental tasks that are subsequently encountered may result in dysfunction, including learned illness behavior.

Given that organisms inevitably experience stress, even very early in life (see Kagan, 1983), the importance of coping is underscored. In a 2-year prospective study of stress and illness in adults, McFarlane, Norman, Streiner, Roy, and Scott (1980) found that perceptions of control and appraisal of one's ability to cope with a particular event determined whether or not one perceived the event as stressful. When both factors were weak, there was an increased chance of experiencing health problems. These findings help explain why the same event might be interpreted very differently across persons. Therefore, the available mechanisms by which the organism handles stress has important implications for psychological and somatic problems and, more generally, for development (S. Cohen & Williamson, 1991; Compas, 1987a).

In an analysis of parental coping and stress, Barnett, Hall, and Bramlett (1989) found that items endorsed on the Passive Appraisal subscale (defined as acceptance of problematic issues with minimal reactivity) of the Family Crisis Oriented Personal Evaluation Scales (McCubbin, Larsen, & Olson, 1981) were significantly related to scores on the Parenting Stress Index (PSI) (Abidin, 1986), including depression, low competence, and isolation. This relationship was deemed important by the authors, since the Passive Appraisal subscale has been found to be related to external locus of control perceptions and low self-efficacy (McCubbin et al., 1981). Overall, the results suggest that passive coping mechanisms are positively correlated with parenting stress, which consequently affected, and was affected by, interactions with the child. The child characteristics that emerged as particularly meaningful to these interactions (as assessed by the PSI) were distractibility and parental perceptions that the child was not experienced as a source of reinforcement. While these findings were not directly related to health indices, they underscore the importance of both parent and child behaviors to ongoing interactions in the family system. To the extent that dysfunctional coping patterns are present, there may be deleterious consequences for the health status of family members.

Although much of the empirical research surrounding coping and health has been conducted with children undergoing painful medical procedures, the results may be generalizable to other forms of pediatric pain (e.g., acute illness, psychosomatic pain). Research in the area of preparation for medical procedures has revealed consistent results regarding mother–child interactions. Specifically, the hospitalized children of mothers who receive interventions that increase support, decrease anxiety, and improve the practice of effective coping strategies show significantly better postoperative behavior than do control children (for a review, see Melamed & Bush, 1985). The children for whom intervention is provided appear less distressed and recover more rapidly.

In another study of children undergoing painful medical procedures, Jay, Ozolins, Elliott, and Caldwell (1983) accounted for a significant portion of the variance in child distress scores with three variables including child's age, the child's previous experience with medical procedures, and, significantly, parental anticipation of child's pain. Furthermore, parental trait anxiety scores correlated significantly and positively with the child distress indices.

Finally, evidence of parental behaviors that may foster or hinder coping was reported in a study of the interactions between mothers and their children during lumbar procedures. Blount, Corbin, Sturges, Wolfe, Prater, and James (1989) revealed that parental behaviors such as apologizing to the child and providing reassurances in the face of pain, as well as criticizing the child, were associated with increases in the level of distress reported by the child. Conversely, distress was minimized when the mothers encouraged the use of coping strategies by their children. Observation of child behaviors demonstrated that following this encouragement, the children engaged in deep breathing and used nonprocedural talk (e.g., they focused their verbalizations on something other than the pain experience). In the absence of such prompts, however, the children failed to engage in such coping strategies. These findings were supported by the results of a questionnaire study in which it was revealed that only one third of children who received coping skills training actually used the procedures in a subsequent medical procedure. With parental prompting, however, this probability increased substantially (Dahlquist, Gil, Armstrong, DeLawyer, Greene, & Wuori, 1986).

These studies point to the influence of adult behaviors on child coping behaviors. Furthermore, the results suggest that coping interventions appear to be beneficial to both the parent and the child. Targeting maternal coping behaviors may be particularly important given that it is the mother who will likely be most involved with caring for the child once the child is sent home from the hospital. Additionally, the effects may generalize to other less severe medical experiences, as was illustrated in a study of nonorganic pain. Specifically, Dunn-Grier, McGrath,

Rourke, Latter, and D'Astous (1986) studied interactions between children with benign intractable pain (e.g., abdominal pain, headaches) and their mothers using a protocol that induced pain in the area of the somatic complaint. There were no differences in the onset of pain across children. The children were divided into "copers" and "noncopers" on the basis of whether or not they continued to fulfill daily obligations of their current developmental stage (e.g., going to school) despite the chronic pain complaints. Pain diaries kept by the children revealed that although both groups experienced similar levels in the intensity, frequency, and duration of pain, the noncopers emitted significantly more negative behaviors during the pain protocol than the copers. That is, the noncopers verbally indicated anger, refusal, or discouragement. Because pain ratings were similar, however, the authors suggested that another factor must also have been operative that distinguished the copers from the noncopers. Specifically, analysis of the maternal behaviors revealed that the mothers of the noncopers discouraged coping behaviors significantly more than the mothers of the copers. Moreover, this variable emerged as most predictive in a discriminant analysis that classified 100% of the copers and 70% of the noncopers. This study demonstrated how the investigation of both child and maternal characteristics was important for a more complete understanding of illness behavior.

Assessing maternal coping behaviors may be particularly important in the case of younger children who may not have had enough relevant experiences to help diversify their own coping repertoires. Instead, they may rely on their mothers as credible models to teach them how to handle stress. According to Maccoby (1983), the ease with which a child returns to a stable state following a stressful event will depend in part on the way in which the mother responds to the child during the stressful experience. Because the mother and child will reciprocally influence each other's behavior, the skill with which the mother can foster active coping efforts on the child's part, while simultaneously engaging in her own coping behaviors, will help determine how well the stressful event is handled. Furthermore, such experiences may be critical to the manner in which subsequent stressful experiences are approached and handled.

In summary, parents must be regarded not only as models of health and illness behaviors, but also as significant models involved in the construction of a copious and diverse coping repertoire for the child. If parents do not provide adequate models and do not encourage their children to engage in such competence-building behavior, the consequences for social, emotional, and behavioral development could be negative. Therefore, while Parmelee (1986) describes how families can socialize health-enhancing behaviors, it is also possible for them to model and socialize health-inhibiting behaviors (Baranowski & Nader, 1985). Given the frequency with which acute illnesses are experienced in childhood, there are ample opportunities for the shaping of positive and negative behaviors. In particular, the child's coping skills and perceptions of control will be crucial to how he or she handles the illness. Furthermore, the amount of control fostered by a particular illness (e.g., acute, chronic, psychosomatic) will have implications for the efficacy of the coping strategies selected.

6.4. Social Learning and Control Perceptions

Although coping is considered a central construct, recall that deficits in one area are hypothesized to have implications for other areas. A particularly important relationship appears to be that between coping and perceptions of control. Just as the type of coping strategy varies according to the nature and appraisal of the stressor, so too do beliefs about the controllability of the stressor. In fact, Levine (1983) suggested that control is perhaps the single most important construct associated with coping. Additionally, perceptions of control can critically influence one's ability to cope with subsequent stressors (Levine, 1983). This finding is particularly cogent when considering evidence that parental locus of control is associated with perceptions of control found in the offspring.

In a longitudinal study of 947 older adolescents and young adults and their parents (80% mothers), Lau (1988) found that parental perceptions of control were a significant predictor of their offsprings' beliefs regarding locus of control. Furthermore, these subjects' beliefs were found to be relatively stable over time (in this study, across a 17-month period), which may suggest that they are reinforced over time. Lau also suggested that the development of positive and negative health experiences was dependent upon whether the locus of control was perceived to be internal or external. Specifically, he hypothesized that those who perceived it to be external (particularly those who attributed control to chance) would interpret an illness as more stressful and debilitating because of a perceived lack of contingency between efforts to change the situation and the outcome associated with those efforts. Lau further posited that with repeated occurrence of symptoms in those who perceived the locus of control to be external, depression could result (akin to the leaned helplessness hypothesis). Therefore, the type of control that is socialized and fostered by the parent can have important and enduring consequences for a child's illness experiences.

6.5. The Coping–Control Relationship

The two constructs discussed above, coping and control, appear particularly amenable to maternal influence. More specifically, it is the relationship between these two variables that has important implications for how stress and illness are experienced. Levine (1983) proposed that the socialization of coping and control begins during infancy when the infant is exposed to experiences of contingencies and control during early mother–child interactions. This proposal was largely based on the work of M. Lewis and Goldberg (1969), who hypothesized (p. 82) that "the mother is important because it is the contingency between the infant's behavior and her responses that enables the infant to learn his behavior does have consequences." This contingency is particularly important for the socialization of health behaviors, since it has been proposed that coping with stress and perceptions of control are directly related to health and illness (Lazarus & Folkman, 1984).

An example of the coping–control relationship was illustrated in the Dunn-Grier et al. (1986) study described in Section 6.3. Recall that mothers of children with greater pain were observed to discourage coping. Furthermore, the mothers of the noncopers were found to be more "intrusive" and "overinvolved" in the pain protocols. That is, it appeared that these mothers were actively fostering dependence instead of encouraging the child to accept responsibility for efforts that might function to reduce pain.

LaMontagne (1984) found that locus of control is related to the coping strategy employed by preoperative children. Children with an internal locus chose active strategies (defined as seeking information about the impending surgery, alertness to threatening aspects, detailed knowledge about the medical problem, and a readiness to discuss the surgery), while children with an external locus engaged in avoidant strategies (defined as having restricted knowledge and an unwillingness to discuss the impending surgical procedure). While these results were not related to surgical outcome, other studies have found a positive relationship between the use of preparatory information (whereby active coping strategies are taught) and postoperative adjustment (Melamed & Siegel, 1975; Peterson & Shigetomi, 1981).

Therefore, it is the relationship between coping and control that appears central to the development of learned illness behavior. Moreover, the socialization of these behaviors may be particularly influenced by maternal negative affect (NA).

7. Maternal Negative Affect and Socialization of Illness Behavior

Thus far, it has been established that the family context is a complex and dynamic system that contributes to child development in multiple ways. Furthermore, social learning appears to be the most important process by which behaviors (both positive and negative) are acquired.

Specifically, parents will serve as the most important models by which the transmission of roles that will be adopted during illness experiences are learned. Finally, the mother's health and psychological status appear to be particularly important for the socialization of child health behaviors, for several reasons. First, the mother is generally the one who appraises and interprets the child's symptom complaints and decides (on behalf of the child) whether or not to seek medical care. Once in the physician's office, the mother will complete symptom checklists or provide verbal descriptions of the child's symptomatology. This information will be used in part by the physician to formulate a diagnosis. Finally, when the child is sent home, the mother is likely to be the one who assumes the responsibility for attending to the symptoms and implementing the prescribed treatment regimen. Of course, with development, the child is expected to assume some of these responsibilities. How these early common childhood illnesses are appraised and treated (when the child is still dependent), however, constitutes an important socializing function for subsequent development of health and other behaviors.

Medical procedures as well as acute illness experiences during the socialization period provide a valuable context for teaching a child to cope with anxiety-arousing stimuli (Melamed & Bush, 1985; Walker & Zeman, 1992). Parmelee (1986) explored the behavioral effects of these acute illnesses and suggested that they serve as a significant socializing event for children, contributing to their overall development (behavioral, cognitive, social, and affective). More specifically, these experiences afford the children the opportunity to expand their repertoire of health-related knowledge.

Moreover, given that children are consistently exposed to parental models, the potential for similarities in the tolerance for a stressor and the manner in which it is dealt with can be communicated to others behaviorally. That is, illness reports can be shaped by the mother, which might explain the consistency and aggregation typically found in health/illness patterns between mother and child (Craig & Prkachin, 1980; R. Johnson, 1971). Consequently, the child who approaches a stressor ill-equipped cognitively, emotionally, and behaviorally might interpret and handle the stressor differently from another child. Repeated experience with such responses to stress may teach an otherwise healthy child that somatic symptoms in the face of stressors are functional. One important contextual variable that will influence the important coping–control process is maternal NA.

During the socialization period, a mother characterized by NA may not be able to conduct a veridical assessment (e.g., appraisal, interpretation, and labeling) of the child's symptomatic behavior. Her perceptions should therefore not be used as the sole index of health status. In general, however, pediatricians look to mothers for information while ignoring their role as important socializing agents whose own emotional status may contribute significantly to the initiation of the visit (Melamed & Bush, 1985). Therefore, because research has demonstrated that child illness is perceived as stressful by parents (Melamed & Bush, 1985), the way in which a mother deals with this apparent stressor may be partially a function of her own emotional status and her ability to deal with other daily stressors. For mothers characterized by NA, it may be quite challenging to deal with their own health status (physical and psychological) while simultaneously responding to another stressor, namely, a sick child's needs. This view is supported by McGrath and Pisterman (1991), who suggested that distressed mothers may contribute to family interaction patterns that hinder the development of coping skills. Therefore, effective coping resources may not be mobilized, a failure that may significantly influence the way in which the child is socialized to deal with stressors. One consequence, then, is that the experience of illness symptoms becomes even more aversive to both the mother and the child (Melamed & Bush, 1985). It is likely, then, that a mother characterized by NA teaches her child to respond to stress in a somatic manner.

A discussion of the etiology of maternal NA is beyond the scope of this chapter. It is important to recognize, however, that whatever factors contribute to maternal NA may also play a central role in the child's development. Models of child health status could therefore begin with maternal NA as an independent variable that affects child developmental variables (particularly coping and control) and could thereby explore one pathway to learned illness behavior and overutilization of medical services.

7.1. The Influence of Maternal Negative Affect on the Coping–Control Relationship

This review suggests that coping and perceptions of control are independently important to health status. It is a negative interactive relationship between these two variables, however, that appears to be influenced by maternal NA during the childhood socialization period. Developmental data indicate that it is in the 9- to 11-year range that "normal" children begin to become more realistic in their perceptions of control and assessment of contingencies (Compas, Banez, Malcarne, & Worsham, 1991b). That is, they become more capable of judging when their own efforts are instrumental (e.g., internal locus) in effecting changes in their environment. It is also approximately at this time that emotion-focused coping skills begin to emerge.

Highlighting the important coping–control relationship, Compas et al. (1988, 1991a,b) illustrated that what appears to be as important as the *type* of coping strategy used is its *match* with perceptions of control (see also Folkman, 1984). That is, a mismatch in the expression of these constructs could result in negative health outcome. Although both problem-focused and emotion-focused strategies are used simultaneously in many situations, it has been suggested that when situations are perceived as malleable, the predominant use of problem-focused coping appears most efficacious. This relationship between problem-focused coping and perceived controllability was found to be significant both in school-age children (Compas et al., 1991a) and in young adolescents (Compas et al., 1988). While the direction of causality has not been documented conclusively, it is most plausible that the relationship is reciprocal; that is, feelings of personal control will result in the employment of problem-focused coping, and problem-focused coping may enhance feelings of control (Compas et al., 1991b).

Conversely, in the face of stressors perceived as uncontrollable with behavioral efforts, the employment of emotion-focused coping strategies appears most effective (Folkman, 1984); that is, such strategies are most effective when the stressor is associated with emotional distress. Moreover, there is evidence that distress also influences the problem-focused/control relationship. That is, distress is exacerbated when *problem*-focused strategies are used when one's perceptions of control are *low* (i.e., when there is a mismatch between coping and control) (Compas et al., 1988, 1991a, b).

The relationship is important for the current model of health status because it has been shown that the relative importance of particular coping strategies may differ according to the nature of the stressor. For example, regarding health and illness (particularly aversive medical procedures), emotion-focused strategies have been found to be especially important (Miller & Green, 1985). Therefore, children not only need to have coping strategies available, but also need to learn how to judge the controllability of the stressor so that the most adaptive strategy is chosen. Weisz (1980, 1986) referred to this learning as a primary developmental task.

As indicated previously, there are developmental differences in the emergence of specific types of coping strategies, with problem-focused strategies becoming manifested earlier while emotion-focused strategies increase with developmental progression. Compas et al. (1991b) hypothesized that the earlier emergence of problem-focused coping may be the result of its easier acquisition due to parental modeling. Given that problem-focused strategies are generally observable behaviors, it follows that such behaviors would be learned more easily than cognitive/emotional-focused strategies.

In summary, when distress is present, health and illness are involved, and perceptions of control tend to be external, employment of emotion-focused strategies may be most efficacious. Interestingly, maternal NA is associated with all three of these variables. Therefore, the role of the mother (as the primary socialization agent) can be important in the etiology and maintenance of the symptoms and learned illness behavior. Hence, the mother's own health status (mental and physical) is paramount in the decisions made on behalf of her child.

Therefore, if the currently proposed model is viable, the presence of maternal NA during the primary socialization period will have important implications for how much control is fostered during a stressful experience and the available coping resources mobilized to handle the stress. In the next section, the various pathways to learned illness behavior will be illustrated using empirical and clinical evidence of nonorganic or functional recurrent abdominal pain (RAP). Though the etiology of nonorganic RAP is currently unknown; it is generally considered an illness amenable to social learning processes. In fact, Walker and Zeman (1992) found a significant main effect for illness type, with children reporting more parental encouragement for illness behavior related to gastrointestinal symptoms than for such behavior related to cold symptoms. The current model will therefore use RAP to illustrate one *potential* pathway to learned illness.

8. Learned Illness Behavior: Recurrent Abdominal Pain as an Exemplar

8.1. Recurrent Abdominal Pain and Social Learning

As suggested earlier, one pathway to illness behavior in children begins with social learning. This pathway can also be applied to RAP. Evidence of social learning comes from the findings that compared to dental patients and healthy controls, children with RAP have parents who also report symptoms of illness behavior (Robinson, Alvarez, & Dodge, 1990). Higher somatization by the parents of RAP children was also found in another study that compared them to parents of children with organic RAP and parents of healthy controls (Walker, Garber, & Greene, 1991).

8.2. Recurrent Abdominal Pain and Maternal Negative Affect

Consistent with the numerous findings in the literature that highly somatic patients exist in a matrix of contexts associated with dysfunction and depression (Mechanic, 1992), there is some evidence that suggests that mothers of children with RAP are indeed characterized by symptoms of NA. For example, several studies have demonstrated elevated levels of depression and anxiety in mothers of RAP children when compared to mothers of healthy controls (Hodges, Kline, Barbero, & Flanery, 1985; Hodges, Kline, Barbero, & Woodruff, 1985; Walker & Greene, 1989; Zuckerman, Stevenson, & Bailey, 1987) and mothers of children with organic RAP (Garber, Zeman, & Walker, 1990). While the RAP mothers in these studies evidenced higher levels of NA than mothers of control samples, they did not differ significantly from mothers of other clinic-referred samples (e.g., behaviorally disordered children). These findings are important in light of the results of Zuckerman et al. (1987) that children may more readily obtain attention from a depressed mother if they complain of somatic sensations. Consequently, these maternal models may shape the learning history of the child to respond to stressors somatically.

Therefore, it appears that a mother's NA and its effect on the socialization experiences of her child can contribute to adverse means of handling stress by the child. Whether the child responds somatically or with negative behavioral reactions, it has been proposed that both types of reactions are ineffective methods of coping with stress (Ryan, 1989). Consistent with the current model, then, RAP children may indeed experience psychopathology as a consequence of their learning history.

8.3. Recurrent Abdominal Pain and Child Psychopathology

Some evidence of child psychopathology comes from clinical reports that suggest that RAP children are anxious and "high-strung" (Apley, 1975; Stone & Barbero, 1970), although empirical studies with RAP children are inconclusive. However, RAP children do appear to experience more stress, anxiety, and negative life events than healthy controls (Hodges & Burbach, 1991; Walker & Greene, 1991). Walker and Greene (1989, 1991) also reported increased levels of depression in RAP children compared to healthy controls, but similar levels were found in the organic RAP group. It was also revealed, however, that stress levels significantly predicted symptom resolution in functional RAP but not in organic RAP. Additional evidence of the influence of stressors on RAP comes from Robinson et al. (1990), who found that compared to healthy children and dental patient controls, children with RAP reported more stressful experiences in the few months preceding the onset of pain.

Stressful life events should not be viewed as etiological for RAP pathology, but should be considered events that can contribute to maladaptive functioning. That is, the relationship is not linear, as it necessarily depends upon one's appraisal of the stimulus. As suggested earlier, NA may have its most profound effects on coping and control variables during socialization. In fact, Mechanic (1977) asserted that the patient's coping abilities may be more significant to the outcome of an illness than any biological indicator that is assessed by the physician. Moreover, Apley (1975) asserted that RAP is indeed a particular response to stress that results from inadequate coping abilities. Therefore, given the episodic nature of RAP, it is important to consider interactions that take place and the types of hassles faced on a daily basis. Whether psychopathology results or not depends upon how the stressors/hassles are appraised and labeled. It follows, then, that poor coping with stress may produce learned illness behavior (Garmezy & Rutter, 1983), such as that seen in RAP.

8.4. Recurrent Abdominal Pain and Primary Care Utilization

At about the age that emotion-focused strategies begin to emerge and realistic perceptions of contingencies develop, concepts about health and illness are also expected to become more sophisticated (Hodges & Burbach, 1991). Furthermore, children are expected to become more independent in health care efforts. Interestingly, this is also the time of the peak incidence of RAP (e.g., 9–11 years of age). Hence, it has been proposed that some RAP children are not equipped with the requisite skills to handle these challenges that are encountered at that point in development (Coleman & Levine, 1986).

One result, then, may be symptoms of psychopathology and consequent overutilization of medical services as a coping mechanism (see Finney, Lemanek, Cataldo, Katz, & Fuqua, 1989). Furthermore, Clyne (1961) suggested that parents may use the child as a "vehicle" to relieve their own distress by utilizing medical services. Utilization may therefore be functional for both parent and child. Specifically, utilization of medical care may function as a largely palliative coping mechanism whereby the mother and child *temporarily* feel better in the face of stress while ignoring the potential psychological underpinnings of the symptoms. Concomitantly, the avoidance of the underlying distress that is fostered by the utilization represents an emotion-focused strategy, whereby somatic complaints are dealt with solely in the medical context. While not specifically studied in RAP children, avoidance coping strategies have been associated with poor health outcome in children with other types of illness (e.g., insulin-dependent diabetes mellitus) (Hanson, Harris, Relyea, Cigrang, Carle, & Burghen, 1989).

The illness report is further shaped and reinforced by the physician, who attempts to understand and validate the symptoms through assessment, testing, diagnosis, and prescription of medication. Mechanic (1977) suggested that this process results in dependency on the physician, thereby delaying the patient's ability to acquire a sense of control over the "illness" (e.g., internal locus of control).

The manifest behavior (e.g., "illness"), then, has multiple determinants, yet, the principal determinants are not recognized by the physician. According to Oski (1981), routine medical examinations have greater potential for identifying psychological problems than they do for diagnosing significant medical problems in patients. The implication, then, is that routine screening for psychological problems could yield a greater prevalence of dysfunctional children than those with only physical disease. Tessler and Mechanic (1978) suggested that the primary care physician is not well equipped to deal with diffuse complaints with no readily verifiable pathology. Consequently, primary care physicians may exacerbate maladaptive and dysfunctional coping behaviors and foster dependency as a result of their limited mental health training. Of course, the physician's diagnosis is constrained by the manner in which the mother interprets and presents the symptoms. Tessler and Mechanic (1978) maintained that this presentation is part of a more fundamental problem whereby patients view health status globally, whereas the physician is concerned with specificity of diagnosis.

8.5. Recurrent Abdominal Pain and Coping and Control

Because of the nature of the stomach complaints (i.e., recurrent), the child is never fully restored to health. In particular, the RAP child is not exposed to the recovery process that is important to the acquisition of health behaviors. The child therefore fails to learn that health-enhancing behaviors are useful, and this lack of coping is reflected in the fact that the organism returns to its prior organizational state (e.g., via the recurrence of the stomachaches) instead of becoming more functional (Maccoby, 1983). That is, if the child continues to rely on external sources of control (e.g., physicians), problem-solving and coping skills do not undergo the normal developmental progression. Recall that Compas et al. (1988, 1991a,b) suggested that distress may be heightened when perceptions of control are low and problem-focused strategies are employed (e.g., physician utilization for "medical" symptoms), as appears to be the case with RAP children. This distress is exacerbated by the use of an ineffective and potentially dangerous emotion-focused coping strategy, namely, avoidance or denial of underlying distress via medical utilization. While such utilization may temporarily succeed in reducing emotional distress, it may simultaneously hinder the child from realistically addressing the problem, thereby deterring adaptive health behavior.

Evidence of avoidance was found in a survey conducted with mothers of children with RAP. Faull and Nicol (1986) found that the majority of mothers were disturbed by the physician's suggestion that the stomach pain, for which no diagnosis could be reached, could be attributable to "nerves." Furthermore, they rejected referrals to mental health facilities.

These biases of interpretation are characteristic of mothers with NA. Hence, they may teach their children to attribute their symptoms to factors other than psychological distress. Furthermore, an avoidant coping pattern also appears to be reflective of a delayed cognitive status. That is, it is not surprising that the illness concepts of children who are exposed to this type of modeling (e.g., denial and avoidance) have not reached the final stage of development according to Bibace and Walsh's taxonomy (i.e., psychophysiological). Lacking this maturation, the children do not acknowledge the potential involvement of psychological factors as instrumental to pain sensations. Therefore, a child who is faced with a math test or feels homesick may not have the cognitive understanding of the role of his or her emotions in the pain experienced. Instead, the child deals with the pain somatically.

Recall that children in the youngest age group of the Ryan (1989) taxonomy relied predominantly upon social support strategies (e.g., characterized by dependence on external agents). This reliance may be a consequence of a child's elementary understanding of health and illness concepts. That is, the child does not have an understanding of the underlying psychological factors associated with her or his stomachache pain and hence does not utilize more diverse cognitive coping strategies. Factors that contribute to the pain are therefore not treated and hence persist. In most children with RAP, the pain is indeed seemingly intractable. While it spontaneously remits in some cases, as many as 25–50% will continue to exhibit similar symptoms in adulthood.

8.6. Interventions: Implications of the Theoretical Model

The child's cognitive status, coping behavior, and control perceptions are also important to treatment approaches for RAP children. Treatment generally consists of increasing dietary fiber, providing relaxation training, or a combination of both. Relaxation training is a physiologically based treatment (i.e., progressive muscle relaxation and autogenic breathing exercises) that typically has a cognitive component (i.e., imagery) that is often prescribed, because of the hypothesized relationship between RAP and the child's poor ability to handle stress. According to the proposed model, however, the cognitive status of children with RAP is less sophisticated as a result of their earlier socialization experiences will illness, specifically the lack of developmental progression in the constructs of coping and internal perceptions of control that is evidenced in normal children. If, upon empirical testing, this hypothesis is correct, then the current model would predict that a physiological treatment with a cognitive component such as relaxation training would be ineffective for children with RAP. Children may need to have concepts characteristic of the psychophysiological stage of cognitive development proposed by Bibace and Walsh (1980) for this type of treatment to be effective.

One recent study sheds some light on the hypothesis that a more "medical" treatment approach may be more effective due to the unsophisticated cognitive status of children with learned illness behaviors like RAP. Specifically, the outcomes of fiber and of relaxation treatments were compared (Edwards, Finney, & Bonner, 1991). Subjects were assigned to fiber treatment if they presented with symptoms of constipation; otherwise, they received a standard relaxation treatment protocol. While the fiber treatment resulted in reduction of stomach pain for all constipated subjects, only minimal effects were found for the relaxation treatment. Moreover, when the fiber treatment was subsequently administered to subjects in the relaxation group, three of six responded positively.

The prescription of fiber may have been effective by affording the child a feeling of some control over his or her symptoms. Hence, this approach produced an appropriate match between perceptions of control and the problem-focused coping strategy of seeking medical care and taking "medication" for the symptoms. Because there are no long-term studies of fiber treatment, it is uncertain whether the fiber functions as a placebo-like treatment. That is, because it does not address the underlying psychological symptoms, the effects may be only temporary. Relaxation training alone, on the other hand, may be too cognitively complex or abstract for these children, who presumably are less sophisticated in their illness conceptions. For relaxation to be effective, it may be necessary for these children to first acquire effective coping patterns that are diverse with regard to cognitive and behavioral strategies before the benefits of relaxation are realized. Acquiring such patterns would require acknowledging the potential effects of psychological variables on somatic sensations. Perhaps the initial effects of fiber treatment and the sense of internal control and increased patient responsibility that it fosters would enable the child to increase her or his understanding of illness etiology. Consequently, this understanding may help the child to reduce distress through more effective coping means. Similarly, it may be efficacious to target coping skill directly.

Support for targeting coping deficits in RAP children comes from a treatment intervention that was delivered in a controlled group design

(Sanders et al., 1989) in which a multicomponent treatment regimen was utilized. Treatment consisted of differential reinforcement of nonillness behavior and cognitive coping skills training. Although both the treatment and the control group experienced pain reduction, the treatment group achieved these reductions more quickly. Moreover, the treatment resulted in a greater number of pain-free subjects at the 3-month follow-up. Furthermore, for the treatment group, the effects generalized to the school environment. While it is impossible to determine which treatment component (i.e., cognitive or behavioral) contributed to the effects or whether the combination was more effective than either component would have been alone, the training of coping skills appeared to be an important component. The absence of such skills may make the prognosis for RAP patients poor. Positive treatment effects have also been found in patients who were taught relaxation training as a coping mechanism in combination with other interventions that addressed directly the contingencies in the child's environment that may have maintained the illness behavior (Finney et al., 1989). In this study, 16 children with RAP who received a multicomponent targeted intervention (e.g., self-monitoring, limited parent attention, relaxation training, increased dietary fiber, and required school attendance) showed significant improvement in symptom resolution and decreases in medical utilization. An untreated comparison group of children with RAP who were matched for RAP symptoms and sex showed no improvement.

8.7. Recurrent Abdominal Pain: Summary

In summary, maternal NA yields a pathway to learned illness in the following way: Psychosomatic complaints may be a manifestation of poor coping whereby RAP children have not developed sufficient strategies to deal with what is demanded of them by the stressful situation (specifically, the regulation of emotional distress). Furthermore, there is a mismatch between their primary coping mechanism (medical utilization and dependence on mother) and the external control that is fostered by this pattern. Additionally, an emotion-focused coping mechanism (namely, avoidance) that has been found to be deleterious to health outcomes in other samples is also employed. Symptomatology and a reliance on external agents, then, are perpetuated by the physician, who continues to seek a medical explanation for the pain. With repeated unsuccessful or only temporarily successful treatments, the stomach pain recurs and the child perceives a lack of contingency between efforts to treat the symptoms and the outcome associated with those efforts. However, these children may receive some reinforcement (e.g., via attention from mother or physician), which may be sufficient to foster a contingent relationship that maintains an external locus of control. As this pattern continues, the child fails to learn self-regulation and self-care skills, and delays in crucial developmental processes (e.g., coping) will determine how subsequent symptoms are labeled, appraised, and experienced. Moreover, with limited coping resources, the child does not experience the relationship between adequate coping and reduced distress, and involvement in symptom remediation is therefore likely to be negligible. Furthermore, if dependency is fostered by external agents' assuming the majority of responsibility, then these children are denied the opportunity to develop their own repertoire of beliefs and behaviors regarding health care.

In addition to socialization experiences, the episodic nature of the RAP illness experience likely contributes to a perceived external health locus of control. While no studies with RAP children were found in the literature that empirically tested this hypothesis, research with other unpredictable diseases provides some tentative support. Shagena et al. (1988) found that children with seizure disorders and orthopedic conditions such as arthritis, in which the symptoms are episodic and unpredictable, had external perception of control. In comparison, equivocal results have been found in studies that have combined several chronic illness categories, including those that are largely pain-free and controllable with treatment adherence (e.g., diabetes), in statistical analyses (for a review, see Wallston & Wallston, 1981). It is possible that illnesses that are largely recurrent and unpredictable (e.g., RAP) foster less control. Therefore, not only do external perceptions (when mismatched with coping strategy) contribute to psychosomatic symptomatology, but also the nature of the illness experience itself maintains the external orientation. Consequently, medical overutilization is likely to persist.

9. Conclusion

Illness experiences in childhood can be seen as positive socialization opportunities that enable a child to acquire the necessary skills to effectively appraise, label, and subsequently contend with the symptoms (whether verified/objective or stress-related). Contrarily, the experience of even minor acute illnesses may reflect delays in the development of important processes—specifically, deficits in coping with daily stressors.

Stressful stimuli alone (in the form of life events) account for only a small portion of the variance in symptom expression (e.g., an average of 15% in cross-sectional studies) (Compas, 1987b). Clearly, then, there is a substantial degree of variability in a child's response to stress and his or her ability to handle somatic sensations. We must therefore go beyond models that assume that stressful stimulation alone is sufficient to result in somatic problems. Instead, it is necessary to consider person–environment variables that interact to account for individual differences in health outcome (Compas, 1987a).

The experience of an illness is not a discrete phenomenon that begins and ends with the presence and absence of symptoms. Instead, it reflects a socialization process that begins early in life. Therefore, a more comprehensive definition of health status is necessary (including both child and maternal variables) to account for learned illness behavior and the consequent variance in utilization. This chapter highlights both theoretical and empirical relations among important child and maternal variables that interact during the socialization period to define health status. Specifically, it demonstrates the importance of what the parent and child bring to the illness experience as well as the nature of the illness experience itself.

Maternal negative affect (NA) is one factor that has been identified in the current model as contributing to the development of illness behavior through the effects it has on the modeling process and through its subsequent influence on the development of important child processes. The illness experience, then, appears to reflect the interactive effects among various response systems including affective, cognitive, and behavioral.

Some of what we have presented has an empirical foundation, while other sections are hypotheses derived from the clinical literature. However, the current model identifies constructs that, because of their presumed importance to development, should not be discounted as trivial to the acquisition of health behaviors (positive or negative). Unfortunately, research in children's health status is in its infancy. Consequently, there are few rigorously designed empirically based studies or theories to support them.

With the current model, then, an attempt has been made to integrate what appear to be distinct and separate literatures surrounding the issues of health status. Specifically, the interactions among three variables (e.g., coping, control, and cognitive appraisal) are hypothesized to have implications for child psychopathology as a consequence of the influence of maternal NA during the socialization period. Furthermore, it is hypothesized that because of these interactions, symptoms associated with psychopathology will be interpreted somatically, resulting in learned illness behavior. The illness behavior will in turn be predictive of overutilization of medical services. This process of somatic interpretation and consequent overutilization of medical services might explain the strong relationship that is typically found between health status and utilization. According to Walker and Zeman (1992, p. 64) such patterns of "exaggerated disability" can interfere with other socialization experiences and may consequently result in learned illness behavior in adulthood.

Importantly, then, factors that contribute to children's health status need to be explored more comprehensively before it is assumed that symptom experience/perceptions of health status and disease pathology are necessarily isomorphic processes (Watson & Pennebaker, 1989). In many studies, however, health status, defined as illness morbidity (via symptom checklists), is entered into regression equations first. Any common variance shared by this and other independent variables is therefore attributed to the illness morbidity (Wolinsky, 1978). However, the interactive effects of other variables such as NA, coping, and locus of control need to be explored, as they may discriminate between somatic symptoms and psychosomatic symptoms that result in learned illness behavior. Studies that do not take account of such interactive effects, employing instead only one or a limited number of psychosocial indices as independent variables, will miss a substantial portion of the variance when predictions about health outcome are made.

Health status is indeed a broad and multidetermined construct. The issues discussed in this chapter are therefore selective, not exhaustive. Empirical tests, particularly studies that capture the dynamic relationships of the mother–child dyad, are needed. Current health intervention programs generally suffer from poor temporal generalization; therefore, instead of targeting only specific health behaviors (e.g., exercise), we need to focus on the underlying variables that influence health behaviors (Quadrel & Lau, 1990). Regarding interventions for children's health status, one solution is to develop and evaluate a primary care model inclusive of mental health services (Finney et al., 1991). An integrated service model has the possibility of achieving the best results for children's health needs.

Furthermore, in addition to child characteristics, other agents in the child's social environment, particularly the mother, should be targeted. In particular, the experimental manipulation of parent behaviors may enable us to better assess the effects on child coping and distress (Blount et al., 1989). A related idea is that if parents expect their children to assume responsibility for resisting engagement in risky behaviors, then they need to provide appropriate socialization experiences to enable them to possess the competencies to effectively deal with risks. Poor socialization experiences with health and illness may render a child vulnerable to such risks.

The origin and expression of health and illness behavior are complex; therefore, the relationships identified in the current model require further exploration and specification. Continued development of the model will require research studies that broaden the conceptual domain within which health status is typically investigated.

10. References

Abidin, R. R. (1986). *Parenting Stress Index: Test manual.* Charlottesville, VA: Pediatric Psychology Press.

American Psychiatric Association (1987). *Diagnostic and statistical manual of mental disorders,* 3rd. ed., revised. Washington, DC: American Psychiatric Association.

Apley, J. (1975). *The child with abdominal pains.* London: Blackwell Scientific Publications.

Band, E. B. (1990). Children's coping with diabetes: Understanding the role of cognitive development. *Journal of Pediatric Psychology, 15,* 27–41.

Bandura, A. (1977). *Social learning theory.* Englewood Cliffs, NJ: Prentice-Hall.

Baranowski, T., & Nader, P. R. (1985). Family health behavior. In D. C. Turk & R. D. Kerns (Eds.), *Health, illness, and families: A life-span perspective* (pp. 51–80). New York: John Wiley.

Barnett, D. W., Hall, J. D., & Bramlett, R. K. (1989). Family factors in preschool assessment and intervention: A validity study of parenting stress and coping measures. *Journal of School Psychology, 28,* 13–20.

Baumann, L. J., Cameron, L. D., Zimmerman, R. S., & Leventhal, H. (1989). Illness representation and matching labels with symptoms. *Health Psychology, 8,* 449–469.

Bibace, R., & Walsh, M. E. (1980). Development of children's concepts of illness. *Pediatrics, 66,* 912–917.

Blount, R. L., Corbin, S. M., Sturges, J. W., Wolfe, V. V., Prater, J. M., & James, L. D. (1989). The relationship between adults' behavior and child coping and distress during BMA/LP procedures: A sequential analysis. *Behavior Therapy, 20,* 585–601.

Brewster, A. (1982). Chronically ill hospitalized children's concepts of their illness. *Pediatrics, 69,* 355–362.

Burbach, D. J., & Peterson, L. (1986). Children's concepts of physical illness: A review and critique of the cognitive–developmental literature. *Health Psychology, 5,* 307–325.

Campbell, J. D. (1975). Illness is a point of view: The development of children's concepts of illness. *Child Development, 46,* 92–100.

Clyne, M. D. (1961). *Night calls: A study in general practice.* London: Tavistock Publishers.

Cockerham, W. C., Kunz, G., & Lueschen, G. (1988). Psychological distress, perceived health status, and physician utilization in America and West Germany. *Social Science and Medicine, 26,* 829–838.

Cohen, F., & Lazarus, R. S. (1983). Coping and adaptation and health and illness. In D. Mechanic (Ed.), *Handbook of health, health care, and the health professions* (pp. 608–635). New York: Free Press.

Cohen, S., & Williamson, G. M. (1991). Stress and infectious diseases in humans. *Psychological Bulletin, 109,* 5–24.

Coleman, W., & Levine, M. (1986). Recurrent abdominal pain: The cost of the aches and the aches of the cost. *Pediatrics in Review, 8,* 143–151.

Compas, B. E. (1987a). Coping with stress during childhood and adolescence. *Psychological Bulletin, 101,* 393–403.

Compas, B. E. (1987b). Stress and life events during childhood and adolescence. *Clinical Psychology Review, 7,* 275–302.

Compas, B. E., Banez, G. A., Malcarne, V., & Worsham, N. (1991a). Perceived control, coping with stress, and depressive symptoms in school-age children. Unpublished manuscript. Burlington: University of Vermont.

Compas, B. E., Banez, G. A., Malcarne, V., & Worsham, N. (1991b). Perceived control and coping with stress: A developmental perspective. *Journal of Social Issues, 47*, 23–34.

Compas, B. E., Davis, G. E., Forsythe, C. J., & Wagner, B. M. (1987). Assessment of major and daily stressful events during adolescence: The Adolescent Perceived Events Scale. *Journal of Consulting and Clinical Psychology, 55*, 534–541.

Compas, B. E., Malcarne, V., & Fondacaro, K. M. (1988). Coping with stressful events in older children and young adolescents. *Journal of Consulting and Clinical Psychology, 56*, 405–411.

Compas, B. E., & Worsham, N. (1991). When mom or dad has cancer: Developmental differences in children's coping with family stress. Paper presented at the Society for Research on Child Development meeting, Seattle, April 1991.

Costello, A. J., Edelbrock, C. S., Dulcan, M. K., Kalas, R., & Klaric, S. H. (1984). *Report on the NIMH Diagnostic Interview Schedule for Children (DIS-C)*. Washington, DC: National Institute of Mental Health.

Costello, E. J., Burns, B. J., Costello, A. J., Edelbrock, C., Dulcan, M. K., & Brent, D. (1988a). Service utilization and psychiatric diagnosis in pediatric primary care: The role of the gatekeeper. *Pediatrics, 82*, 435–441.

Costello, E. J., Edelbrock, C., Costello, A. J., Dulcan, M. K., Burns, B. J., & Brent, D. (1988b). Psychopathology in pediatric primary care: The new hidden morbidity. *Pediatrics, 82*, 415–424.

Craig, K. D., & Prkachin, K. M. (1980). Social influences on public and private components of pain. In I. G. Sarason & C. D. Speilberger (Eds.), *Stress and anxiety* (pp. 57–72). Washington, DC: Hemisphere.

Croyle, R. T., & Uretsky, M. B. (1987). Effects of mood on self-appraisal of health status. *Health Psychology, 6*, 239–253.

Dahlquist, L. J., Gil, K. M., Armstrong, D., DeLawyer, D. D., Greene, P., & Wuori, D. (1986). Preparing children for medical examinations: The importance of previous medical experience. *Health Psychology, 5*, 249–259.

Dielman, T. E., Leech, S., Becker, M. H., Rosenstock, I. W., Horvath, W. J., & Radius, S. M. (1982). Parental and child health beliefs and behaviors. *Health Education Quarterly, 9*, 60–77.

Dunn-Grier, B. J., McGrath, P. J., Rourke, B. P., Latter, J., & D'Astous, J. (1986). Adolescent chronic pain: The ability to cope. *Pain, 26*, 23–32.

Edwards, M. C., Finney, J. W., & Bonner, M. J. (1991). Matching treatment with recurrent abdominal pain symptoms: An evaluation of dietary fiber and relaxation treatments. *Behavior Therapy, 22*, 257–267.

Eiser, C. (1990). Psychological effects of chronic disease. *Journal of Child Psychology and Psychiatry, 31*, 85–98.

Faull, C., & Nicol, A. (1986). Abdominal pain in a six-year old: An epidemiological study in a new town. *Journal of Child Psychology and Psychiatry, 27*, 251–260.

Fiese, B. H., & Sameroff, A. J. (1989). Family context in pediatric psychology: A transactional perspective. *Journal of Pediatric Psychology, 114*, 293–314.

Finney, J. W., Lemanek, K. L., Cataldo, M. F., Katz, H. P., & Fuqua, R. W. (1989). Pediatric psychology in primary health care: Brief targeted therapy for recurrent abdominal pain. *Behavior Therapy, 20*, 283–291.

Finney, J. W., Riley, A. W., & Cataldo, M. F. (1991). Psychology in primary health care: Effects of brief targeted therapy on children's medical care utilization. *Journal of Pediatric Psychology, 16*, 447–461.

Folkman, S. (1984). Personal control and stress and coping processes: A theoretical analysis. *Journal of Personality and Social Psychology, 46,* 839–852.

Garber, J., Zeman, J., & Walker, L. S. (1990). Recurrent abdominal pain in children: Psychiatric diagnoses and parental psychopathology. *Journal of the American Academy of Child and Adolescent Psychiatry, 29,* 648–656.

Garmezy, N., & Rutter, M. (1983). *Stress, coping, and development in children.* New York: McGraw-Hill.

Gochman, D. S., & Parcel, G. (1982). Introduction to special issue. *Health Education Quarterly, 9,* 5–7.

Green, L. W. (1979). Status identity and preventive health behavior. *Pacific Health Education Report, 1,* 1–130.

Hanson, C. L., Harris, M. A., Relyea, G., Cigrang, J. A., Carle, D. L., & Burghen, G. A. (1989). Coping styles in youths with insulin-dependent diabetes mellitus. *Journal of Consulting and Clinical Psychology, 57,* 644–651.

Haskins, R., Hirschibiel, P. O., Collier, A. M., Sanyal, M. A., & Finkelstein, N. W. (1981). Minor illness and social behavior of infants and caregivers. *Journal of Applied Developmental Psychology, 2,* 117–128.

Hodges, K., & Burbach, D. J. (1991). Recurrent abdominal pain. In J. P. Bush & S. W. Harkins (Eds.), *Children in pain: Clinical and research issues from a developmental perspective* (pp. 251–273). New York: Springer-Verlag.

Hodges, K., Kline, J., Barbero, G., & Flanery, R. (1985). Depressive symptoms in children with recurrent abdominal pain and in their families. *Journal of Pediatrics, 107,* 622–626.

Hodges, K., Kline, J., Barbero, G., & Woodruff, C. (1985). Anxiety in children with recurrent abdominal pain and their parents. *Psychosomatics, 26,* 859–866.

Jacobson, A. M., Goldberg, I. D., & Burns, B. J. (1980). Diagnosed mental disorder in children and use of health services in four organized health care settings. *American Journal of Psychiatry, 137,* 559–565.

Jay, S. M., Ozolins, M., Elliott, C. H., & Caldwell, S. (1983). Assessment of children's distress during painful medical procedures. *Health Psychology, 2,* 133–147.

Johnson, C. C., Nicklas, T. A., Arbeit, M. L., Franklin, F. A., & Berenson, G. S. (1988). A comprehensive model for maintenance for family health behaviors: The "Heart Smart" Family Health Promotion Program. *Family and Community Health, 11,* 1–7.

Johnson, J. H., & Sarason, I. G. (1978). Life stress, depression and anxiety: Internal–external control as a moderator variable. *Journal of Psychosomatic Research, 22,* 205–208.

Johnson, R. (1971). Maternal influence on child behavior in a dental setting. *Psychiatry in Medicine, 2,* 211–228.

Kagan, J. (1983). Stress and coping in early development. In N. Garmezy & M. Rutter (Eds.), *Stress, coping, and development in children* (pp. 191–216). New York: McGraw-Hill.

Kaplan, R. M. (1990). Behavior as the central outcome in health care. *American Psychologist, 45,* 1211–1220.

Katon, W. (1984). Depression: Relationship to somatization and chronic medical illness. *Journal of Clinical Psychiatry, 45,* 4–11.

LaMontagne, L. (1984). Children's locus of control beliefs as predictors of preoperative coping behavior. *Nursing Research, 33,* 76–87.

Lau, R. R., (1988). Beliefs about control and health behavior. In D. Gochman (Ed.), *Health behavior: Emerging research perspectives* (pp. 43–63). New York: Plenum Press.

Lau, R. R., & Hartman, K. A. (1983). Common sense representations of common illness. *Health Psychology, 2,* 167–185.

Lau, R. R., & Klepper, S. (1988). The development of illness orientations in children aged 6–12. *Journal of Health and Social Behavior, 29,* 149–168.

Lau, R. R., Quadrel, M. J., & Hartman, K. A. (1990). Development and change of young adults' preventive health beliefs and behavior: Influence from parents and peers. *Journal of Health and Social Behavior, 31,* 240–259.

Lazarus, R. S., & Folkman, S. (1984). Coping and adaptation. In W. D. Gentry (Ed.), *The handbook of behavioral medicine* (pp. 282–385). New York: Guilford Press.

Leventhal, H. W., Meyer, D., & Nerenz, D. (1980). The common sense representation of illness danger. In S. Rachman (Ed.), *Medical psychology* (pp. 7–30). Elmsford, NY: Pergamon Press.

Levine, S. (1983). A psychobiological approach to the ontogeny of coping. In N. Garmezy & M. Rutter (Eds.), *Stress, coping and development in children* (pp. 107–131). New York: McGraw-Hill.

Levy, J. C. (1980). Vulnerable children: Parents' perspectives and the use of medical care. *Pediatrics, 65,* 956–963.

Lewis, C. E., Lewis, M. A., Lorimer, A. A., & Palmer, B. B. (1977). Child-initiated care: The use of school nursing services in an adult-free system. *Pediatrics, 60,* 499–507.

Lewis, M., & Goldberg, S. (1969). Perceptual–cognitive development in infancy: A generalized expectancy model as a function of the mother–infant interaction. *Merill-Palmer Quarterly, 15,* 81–100.

Liebman, R., Honig, P., & Berger, H. (1976). An integrated treatment program for psychogenic pain. *Family Process, 15,* 397–405.

Littman, B., & Parmelee, A. H., Jr. (1978). Medical correlates of infant development. *Pediatrics, 61,* 470–474.

Maccoby, E. E. (1983). Social–emotional development and response to stressors. In N. Garmezy & M. Rutter (Eds.), *Stress, coping and development in children* (pp. 217–234). New York: McGraw-Hill.

Maddux, J. E., Roberts, M. C., Sledden, E. A., & Wright, L. (1986). Developmental issues in child health psychology. *American Psychologist, 41,* 25–34.

Maiman, L. A., Becker, M. H., & Katlic, A. W. (1985). How mothers treat their children's physical symptoms. *Journal of Community Health, 10,* 136–155.

Manning, W. G., & Wells, K. B. (1992). The effects of psychological distress and psychological well-being on use of medical services. *Medical Care, 30,* 541–553.

McCubbin, H. I., Larsen, A., & Olson, D. H. (1981). *Family Crisis Oriented Personal Evaluation Scales.* Madison: University of Wisconsin.

McFarlane, A. H., Norman, G. R., Streiner, D. L., Roy, R., & Scott, D. J. (1980). A longitudinal study of the influence of the psychosocial environment on health status: A preliminary report. *Journal of Health and Social Behavior, 21,* 124–133.

McGrath, P. J., & Pisterman, S. (1991). Developmental issues: Adolescent pain. In J. P. Bush & S. W. Harkins (Eds.), *Children in pain: Clinical and research issues from a developmental perspective* (pp. 231–250). New York: Springer-Verlag.

Mechanic, D. (1964). The influence of mothers on their children's health attitudes and behavior. *Pediatrics, 33,* 444.

Mechanic, D. (1972). Social–psychological factors affecting the presentation of bodily complaints. *New England Journal of Medicine, 286,* 1132–1139.

Mechanic, D. (1977). Illness behavior, social adaptation, and the management of illness. *Journal of Nervous and Mental Disease, 165,* 79–87.

Mechanic, D. (1983). The experience and expression of distress: The study of illness behavior and medical utilization. In D. Mechanic (Ed.), *Handbook of health, health care, and the health professions* (pp. 591–607). New York: Free Press.

Mechanic, D. (1992). Health and illness behavior and patient–practitioner relationships. *Social Science and Medicine, 34,* 1345–1350.

Melamed, B. G., & Bush, J. P. (1985). Family factors in children with acute illness. In D. C.

Turk & R. D. Kerns (Eds.), *Health, illness and families: A life-span perspective* (pp. 183–219). New York: John Wiley.

Melamed, B. G., & Siegel, L. J. (1975). Reduction of anxiety in children facing hospitalization and surgery by use of filmed modeling. *Journal of Consulting and Clinical Psychology, 43*, 511–521.

Meyer, R. J., & Haggerty, R. J. (1962). Streptococcal infections in families. *Pediatrics, 29*, 539–549.

Miller, S. M., Brody, D. S., & Summerton, J. (1988). Styles of coping with threat: Implications for health. *Journal of Personality and Social Psychology, 54*, 142–148.

Miller, S. M., & Green, M. L. (1985). Coping with stress and frustration: Origins, nature, and development. In M. Lewis & C. Saarni (Eds.), *The socialization of emotions* (pp. 263–314). New York: Plenum Press.

Minuchin, S., Baker, L., Rosman, B. L., Liebman, R., Milman, L., & Todd, T. C. (1975). A conceptual model of psychosomatic illness in children: Family organization and family therapy. *Archives of General Psychiatry, 32*, 1031–1038.

Natapoff, J. N. (1982). A developmental analysis of children's ideas of health. *Health Education Quarterly, 9*, 34–45.

Newacheck, P. W., & Halfon, N. (1986). The association between mother's and children's use of physician services. *Medical Care, 24*, 30–38.

Nielson, A. C., & Williams, T. A. (1980). Depression in ambulatory medical patients. *Archives of General Psychiatry, 37*, 999–1004.

Olson, D. H., Portner, J., & Bell, R. (1986). Family Adaptability and Cohesion Evaluation Scales. In D. H. Olson, H. I. McCubbin, H. Barnes, A. Larsen, M. Muxen, & M. Wilson (Eds.), *Family inventories* (pp. 5–24). St. Paul: Family Social Science, University of Minnesota.

Osborne, R. B., Hatcher, J. W., & Richtsmeier, A. J. (1989). The role of social modeling in unexplained pediatric pain. *Journal of Pediatric Psychology, 14*, 43–61.

Oski, M. (1981). Comment on article by Sturner et al. In F. A. Oski & J. A. Stockman (Eds.), *Yearbook of pediatrics* (p. 400). Chicago: Year Book Medical Publishers.

Palmer, B. B., & Lewis, C. E., (1976). Development of health attitudes and behaviors. *Journal of School Health, 46*, 401–402.

Parcel, G. S., & Meyer, M. P. (1978). Development of an instrument to measure children's health locus of control. *Health Education Monographs, 6*, 149–159.

Parmelee, A. H. (1986). Children's illnesses: Their beneficial effects on behavioral development. *Child Development, 57*, 1–10.

Patterson, T. L., Sallis, J. F., Nader, P. R., Kaplan, R. M., Rupp, J. W., Atkins, C. J., & Senn, K. L. (1989). Familial similarities of changes in cognitive, behavioral, and physiological variables in a cardiovascular health promotion program. *Journal of Pediatric Psychology, 14*, 277–292.

Pennebaker, J. W., & Watson, D. (1988). Blood pressure estimation and beliefs among normotensives and hypertensives. *Health Psychology, 7*, 309–328.

Perrin, E. C., & Gerrity, P. S. (1981). There's a demon in your belly: Children's understanding of illness. *Pediatrics, 67*, 841–849.

Peterson, L., & Shigetomi, C. (1981). The use of coping techniques to minimize anxiety in hospitalized children. *Behavior Therapy, 12*, 1–14.

Phipps, S. A. (1991). Family systems functioning, family health roles, and utilization of physician health services. *Lifestyles, 12*, 23–41.

Piaget, J. (1929). *The child's conception of the world.* New York: Harcourt Brace.

Pratt, L. (1973). Child rearing methods and children's health behavior. *Journal of Health and Social Behavior, 14*, 61–69.

Quadrel, M. J., & Lau, R. R. (1990). A multivariate analysis of adolescents' orientations toward physician use. *Health Psychology, 9*, 750–773.

Radius, S. M., Dillman, T., Becker, M. H., Rosenstock, I. M., & Horvath, W. J. (1980). Adolescent perspectives on health and illness. *Adolescence, 15*, 375–384.

Rickard, K. (1988). The occurrence of maladaptive health-related behaviors and teacher-rated conduct problems in children of chronic low back pain patients. *Journal of Behavioral Medicine, 11*, 107–116.

Riley, A. W., Finney, J. W., Mellitus, E. D., Starfield, B., Kidwell, S., Quaskey, S., Cataldo, M. F., Filipp, L., & Shematek, J. P. (1993). Determinants of children's health care use: An investigation of psychosocial factors. *Medical Care, 31*, 761–783.

Robinson, J. O., Alvarez, J. H., & Dodge, J. A. (1990). Life events and family history in children with recurrent abdominal pain. *Journal of Psychosomatic Research, 34*, 171–181.

Ross, D. & Ross, S. (1984). Childhood pain: The school-aged child's viewpoint. *Pain, 20*, 179–191.

Rutter, M. (1981). Stress, coping, and development: Some issues and some questions. *Journal of Child Psychology and Psychiatry, 22*, 323–356.

Ryan, N. (1989). Stress-coping strategies identified from school age children's perspective. *Research in Nursing and Health, 12*, 111–122.

Sallis, J. F., & Nader, P. R. (1988). Family determinants of health behaviors. In D. S. Gochman (Ed.), *Health behavior: Emerging research perspectives* (pp. 107–124). New York: Plenum Press.

Salovey, P., & Birnbaum, D. (1989). Influence of mood on health-relevant cognitions. *Journal of Personality and Social Psychology, 57*, 539–551.

Sanders, M. R., Regbetz, M, Morrison, M., Bor, W., Cordon, A., Dadds, M., & Shepard, R. (1989). Cognitive–behavioral treatment of recurrent nonspecific abdominal pain in children: An analysis of generalization, maintenance, and side effects. *Journal of Consulting and Clinical Psychology, 57*, 294–300.

Schor, E. (1986). Impact of presumably stressful life transitions on pediatric service use. *Pediatrics, 77*, 834–841.

Schor, E., Starfield, B., Stidley, C., & Hankin, J. (1987). Family health: Utilization and effects of family membership. *Medical Care, 25*, 616–626.

Shagena, M. M., Sandler, H. K., & Perrin, E. C. (1988). Concepts of illness and perception of control in healthy children and in children with chronic illnesses. *Developmental and Behavioral Pediatrics, 9*, 252–256.

Silver, R. L., & Wortman, C. B. (1980). Coping with undesirable life events. In J. Garber & M. E. P. Seligman (Eds.), *Human helplessness: Theory and applications* (pp. 279–340). New York: Academic Press.

Simeonsson, R. J., Buckley, L., & Monson, L. (1979). Conceptions of illness causality in hospitalized children. *Journal of Pediatric Psychology, 4*, 77–84.

Sklar, L. S., & Anisman, H. (1981). Stress and cancer. *Psychological Bulletin, 89*, 369–406.

Stone, R., & Barbero, G. (1970). Recurrent abdominal pain in childhood. *Pediatrics, 45*, 732–738.

Strickland, B. R. (1978). Internal–external expectancies and health-related behaviors. *Journal of Consulting and Clinical Psychology, 46*, 1192–1211.

Susser, M., Hopper, K., & Richman, J. (1983). Society, culture, and health. In D. Mechanic (Ed.), *Handbook of health, health care, and the health professions* (pp. 591–607). New York: Free Press.

Tessler, R., & Mechanic, D. (1978). Psychological distress and perceived health status. *Journal of Health and Social Behavior, 19*, 254–262.

Tessler, R., Mechanic, D., & Diamond, M. (1976). The effect of psychological distress on physician utilization: A prospective study. *Journal of Health and Social Behavior, 17,* 353–364.

Tinsley, B. J. (1987). The effect of maternal health beliefs on utilization of childhood preventive health services and child health. Paper presented at the biannual meeting of the Society for Research on Child Development, Baltimore, April 1987.

Tinsley, B. J. (1992). Multiple influences on the acquisition and socialization of children's health attitudes and behavior. An integrative review. *Child Development, 63,* 1043–1069.

Tinsley, B. J., & Holtgrave, D. R. (1989). Parental health beliefs, utilization of childhood preventive health services and infant health. *Journal of Developmental Behavioral Pediatrics, 10,* 236–241.

Walker, L. S., Garber, J., & Greene, J. W. (1991). Somatization symptoms in pediatric abdominal pain patients: Relation to chronicity of abdominal pain and parent somatization. *Journal of Abnormal Child Psychology, 19,* 379–394.

Walker, L. S., & Greene, J. W. (1989). Children with recurrent abdominal pain and their parents: More somatic complaints, anxiety, and depression than other patients? *Journal of Pediatric Psychology, 14,* 231–293.

Walker, L. S., & Greene, J. W. (1991). Negative life events and symptom resolution in pediatric abdominal pain patients. *Journal of Pediatric Psychology, 16,* 39–57.

Walker, L. S., & Zeman, J. L. (1992). Parental response to child illness behavior. *Journal of Pediatric Psychology, 17,* 49–72.

Wallston, K. A., & Wallston, B. S. (1981). Health locus of control scales. In H. Lefcourt (Ed.), *Research with the locus of control construct* (pp. 189–243). Orlando, FL: Academic Press.

Wallston, K. A., Wallston, B. S., & DeVellis, R. (1978). Development of the Multidimensional Health Locus of Control (MHLC) Scales. *Health Education Monograph, 6,* 161–170.

Watson, D. (1988). Intraindividual and interindividual analyses of positive and negative affect: Their relation to health complaints, perceived stress, and daily activities. *Journal of Personality and Social Psychology, 54,* 1020–1030.

Watson, D., & Clark, L. A. (1984). Negative affectivity: The disposition to experience aversive emotional states. *Psychological Bulletin, 96,* 465–490.

Watson, D., & Pennebaker, J. W. (1989). Health complaints, stress, and distress: Exploring the central role of negative affectivity. *Psychological Review, 96,* 234–254.

Weisz, J. R. (1980). Developmental change in perceived control: Recognizing noncontingency in the laboratory and perceiving it in the world. *Developmental Psychology, 16,* 385–390.

Weisz, J. R. (1986). Understanding the developing understanding of control. In M. Perlmutter (Ed.), *Cognitive perspectives on children's social and behavioral development: The Minnesota symposium on child psychology* (pp. 219–275). Hillsdale, NJ: Erlbaum Associates.

Whitehead, W. E., Busch, C. M., Heller, B. R., & Costa, P. T. (1986). Social learning influences on menstrual symptoms and illness behavior. *Health Psychology, 5,* 13–23.

Wolf, T. M., Sklov, M. C., Hunter, S. M., & Berenson, G. S. (1982). Factor analytic study of the Children's Nowicki–Strickland Locus of Control Scale. *Education and Psychological Measurement, 42,* 333–337.

Wolinsky, F. D. (1978). Assessing the effects of predisposing, enabling, and illness–morbidity characteristics on health service utilization. *Journal of Health and Social Behavior, 19,* 384–396.

Zuckerman, B., Stevenson, J., & Bailey, V. (1987). Stomachaches and headaches in a community sample of preschool children. *Pediatrics, 79,* 677–682.

8

New Directions in Behavioral Family Intervention with Children

Matthew R. Sanders

1. Introduction

Behavioral family intervention (BFI) has had a major influence in the field of child psychopathology and has become a dominant paradigm in the treatment of many childhood disorders (Lochman, 1990). During the past three decades, BFI has evolved as a viable, empirically supported approach to working with oppositional and conduct-disordered children (Forehand & Long, 1988; Forehand & McMahon, 1981; Sayger, Horne, Walker, & Passmore, 1988; Twardosz & Nordquist, 1988; Webster-Stratton, Kolpacoff, & Hollinsworth, 1988; Wells & Egan, 1988) and, to a lesser extent, children with attention-deficit disorders (Barkley, Guevremont, Anastopoulos, & Fletcher, 1992; Pisterman, McGrath, Firestone, Goodman, Webster, & Mallory, 1989). BFI is also widely used with abused and neglected children as a component of a multicomponent intervention protocol (Lutzker, 1992). Parent training has become an integral part of services for children with autism and developmental disabilities (Schreibman, Kaneko, & Koegel, 1991; Harrold, Lutzker, Campbell, & Touchette, 1992). Children with language problems (Laski, Charlop, & Schreibman, 1988; Alpert & Kaiser, 1992) and academic learning difficulties (McNaughton, Glynn, & Robinson, 1987) have also been shown to benefit from this approach, and behavioral techniques have been successfully employed with a variety of common behavior problems of otherwise normal children such as bedtime and mealtime

Matthew R. Sanders • Behaviour Research and Therapy Centre, Department of Psychology, University of Queensland, Brisbane, Queensland 4072, Australia.

Advances in Clinical Child Psychology, Volume 18, edited by Thomas H. Ollendick and Ronald J. Prinz. Plenum Press, New York, 1996.

problems (Dadds, Sanders, & Bor, 1984; Hall, Axelrod, Tyler, Grief, Jones, & Robertson, 1972; Sanders, Dadds, & Bor, 1989a) and problems on shopping trips or in restaurants (Clark, Greene, Macrae, McNees, Davis, & Risley, 1977).

The success of BFI has prompted broader application of its methods. Justification for this extension comes in part from studies showing that family dysfunction is a generic risk factor for a range of psychological problems in childhood (Dadds, 1987; Rutter, 1985a; Rutter & Quinton, 1984). Despite these findings, there is little evidence showing that specific patterns of family interaction are uniquely associated with specific disorders. Recent research has pointed to the potential benefits of BFI for other groups of children. These include children from maritally discordant homes (Dadds, Schwartz, & Sanders, 1987b), children whose parents have divorced (Grych & Fincham, 1992), children from stepfamilies (Lawton & Sanders, 1984), children with somatic complaints such as recurrent pain syndromes (Beames, Sanders, & Bor, 1992; Sanders et al., 1989c), feeding and sleeping difficulties (Werle, Murphy, & Budd, 1993), habits such as nail biting, thumbsucking (Christensen & Sanders, 1985), and obesity (Graves, Meyers, & Clarke, 1988), and children with anxiety disorders (Ollendick & Francis, 1988). This extensive empirical base supports the basic conclusion that when parents are trained to implement behavior change strategies, there is often a corresponding improvement in their children's behavior and adjustment.

This chapter reviews recent evidence concerning the extension and enhancement of family intervention methods with preadolescent children. As the family intervention literature is so extensive, this review is necessarily selective and focuses on innovative applications with four groups of children: children with somatic complaints, children with anxiety disorders, children with conduct problems, and children from distressed or second marriages.

2. What Is Behavioral Family Intervention?

"Behavioral family intervention" is a generic term used herein to describe a therapeutic process that aims to effect change in a child's behavior and adjustment through corresponding changes in aspects of the family environment that affect the child's problem behavior (Sanders & Dadds, 1993). It targets interactional processes that are assumed to be related to the etiology, maintenance, exacerbation, or relapse of a child's functioning. The focus of intervention frequently involves an attempt to change the parents' behavior toward their children, although it can include changing other aspects of family functioning such as the parents' marital relationships, the behavior of siblings, grandparents, and child-minders, the division of labor among caregivers, and the provision of age-appropriate activities in the home. Although parental behavior change has been the focus of much BFI research, changes in parental perceptions, expectations, beliefs, assumptions, attributions, and self-talk are legitimate targets of intervention. The term BFI is used in preference to other terms—such as behavior parent training, child management training, parent management training, parent–child interaction therapy, or functional family therapy—to more accurately reflect the role of family intervention in both treatment and prevention efforts and to emphasize that the targets of family interventions extend beyond parenting skills to the family system as a whole.

2.1. Conceptual Framework

Contemporary BFI had its roots within the applied behavior analysis traditions, an approach that emphasized the importance of involving parents, teachers, and other significant persons (e.g., daycare or institution staff) as "mediators" or "behavior change agents" to bring about lasting therapeutic change (Patterson, 1969; Tharp & Wetzel, 1969). Behavior analysts argue that effective intervention with children must access the aspects of the child's social environment that contribute to problem behavior (Patterson, 1982; Wahler, 1969). There is substantial evidence that implicates parents and other family members in both the development and the maintenance of a variety of disturbed child behaviors (e.g., Dadds, 1987, 1995; Hetherington & Martin, 1979; Patterson & Reid, 1984). Training parents to provide different social contingencies for specific problem behaviors as a therapeutic approach provides direct and immediate access to particular social interaction factors within the family that maintain problem behaviors. Many of the management techniques used in BFI were directly derived from contemporary learning theory, particularly models of operant behavior (Baer, Wolf, & Risley, 1968; Skinner, 1953), and to a lesser extent from social learning theory (Bandura, 1977) and developmental theory (Bijou & Baer, 1961; Harris & Ferrari, 1983; Forehand & Wierson, 1993).

Other theoretical perspectives became evident in the literature as BFI began to investigate the mechanisms responsible for therapeutic change, the reasons some families fail to respond to treatment, and the ways in which the broader social contexts of children and families affect outcome. These perspectives include Bandura's cognitive social learning theory (Bandura, 1977), functional contextualism (Biglan, 1992, 1993), attribution theory (Smith & O'Leary, 1995), systems theory (Robins & Foster, 1989), and developmental theory (Forehand & Wierson, 1993). These expanded theoretical perspectives have led to making cognitive and affective dimensions of parent–child relationships as well as behavior the targets of intervention. It would probably be more accurate to refer to contemporary BFI as "cognitive–behavioral family intervention." Whether these expanded theoretical perspectives actually improve the long-term efficacy of BFI remains to be seen.

2.2. Therapeutic Options

The clinical practice of BFI is not a single therapeutic modality, but rather includes several different types of intervention. The appropriateness of each intervention depends on the nature and complexity of the presenting problem and its maintaining conditions (Sanders & Dadds, 1993). Table 1 outlines five levels of intervention that vary in complexity and the level of clinical sophistication required to effect change. They range from brief, focal interventions using written materials that parents implement with minimal or no training (Azrin & Foxx, 1974) to more complex intervention programs that concurrently address a variety of other family issues (e.g., marital problems, maternal depression, parental stress, financial difficulties, social isolation of parents) in addition to child management problems (e.g., Dadds et al., 1987b).

All interventions share an emphasis on producing child behavior change by modifying patterns of family interaction, particularly the reciprocal patterns of antecedents and consequences of problem child behavior and dysfunctional parenting. The therapeutic centerpiece of much of the family intervention literature is parent training. Much of the empirical research has concentrated on the evaluation of parent training (level 3 and 4 interventions).

An important research priority is to determine which type of intervention is required for different parents and children (Blechman, 1981; Embry, 1984; Prinz, 1992). For example, the mother of an otherwise healthy 2-year-old with a relatively uncomplicated problem of sleep disturbance is unlikely to require extensive skills training to implement a new nighttime routine that incorporates planned ignoring of crying once the child is put to bed. A simple written protocol presented by the family doctor may suffice (Sanders & Markie-Dadds, 1995). On the other hand, if the child's mother and father frequently argue over the handling of the child's nighttime crying, an intervention to address the associated marital conflict may be essential to ensure that the treatment plan is accurately implemented and the child's difficulty is resolved.

TABLE 1

Therapeutic Options in Behavioral Family Intervention with Children

Description of option	Intervention methods	Possible target behaviors	Examples in the literature
1. Specific advice	Brief written instructions on videomodeling on how to solve specific child problems. No therapist contact.	Sleep disturbances, toilet training, supermarket behavior problems	Seymour, Brock, During, & Poole (1989); McManmon, Peterson, Metelenis, McWhinter, & Clark (1982); Endo, Sloane, Hawkes, McLoughlin, & Jenson (1991a)
2. Specific advice plus minimal therapist contact	Written instructions combined with brief therapist contact (live or telephone).	Mealtime behavior problems, bedtime disruption, thumbsucking	Christensen & Sanders (1987); Sanders, Bor & Dadds (1984)
3. Specific advice plus active training	Combination of instructions, modeling, rehearsal, and feedback focused on teaching parents how to manage specific problems.	Temper tantrums, aggression, noncompliance	Dadds et al. (1984)
4. Intensive behavioral parent training	Training methods similar to level 3 above, but focus is on parent–child interaction and the application of diverse parenting skills to a variety of child problems. Includes training in antecedent stimulus control and contingency management techniques.	Oppositional behavior or aggression as a response class	Forehand & McMahon (1981); Sanders & Plant (1989); Koegel et al. (1978)
5. Behavioral family intervention	May involve all of the above, but in addition, other family problems are addressed, such as marital problems, stress, depression, and anger management.	Concurrent child and parent problems, severe conduct disorder, child depression, mixed depression and anxiety disorders	Dadds et al. (1987b); Sanders & Dadds (1993); Wahler et al. (1993)

2.3. Consultation Skills

BFI has always emphasized the value of active training methods such as instructions, modeling, rehearsal, feedback, and structured homework assignments. However, as attention has shifted to analyzing what actually transpires in therapy sessions with families, there has been greater emphasis on the interpersonal context of therapy and process issues (Patterson & Stoolmiller, 1995). BFI practitioners clearly use a wider range of clinical skills than are typically acknowledged or reported in research papers or in treatment manuals (Webster-Stratton & Herbert, 1993; Sanders & Lawton, 1993). How experienced clinicians tackle tasks such as communicating assessment findings with parents without provoking excessive defensiveness, how they respond to parental distress or resistance, and how they challenge parents' maladaptive views on the nature of the child's problems are extremely important yet underresearched aspects of the technology. Table 2 provides an overview of the consultation process used in the Family Intervention Program at the Behaviour Research and Therapy Centre at the University of Queensland in Australia. A detailed description of this program can be found in Sanders and Dadds (1993). The specific role of process variables in influencing treatment outcome in BFI is an important yet relatively neglected area of research.

3. Applications with Health-Related Problems

An important new area of application of BFI methods involves working with the families of children with somatic complaints or physical illnesses that may or may not have an organic basis. These children typically present to pediatric settings, and intervention is often multidisciplinary. This section discusses four problem areas in which family interventions show promise as components of a child's treatment: recurrent and acute pain, persistent feeding difficulties, sleep disturbance, and chronic illness.

3.1. Pain Management

Pain is an unpleasant sensory and emotional experience. Like adults, children experience a variety of different types of pain that vary in strength, quality, location, duration, and affective components (McGrath, 1990). Considerable progress has been made in the assessment and treatment of children's pain in recent years, and social learning processes in the family have been a target of intervention efforts.

TABLE 2

Therapeutic Tasks of Each Phase of Behavioral Family Intervention[a]

INITIAL PHASE Assessment and feedback	MIDDLE PHASE Behavior change	FINAL PHASE Termination
Behavioral analysis Hypothesis generation and testing Formulation of problems in terms of behavioral excesses, deficits, and inappropriate or inadequate stimulus control Identification of obstacles to treatment and resources available Initial formulation of treatment plan	*Implementation of treatment plan* Teaching positive family interaction and child management skills via provision of verbal and written information, and modeling Behavior rehearsal and feedback Implementation in clinic and natural environment	*Generalization and maintenance* Identification of obstacles to generalization (behavioral, cognitive, affective, social, and environmental) Identification of high-risk settings for relapse Problem solving and implementation of management strategies in high-risk settings Specification of contingencies for returning to therapy to prevent relapse
Development of therapeutic relationship and commitment for change Discussion of assessment findings Establishing joint understanding of the nature of the problem Formulation of mutually determined treatment plan	*Monitoring and evaluation of progress* Use of observational and self-report measures to assess change in targeted and nontargeted behaviors Reformulation of treatment plan as required Further teaching, behavioral rehearsal, and feedback as required	*Facilitation of independence* Fading of artificial prompts Teaching self-management skills (goal setting, self-monitoring, etc.)

[a]Adapted from Kanfer and Schefit (1988) and Sanders and Dadds (1993).

Recurrent abdominal pain (RAP) is a common pediatric complaint affecting an estimated 10–15% of elementary-school-age children (Apley, 1975). It involves chronic intermittent pain in the periumbilical or midepigastric region, which causes the child significant distress and interferes with the child's usual activities. Typically, the child is physically well between episodes but as many as one third are vulnerable to recurrences of the pain over several years. An identifiable organic cause can be found in only 5–10% of children with RAP. Due to its etiological uncertainty and the lack of empirically validated treatments, the disorder generates considerable parental anxiety, and it is associated with frequent use and occasional abuse of medical services (Finney, Lemanek, Cataldo, Katz, & Fuque, 1989) (also see Chapter 7).

The conceptual justification for BFI methods for RAP stems from the pain literature, in which family interactions have been hypothesized to influence pain behavior (Payne & Norfleet, 1986). In the case of children, maternal caregiving is particularly important, since mothers are more likely to have the responsibility of caring for a sick child during episodes of illness (Turk, Litt, Salovey, & Walker, 1985). Although empirical support for the relationship between family interaction and RAP is limited, family interactions may affect children with RAP via two interacting mechanisms. First, family conflict (e.g., marital discord) and parental distress (e.g., excessive anxiety or depression) can constitute a source of stress that might precipitate or prolong an episode of RAP. There is little evidence to show that parents of children with RAP have more marital problems than other parents. Some evidence, however, shows higher levels of anxiety, depression, and somatization (Walker & Greene, 1989) and migraine headaches (Mortimer, Kay, Jaron, & Good, 1992) in parents of children with RAP than in parents of pain-free children. Few studies, however, have found parental characteristics that differentiate parents of children with nonorganic pain and parents of children with organic pain. It is quite possible that unresolved pain in a child may generate parental anxiety that in turn exacerbates the child's pain.

Second, illness behaviors may develop or be maintained through a process whereby parents inadvertently model, prompt, and reinforce illness behaviors and in other ways discourage a child from active coping. Support for this hypothesis comes from treatment studies that show that training parents to alter their contingent reactions to their child's pain behavior can be successful in reducing RAP symptoms (e.g., A. J. Miller & Kratochwill, 1979; Sanders et al., 1989c; Sanders, Shepherd, Cleghorn, & Woolford, 1994b). Consistent with cognitive behavioral models of pain, which emphasize the role of contingent solicitous attention as a reinforcer of pain behavior (e.g., Fordyce, 1976), Sanders, Woolford, Turner, Shepherd, and Cleghorn (1995) found that mothers of children with RAP showed greater preference for providing sympathetic attention to a child in pain than did parents of pain-free children. Interestingly, parents, regardless of diagnostic group, rated ignoring as their least preferred reaction. This finding has obvious implications for cognitive behavioral programs that emphasize the importance of minimizing attention to pain behaviors. Mothers appear to believe that it is important to respond sensitively and with concern when a child is in distress. Unfortunately, such attending may inadvertently reinforce pain behavior, rather than empower children to manage their anxiety or pain more effectively.

The treatment of children with RAP generally includes some form of coping skills training for children with RAP. The usefulness of this approach has been suggested by uncontrolled clinical case reports (Linton, 1986) in which relaxation training as a specific coping skill has been used in conjunction with other behavioral and dietary interventions (e.g., Edwards, Finney, & Bonner, 1991; Finney et al., 1989). However, controlled studies are lacking, and no studies have examined whether changes in children's coping strategies are responsible for the improvement in the children's pain.

Interest in involving parents stems from the observation that parents may influence a child's capacity to implement adaptive coping skills (Dolgin & Phipps, 1989; Dunn-Geier, McGrath, Rourke, Latter, & D'Astous, 1986). Training parents to alter attending behaviors that reinforce pain behaviors and to support their children's well behavior or active coping (e.g., positive self-talk, persistence with tasks, relaxation, or distraction) may be useful. Parents can be trained to prompt self-coping skills and to withhold reinforcement for pain behavior (extinction). Such parent–child collaboration may improve children's implementation of coping skills, decrease the likelihood of relapse, and at the same time decrease parents' anxiety and uncertainty about how to help their child.

Several case studies have shown that modifying the social consequences of pain behavior can be effective in treating RAP symptoms (e.g., A. J. Miller & Kratochwill, 1979; Sank & Biglan, 1974), and two group comparison studies have evaluated cognitive behavioral programs for RAP that incorporate systematic training of parents (Sanders et al., 1989b). Sanders et al. (1989b) evaluated an 8 session program that involved training children to employ self-management skills (viz., relaxation, distraction, positive imagery, and coping self-statements) and training the parents to prompt and reinforce their children's use of these skills. Compared to a waitlist control condition, more children in the cognitive behavioral condition were completely pain-free at a 3-month follow-up. They responded more quickly, and cognitive behavioral treatment was associated with greater improvement in the school setting.

However, this study had only a short (3-month) follow-up and did not control for therapist contact or parents' pretreatment expectancies for change.

Sanders et al. (1994b) extended earlier work by evaluating the effects of a cognitive–BFI (CBFI) program on children's pain, the extent of relapse, and the degree of interference of the pain with the child's activities. The Sanders and Dadds (1993) model of BFI was adapted for use with pain patients. The model involves conducting a comprehensive functional analysis of the child's behavior and family interactions; discussing assessment findings with parents and challenging, where necessary, maladaptive attributions or explanations; presenting a social learning explanation for the pain; and providing active skills training via instructions, modeling, rehearsal, feedback, and homework assignments to train parents to implement behavior change strategies with children in the home. Individual skills training intervention is provided to children on an as-required basis. Treatment involved 6 sessions.

On the most stringent criterion of clinical improvement (being pain-free), children receiving CBFI had significantly lower levels of RAP than children receiving standard pediatric care (SPC) at posttreatment and 6-month and 12-month follow-up assessments. Both the child and the mother reported fewer relapse episodes in the 3 months preceding the 12-month follow-up assessment. The children's remaining pain was less severe, and parents were more satisfied with treatment, than those receiving SPC.

As treatment involved teaching the child and his or her mother new ways of coping with the child's pain, the study sought to identify whether children's coping and mothers' caregiving skills predicted clinical outcome. Regression procedures were used to examine whether the child's active coping and the mother's adaptive caregiving predicted the child's level of pain following treatment. After controlling for the child's initial level of pain on entry to the trial, the mother's use of adaptive caregiving was a significant independent predictor of the child's posttreatment level of pain. Furthermore, the child's posttreatment level of pain behavior was also significantly predicted by the child's active self-talk, the mother's adaptive caregiving, and reductions in the mother's use of sympathy, seeking external medical help, and anger.

Sanders, Cleghorn, Shepherd, and Patrick (1993a) subsequently examined pretreatment predictors of the amount of change in the child's pain scores and the degree of interference of the pain in the child's life. Having a stress-related mode of onset for RAP and higher levels of adaptive maternal caregiving were significant predictors of the extent of change on the measure of pain.

These findings showed that the modification of family interactions is effective in treating RAP. Similar treatment methods have been successfully employed in the treatment of pediatric headache (Beames et al., 1992). As child and parent have been trained concurrently in much of this research, the unique contribution of parent training to outcome over and above the effects of child coping skills is unclear. Future pain management studies could usefully compare the effects of child coping training alone with child coping combined with adjunctive parent training and with parent training alone. Our clinical impression has been that most parents require relatively minimal training to prompt and support their child's self-coping efforts. In cases in which parents themselves have significant health problems (e.g., chronic illness or chronic pain), however, a purely child-focused intervention may be inadequate.

3.1.1. Acute Pain

Another application of parent training interventions involves helping parents to coach their children to cope with painful medical procedures such as injections or with even more invasive procedures such as bone marrow aspirations, lumbar punctures, or surgery (e.g., Jay, 1988). Young children can become quite distressed during medical procedures. Parents themselves are often uncertain about how to assist their child or indeed to manage their own anxiety.

Blount et al. (1992) compared the effects of a combined child and parent training intervention with routine care in preschool children receiving routine immunization injections. Children were taught to distract themselves and to blow up a balloon as a form of deep breathing. Parents were taught to coach their children. Observational measures of children's distress during the procedure showed that trained parents were more likely to use the coaching skills, and their children were less distressed during the procedure on two of three observational measures than were children of untrained parents.

3.2. Chronic Food Refusal

Feeding difficulties are common in young children, with an estimated one in five preschoolers being reported by their parents to be problem feeders (Fergusson, Horwood, & Shannon, 1985). Childhood eating disorders are estimated to account for 25–35% of referrals to outpatient pediatric and mental health clinics (Archer & Szatmari, 1990) and up to 5% of pediatric hospital admissions (Wittenberg, 1990).

Difficulties range from minor, transient problems to longer-term difficulties, including total food refusal with resulting grave implications for the child's health and adequate growth (Luiselli, 1989). Problems at mealtimes can include picky or messy eating, noisy or disruptive behavior, refusal to remain seated at the table (Sanders, Patel, Le Grice, & Shepherd, 1993b), throwing food, not using utensils, being easily distracted, refusing to eat meals (but demanding snacks), and crying or throwing tantrums during meals (Finney, 1986). Some feeding problems affect the child's dietary intake and may lead to failure to thrive. Problems that affect growth include food refusal and selectivity, limited food intake, self-feeding deficits and improper pacing (Luiselli, 1989), difficulties taking solids, gagging (Archer & Szatmari, 1990), resistance to feeding, disinterest, anorexia, rumination, and vomiting (Larson, Ayllon, & Barrett, 1987). Children with feeding difficulties are at risk of delayed social development or otherwise atypical development (e.g., lack of acceptance in peer and school environments). Parents can be extremely anxious about their children's abnormal eating, even when the children's physical growth is not impaired.

Many feeding problems are multidetermined, involving both organic and psychological factors. Organic problems include physiological anomalies (e.g., cleft palate, short-gut syndrome, esophageal stricture), metabolic disorders (e.g., cystic fibrosis, diabetes, celiac disease, congenital heart disease, enzyme deficits), absorption or utilization deficits (e.g., prolonged vomiting from gastroesophageal reflux, vomiting and diarrhoea from gastroenteritis or chronic infection, food allergies or intolerances), and mechanical or neuromotor dysfunction (e.g., cerebral palsy, swallowing disorders, perinatal trauma such as anoxia, asphyxia, and other causes of central nervous system damage) (Denton, 1986; Luiselli, 1989).

Family interaction factors also contribute to the development and maintenance of feeding problems. Parents' feeding practices (e.g., absence of effective prompts for age-appropriate eating, failure to model appropriate mealtime behavior, inadequate consequences for appropriate eating and problem mealtime behaviors) and failure to establish a conducive eating environment (e.g., irregular mealtimes, unrestricted access to food between meals, presenting meals in an environment containing distractions such as toys and television, and unrealistic or inappropriate expectations of age-appropriate dietary intake and mealtime behavior) have been proposed to account for the development and maintenance of feeding problems (Sanders et al., 1993b).

Sanders et al. (1993b) examined the family interactions of feeding-disordered children and non-problem eaters and found that parents of problem eaters were more negative and coercive and engaged in higher rates of aversive instruction giving, aversive prompting, and negative comments related to eating than did parents of non-problem eaters.

Coercive parental behaviors were found to be significantly associated with food refusal and noncompliance in children.

Behavioral techniques such as verbal instructions, manual prompts, shaping, modeling, differential reinforcement or reward and punishment contingencies, stimulus control techniques, extinction, and time out have been successfully used to modify feeding behavior in children with developmental disabilities (Iwata, Riordan, Wohl, & Finney, 1982; Luiselli, 1989; Sisson & Dixon, 1986), with organic problems such as cystic fibrosis (Stark, Bowen, Tyc, Evans, & Passero, 1990) and short-gut syndrome (Linscheid, Tarnowski, Rasnake, & Brams, 1987), with food refusal and failure to thrive in the absence of organicity (Larson et al., 1987; Ramsay & Zelazo, 1987) or following the correction or remission of organic problems such as gastroesophageal reflux (Greer, Dorow, Williams, McCorkle, & Asnes, 1991; Koepke & Thyer, 1985), and with disruptive behavior problems (Dadds et al., 1984).

For example, Werle et al. (1993) used a multiple-baseline, across-subjects design to evaluate the effects of a home-based parent training program with three families. Parents were trained to regularly offer children previously rejected food, to give clear prompts, to increase contingent positive attention, and to use planned ignoring and terminating instructions for attempts to leave the meal area. Results showed that training was effective in increasing the mother's offerings of target foods and positive attention and increasing children's eating on their own and consuming targeted foods. The authors also reported that some training difficulties arose due to competing child care responsibilities in the home.

Because of the complex interrelationships between physiological and environmental influences, individual treatment should be based on a careful functional analysis of variables that are maintaining the problem (Luiselli, 1989; Sisson & Dixon, 1986). Treatment plans often follow direct observation of parent–child mealtime interactions, with subsequent parent training addressing the goals determined by the observations (Iwata et al., 1982; Finney, 1986). Most studies, however, have been case reports or single case studies. There is a need for randomized group comparison studies involving direct comparisons of active alternative treatments. One important treatment option in research on feeding disorders is the provision of dietary guidance and advice, as dietitians are frequently involved in multidisciplinary teams treating children with feeding problems. Consequently, it is important to determine whether parent training is more effective than dietary intervention alone.

Turner, Sanders, and Wall (1994) sought to address these limitations by comparing the effects and acceptability of a parent training intervention and a nutrition education procedure commonly used in pediatric care. Measures of mealtime interaction, feeding behavior, nutritional status, and adjustment of preschool-age children with persistent feeding problems were taken. The parent training condition sought to modify dysfunctional parental feeding practices and to teach parents effective management of children's eating and mealtime behavior. Dietary education focused on educating parents about children's nutritional requirements, without specific skills training in the implementation of behavior change techniques. Children in both treatment conditions showed improvement on the child behavior measures (e.g., food refusal, disruptive behavior during mealtimes) at home and in mealtime observations in the clinic. Children in both conditions also showed at follow-up an increase in the variety of foods sampled. Following treatment, mothers who received parent training showed more positive mother–child interaction during mealtimes and were more satisfied with treatment than mothers who received dietary education. All treatment effects were maintained at 3-month follow-up assessment. The main limitation of this study was lack of a waitlist control condition to control for maturational effects; also limiting was the relatively small sample size, which made it difficult to detect statistically significant differences between groups.

Theses studies provide preliminary evidence that parent training interventions are useful in the management of children with persistent feeding difficulties. There is need, however, for a large-scale randomized trial that includes appropriate comparison groups, including a waitlist control condition. At the time of writing, we are currently completing the follow-up assessments of children in a study that addresses many of these methodological limitations.

3.3. Infant Sleep Disturbance

Sleep disturbance is a common problem in young children. Problems such as refusal to go to bed, sleep-onset delay, and night waking with crying affect 15–35% of preschool-age children (Blampied & France, 1993). Night waking occurs in approximately one fifth to one half of all infants in the 6- to 24-month age group (Richman, 1981a,b). Persistent sleep disturbance is often stressful for parents and is associated with increased maternal depression, marital discord, and child abuse (Seymour, 1987). Although the causes of sleep disturbance have not been firmly established, Blampied and France (1993) argued that physiological, maturational, and parenting factors all play a role. Intermittent parent attention following night waking has been proposed as a maintenance factor, and suggestive evidence comes from studies in which parents have modified sleep disruption by withholding attention and using stimulus control interventions such as regular, predictable bedtime routines (e.g., Richman, Douglas, Hunt, Lansdown, & Levene, 1985; Sanders, Bor, & Dadds, 1984).

In a carefully designed study, France and Hudson (1990) successfully trained the parents of seven infants (age range 8–20 months) with recurrent sleep difficulties to employ extinction and stimulus control procedures. Using a multiple-baseline, across-subjects design, the results showed that all children had decreased frequency and duration of night waking that maintained at 3- and 24-month follow-up.

The management of sleep disturbance can be a controversial issue. Planned ignoring is not acceptable to all parents of infants who cry persistently. France (1994) discussed a number of concerns that have been raised by both professionals and parents about the use of behavioral treatment methods for infant sleep disturbance. These include the beliefs that the use of extinction is harmful, that sleep disturbance is normal and inevitable, that it should be tolerated by parents, and that treating sleep disturbance is treating the symptom, not the cause. As France points out, however, many of parents' concerns are based on misinformation about the nature, seriousness, causes, and effects of sleep disturbance; this difficulty is best dealt with through a combination of accurate information in the context of a collaborative professional relationship. Other studies with older preschool children have shown that the combination of stimulus control and standard contingency management procedures is useful for managing refusal to go to bed and nighttime wakefulness (e.g., Sanders et al., 1984).

3.4. Relatively Neglected Areas

Children with chronic illness are another group who might benefit from family intervention. Approximately 10–15% of children suffer from a chronic illness (Gortmaker, 1985). Contemporary pediatric practice increasingly involves the management of chronic illnesses and the psychosocial complications of these illnesses rather than acute or infectious disease. Illnesses such as juvenile rheumatoid arthritis, cancer, insulin-dependent diabetes mellitus, and cystic fibrosis are all conditions that have psychosocial complications that may compromise the child's treatment and clinical status. These illnesses often impose a considerable burden of care on a child's family, particularly the child's mother. Caring for a chronically ill child often entails seemingly endless medical appointments, hospitalizations, injections, physiotherapy, and special diets. Some evidence has linked parent–child interaction processes to children's clinical status. Miller-Johnson, Emery, Marvin, Clarke, Lovinger, and Martin (1994), in a study of 88 children and adolescents attending pediatric endocrinology clinics, found that parent–child conflict as independently reported by both child and parent on a self-report measure was associated with parents' ratings of adherence and to measures of the child's metabolic control. Conflict appeared to affect metabolic control indirectly by affecting the child's adherence to the treatment regimen.

Parents often need information and advice about behavior management, as well as knowledge about the disease process, management of illness-related anxiety, means of promoting adherence to medical treatments, and the integration of the illness and its treatment into the family's everyday life (Eiser, 1990).

A recent example of the value of parent training as part of a multicomponent intervention strategy stems from the work of Stark et al. (1993) on cystic fibrosis. Cystic fibrosis is a life-threatening, genetically transmitted disease involving generalized dysfunction of the exocrine system affecting the respiratory, gastrointestinal, pancreatic, hepatic, and reproductive systems (Matthews & Drotar, 1984). A major concern in the management of these children is that they will be inadequately nourished. Parents underwent group training that involved receiving nutritional information, specific suggestions about meal preparation, and training in behavior management principles, praise, differential attention, and contingent withdrawal of privileges. Children also attended a group. Results showed that children's caloric intake increased and was maintained at 2-year follow-up, and children's growth rates were higher following intervention than in the previous year.

Finney and Bonner (1992) argued that family systems models have dominated the writings on the role of the family in chronic illness. They pointed out that there is little supportive empirical research documenting the effectiveness of any form of family therapy with medically ill children. There is also a paucity of BFI studies, and such studies remain an important area for future research.

4. Applications with Childhood Anxiety Disorders

It is now recognized that children suffer from anxiety and stress-related problems (Kendall, 1992) and that family interactions can play a role in the development and maintenance of anxiety. Children may imitate the fears and anxieties of their parents, and parents may inadvertently reward anxious behavior by providing contingent comfort and reassurance and by removing aversive stimuli (threats, chores, separation) (King, Hamilton, & Ollendick 1988). Goodyer (1990) argued that children's anxiety and depression are related to mothers' high levels of emotional distress and lack of intimate social support. The degree of anxiety experienced by nonclinic children is positively correlated with parents' marital problems (Dadds & Powell, 1991). Krohne, Kohlmann, and colleagues hypothesized that anxiety in children is associated with restrictive parental behavior that fosters deficits in child competence and negative self expectancies and evaluations. Krohne and Hock (1991) observed mother–child dyads solving a wooden block puzzle. Independent raters scored the duration of individual vs. cooperative working and transitions from one mode to the other. The results showed that the degree of self-reported trait anxiety in the child was associated with the extent to which the mother cooperated vs. restricted the child's engagement in the task.

Recent studies by Dadds and colleagues hypothesized that anxiety could be modeled or promulgated within a family unit through a specific series of interpersonal behaviors and interactions. Children and their parents are asked separately to interpret an ambiguous yet potentially threatening social situation and then state how they would respond to it. After each person has responded to these items, parent(s) and child discuss the ambiguous situation together. After 5 minutes of discussion, the child again answers two questions: "What do you think is happening?" and "What will you do?" Anxious children made more threat interpretations and more avoidant responses than non-anxious children. Moreover, a significant proportion of the anxious children were found to switch from a proactive plan (e.g., "I will join in the game") to an avoidant plan (e.g., "I will stay away from them") after discussing the problem with their parents (Barrett, Rapee, Dadds, & Ryan, 1995). The change to a more avoidant plan was found to be negatively related to the extent to which the parents listened to the child and rewarded proactive plans and positively related to the extent to which parents reciprocated avoidant plans in the child. Thus, anxious children appear to learn to emphasize threat avoidance through interaction with their parents.

Some research has evaluated the efficacy of focusing on parenting skills and family interaction processes. Several single case studies have shown that parents can modify children's phobias (Dadds, Heard, & Rapee, 1991). Only one controlled treatment study has evaluated the role of family variables in the remediation of child anxiety. Barrett, Dadds, and Rapee (1993) treated a large group of anxious children (overanxious, avoidant, separation anxiety) who were randomly assigned to either a cognitive–behavioral treatment (CBT) based on Kendall's model or the same CBT model plus a family intervention that ran in parallel over a 14-week period. The family intervention involved three phases: (1) parent skills for managing child distress and avoidance, (2) parent skills for managing their own anxiety, and (3) parent communication and problem-solving skills.

Following treatment, 61% of children in the CBT group no longer met a DSM-III-R diagnosis, compared with 88% in the combined treatment and fewer than 30% in the waitlist control group. At 12-month follow-up, the relative success rates for the two treatment groups were 80% and 100%, respectively. Thus, it appears that the modification of parent skills can have a significant effect on anxiety in children when combined with a CBT program for the child. It is not clear, however, whether changing parent skills on its own will result in an improvement in child behavior, and it is not clear which aspect of the parental intervention was associated with the extra improvements. The Barrett et al. (1993) study also examined whether the CBT plus family intervention changed the way parents of anxious children taught their children to interpret and respond to threat. As discussed above, these parents were found to ask more questions of their children and to reinforce more avoidance in their children when faced with an ambiguous threat situation than were parents of nonclinic and clinic nonanxious children. At the end of treatment, this tendency had greatly diminished. That is, after treatment, parents of anxious children were no longer focusing so much of their child's attention on threat and avoidance strategies. Thus, it appears that this mechanism may be an important factor in the development and treatment of these disorders.

4.1. Overview

Collectively, the studies examining the role of family intervention in the treatment of stress-related somatic complaints (e.g., RAP) and anxiety problems in children have used similar treatment methods. The concurrent training of children in the use of active coping skills and preparation of parents in how to support their child's efforts through modeling, prompting of self coping, and social reinforcement procedures appears to be an effective combination and may have broader application.

5. Applications with Conduct-Problem Children

5.1. Effectiveness

Parent disciplinary practices have been repeatedly shown to be related to the origins and maintenance of conduct problems in children (Patterson, 1982). These problems continue to be a focus of much of the empirical and theoretical literature on BFI. This emphasis is justifiable, given the prevalence of the disorders, the chronic nature of the problem, and the significance of the social, personal, and community costs of juvenile delinquency. Between a third and a half of all children referred to mental health facilities have conduct problems (Kazdin, 1987).

The strongest evidence attesting to the efficacy of BFI with conduct problems is with preadolescent children with oppositional behavior problems. Several recent reviews of the parent training literature show that parents of conduct-problem children can produce clinically significant changes in their own and their children's behavior when they receive appropriate training in the application of behavior change procedures (e.g., Kendziora & O'Leary, 1993; McMahon, 1994; McMahon & Wells, 1989; G. E. Miller & Prinz, 1990; Patterson, Dishion, & Chamberlain, 1993; Webster-Stratton, 1993). Commonly employed techniques include the use of consequences such as contingent social attention, praise, time out, and response cost contingencies and antecedent or setting event interventions such as using clear instructions, rules, and the provision of age-appropriate activities (Berkowitz & Graziano, 1972; Graziano, 1977; Kazdin, 1987).

A range of training methods have been shown to be effective (O'Dell, 1974; Sutton, 1992); however, most successful programs with children with clinically significant levels of antisocial behavior provide clear written and verbal instructions to parents, model parenting skills, use behavioral rehearsal procedures to practice skills, and provide contingent feedback following direct observation of parent–child interaction. Videomodeling is a particularly effective training method, although maintenance of treatment effects has been poor with use of videomodeling alone (Webster-Stratton, Hollinsworth, & Kolpacoff, 1989).

Not only is the effectiveness of parent training interventions for conduct-problem children attested to by changes in children's disruptive behavior, but also there are often wide-ranging positive effects in other aspects of the families' functioning. These effects include improvements in mothers' sense of parenting competence (Pisterman et al., 1992) and attitudes toward children. Other research shows that BFI is associated with reductions in parenting stress, depression, and marital conflict. Little evidence of any negative side effects of treatment has emerged.

Parents undergoing BFI are generally satisfied consumers and view the specific techniques taught in these training programs (e.g., praise, time out) as both effective and acceptable (McMahon & Forehand, 1983; Webster-Stratton, 1989a). Webster-Stratton (1989a) found that ignoring misbehavior was rated as more difficult to use and less useful than other techniques taught in her program (e.g., use of rewards and time out).

Heffer and Kelley (1987) found that low-income families rated time out as being significantly less acceptable than did high-income families. However, parents' ratings of acceptability appear to be affected by the severity of the child's problem behavior (Frentz & Kelley, 1986). Much less is known about how children view the treatment process, although Dadds, Adlington, and Christensen (1987a) found that both nonclinic and oppositional children rated time out as an acceptable strategy for parents to use.

While parent training is effective with many families, it is not a panacea, given that an estimated 30–50% of children after intervention remain in the clinically disturbed range on measures of child adjustment (Patterson et al., 1993; Webster-Stratton et al., 1989). Intervention effects are less impressive with older severely conduct-disordered children, particularly adolescents, or children with attention-deficit disorders (e.g., Barkley et al., 1992).

One criterion of effectiveness that is rarely discussed outside the behavior therapy field concerns the generalization of treatment effects. Clients frequently need to generalize their skills to conditions outside the initial training setting in which the skills were first learned (Stokes & Osnes, 1989). This generalization might involve the parents' applying a behavior change strategy acquired for one child in the family to a sibling who displays similar problem behavior (sibling generalization). There is some evidence to show that siblings of conduct-disordered children often display levels of oppositional behavior similar to those of the referred children (Dadds, Sanders, Morrison & Rebgetz, 1992). Generalization enhancement might involve the parents' learning to deal with out-of-home situations (e.g., in a supermarket) in which a child is disruptive in the same or a very similar way (setting generalization). Alternatively, the child who is taught to speak pleasantly when making requests of one adult (e.g., the father) should be able to display similar polite behavior when speaking to other adults such as the mother (person generalization). At the same time, parents and children also need to learn to discriminate conditions in which generalization is not desirable (Sanders, 1984). For example, it is inappropriate to use with a teenager the same token reinforcement program used with a preschooler.

Research indicates that generalized implementation of new parenting strategies is a realistic and feasible clinical goal, particularly when the parents receive comprehensive training in the use of a variety of behavioral skills (e.g., Koegel, Glahn, & Nieminen, 1978; S. J. Miller & Sloane, 1976; Powers, Singer, Stevens, & Sowers, 1992; Sanders & Dadds, 1982; Sanders & Glynn, 1981; Sanders & Plant, 1989). Some parents generalize their implementation of behavioral skills across different child care settings with no or relatively minimal prompting, while others need supplementary interventions to promote generalization (Sanders & Glynn, 1981). Furthermore, there is some evidence that reductions in negative parental behavior seem to generalize and maintain better than increases in positive or nonaversive parent behavior (Sanders & Dadds, 1982).

The extent to which BFI produces child behavior changes that generalize to the school setting is an important issue for many conduct-problem children, who can have significant learning and behavioral difficulties at school. McNeil, Eyberg, Eisenstadt, Newcomb, and Funderburk (1991) reported some encouraging findings showing the beneficial effects of parent training for children with behavior problems at school. Children whose parents received parent training interventions showed improvements on measures of oppositional behavior in the classroom, even though there were no specific school-based interventions. A limitation of the training was that there was no effect on measures of hyperactivity, inattention, or peer relationships, highlighting the importance of specifically assessing the generalization effects across different response domains. Research has yet to adequately explain why generalization effects occur, and there appears to be less interest in pursuing the issue than there was a decade ago (Sanders & James, 1983).

Several studies have examined the durability of treatment effects (Forehand & Long, 1988; Long, Forehand, Wierson, & Morgan, 1994; Webster-Stratton, 1990). In general, these studies have shown good gains in maintenance of treatment, particularly when the child's problem is not complicated by parent-related difficulties or significant social adversity. A long-term follow-up study of adolescents who participated in the treatment program employed by Forehand and colleagues showed that on most measures of adolescent functioning, treated children were indistinguishable from a comparison group of nonclinic adolescents. However, one third of the treated group had received other treatment since leaving the program and were showing significantly poorer academic performance at school. These findings highlight the importance of school-based intervention with conduct-problem children. The parents of the treated children were functioning just as well as parents of nonclinic adolescents on measures of depression, marital adjustment, and parenting competence.

A further follow-up of these same children by Long et al. (1994) when they were in late adolescence or early adulthood showed that they were not significantly different from a matched community sample on measures of delinquency, emotional adjustment, academic progress, or relationships with parents. These results are suggestive of the beneficial long-term effects of early intervention; however, the absence of a control group precludes definitive conclusions about the variables responsible for the maintenance effects observed.

Webster-Stratton (1990) followed up 83 mothers and 51 fathers who had participated in one of three different parent training programs 3 years earlier. Only parents who had received a videotape modeling program with a therapist-led group discussion maintained stable treatment gains. Parents receiving a self-directed videotape program failed to maintain initial gains. Overall, children who failed to maintain improvements were from more disadvantaged circumstances. They were more likely to come from single-parent homes, were lower income, and had increased alcoholism, drug abuse, and depression in the immediate family.

Other research shows that BFI has limited long-term effects in cases in which there is a concurrent unresolved marital problem (Dadds et al., 1987b), in which the mother suffers from depression (McMahon, Forehand, Griest, & Wells, 1981; Webster-Stratton, 1990, 1992), in which the family lives in adverse socioeconomic circumstances (Dumas, 1986; Webster-Stratton, 1985), and in which the mother has a low level of social support available to her (Wahler, 1980) or is a single parent (Webster-Stratton, 1992). No studies have examined the effects of treatment with severely clinically depressed children. Outcome is also poorer in some programs when trainee therapists are used (Frankel & Simmons, 1992). Of course, many of the aforementioned factors are risk factors for the development of conduct problems in the first place.

5.2. Enhancing Treatment Outcome

There is now general agreement that due to the pervasive nature and multidetermined etiology of conduct problems, effective family intervention must be based on careful assessment of the broader social and interpersonal context within which families live. Numerous authors have proposed ways to improve the outcome of treatment with multi-distressed families by expanding the focus of treatment to address either parents' own personal concerns (G. E. Miller & Prinz, 1990; Wahler, 1980) or children's deficits in peer relationships, academic achievement, or social problem solving (e.g., Kazdin, Siegel, & Bass, 1992). Parent-focused interventions include teaching parents self-management skills (Griest, Forehand, Rogers, Breiner, Furey, & Williams, 1982), providing concurrent marital therapy (Dadds et al., 1987b), providing training in the selection and arrangement of activities for children in high-risk situations (Sanders & Dadds, 1982; Sanders & Christensen, 1985), anger management (Goldstein, Keller, & Erne, 1985), social support training (Dadds & McHugh, 1992), and the development of better home–school liaison for the management of school-based behavioral problems (Blechman, 1984). Unfortunately, much of this research has failed to document that families receiving adjunctive procedures actually had deficits in the skills or problems the additional interventions were designed to correct. 306To avoid the "shotgun" approach to therapy, adjunctive treatments are most usefully applied when there is clear evidence to link the additional problem (e.g., depression, marital distress) to the parents' capacity to alter dysfunctional parenting practices. Such evidence is not readily available.

Nevertheless, some evidence shows that more broadly focused family interventions enhance treatment outcome. Webster-Stratton (1994) showed that the addition of a 14-week adjunctive intervention that provided training for the parents in self-control skills, communication skills, problem solving, and social support skills, after a 12-week standard parent training program, led to significant extra improvements on measures of parents' problem solving, communication, and consumer satisfaction. There was no additional benefit for children. Both the standard and the combined treatment were effective in reducing problem behavior.

Another recent study also demonstrated the value of attending to parents' additional concerns in reducing dropout from treatment. Prinz and Miller (1994) randomized families to either standard treatment or an enhancement intervention that spent part of each session discussing parental expectations, feelings, and other concerns (e.g., work pressures). The discussion apparently encouraged parental problem solving. There was a significantly lower level of dropout with the enhanced treatment (29%) than with the standard family intervention procedure (46%). The dropout rates for the standard treatment, however, were higher than those reported in other programs.

An alternative approach to enhancing outcome with multidistressed parents involves training mothers to respond differently to external stressors in their lives. Wahler, Cartor, Fleischman, and Lambert (1993) evaluated the effects of a parent training program that incorporated "synthesis training" with 29 children with severe conduct problems from multidistressed families. This enhancement procedure involved a conversational format designed to increase parents' ability to discriminate between child-focused issues and social exchanges involving others, rather than to view them as a collective set. This process was predicted to result in a more consistent application of parenting skills. The results of the study showed that the intervention had no effect on clinic observation measures. However, observation of mother–child interaction at home showed that mothers receiving synthesis training had lower levels of indiscriminate parenting at follow-up, and their children engaged in less aversive child behavior, compared to the standard training condition. Although the results were consistent with the authors' theoretical position, no objective measure of the hypothesized mechanisms of change was reported. It is quite plausible that the increased empathic attention mothers received for discussing other problems in their lives may have produced the apparent additive treatment effect.

Spaccarelli, Cotler, and Penman (1992) found that the addition of problem-solving skills training for parents enhanced the effects of parent training. Their study controlled for the amount of contact parents received in the adjunctive treatment. While both treatments resulted in significant improvements in parenting behaviors and child aversiveness, the problem-solving group also resulted in additional improvements on measures of parenting stress and parental attitudes to the child's adjustment. These groups' differences did not maintain at follow-up, and there was no measure of how well parents actually learned or implemented the problem-solving skills they were taught.

There is some evidence showing that outcome with older children can be improved by teaching children problem-solving skills. Kazdin et al. (1992) found that an intervention that combined parent management training and child-focused problem-solving skills training was significantly more effective with 7- to 13-year-old conduct-problem children than was either treatment alone. Greater effects on measures of child aggression, antisocial behavior, and delinquency were noted for the combined treatment. At 1-year follow-up assessments, the combined treatment resulted in a significantly higher proportion of children being in the nonclinical range on measures of child adjustment.

Conduct-problem children often have deficiencies in peer relationships (Dumas, Blechman, & Prinz, 1994; Patterson et al., 1993; Prinz, Blechman, & Dumas, 1994). Prinz et al. (1994) used a peer coping skills training intervention based on a coping-competency model with aggressive children in grades 1–3. The program involved teaching children prosocial communication skills and emphasized teaching communication skills (information exchange) rather than formal social problem-solving skills. Children receiving the intervention showed improvements in children information exchange, social skills, and, to a lesser extent, aggression. It remains to be seen whether such interventions enhance the effects of family intervention programs.

Another approach to dealing with social skills deficits is to use parents as social skills trainers (Budd & Itzkowitz, 1990). Relatively little work has focused on using family interventions to promote socially competent or prosocial behavior in children. Parents can be taught how to model, prompt, and reinforce prosocial or socially competent behaviors, particularly in young children. Important relationship-enhancing skills include behaviors such as giving and receiving positive affection and soliciting children's opinions and ideas about family activities or the child's own experiences, and modeling, prompting, and reinforcing constructive communication in resolving conflict could provide a support environment for social skills programs targeted at children.

5.3. Overview

There has been an increasing convergence of opinion in the literature that children with severe conduct problems, once they start school, require prolonged, multifaceted interventions at home, at school, and in the peer group (Kazdin, 1987; Prinz et al., 1994). Prior to school entry, BFI alone appears to be effective. If this conclusion is correct, it is likely that the models of intervention that evolve will be expensive. The costs of such interventions must be balanced by the savings potentially realizable from reduced antisocial behavior. An alternative approach to clinical management after a disorder has developed involves moving toward a public health perspective in the delivery of prevention focused programs.

A great deal of empirical work is required to determine the appropriate strength of intervention needed to produce clinically significant treatment effects. For some children with severe conduct problems whose parents are unwilling or unable to be involved, a completely different kind of parent training may be required. Moore and Chamberlain (1994) (see also Chapter 2) described a model of community foster care for severely disturbed adolescents that combined specific training of foster parents in the use of behavior change techniques, school consultation, individual therapy for children, and family intervention with the child's own family based on Patterson's work (e.g., Patterson, Reid, Jones, & Conger, 1975).

6. Applications with Maritally Distressed and Remarried Families

6.1. Children in Conflictual Marriages

Reviewing the literature on the relationship between marital conflict and children's adjustment, Grych and Fincham (1990) concluded that measures of marital conflict are more closely related to children's adjustment problems than are measures of marital satisfaction. The specific effects of discord on children depended on the type of conflict involved, with more frequent and intense conflict producing more distress in children. The combination of verbal and physical violence is associated with higher levels of conduct problems in children than is verbal abuse alone (Fantuzzo, DePaola, Lambert, Martino, Anderson, & Sutton, 1991).

Grych and Fincham (1990) proposed that understanding the effects of marital distress on children's adjustment depends not only on the type of distress, but also on the child's coping strategies in dealing with the conflict and other contextual factors such as the child's prior experience with conflict, the child's perceptions of the emotional climate of the home, and the child's temperament and gender. Although empirical support for this model is limited at present, the model points to the importance of careful assessment of the marital or relationship context within which children's behavior problems occur.

However, the strength of the relationship between marital discord and children's adjustment is influenced by who the informant is, with stronger associations between reports of marital discord and child adjustment by mothers than by fathers or children (Burman, John, & Margolin, 1987). Children from highly discordant families compared to low-discord families are more likely to believe that both mothers and fathers would and should use coercive discipline in hypothetical discipline situations (Dadds, Sheffield, & Holbeck, 1990).

Marital conflict is not only a generic risk factor for the development of behavior problems in children (Rutter, 1985a), but also a risk factor for treatment failure (Dadds et al., 1987b). Numerous authors have noted that maritally discordant couples are difficult to treat and that successful teaching of child management skills to mothers may not reduce negative communication between spouses.

There is increasing evidence of the value of assessing and treating marital discord directly in the context of BFI programs. Sayger, Horne, and Glasser (1993) found that families with low marital satisfaction scores showed significant improvement in marital adjustment in a family-focused social learning intervention for aggressive children. The multicomponent program involved an emphasis on teaching family communication skills to all family members, not just the target child, as well as child management strategies. Dadds et al. (1987b), using a factorial design, found that when maritally distressed parents of behaviorally disturbed children received training only in parenting skills, they tended to relapse following initially successful training. In contrast, maritally discordant couples who received communication training, known as "partner support," maintained their treatment gains as well as nonmaritally distressed couples with a behavior-problem child. These studies encouragingly note that child-focused treatments can still be successful in treating children's behavior, despite the presence of discord.

One of the major obstacles to addressing marital issues in child cases is the relatively low participation rates of fathers in parent training (Coplin & Houts, 1991). It is not uncommon for parents of disruptive children to have markedly divergent views on the nature, significance, causes, and remediation of a child's behavior problem.

6.2. Children in Remarried Families

Stepfamilies formed after the divorce of one partner are becoming increasingly common (Baa, Sweet, & Martin, 1990). An estimated 35% of children born in the United States in the 1980s will experience the divorce and remarriage of their custodial parent (Glick, 1989). Children living in remarried families appear to have higher than normal rates of behavior problems and other psychopathology (Bray, 1988; Wadsworth, Burnell, Taylor, & Butler, 1985; Zill, 1988). Clinical research with this population is limited, and as yet no controlled trials have examined the efficacy of family interventions with stepfamilies, even though there are indications that a modified type of BFI may be a useful approach with these families.

Children from stepfamilies have been found to display higher rates of aggressive, impulsive, antisocial behavior than children from intact families. In addition, parents and teachers report that children from stepfamilies, especially girls, are more likely than their peers to be depressed, moody, or withdrawn. Compared with children from intact families, these children perform less well academically, experiencing more school absences, tardiness, and discipline problems. Children from remarried families also appear to be at greater risk for health problems and accidental injury than children living with both biological parents.

Research comparing adolescents from remarried families with adolescents from intact 2-parent families has found evidence of greater delinquency and other long-term negative consequences in the former. Parental remarriage was associated with early sexual activity, home leaving, and dropout from education. Adolescents from stepfamilies reported higher rates of substance use, and community surveys suggest that they are overrepresented among homeless youth (O'Connor, 1989). Girls may be at greater risk for poor long-term outcome than boys, especially in relation to leaving home early and early dropout from formal education.

Child adjustment following remarriage in some studies appears to be related to the child's age, gender, and family type. Several studies show that girls are less well adjusted than boys following parental remarriage (e.g., Hetherington, Cox, & Cox, 1982), although other studies have failed to replicate this finding (e.g., Zill, 1988). Over time, boys appear to benefit from having an additional parent in the household (Hetherington, Cox, & Cox, 1985; Santrock, Warshak, Lindbergh, & Meadows, 1982). While cross-sectional research suggests that young children and adolescents show the greatest deterioration in behavior (Zill, 1988), this picture is not supported by longitudinal studies. After initial disruptions, young children (early school age and younger) appear to adjust better to their parent's remarriage than older children (Hetherington et al., 1982).

Lawton and Sanders (1994) argued that traditional parent training interventions need to be modified to be acceptable to and effective with parents living in stepfamilies. They developed a behavioral stepfamily intervention that included training in parenting skills, partner support, shared family activities, and problem solving skills. This intervention was more effective in reducing oppositional behavior than a self-directed version of the same parenting program or a waitlist control. However, the therapist-delivered BFI was more effective for children with oppositional disorders than for children with more severe conduct disorders.

A critical issue that needs addressing in work with remarried families is the nature of the custodial parent's contact with the noncustodial parent. It is not uncommon for one parent to support the child's involvement in therapy while the other is bitterly opposed to it. Much greater attention needs to be given to evaluating preventive interventions with remarrying couples who have children, to reduce the risk of marital relationship breakdown.

7. Issues and Future Directions

7.1. The Importance of Process Variables

The therapist–client relationship in behavior therapy has received increased attention in recent times (e.g., Dadds, 1989; Horne, 1990; Patterson, 1985; Patterson & Chamberlain, 1995; Sanders & Dadds, 1993; Sweet, 1987; Twardosz & Nordquist, 1988). Early descriptions of BFI largely ignored the role of process variables that affect families' engagement in therapy and the acceptability of the parenting techniques advocated by therapists (e.g., Forehand & McMahon, 1981; Patterson et al., 1975). These variables include a diverse range of clinical and interpersonal skills that provide the relationship context within which family intervention takes place.

BFI can be conceptualized as involving a series of interrelated consultation tasks and consultation skills, the former being the process tasks that clinicians undertake, the latter being the interpersonal, communication, and therapeutic skills to carry out the required tasks. While the precise form of the intervention should depend substantially on the results of a comprehensive clinical assessment and behavioral analysis, the basic consultation tasks involved remain fairly constant. Table 3 summarizes the key consultation tasks and associated clinical skills described by Sanders and Dadds (1993) as being required of therapists in carrying out an intervention plan.

We and others have previously emphasized the importance of developing a shared collaborative relationship with parents during parent training (Sanders & Dadds, 1993). Sanders and Lawton (1993) described a guided participation model of information transfer for use in discussing assessment findings with families. The model involves a series of communicative tasks during which the therapist and the client review assessment information to arrive at a shared perspective regarding the nature and the causes of the problem and to establish goals for treatment. Descriptive information is presented in a sequenced manner with provision for parents to process, react to, and challenge the therapist's views. The model assumes that parental compliance with therapy depends in part on the extent to which parents are able to (1) reach reasonable agreement with the therapist about the nature of the problem, (2) understand the causes or explanations of the problem provided by the therapist, and (3) accept the relationship between their own actions and their child's behavior.

Webster-Stratton and Herbert (1993) also argued for the importance of effective communication with families and identified six skill domains that they believe characterize successful therapy: (1) building a supportive relationship, (2) empowering parents through behaviors such as reinforcing and validating parental insights, (3) using active teaching skills (e.g., videomodeling, rehearsal, and feedback), (4) interpreting (e.g., using analogies and metaphors), (5) leading and challenging (e.g., dealing with resistance), and (6) prophesy (e.g., anticipating setbacks).

Research by Patterson and colleagues has highlighted the critical importance of the way in which therapists respond to client "resistance" in therapy. In one of the earliest observational studies of the family intervention process, Patterson and Forgatch (1985) showed that when therapists began to teach or confront parents, there was an increase in parental resistant behaviors. Resistive behavior decreased when therapists were more nondirective. If therapists avoid confronting parents about maladaptive parenting practices, however, little change in parental behavior can be expected. Parental resistance is a major cause of premature dropout from therapy and poor treatment outcome and can take many different forms.

TABLE 3
Consultation Tasks and Clinical Skills

Consultation tasks	Important clinical skills
1. Creating a therapeutic alliance.	1. Effective listening, empathic, and other interviewing and rapport-building skills.
2. Negotiating an assessment protocol.	2. Translating vague or nonspecific concerns of clients into concrete, specific goals for change.
3. Discussing assessment results.	3. Providing a rationale for data collection tasks.
4. Negotiating goals of intervention.	4. Negotiating with parents and school personnel regarding data collection requirements.
5. Designing an intervention.	5. Conveying assessment results clearly and succinctly; dealing with client defensiveness and resistance.
6. Implementing treatment.	6. Formulating with the parent a shared explanation for the problem behavior.
7. Monitoring and evaluating progress.	7. Conducting a behavioral rehearsal with the parent as a skill training negative.
8. Programming for generalization and maintenance of therapeutic gains.	8. Providing constructive negative feedback without being critical.
	9. Dealing with dependency problems.

In a subsequent study, Patterson and Stoolmiller (1995) examined the role of parental resistance in predicting long-term clinical outcome in 70 cases of children referred for the treatment of antisocial behavior. Six treatment sessions were videotaped (corresponding to the beginning, midpoint, and end of therapy) and coded to record the occurrence of four negative parent behaviors (including confront, hopeless, sidetrack, and defend). There emerged from this study several important findings that highlighted the relationship between parents' within-session cooperation and their partners' use of discipline techniques. First, fathers' confrontational behavior during therapy predicted mothers' effective use of parental discipline. Specifically, fathers who showed an increase in confrontational behavior during treatment had partners who showed less change in effective discipline strategies. This finding highlighted the importance of effectively dealing with fathers' tendency to challenge the therapist. There was also a significant correlation between mothers' hopeless and defending behavior and changes in fathers' discipline practices.

In another study, Patterson and Chamberlain (1995) showed that parental social disadvantage, antisocial behavior, and depression were associated with increased parental resistance throughout parent training. They argued that parental resistance could result from four factors: (1) a history of defeats in discipline encounters with their child; (2) parental psychopathology, particularly depression and antisocial behavior; (3) stress and social disadvantage; and (4) the therapist's clinical skills in teaching and confronting parents.

Not all clinical problems are associated with the same process problems. Indeed, Patterson has argued that their general formulation may be applicable only to working-class parents of antisocial children. Fewer resistance problems are experienced in working with the families of children with stress and anxiety problems than in working with the chaotic, dysfunctional families of conduct-problem children. The former are on time or early, rarely miss appointments, and are generally cooperative with homework tasks. Consequently, process difficulties need to be studied with different populations and will also vary depending on the type of family intervention being employed (e.g., group vs. individual treatment, therapist-assisted vs. self-help programs).

7.2. Intervening across Multiple Settings

Clinical treatments with conduct-problem children are often limited by the difficulty of intervening across a range of settings in the child's life. While it is somewhat easier to work with childhood problems that are limited to one setting, such as noncompliance in the home, many children's problems occur in a range of home and community settings, and generally this circumstance is predictive of a poorer prognosis for the child (Kazdin, 1987). A common source of frustration for clinicians working with children with generalized problems is the uncoordinated involvement of several agencies in this case. Effective communication and coordination of services between agencies is critical to providing the most appropriate intervention with the minimum use of resources and at lowest cost to the community. All clinical services operate within a larger mental health system, and resources need to be devoted to establishing effective liaison with related services (including staff training).

7.3. Applying High-Power Interventions

Kazdin (1987) argued that the power of a clinical intervention needs to be matched to the severity and chronicity of the presenting problem. Children referred to mental health services for adjustment problems present with a variety of complex interrelated problems in areas of social, emotional, language, cognitive, and academic functioning. For example, children referred for disruptive behavior problems such as aggression, noncompliance, tantrums, and destructiveness often have problems of impulse control as well as problems such as anxiety, depression, and poor school performance. They may also be engaged in secretive or covert behaviors such as stealing, truanting, or lying that bring them into conflict with school authorities or the police. Such children can be markedly lacking in social skills and have few friends. The children's behavior frequently brings them into conflict with parents or other authority figures.

It is pointless to offer minimal interventions to children and families with severe and persistent problems. Research on the effectiveness of various methods for training parents to implement child management skills has clearly indicated that a combination of information provision, modeling, and rehearsal plus feedback is often required to teach basic parenting skills such as praising a child or using time out effectively.

Some families require more intensive home-based training. For example, single parents having difficulties with nighttime routines (e.g., dinnertime, bedtime) who have additional problems of lack of social support and confined living circumstances often benefit from a training session followed by a series of home visits in which the therapist models skills, prompts the parent's implementation of skills, and provides supportive, constructive feedback.

When a child's problem is complicated by additional parent-related problems such as marital distress, depression, or alcohol abuse, a major future challenge is to develop and evaluate adjunctive interventions that attend specifically to the type of dysfunction evident in the family. Fortunately, progress is being made in this area; however, "enhanced" interventions do not necessarily improve outcome. For example, McFarland and Sanders (1993) developed an enhanced version of their basic BFI intervention, which included cognitive therapy designed to treat depressed mothers of conduct-problem children. By 6-month follow-up, however, both the standard and the enhanced treatment were equally effective in reducing disruptive behavior and in reducing depression.

7.4. Dealing with Educational and Learning Problems

Conduct problems and learning difficulties go hand in hand for many children, and a comprehensive approach to helping distressed children must include a focus on the interaction of the two (Loeber, 1990). This requirement has clear clinical implications.

First, it is important that child and family therapists either be skilled in the assessment and treatment of childhood learning problems or be able to liaise effectively with staff who possess these skills. Second, it is important that treatment planning incorporate a comprehensive focus on the interrelationship of learning and behavioral problems. Third, treatment effectiveness will be enhanced by cooperation between intervention agents who are operating in different settings and on different aspects of the child's problems. For example, a number of studies have provided evidence that reinforcement contingencies that span home and school settings are effective in decreasing generalized problems in children (Shapiro, 1987). A teacher may be trained to provide contingencies for parental reports of improvements in child behavior in the home setting. Alternatively, a teacher can send home reports of the child's behavior and achievement in the classroom to parents who have been trained to apply effective contingencies (Kelley, 1990). Interventions such as these that span learning and home settings show considerable promise, and further research and development should be encouraged in this area.

7.5. Applications That Combine Individual and Family-Focused Interventions

The model of BFI described in this chapter focuses primarily on working with children through their parents. As children move toward adolescence, they may benefit from concurrent individual therapy sessions. For example, children with anger control, depression, or anxiety problems can be taught self-coping, self-management, or problem solving skills relevant to the problem. Such individual therapy often works most effectively, however, if parents can be trained to support and encourage children's application of skills they have acquired during individual therapy. Future research needs to determine what combinations of child- and family-focused treatments might be effective in the treatment of a variety of disorders.

7.6. Rural and Isolated Families

Families living in rural and remote areas experience mental health problems at a rate similar to that experienced by their urban counterparts (Connell, Irvine, & Rodney, 1982). However, children with behavioral or emotional problems are less likely to access mental health services of any type due to physical isolation from services, stigma associated with seeking assistance for psychological problems, and difficulties in recruiting and retaining qualified mental health professionals. Several authors have written of the specific problems encountered by poor families in rural areas (Kelleher, Taylor, & Rickert, 1992; Reid & Solomon, 1992).

Connell, Sanders, and Markie-Dadds (1994) developed a brief intervention for parents living in rural and remote areas of Queensland in Australia. A 10-week self-directed program involved provision of a commercially available parenting book (*Every Parent: A Positive Approach to Children's Behavior*) and a self-directed implementation guide (Sanders, Lynch, & Markie-Dadds, 1994a), supplemented by brief weekly, then fortnightly, telephone contact that emphasized parent self-sufficiency. Evaluation of the program is ongoing, although preliminary data show that compared to children in a waitlist control condition, children whose parents received the intervention showed lower levels of disruptive behavior immediately posttreatment and reported a high level of satisfaction with the treatment.

7.7. Toward a Public Health Perspective on Family Intervention

Children's psychological problems in general and conduct disorder in particular are major social problems with enormous social and economic costs to the community and the judicial, social welfare, and health care systems and as such constitute a major public health problem (Offord, 1989; Webster-Stratton, 1993). There has been renewed interest recently in the possibility of preventing behavior disorders in children, and there are now several well-controlled prevention trials (primary or secondary) under way that deal specifically with behavioral or emotional problems. These trials invariably involve multicomponent interventions addressing family, school, and social relationship difficulties of school-age children who are at high risk for conduct disorder (e.g., McMahon, 1994). Similar preventively focused programs based on population screening at school must be undertaken for other disorders as well, such as children at risk for anxiety disorders (see Sanders & Dadds, 1995).

In the search for preventive interventions, it is important not to lose sight of economic imperatives that demand the development of the most cost-effective solutions that are capable of solving the problem. No prevention program, even if it is successful in a demonstration project, will be effectively disseminated if it is perceived to be too costly, unnecessarily complex, or cluttered. Programs focused on prevention should fully explore the idea of using brief self-directed programs that can access entire populations, with more intensive interventions reserved for nonresponders.

Research has indicated that it is often the families most in need of help with emotional and behavioral problems who do not have or seek access to mental health services (Sarason, 1974). Families who are socially and economically disadvantaged may be less likely to refer themselves for help and typically do not fare as well in treatment compared with middle-class populations (Dumas, 1986; Webster-Stratton, 1985). Many disadvantaged families will not access the service, and the ones who do may see the service as coercive and intrusive rather than helpful (Wahler, 1980).

Hence, an important area for future research is to improve our understanding of methods for encouraging high-risk families to access available clinical services. Means of accessing families in lower socioeconomic groups include making information about services more readily accessible at nontreatment points of contact with families (e.g., in family doctors' waiting rooms; at daycare, preschool, and school facilities; at community health centers or neighborhood centers; or through community service announcements on television and radio). Services are required that are low-cost, readily accessible, and available on a continuing basis over the course of the child's early development. It is preferable that these services be delivered as part of comprehensive "well child" care to avoid any stigma associated with contacting helping agencies.

7.8. The Role of the Media in Family Intervention

There is a vast untapped potential for the use of mass media interventions to promote children's mental health. The possible advantages of mass media programs to promote competent child-rearing practices and family mental health are that they reach a large proportion of the population, they reach groups who are difficult to access through other means, and they are relatively inexpensive ways of exposing the parenting population to health-enhancing messages. They can package messages in a sophisticated and powerful way and can provide support for interventions targeted at the individual level or at high-risk families.

Evidence from the public health field has shown media strategies to be effective in increasing community awareness and helpful in modifying damaging behaviors and attitudes associated with cigarette smoking, obesity, stress, hypertension, and AIDS (Flay, 1987). Media messages concerning parenting could be pitched at increasing community awareness of children's behavior difficulties, early detection of at-risk children, and encouragement to access appropriate services. In addition, families could be given practical advice on the management of specific problems, backed up with more detailed written information or advice.

The development and dissemination of child-rearing information through public television represent a whole new set of challenges for clinical psychologists. There are many issues and obstacles to attend to, including gaining media support and developing high-impact but entertaining messages about child rearing that lead to broad acceptance and community support.

8. Conclusion

BFI is an effective intervention with many families seeking assistance for their child because of behavioral and emotional problems. Graziano (1977) argued that the approach has revolutionized clinical services for children and is now widely used in many clinical settings. This approach involves a consultative process that requires effective communication among the child's family, the therapist, and other significant persons in the child's social network. While techniques of behavior change constitute the therapeutic centerpiece of the intervention, the consultation process strongly influences the acceptability of treatment to parents and therefore has an important role in the overall therapeutic strategy. Future research on BFI should attempt to define the specific strategies that therapists employ in dealing with issues such as client nonadherence to therapeutic tasks and other types of client behavior that create obstacles for the smooth progression of therapy. Skill in dealing with such problems should not be explained away as simply reflecting a therapist's experience, intuition, or personal qualities. Some strategies may work more effectively than others and are clearly worthy of empirical study in their own right.

There are several major challenges in delivering better treatment services to children and families. These challenges concern the need to develop more effective ways of accessing the many high-risk families who at present receive no treatment at all. Unless disadvantaged families can be encouraged to seek help, it will not be possible to investigate methods of improving services to such families. Effective treatment is also limited to the extent that we can liaise with other relevant treatment agencies and provide, across a range of childhood problems, treatments that are sensitive to the developmental aspects of the child's problems and that are appropriately matched in power to the severity of the child's problems.

There is need for research that examines the specific types of obstacles disadvantaged groups experience in accessing services. A variety of initiatives may improve access by reducing possible obstacles. These obstacles can be structural and cultural. Structural obstacles, such as inflexible clinic hours that make it difficult for working parents to attend, can be modified. The systematic use of prompting and reminder systems to facilitate appointment keeping, the provision of services in peoples' homes, and the provision of child care and assistance with transportation may help decrease obstacles that families encounter. However, families who are finding it difficult to provide regular meals for their children, who live in unsafe environments, or who have members with drug addiction problems have a different set of priorities, concerned with simple daily survival, than do parents whose basic physical needs are met but who are worried about their child's behavior. Unless more basic family needs are met, child-focused participation in parenting programs will remain of secondary importance.

Cultural obstacles to accessing services include culturally based differences in how disturbed behavior is viewed (i.e., whether it is a problem), families' causal attributions of children's behavior, rigid adherence to traditional sex role stereotypes in some cultures, and also culturally acceptable methods of resolving such problems. Family intervention services need to become more culturally informed and appropriate to become accessible to indigenous and ethic minority groups. This adaptation will involve much more than translating programs that work for middle-class families into other languages.

While prevention of children's psychological and behavioral problems sounds like an attractive alternative, it is by no means clear whether preventative interventions will in fact reduce the prevalence of children's behavioral problems in the community. More research and creative development of preventative programs is clearly needed to address the aforestated limitations.

9. References

Alpert, C. L., & Kaiser, A. P. (1992). Training parents as milieu language teachers. *Journal of Early Intervention*, *16*, 31–52.

Apley, J. (1975). *The child with abdominal pains*. London: Blackwell Scientific Publications.

Archer, L. A., & Szatmari, P. (1990). Assessment and treatment of food aversion in a four year old boy: A multidimensional approach. *Canadian Journal of Psychiatry*, *35*, 501–505.

Azrin, N. H., & Foxx, R. M. (1974). *Toilet training in less than a day*. New York: Simon & Schuster.

Baa, I., Sweet, J., & Martin, T. C. (1990). Changing patterns of remarriage. *Journal of Marriage and the Family*, *52*, 747–756.

Baer, D. M., Wolf, M. M., & Risley, T. R. (1968). Some current dimensions of applied behavior analysis. *Journal of Applied Behavior Analysis*, *1*, 91–97.

Bandura, A. (1977). *Social learning theory*. Englewood Cliffs, NJ: Prentice-Hall.

Barkley, R. A., Guevremont, D. C., Anastopolus, A. D., & Fletcher, K. E. (1992). A comparison of three family therapy programs for treating family conflicts in adolescents with attention-deficit hyperactivity disorder, *Journal of Consulting and Clinical Psychology*, *60*, 450–462.

Barrett, P. M., Dadds, M. R., & Rapee, R. M. (1993). Family intervention for childhood anxiety: A controlled trial. Paper presented at the 27th Annual Convention of the Association for Advancement of Behavior Therapy, Atlanta, GA.

Barrett, P. M., Rapee, R. M., Dadds, M. R., & Ryan, S. M. (1995). Family enhancement of cognitive style in anxious and aggressive children: Threat bias and the FEAR effect (submitted).

Beames, L., Sanders, M. R., & Bor, W. (1992). The role of parent training in the cognitive behavioral treatment of children's headaches. *Behavioural Psychotherapy*, *20*, 167–180.

Berkowitz, B. P., & Graziano, A. M. (1972). Training parents as behavior therapists: A review. *Behavior Research and Therapy*, *10*, 297–317.

Biglan, A. (1992). Family practices and the larger social context. *New Zealand Journal of Psychology*, *21*, 37–43.

Biglan, A. (1993). A fuctional contextualist framework for community intervention. In S. C. Hayes, L. J. Hayes, H. W. Reese, & T. R. Sarbin (Eds.), *Varieties of scientific contextualism* (pp. 251–276). Reno: Context Press.

Bijou, S. W., & Baer, D. M. (1961). *Child development: A systematic and empirical theory*, Vol. 1. New York: Appleton.

Blampied, N. M., & France, K. G. (1993). A behavioral model of infant sleep disturbance. *Journal of Applied Behavior Analysis*, *26*, 477–492.

Blechman, E. A. (1981). Toward comprehensive behavioral family intervention: An algorithm for matching families and interventions. *Behavior Modification*, *5*, 221–236.

Blechman, E. A. (1984). Competent parents, competent children: Behavioral objectives of parent training. In R. F. Dangel & R. A. Polster (Eds.), *Parent training: Foundations of research and practice* (pp. 34–63). New York: Guilford Press.

Blount, R. L., Bachanas, P. J., Powers, S. W., Cotter, M. C., Franklin, A., Chaplin, W., Mayfield, J., Henderson, M., & Blount, S. D. (1992). Training children to cope and parents to coach them during routine immunizations: Effects on child, parent, and staff behaviors. *Behavior Therapy*, *23*, 689–705.

Bray, J. H. (1988). Children's development during early remarriage. In E. M. Hetherington & J. D. Arasteh (Eds.), *Impact of divorce, single parenting and stepparenting on children* (pp. 299–324). Hillsdale, NJ: Erlbaum Associates.

Budd, K. S., & Itzkowitz, J. S. (1990). Parents as social skills trainers and evaluators of children. *Child and Family Behavior Therapy*, *12*, 13–30.

Burman, B., John, R. S., & Margolin, G. (1987). Effects of marital and parent–child relations on children's adjustment. *Journal of Family Psychology, 1*, 91–108.

Christensen, A. P., & Sanders, M. R. (1987). Habit reversal and differential reinforcement of other behavior in the treatment of thumbsucking: An analysis of generalization and side-effects. *Journal of Child Psychology and Psychiatry, 28*, 281–295.

Clark, H. B., Greene, B. F., Macrae, J. W., McNees, M. P., Davis, J. L. & Risley, T. R. (1977). A parent advice package for family shopping trips: Development and evaluation. *Journal of Applied Behavior Analysis, 10*, 605–624.

Connell, S., Irvine, L., & Rodney, J. (1982). The prevalence of psychiatric disorder in rural school children. *Australian and New Zealand Journal of Psychiatry, 16*, 43–46.

Connell, S., Sanders, M. R., & Markie-Dadds, C. (1994). Triple P goes bush. Poster presented at the Second Annual Behavior Therapy Update of the Australian Behavior Modification Association, Eumundi, Queensland, May 1994.

Coplin, J. W., & Houts, A. C. (1991). Father involvement in parent training for oppositional child behavior: Progress or stagnation. *Child and Family Behavior Therapy, 13*, 29–51.

Dadds, M. R. (1987). Families and the origins of child behavior problems. *Family Process, 26*, 341–357.

Dadds, M. R. (1989). Child behavior therapy and family context: Suggestions for research and practice with maritally discordant families. *Child and Family Behavior Therapy, 11*, 27–44.

Dadds, M. R. (1995). *Families, children and the development of dysfunction.* New York: Sage.

Dadds, M. R., Adlington, F. M., & Christensen, A. P. (1987a). Children's perceptions of time out. *Behaviour Change, 4*, 3–13.

Dadds, M. R., Heard, P. M., & Rapee, R. M. (1991). Anxiety disorders in children. *International Review of Psychiatry, 3*, 231–241.

Dadds, M. R., & McHugh, T. A. (1992). Social support and treatment outcome in behavioral family therapy for child conduct problems. *Journal of Consulting and Clinical Psychology, 60*, 252–259.

Dadds, M. R., & Powell, M. B. (1991). The relationship of interpersonal conflict and marital adjustment to aggression, anxiety and immaturity in aggressive and nonclinic children. *Journal of Abnormal Child Psychology, 19*, 553–567.

Dadds, M. R., Sanders, M. R., & Bor, W. (1984). Training children to eat independently: Evaluation of mealtime management training for parents. *Behavioral Psychotherapy, 12*, 356–366.

Dadds, M. R., Sanders M. R., Morrison, M., & Rebgetz, M. (1992). Childhood depression and conduct disorder: II. An analysis of family interaction patterns in the home. *Journal of Abnormal Psychology, 101*, 505–513.

Dadds, M. R., Schwartz, S., & Sanders, M. R. (1987b). Marital discord and treatment outcome in the treatment of childhood conduct disorders. *Journal of Consulting and Clinical Psychology, 55*, 396–403.

Dadds, M. R., Sheffield, J. K., & Holbeck, J. F. (1990). An examination of the differential relationship of marital discord to parents' discipline strategies for boys and girls. *Journal of Abnormal Psychology, 18*, 121–129.

Denton, R. (1986). An occupational therapy protocol for assessing infants and toddlers who fail to thrive. *American Journal of Occupational Therapy, 40*, 352–358.

Dolgin, M. J., & Phipps, S. (1989). Pediatric pain: The parents' role. *Pediatrician, 16*, 103–109.

Dumas, J. E. (1986). Indirect influence of maternal social contacts on mother–child interactions: A setting event analysis. *Journal of Abnormal Child Psychology, 14*, 205–216.

Dumas, J. E., Blechman, E. A., & Prinz, R. J. (1994). Aggressive children and effective communication. *Aggressive Behavior, 20*, 347–358.

Dunn-Geier, B., McGrath, P. J., Rourke, B. P., Latter, J., & D'Astous, J. (1986). Adolescent chronic pain: The ability to cope. *Pain, 26*, 23–32.

Edwards, M. C., Finney, J. W., & Bonner, M. (1991). Matching treatment with recurrent abdominal pain symptoms: An evaluation of dietary fiber and relaxation treatments. *Behavior Therapy, 22*, 257–267.

Eiser, C. (1990). *Chronic disease management: An introduction to psychological theory and research*. Cambridge: Cambridge University Press.

Embry, L. H. (1984). What to do? Matching client characteristics and intervention techniques through a prescriptive taxonomic key. In R. F. Dangel., & R. A. Polster (Eds.), *Parent training: Foundations of research and practice* (pp. 443–473). New York: Guilford Press.

Endo, G. T., Sloane, H. N., Hawkes, T. W., & Jenson, W. R. (1991a). Reducing child whining through self-instructional parent training materials. *Child and Family Behavior Therapy, 13*, 41–59.

Endo, G. T., Sloane, H. N., Hawkes, T. W., McLoughlin, C., & Jenson, W. R. (1991b). Reducing child tantrums through self-instructional parent training materials. *School Psychology International, 12*, 95–109.

Fantuzzo, J. W., DePaola, L. M., Lambert, L., Martino, T., Anderson, G., & Sutton, S. (1991). Effects of interparental violence on the psychological adjustment and competencies of young children. *Journal of Consulting and Clinical Psychology, 59*, 258–265.

Fergusson, D. M., Horwood, L. J., & Shannon, F. T. (1985). Relationship between family life events, maternal depression and childe-rearing problems. *Pediatrics, 73*, 773–788.

Finney, J. W. (1986). Preventing common feeding problems in infants and young children. *Pediatric Clinics of North America, 33*, 775–788.

Finney, J. W., & Bonner, M. J. (1992). The influence of behavioral family intervention on the health of chronically ill children. *Behavior Change, 9*, 157–170.

Finney, J. W., Lemanek, K. L., Cataldo, M. F., Katz, H. P., & Fuque, R. W. (1989). Pediatric psychology in primary health care: Brief targeted therapy for recurrent abdominal pain. *Behavior Therapy, 20*, 283–291.

Flay, B. R. (1987). Mass media and smoking cessation: A critical review. *American Journal of Public Health, 77*, 153–160.

Fordyce, W. E. (1976). *Behavioral methods for chronic pain and illness*. St. Louis: C. V. Mosby.

Forehand, R. L., & Long, N. (1988). Outpatient treatment of the acting out child: Procedures, long term follow-up data, and clinical problems. *Advances in Behavior Research and Therapy, 10*, 129–177.

Forehand, R., & McMahon, R. J. (1981). *Helping the non-compliant child: A clinician's guide to parent training*. New York: Guilford Press.

Forehand, R., & Wierson, M. (1993). The role of developmental factors in planning behavioral interventions for children: Disruptive behavior as an example. *Behavior Therapy, 24*, 117–141.

France, K. G. (1994). Handling parents' concerns regarding the behavioral treatment of infant sleep disturbance, *Behavior Change, 11*, 101–109.

France, K. G., & Hudson, S. M. (1990). Behavior management of infant sleep disturbance. *Journal of Applied Behavior Analysis, 23*, 91–98.

Frankel, F., & Simmons, J. Q. (1992). Parent behavioral training: Why and when some parents drop out. *Journal of Clinical Child Psychology, 21*, 332–330.

Frentz, C., & Kelley, M. L. (1986). Parents' acceptance of reductive treatment methods: The influence of problem severity and perception of child behavior. *Behavior Therapy, 17*, 75–81.

Glick, P. C. (1989). Remarried families, stepfamilies and stepchildren: A brief demographic profile. *Family Relations, 38*, 24–27.

Goldstein, A. P., Keller, H., & Erne, D. (1985). *Changing the abusive parent.* Champaign, IL: Research Press.

Goodyer, I. M., (1990). Family relationships, life events and childhood psychopathology. *Journal of Child Psychology and Psychiatry and Allied Disciplines, 31,* 161–192.

Gortmaker, S. L. (1985). Demography of chronic childhood diseases. In N. Hobbs & J. M. Perrin (Eds.), *Issues in the care of children with chronic illness: A sourcebook on problems, services and policies* (pp. 135–154). San Fransisco: Jossey-Bass.

Graves, T., Meyers, A. W., & Clark, L. (1988). An evaluation of parental problem solving training in the behavioral treatment of childhood obesity. *Journal of Consulting and Clinical Psychology, 56,* 246–250.

Graziano, A. M. (1977). Parents as behavior therapists. *Progress in Behavior Modification, 4,* 251–298.

Greer, R. D., Dorow, L., Williams, G., McCorkle, N., & Asnes, R. (1991). Peer-mediated procedures to induce swallowing and food acceptance in young children. *Journal of Applied Behavior Analysis, 24,* 783–790.

Griest, D. L., Forehand, R., Rogers, T., Breiner, J., Furey, W., & Williams, C. A. (1982). Effects of parent enhancement therapy on the treatment outcome and generalization of a parent training program. *Behavior Research and Therapy, 20,* 429–436.

Grych, J. H., & Fincham, F. D. (1990). Marital conflict and children's adjustment: A cognitive–contextual framework. *Psychological Bulletin, 108,* 267–290.

Grych, J. H., & Fincham, F. D. (1992). Interventions for children of divorce: Toward greater integration of research and action. *Psychological Bulletin, 111,* 434–454.

Hall, R. V., Axelrod, S., Tyler, L., Grief, E., Jones, F. C., & Robertson, R. (1972). Modification of behavior problems in the home with a parent as observer and experimenter. *Journal of Applied Behavior Analysis, 5,* 53–64.

Harris, S. L., & Ferrari, M. (1983). Developmental factors in child behavior therapy. *Behavior Therapy, 14,* 54–72.

Harrold, M., Lutzker, J. R., Campbell, R. V., & Touchette, P. E. (1992). Improving parent–child interactions for families with developmental disabilities. *Journal of Behavior Therapy and Experimental Psychiatry, 23,* 89–100.

Heffer, R. W., & Kelley, M. L. (1987). Mothers' acceptance of behavioral interventions for children: The influence of parent race and income. *Behavior Therapy, 18,* 153–163.

Hetherington, E. M., Cox, M., & Cox, R. (1982). Effects of divorce on parents and children. In M. E. Lamb (Ed.), *Nontraditional families: Parenting and child development* (pp. 233–288.). Hillsdale, NJ: Erlbaum Associates.

Hetherington, E. M., Cox, M., & Cox, R. (1985). Long term effects of divorce and remarriage on the adjustment of children. *Journal of the Academy of Child Psychiatry, 24,* 518–530.

Hetherington, E. M., & Martin, B. (1979). Family interaction. In H. C. Quay. & J. S. Werry (Eds.), *Psychopathological disorders of childhood,* 2nd ed. (pp. 247–302). New York: John Wiley.

Horne, A. M. (1991). Social learning family therapy. In A. M. Horne & J. L. Passmore (Eds.), *Family counselling and therapy,* 2nd ed. (pp. 463–497). Itasca, IL: Peacock Publishing.

Iwata, B. A., Riordan, M. M., Wohl, M. K., & Finney, J. W. (1982). Pediatric feeding disorders: Behavioral analysis and treatment. In P. J. Accardo (Ed.), *Failure to thrive in infancy and early childhood: A multidisciplinary team approach* (pp. 297–329). Baltimore: University Park Press.

Jay, S. M. (1988). Invasive medical procedures: Psychological interventions and assessment. In D. K. Routh (Ed.), *Handbook of pediatric psychology* (pp. 401–425). New York: Guilford Press.

Kanfer, F. H., & Schefft, B. K. (1988). *Guiding the process of therapeutic change*. Champaign, IL: Research Press.

Kazdin, A. E. (1987). *Conduct disorder in childhood and adolescence*. Newbury Park, CA: Sage Publications.

Kazdin, A. E., Siegal, T. C., & Bass, D. (1992). Cognitive problem-solving skills training and parent management training in the treatment of antisocial behavior in children. *Journal of Consulting and Clinical Psychology, 5*, 733–747.

Kelleher, K. J., Taylor, J. L., & Rickert, V. I. (1992). Mental health services for children and adolescents. *Clinical Psychology Review, 12*, 841–852.

Kelley, M. L. (1990). *School–home notes: Promoting children's classroom success*. New York: Guilford Press.

Kendall, P. C. (1992). Childhood coping: Avoiding a lifetime of anxiety. *Behavior Change, 3*, 70–73.

Kendziora, K. T., & O'Leary, S. G. (1993). Dysfunctional parenting as a focus for prevention and treatment of child behaviour problems. *Advances in Child Clinical Psychology, 15*, 175–206.

King, N. J., Hamilton, D. I., & Ollendick, T. H. (1988). *Children's fears and phobias: A behavioral perspective*. Chichester: John Wiley.

Koegel, R. L., Glahn, T. J., & Nieminen, G. S. (1978). Generalization of parent training results. *Journal of Applied Behavior Analysis, 11*, 95–109.

Koepke, J., & Thyer, B. (1985). Behavioral treatment of failure to thrive in a two-year-old. *Child Welfare, 64*, 511–516.

Krohne, H. W., & Hock, M. (1991). Relationships between restrictive mother–child interactions and anxiety of the child. *Anxiety Research, 4*, 109–124.

Larson, K. L., Ayllon, T., & Barrett, D. H. (1987). A behavioral feeding program for failure-to-thrive infants. *Behavior Research and Therapy, 25*, 39–47.

Laski, K., Charlop, M. H., & Schreibman, L. (1988). Training parents to use the natural language paradigm to increase their autistic children's speech. *Journal of Applied Behavior Analysis, 21*, 391–400.

Lawton, J. M., & Sanders, M. R. (1994). Designing effective behavioral family interventions for stepfamilies. *Clinical Psychology Review, 14*, 463–496.

Linscheid, T. R., Tarnowski, K. J., Rasnake, L. K., & Brams, J. S. (1987). Behavioral treatment of food refusal in a child with short-gut syndrome. *Journal of Pediatric Psychology, 12*, 451–459.

Linton, S. J. (1986). A case study of the behavioral treatment of chronic stomach pain in a child. *Behaviour Change, 3*, 70–73.

Loeber, R. (1990). Development and risk factors of juvenile antisocial behavior and delinquency. *Clinical Psychology Review, 10*, 1–41.

Long, P., Forehand, R., Wierson, M., & Morgan, A. (1994). Does parent training with young noncompliant children have long-term effects? *Behavior Research and Therapy, 32*, 101–107.

Luiselli, J. K. (1989). Behavioral assessment and treatment of pediatric feeding disorders in developmental disabilities. *Progress in Behavior Modification, 24*, 91–131.

Lutzker, J. R. (1992). Developmental disabilities and child abuse and neglect: The ecobehavioral imperative. *Behavior Change, 9*, 149–156.

Matthews, L. W., & Drotar, D. (1984). Cystic fibrosis—A challenging long-term chronic disease. *Pediatric Clinics of North America, 31*, 133–152.

McFarland, M., & Sanders, M. R. (1993). A comparison of behavioral and cognitive–behavioral family intervention with maternally depressed families of disruptive children. Paper presented at the 27th annual convention of the Association for the Advancement of Behavior Therapy, Atlanta, November 1993.

McGrath, P. A. (1990). *Pain in children: Nature, assessment and treatment.* New York: Guilford Press.

McMahon, R. J. (1994). Diagnosis, assessment and treatment of externalizing problems in children: The role of longitudinal data. *Journal of Consulting and Clinical Psychology, 62,* 901–917.

McMahon, R. J., & Forehand, R. L. (1983). Consumer satisfaction in behavioral treatment of children: Types, issues and recommendations. *Behavior Therapy, 14,* 209–225.

McMahon, R. J., Forehand, R., Griest, D. L., & Wells, K. C. (1981). Who drops out of therapy during parent behavioral training? *Behavior Counseling Quarterly, 1,* 79–85.

McMahon, R. J., & Wells, K. (1989). Conduct disorders. In E. J. Marsh & R. A. Barkley (Eds.), *Treatment of childhood disorders* (pp. 73–134) New York: Guilford Press.

McManmon, L., Peterson, C. R., Metelinis, L., McWhirter, J., & Clark, H. B. (1982). The development of a parental advice protocol for enhancing family mealtime. *Behavioral Counselling Quarterly, 2,* 156–167.

McNaughton, S., Glynn, T., & Robinson, V. M. J. (1987). *Parents as remedial tutors: Issues for home and school.* Wellington, New Zealand: NZCER.

McNeil, C. B., Eyberg, S., Eisenstadt, T. H., Newcomb, K., & Funderburk, B. (1991). Parent–child interaction therapy with behavior problem children: Generalization of treatment effects to the school setting, *Journal of Clinical and Child Psychology, 20,* 140–151.

Miller, A. J., & Kratochwill, T. R. (1979). Reduction of frequent stomach complaints by time out. *Behavior Therapy, 10,* 211–218.

Miller, G. E., & Prinz, R. J. (1990). Enhancement of social learning family interventions for childhood conduct disorder. *Psychological Bulletin, 108,* 291–307.

Miller, S. J., & Sloane, H. N. (1976). The generalization of parent training across stimulus settings. *Journal of Applied Behavior Analysis, 9,* 355–370.

Miller-Johnson, S., Emery, R. E., Marvin, R. S., Clarke, W., Lovinger, R., & Martin, M. (1994). Parent–child relationships and the management of insulin-dependent diabetes mellitus. *Journal of Consulting and Clinical Psychology, 62,* 603–610.

Moore, K. J., & Chamberlain, P. (1994). Treatment foster care: Toward development of community-based models for adolescents with severe emotional and behavioral disorders. *Journal of Emotional and Behavioral Disorders, 2,* 22–30.

Mortimer, M. J., Kay, J., Jaron, A., & Good, P. A. (1992). Does a history of maternal migraine or depression predispose children to headache and stomach-ache? *Headaches, 32,* 353–355.

O'Connor, I. (1989). *Our homeless children: Their experiences.* Report to the National Inquiry into Homeless Children by the Equal Rights and Equal Opportunity Commission, Sydney.

O'Dell, S. (1974). Training parents in behavior modification: A review. *Psychological Bulletin, 81,* 418–433.

Offord, D. R. (1989). Conduct disorder: Risk factors and prevention. In: *Prevention of mental disorders, alcohol and other drug use in children and adolescents* (DHHS Publication No. ADM 89–1646) (pp. 273–307). Washington, DC: Alcohol, Drug Abuse and Mental Health Administration.

Ollendick, T. H., & Francis, G. (1988). Behavioral assessment and treatment of childhood phobias. *Behavior Modification, 12,* 165–204.

Patterson, G. R. (1969). Behavioral techniques based on social learning: An additional base for developing behavior modification technologies. In C. M. Franks (Ed.), *Behavior therapy: Appraisal and status* (pp. 341–374). New York: McGraw-Hill.

Patterson, G. R. (1982). *Coercive family process.* Eugene, OR: Castalia Pres.

Patterson, G. R. (1985). Beyond technology: The next stage in developing an empirical base for parent training. In L. L'Abate (Ed.), *Handbook of family psychology and therapy* (pp. 1344–1379). Homewood, IL: Dorsey.

Patterson, G., & Chamberlain, P. (1995). A functional analysis of resistance during parent training therapy (submitted).

Patterson, G. R., Dishion, T. J., & Chamberlain, P. (1993). Outcomes and methodological issues relating to treatment of antisocial children. In T. G. Giles (Ed.), *Handbook of effective psychotherapy* (pp. 43–87). New York: Plenum Press.

Patterson, G. R., & Forgatch, M. S. (1985) Therapist behavior as a determinant for client noncompliance: A paradox for the behavioral modifier. *Journal of Consulting and Clinical Psychology, 53*, 846–851.

Patterson, G. R. & Reid, J. B. (1984). Social interactional processes in the family: The study of the moment by moment family transactions in which human social development is embedded. *Journal of Applied Developmental Psychology, 5*, 237–262.

Patterson, G. R., Reid, J. B., Jones, R. R., & Conger, R. W. (1975). *A social learning approach to family intervention.* Eugene, OR: Castalia.

Patterson, G. R., & Stoolmiller, M. (1995). Relationship of changes in parental resistance and discipline practices to future clinical outcomes. *Behavior Therapy* (in press).

Payne, B., & Norfleet, M. A. (1986). Chronic pain and the family. *Pain, 26*, 1–22.

Pisterman, S., Firestone, P., McGrath, P., Goodman, J. T., Webster, I., Mallory, R., & Goffin, B. (1992). The effects of parent training on parenting stress and sense of competence. *Canadian Journal of Behavioral Science, 24*, 41–58.

Pisterman, S., McGrath, P., Firestone, P., Goodman, J. T., Webster, I., & Mallory, R. (1989). Outcome of parent-mediated treatment of preschoolers with attention-deficit disorder with hyperactivity. *Journal of Consulting and Clinical Psychology, 57*, 628–625.

Powers, L. E., Singer, G. H. S., Stevens, T., & Sowers, J. (1992). Behavioral parent training in home and community generalization settings, *Education and Training in Mental Retardation, 27*, 13–27.

Prinz, R. J. (1992). Overview of behavioral family interventions with children: Achievements, limitations and challenges. *Behavior Change, 9*, 120–125.

Prinz, R. J., Blechman, E. A., & Dumas, J. E. (1994). An evaluation of peer coping-skills training for childhood aggression. *Journal of Clinical Child Psychology, 23*, 193–203.

Prinz, R. J., & Miller, G. E. (1994). Family-based treatment for childhood antisocial behavior: Experimental influences on dropout and engagement. *Journal of Consulting and Clinical Psychology, 62*, 645–650.

Ramsay, M., & Zelazo, P. R. (1987). Food refusal in failure-to-thrive infants: Nasogastric feeding combined with interactive–behavioral treatment. *Journal of Pediatric Psychology, 13*, 329–347.

Reid, M., & Solomon, S. (1992). Improving Australia's rural health and aged care services. National Health Strategy Background Paper No. 11.

Richman, N. (1981a). A community survey of characteristics of one-to-two year olds with sleep disruptions. *Journal of the American Academy of Child Psychiatry, 20*, 281–291.

Richman, N. (1981b). Sleep problems in young children. *Archives of Diseases in Childhood, 56*, 491–493.

Richman, N., Douglas, J., Hunt, H., Lansdown, R., & Levene, R. (1985). Behavioral methods in the treatment of sleep disorders: A pilot study. *Journal of Child Psychology and Psychiatry, 26*, 581–590.

Robins, A. L., & Foster, S. (1989). *Negotiating parent–adolescent conflict. A behavioral family systems approach.* New York: Guilford Press.

Rutter, M. (1985a). Family and school influences on behavioral development. *Journal of Child Psychology and Psychiatry, 26*, 349–368.

Rutter, M. (1985b). Resilience in the face of adversity: Protective factors and resistance to psychiatric disorder. *British Journal of Psychiatry, 47*, 598–611.

Rutter, M. (1989). Pathways from childhood to adult life. *Journal of Child Psychology and Psychiatry, 30*, 23–51.

Rutter, M., & Quinton, D. (1984). Parental psychiatric disorder: Effects on children. *Psychological Medicine, 14*, 853–880.

Sanders, M. R. (1984). Clinical strategies for enhancing generalization in behavioral parent training: An overview. *Behavior Change, 1*, 25–35.

Sanders, M. R., Bor, W., & Dadds, M. R. (1984). Modifying bedtime disruptions in children using stimulus control and contingency management procedures. *Behavioural Psychotherapy, 12*, 130–141.

Sanders, M. R. & Christensen, A. P. (1985). A comparison of the effects of child management and planned activities training in five parenting environments. *Journal of Abnormal Child Psychology, 13*, 101–117.

Sanders, M. R., Cleghorn, G., Shepherd, R. W., & Patrick, M. (1993a). Predictors of clinical improvement in children with recurrent abdominal pain. Unpublished manuscript. Herston: Behaviour Research and Therapy Centre, University of Queensland.

Sanders, M. R., & Dadds, M. R. (1982). The effects of planned activities and child management training: An analysis of setting generality. *Behavior Therapy, 13*, 1–11.

Sanders, M. R., & Dadds, M. R. (1993). *Behavioral family intervention*, Needham Heights, MA: Allyn & Bacon.

Sanders, M. R., & Dadds M. R. (1995). The prevention of anxiety disorders in children. In B. Raphael & G Burrows (Eds.), *Handbook of preventive psychiatry*. Amsterdam: Elsevier (in press).

Sanders, M. R., Dadds, M. R., & Bor, W. (1989a). A contextual analysis of oppositional child behavior and maternal aversive behavior in families of conduct disordered children. *Journal of Clinical Child Psychology, 18*, 72–83.

Sanders, M. R., & Glynn, T. (1981). Training parents in behavioral self management: An analysis of generalization and maintenance. *Journal of Applied Behavior Analysis, 14*, 223–237.

Sanders, M. R., Gravestock, F., & Wanstall, K. (1990). *Cystic fibrosis: A parent's handbook for dealing with compliance problems*. Brisbane: Behaviour Research and Therapy Centre, University of Queensland.

Sanders, M. R., & James, J. E. (1983). The modification of parent behavior: A review of generalization and maintenance. *Behavior Modification, 7*, 3–27.

Sanders, M. R., & Lawton, J. M. (1993). Discussing assessment findings with families: A guided participation model for information transfer. *Child and Family Behavior Therapy, 15*, 5–35.

Sanders, M. R., Lynch, M. E., & Markie-Dadds, C. (1994a). *Every parent's workbook: A practical guide to positive parenting*. Brisbane: Australian Academic Press.

Sanders, M. R., & Markie-Dadds, C. (1995). Managing common childhood behavior problems. In M. R. Sanders, C. Mitchell, & G. Byrne (Eds.), *Medical consultation skills: A practical handbook*. Sydney: Addison-Wesley (in press).

Sanders, M. R., Patel, R. K., Le Grice, B., & Shepherd, R. W. (1993b). Children with persistent feeding difficulties. An observational analysis of the feeding interactions of problem and non-problem eaters. *Health Psychology, 12*, 64–73.

Sanders, M. R., & Plant, K. (1989). Programming for generalization to high and low risk parenting situations in families with oppositional developmentally disabled preschoolers. *Behavior Modification, 13*, 283–305.

Sanders, M. R., Rebgetz, M., Morrison, M., Bor, W., Gordon, A., Dadds, M. R., & Shephard, R. (1989b). Cognitive–behavioral treatment of recurrent nonspecific abdominal pain in children: An analysis of generalization and side effects. *Journal of Consulting and Clinical Psychology, 57,* 294–300.

Sanders, M. R., Shepherd, R. W., Cleghorn, G., & Woolford, H. (1994b). The treatment of recurrent abdominal pain in children: A controlled comparison of cognitive–behavioral family intervention and standard pediatric care. *Journal of Consulting and Clinical Psychology, 62,* 306–314.

Sanders, M. R., Woolford, H., Turner, K. M. T., Shepherd, R. W., & Cleghorn, G. (1995). Maternal caregiving, child coping and recurrent abdominal pain. A comparison of children with recurrent abdominal pain, organic pain and pain free controls (submitted).

Sank, L. I., & Biglan, A. (1974). Operant treatment of a case of recurrent abdomination in a 10-year-old boy. *Behavior Therapy, 5,* 677–681.

Santrock, J. W., Warshak, R. A., Lindbergh, C., & Meadows, L. (1982). Childrens' and parents' observed social behavior in stepfather families. *Child Development, 53,* 472–480.

Sarason, S. B. (1974). *The psychological sense of community: Prospects for a community psychology.* San Francisco: Jossey-Bass.

Sayger, T. V., Horne, A. M., & Glaser, B. A. (1993). Marital satisfaction and social learning family therapy for child conduct problems: Generalization of treatment effects. *Journal of Marital and Family Therapy, 19,* 393–402.

Sayger, T. V., Horne, A. M., Walker, J. M., & Passmore, J. L. (1988). Social learning family therapy with aggressive children: Treatment outcome and maintenance. *Journal of Family Psychology, 3,* 261–285.

Schreibman, L., Kaneko, W. M., & Koegel, R. L. (1991). Positive affect of parents of autistic children: A comparison across two teaching techniques. *Behavior Therapy, 22,* 479–490.

Seymour, F. W. (1987). Parent management of sleep difficulties in young children. *Behavior Change, 4,* 39–48.

Seymour, F. W., Brock, P., During, M., & Poole, G. (1989). Reducing sleep disruptions in young children: Evaluation of therapist-guided and written information approaches: A brief report. *Journal of Child Psychology and Psychiatry, 30,* 913–918.

Shapiro, E. S. (1987). Academic problems. In M. Hersen & V. B. Van Hasselt (Eds.), *Behavior therapy with children and adolescents: A clinical approach* (pp. 362–384). New York: John Wiley.

Sisson, L. A., & Dixon, M. J. (1986). A behavioral approach to the training and assessment of feeding in multihandicapped children. *Applied Research in Mental Retardation, 7,* 149–164.

Smith, A. M., & O'Leary, S. G. (1995). Attributions and arousal as predictors of maternal discipline. *Cognitive Therapy and Research* (in press).

Spaccarelli, S., Cotler, S., & Penman, D. (1992). Problem-solving skills training as a supplement to behavioral parent training. *Cognitive Therapy and Research, 16,* 1–18.

Stark, L. J., Bowen, A. M., Tyc, V. L., Evans, S., & Passero, M. A. (1990). A behavioral approach to increasing calorie consumption in children with cystic fibrosis. *Journal of Pediatric Psychology, 15,* 309–326.

Stokes, T. R. & Osnes, P. G. (1989). An operant pursuit of generalization. *Behavior Therapy, 20,* 337–355.

Sutton, C. (1992). Training parents to manage difficult children: A comparison of methods. *Behavioural Psychotherapy, 20,* 115–139.

Sweet, A. A. (1987). The therapeutic relationship in behavior therapy. *Clinical Psychology Review, 4,* 253–272.

Tharp, R. G., & Wetzel, R. J. (1969). *Behavior modification in the natural environment.* New York: Academic Press.

Turk, D. C., Litt, M. D., Salovey, P., & Walker, J. (1985). Seeking urgent pediatric treatment: Factors contributing to frequency, delay, and appropriateness. *Health Psychology*, 4, 43–59.

Turner, K. M. T., Sanders, M. R., & Wall, C. (1994). A comparison of behavioural parent training and dietary education in the treatment of children with persistent feeding difficulties. *Behaviour Change*, 4, 242–258.

Twardosz, S., & Nordquist, V. M. (1988). Parent training. In M. Hersen & V. B. Van Hasselt (Eds.), *Behavior therapy with children and adolescents: A clinical approach* (pp. 75–104). New York: John Wiley.

Wadsworth, J., Burnell, I., Taylor, B., & Butler, N. (1985). The influence of family type on children's behavior and development at five years. *Journal of Child Psychology and Psychiatry*, 26, 245–254.

Wahler, R. G. (1969). Oppositional children: A quest for parental reinforcement control. *Journal of Applied Behavior Analysis*, 2, 159–170.

Wahler, R. G. (1980). The insular mother: Her problems in parent–child treatment. *Journal of Applied Behavior Analysis*, 13, 207–219.

Wahler, R. G., Cartor, P. G., Fleischman, J., & Lambert, W. (1993). The impact of synthesis teaching and parent training with mothers of conduct-disordered children. *Journal of Abnormal Child Psychology*, 21, 425–441.

Walker, L. S., & Greene, J. W. (1989). Children with recurrent abdominal pain and their parents: More somatic complaints, anxiety, and depression than other patient families? *Journal of Pediatric Psychology*, 14, 231–243.

Webster-Stratton, C. (1985). Predictors of outcome in parent training dor conduct disordered children. *Behavior Therapy*, 16, 223–243.

Webster-Stratton, C. (1989a). Systematic comparison of consumer satisfaction of three cost-effective parent training programs for conduct problem children. *Behavior Therapy*, 20, 103–115.

Webster-Stratton, C. (1989b). The relationship of marital support, conflict, and divorce to parent perceptions, behaviors, and childhood conduct problems. *Journal of Marriage and the Family*, 51, 417–430.

Webster-Stratton, C. (1990). Long-term follow-up of families with young conduct problem children: From preschool to grade school. *Journal of Clinical Child Psychology*, 19, 144–149.

Webster-Stratton, C. (1992). *The incredible years: A trouble-shooting guide for parents of children aged 3–8*. Toronto, Ontario: Umbrella Press.

Webster-Stratton, C. (1993). Strategies for helping early school-age children with oppositional defiant disorders: The importance of home–school partnerships. *School Psychology Review*, 22, 437–457.

Webster-Stratton, C. (1994). Advancing videotape parent training: A comparison study. *Journal of Consulting and Clinical Psychology*, 62, 583–593.

Webster-Stratton, C., & Herbert, M. (1993). What really happens in parent training? *Behavior Modification*, 17, 407–456.

Webster-Stratton, C., Hollinsworth, T., & Kolpacoff, M. (1989). The long-term effectiveness and clinical significance of three cost-effective training programs for families with conduct-problem children. *Journal of Consulting and Clinical Psychology*, 57, 550–553.

Webster-Stratton, C., Kolpacoff, M., & Hollinsworth, T. (1988). Self-administered videotape therapy for families with conduct-problem children: Comparison with two cost-effective treatments and a control group. *Journal of Consulting and Clinical Psychology*, 56, 558–566.

Wells, K. C., & Egan, J. (1988). Social learning and systems family therapy for childhood oppositional disorder: Comparative treatment outcome. *Comprehensive Psychiatry*, 29, 138–146.

Werle, M. A., Murphy, T. B., & Budd, K. S. (1993). Treating chronic food refusal in young children: Home-based parent training. *Journal of Applied Behavior Analysis, 26*, 421–433.

Wittenberg, J. P. (1990). Feeding disorders and infancy: Classification and treatment considerations. *Canadian Journal of Psychiatry, 35*, 529–533.

Zill, N. (1988). Behavior, achievement and health problems among children in stepfamilies. In E. M. Hetherington & J. D. Arasteh (Eds.), *Impact of divorce, single parenting and stepparenting on children* (pp. 325–368). Hillsdale, NJ: Erlbaum Associates.

9

Emerging Trends in Child and Adolescent Mental Health Services

DONALD P. OSWALD AND NIRBHAY N. SINGH

1. Introduction

Child mental health service delivery systems in the United States are in the midst of change. Child advocates have decried the sad state of the service systems and have called for sweeping and fundamental reforms. Mental health professionals and policy makers have endorsed that call and are actively supporting reform initiatives across the country. In this chapter, we describe briefly some of the major historical events in the field of child mental health, summarize the trends emerging from the reform initiatives, and anticipate the direction in which the field is likely to evolve. Before beginning, we note that this chapter will follow the convention of using the terms "child," "children," and "youth" to refer to children and adolescents under the age of 18 years.

1.1. Child Mental Health Services Reform

The 1964 Joint Commission on Mental Health of Children convened to study services for emotionally disturbed children. In their report, *Crisis in Child Mental Health: Challenge for the 1970s* (Joint Commission on Mental Health of Children, 1969), they were among the first to sound an alarm about the state of child mental health service delivery systems. This report marked the beginning of an emphasis on advocacy and on the development of a continuum of care in the community (Behar, 1985). Nearly a decade after the Joint Commission's report, the report of the

DONALD P. OSWALD AND NIRBHAY N. SINGH • Department of Psychiatry, Medical College of Virginia, Virginia Commonwealth University, Richmond, Virginia 23298.

Advances in Clinical Child Psychology, Volume 18, edited by Thomas H. Ollendick and Ronald J. Prinz. Plenum Press, New York, 1996.

President's Commission on Mental Health (1978) echoed these themes, lamenting the scarcity and fragmentation of child mental health services.

As with many social changes in recent years, the spark that ignited child mental health services reform was a lawsuit. In 1980, the Willie M. v. Hunt class action suit mandated that the state of North Carolina develop a complete continuum of care within local mental health programs for seriously disturbed and assaultive children who were at risk for institutionalization (Willie M. et al. v. James B. Hunt, Jr. et al., 1980). The state set out to provide an integrated, full-range service delivery system to a group of children who had been failed by every existing service program of the day (Behar, 1985). Subsequently, the national call to arms was sounded by Jane Knitzer (1982) with the publication of *Unclaimed Children*. While some have criticized the work as long on conclusions and emotional appeal and short on data, it had unquestionable impact. The author advocated the creation of public mental health services for children that are based in the community and are centered on the needs of the families.

In 1983, the Child and Adolescent Service System Program (CASSP) was founded as a branch of the National Institute of Mental Health (NIMH). The initial goal of CASSP was to facilitate the development of multiagency, coordinated, community-based systems of care for children. A year later, NIMH funded the first ten CASSP state demonstration programs, and in the last 10 years, federal efforts have increased substantially, with CASSP emerging as an important leader in the movement to reform child mental health services.

In 1988, the Robert Wood Johnson Foundation launched the Mental Health Services for Youth Initiative, a privately funded program developed to improve mental health services for children. The following year, 12 1-year development grants were awarded to state agencies for organization, reform, and start-up support for community-based services (Beachler, 1990).

The United States Congress passed P.L. 99-660 in 1987 requiring all states to develop plans for an organized community-based system of care for children with emotional and behavioral disorders. States were mandated to demonstrate substantial implementation of their plans by 1992 or face a reduction in block grant funds (Behar & Munger, 1993). There is little doubt that this federal mandate played a major role in the explosion of reform efforts seen in this country during the last 5 years.

1.2. Estimates of Need

While it is generally agreed that there is a substantial unmet need for child mental health treatment services, it has been very difficult to estimate this need in quantifiable terms. Epidemiological studies offer the broadest estimates of need for psychiatric services. In nonclinic samples, about 20% of children are typically found to meet the criteria for one or more psychiatric diagnoses (Costello, 1989). While it is not evident that all the children so identified require, or would benefit from, mental health services, recent studies indicate that one half to one third of children with a DSM diagnosis show significant impairments in functioning in some aspect of their lives (Costello, Burns, Angold, & Leaf, 1993). A recent report from the United States Office of Technology Assessment (1986) offered a somewhat more liberal estimate and asserted that at least 12% of children in the United States require mental health intervention. The prevalence of "serious" emotional disorder is generally considered to be somewhat lower. For example, Knitzer (1982) estimate the prevalence rate to be about 5%, although the problem of adequately defining the term has resulted in widely ranging prevalence figures.

Establishing unmet needs requires not only an estimate of overall prevalence but also an estimate of current service utilization rates. How many of the children in need are receiving mental health services of some kind? By the most obvious measures, the answer is clearly "only a fraction." A comparison of estimated prevalence rates of emotional disturbance in children and the 1986 mental health service utilization figures (Burns, Thompson, & Goldman, 1993) suggests that the mental health needs of 63–84% of these children are not met (Burns, 1991). However, this estimate does not take into account the number of children receiving mental-health–related services in primary care or school settings. Although as many as 6% of the population of children are receiving such services (Costello et al., 1993), few would argue that their mental health needs are being adequately addressed. In any case, it is difficult to arrive at a reasonable estimate of utilization rates for mental-health-related services. Striking as they are, estimates of unmet need have provided only some of the impetus for reform in child mental health services. The major impetus for reform came from child advocates who emphasized providing not only *more* services but also fundamentally *different* services. Their call for a fundamental change was based on their conviction that the system contained basic and fatal flaws that constituted serious barriers to appropriate and effective services for children.

1.3. Barriers to Appropriate and Effective Services

A review of the systemic barriers to appropriate and effective services reveals a number of common themes, the four most serious of which are described below.

1.3.1. Fragmented Community Services

The lack of coordination of local community services arises through the inertia inherent in separate local service systems and through statutory limitations that preclude effective collaboration (Collins & Collins, 1994). Behar (1985, p. 191) noted that prior to the implementation of the Willie M. program, the North Carolina child service system was characterized by ". . . the lack of linkages, that is, the lack of planned, coordinated movement through the various agencies." We may safely assume that this state of affairs was not unique to North Carolina in the 1980s, indeed, the description still applies to most communities today.

1.3.2. Overreliance on Institutional Care

The absence of an intermediate level of services in many communities has contributed to the persistent overuse of restrictive institutional care because many professionals and parents are opting for these more readily available services in the interest of safety and risk management. The reliance on restrictive services may also be a part of a self-perpetuating cycle that involves strengthening family and professional attitudes about the necessity for frequently using such services and bolstering funding mechanisms that disproportionately support the more restrictive end of the service continuum (Collins & Collins, 1994).

1.3.3. Organizational Structures and Practices That Impede Collaboration

Organizational features that reduce the likelihood of agency–agency and agency–family collaboration are common throughout most service systems. One of the most pernicious examples is the common practice of requiring parents to give up custody of their child in order for the child to access a state-funded, out-of-home program. For example, Cohen, Harris, Gottlieb, and Best (1991) reported that most states require a transfer of custody as a prerequisite to the family's receiving financial assistance for the treatment of their child. However, the federal law that is often cited to support such a practice clearly states that a voluntary placement agreement is an acceptable alternative to the transfer of custody (Cohen, Preiser, Gottlieb, Harris, Baker, & Sonenklar, 1993). State and local service agencies have long histories of relatively independent action resulting in duplication of efforts, administrative redundancies, turf battles, and considerable mistrust and resistance to collaboration (MacBeth, 1993).

1.3.4. Exclusion of the Child's Family from the Process

Failure to successfully incorporate families into the planning and implementation of services has been cited as one of the major flaws of child mental health service systems. This failure is a result of efforts that have (1) focused on the child as the unit of service, rather than on the family; (2) emphasized mental health to the exclusion of other family needs; (3) emphasized formal services to the exclusion of informal support from other community social institutions; and (4) failed to use the resources and expertise of family members (Friesen & Koroloff, 1990).

1.4. Social and Demographic Trends

The response of service systems to child mental health needs and to existing barriers is further complicated by the expectation that the current trend of an increasing population of children in the United States will continue for at least the next decade. The number of school-age children will reach over 55.5 million by the year 2004, representing an increase of about 15% from 1992 (National Center for Education Statistics, 1993a). Further, the ethnic composition of the child population is also changing. For example, the nonwhite portion of public elementary and secondary school enrollment increased from 29.6% in 1986 to 32.6% in 1991. The group showing the largest increase was children of Hispanic ethnicity, increasing from 9.9% to 11.8% over the same period (National Center for Education Statistics, 1993b). Growth in the African-American and Hispanic populations is forecast to continue and, depending on immigration patterns, may even accelerate (Ward, 1992).

The impact of these demographic trends is only beginning to be felt in the human services system. The growing school-age population will increase the shortage of child mental health professionals in the coming years (Wohlford, 1990). The changing ethnic composition also increases the need for minorities in the mental health and child welfare professions. Cultural competence is of particular importance in dealing with minority families of children with emotional and behavioral disorders (Kavanagh & Kennedy, 1992). In the child service systems, the most basic principles of cultural sensitivity, such as providing a clinician who can communicate with children and families in their first or preferred language, are frequently violated. Language barriers and cultural insensitivity are likely to exacerbate the low utilization rates of mental health services found in some ethnic minority groups, such as Asian-Americans. These population trends emphasize the urgent need for the mental health community to develop treatment methods that recognize and build on the strengths of diverse cultural groups. What is required is the incentive and the means to educate child mental health professionals in cultural competence (Chin, 1990).

2. New Directions

The problems facing child mental health service systems have not gone unheeded over the past quarter century. Indeed, this period has been the most fruitful in history in terms of the development of more progressive conceptual frameworks and practices. We turn next to the identification and analysis of these developments.

2.1. The Importance of "Place"[1]

Human services professionals have become increasingly sensitized to the significance of "place" over the past several decades. In judging the merits of service programs, "Where is the child?" has become almost as important a question as "What are we doing for the child?" The current focus on inclusion in special education is only one of the most recent manifestations of this notion. However, an analysis of the meaning of place in the history of this country goes well beyond the domain of special education placement. A true understanding of the meaning of place must take into account the cultural and emotional loading that has accrued over the years. The battle for school desegregation was fought over issues of place, as was the deinstitutionalization movement (Kauffman & Lloyd, 1995).

Thus, it is not surprising that calls to reform child mental health services include a strong theme of place. Of the barriers to appropriate and effective care most discussed in the literature, those that elicit the most emotional response are related to the place where services are provided to children with emotional and behavioral disorders. Although the outcome literature on restrictive treatment settings is equivocal at best (Maluccio & Marlow, 1992), a careful analysis of the advocacy argument reveals that overreliance on institutional placements is censured not so much on the basis of ineffectiveness as on philosophical grounds. There is an emerging consensus that needed services should be brought to the child's natural setting rather than that the child should be taken to a restrictive, intensive treatment site (England & Cole, 1992). The question as to the relative *effectiveness* of services in institutional settings is secondary to the fundamental value judgment that, by their very nature, institutions are unacceptable.

---

[1] The authors are indebted to Kauffman and Lloyd (1995) for inspiring the title and many of the central ideas of this section.

The significance of place emerges most powerfully in the argument over the appropriateness and effectiveness of residential treatment for children. Advocates proclaiming an overutilization of institutional care point to a dramatic increase in the use of residential treatment centers during the 1970s and 1980s. Indeed, residential treatment admissions increased by 66% between 1975 and 1986 (Burns, 1991). A critical context for this comparison, however, is that outpatient services for adolescents showed a similar increase (62%) during the same period (Burns, 1991). Frank and Dewa (1992) reported that while residential treatment of children (including inpatient hospitalization) grew between 1970 and 1986, ambulatory care grew even faster; thus, the proportion of all children provided residential mental health services actually declined slightly during that time. Clearly, residential treatment is expensive and consumes a disproportionate amount of the resources devoted to mental health treatment (Burns, 1991), but precisely how much of the available resources should be devoted to residential treatment remains to be determined.

The data on patient demographics in the various treatment places has revealed a surprising trend related to race and social class. Hospital-based care actually declined for disadvantaged children between 1970 and 1986 due to the downsizing or closing of many state psychiatric facilities. Consequently, the number of private hospital beds increased, but private beds are generally not available to those without insurance. Thus, residential treatment centers may be fulfilling the role in the system that was previously filled by state mental hospitals (Frank & Dewa, 1992).

Although national data on residential treatment use are not yet available for the years after 1986, it is clear that communities or states that instituted demonstration projects aimed at reducing the use of costly restrictive care showed substantial decreases in residential treatment (Burns et al., 1993; Jordan & Hernandez, 1990). Efforts to reduce reliance on residential treatment are increasing, and organizational changes in systems of care have been effective in achieving such reductions. However, the impact of these efforts in terms of clinical and social outcomes for the children is largely unknown.

Inpatient (hospital) treatment settings, particularly state hospitals for children, have also been the focus of increased attention in recent years. Child inpatient services have been attacked as unnecessary, ineffective, expensive, and excessively restrictive (Burns, 1991; Feldman, 1993). Utilization rates for inpatient psychiatric treatment have been more variable than those for residential treatment centers. Burns (1991) reported that adolescent use of inpatient services declined slightly between 1975 and 1980, then increased 33% between 1980 and 1986. Like residential treatment, inpatient hospitalization can be significantly reduced by changes in local systems of care (Burns et al., 1993).

Use of inpatient treatment is responsive to other pressures as well, including changing insurance benefits. For example, in a study of children enrolled as dependents in a federal employees program, Patrick, Padgett, Burns, Schlesinger, and Cohen (1993) investigated the effects of changes in benefits over a 5-year period. Families enrolled in the program could choose high- or low-option plans that included more or less coverage for inpatient treatment. Both plans changed in the direction of less generous benefits during the period under study. A substantial drop occurred in the rate at which these dependents with a psychiatric diagnosis were hospitalized and in the mean number of days hospitalized. More striking, however, were the comparisons between high- and low-option enrollees. By the end of the study period, children and youth in families enrolled in the more generous plan were over twice as likely to be hospitalized as were those from families choosing the low-option plan. While other predictors were also significant, Patrick et al. (1993) concluded that child inpatient care is clearly responsive to changes in insurance benefits.

The importance of place is a strong philosophical undercurrent in much of the child mental health treatment reform. The philosophical stance favoring reduction in the use of restrictive treatment has been bolstered by economic pressure to control costs and has created a momentum that is unlikely to be altered. Rightly or wrongly, economic pressure is the motivating force that drives many of the reform efforts throughout the country.

2.2. Development of Home-Based Services

One response to the growing concern over issues of place in the treatment of children with serious emotional and behavioral disorders has been the development of home-based service programs. The notion of home-based services, also known as "family preservation services," began in the early 1970s with the introduction of the Homebuilders Program in Washington and Kaleidoscope in Illinois. Home-based programs are frequently intended to prevent children from being placed in foster homes, residential treatment centers, or psychiatric hospitals, and have grown and evolved over the years to occupy a central place in many local child mental health services systems. Although they differ in detail, most home-based programs share three primary goals: (1) to preserve the integrity of the family and to prevent unnecessary out-of-home placement; (2) to link the child and family with appropriate community agencies and individuals, and to create an ongoing community

TABLE 1
Major Features of Home-Based Services[a]

---

1. The intervention is delivered primarily in the family's home.
2. Home-based services have a family focus, and the family unit is viewed as the client.
3. The services have an "ecological" perspective and involve working with the community system to access and coordinate needed services and supports.
4. Home-based service programs are committed to family preservation and reunification unless there is clear evidence that this is not in the child's best interest.
5. The hours of service delivery are flexible in order to meet the needs of families, and 24-hour crisis intervention is provided.
6. Home-based services are multifaceted and include counseling, skill training, and helping the family to obtain and coordinate necessary services, resources, and supports.
7. Services are offered along a continuum of intensity and duration based on the goals of the program and the needs of the family.
8. Staff have small caseloads to permit them to work actively and intensively with each family.
9. The relationship between the home-based worker and the family is uniquely close, intense, and personal.
10. The programs are committed to empowering the families, instilling hope in families, and helping families to set and achieve their own goals and priorities.

---

[a]From Stroul and Goldman (1990). Used by permission.

support system; and (3) to strengthen the family's ability to cope and their capacity to function effectively in the community (Stroul & Goldman, 1990).

The major features of home-based services vary significantly from one program to another. As shown in Table 1, however, Stroul and Goldman (1990) presented a set of characteristics that describe an emerging consensus on the components of home-based services. These characteristics relate to the philosophy, conceptual base, policy, and attitudes associated with such services and reflect many of the current trends in child mental health service delivery systems. Home-based service programs have evolved in many directions in recent years. The range of specific activities included in home-based services has increased according to the creativity of the therapists involved. Providing a variety of mental-health-related services to children and families in their homes has become a basic tenet of many of the systems of care programs emerging across the country.

2.3. Systems of Care in the Community

Changing the location of child mental health services from institutional to community and home settings gained momentum in the service systems of the 1970s and 1980s. The philosophy of the inherent superiority of community-based services has played an important role in the initiation of mental health service reform. Experience has taught us, however, that a philosophical stance alone will not sustain a reform movement in the face of entrenched political and economic forces and that merely moving traditional services to the community, without systemic reform, generally results in those services becoming yet another disconnected piece of a fragmented system. As a result of this experience, a concept has emerged over the past 15 years that guides much of the current thinking regarding mental health services for children, particularly children with serious emotional and behavioral problems. Generally known as "systems of care in the community," this idea is based on the assumption that mental health services should come to the child, both literally and metaphorically, rather than that the child should go to the service settings.

Stroul and Friedman (1986, p. iv) have described a system of care as "a comprehensive spectrum of mental health and other necessary services which are organized into a coordinated network to meet the multiple and changing needs of seriously emotionally disturbed children." Further, they presented a framework of services that should surround the identified child and family, including mental health, social, education, health, vocational training, recreation, and operational services. Within these categories, Stroul and Friedman enumerated 50 specific service components that could be expected to comprise the system. Examples of component services include outpatient treatment, emergency services, respite care, self-contained special education, primary health care, vocational skills training, summer camps, and transportation. The categories within Stroul and Friedman's framework reflect, and in some ways reinforce, traditional agency divisions and their separate missions. An alternative approach is the Functional Model of Systems of Care Services that was developed as a part of the planning for the Virginia Comprehensive Services Act (see Table 2). This approach was intended to encourage more community agency flexibility in the development, location, and operation of the component services (MacBeth, 1993).

The systems of care model has had a profound influence on child mental health services. The core principles of comprehensive, community-based treatment for children with emotional and behavioral disorders

TABLE 2
Functional Model of Systems of Care Services[a]

Therapeutic
  Early identification
  Counseling and therapy services
  Home-based services
  Day treatment
  Therapeutic nursery program
  Nonresidential emergency services
  Adoption
Instructional
  Regular classroom
  Special education
  Resource room
  Self-contained classroom
  Special and alternative schools
  Homebound instruction
  Related services
  Life skills training
Health care
  Health promotion
  Primary care and screening
  Acute medical care
  Chronic medical care
  Dental care
Vocational
  Career education
  Vocational assessment
  Job survival skills training
  Vocational skills training
  Work experiences
  Job finding, placement, and
    retention services
  Supported employment
Recreational/social
  Neighborhood programs
  After-school programs
  Summer camps
  Special recreational projects
  Self-help and support groups
Human resource development
  Staff recruitment and training
  Volunteer recruitment and training

Family
  Parent education and family
    support
  Mediation
  Family and parent counseling
  Home aide services
  Respite care
  Adoption
Supervisory/protective
  Probation
  Intensive supervision services
  Outreach detention
  Postdispositional detention
Residential
  Independent living
  Therapeutic foster care
  Therapeutic group care
  Residential treatment
  Inpatient hospitalization
  Therapeutic camp
  Crisis residential
  Foster care
  Shelter
  Residential schools
  Diagnostic center
  Learning center
  Secure detention
Operational mechanisms
  Assessment
  Service planning
  Case management
  Advocacy
  Transportation
  Legal services
Sustenance
  Housing
  Food
  Clothing
  Financial services (e.g., food
    stamps, AFDC, Medicaid,
    fuel assistance, WIC, SSI)

[a]From MacBeth (1993). Used by permission. This list of service components is not all-inclusive. Communities may identify and develop other service modalities that are compatible with this model.

include individualized treatment planning, intensive case management, family-centered services, and interagency collaboration. Programs, initiatives, or systems that embody these core principles have come to be known as "community-based systems of care."

Support for the development of systems of care has come from several sources. For example, by the end of 1989, 47 of 50 states had received some grant funding through CASSP for planning and development. Further, CASSP has been quite successful in getting states to endorse a policy focus on the needs of severely emotionally and behaviorally disturbed children and in creating a vision of how such systems should be constituted (Duchnowski & Friedman, 1990). In addition, the Robert Wood Johnson Foundation awarded service implementation grants to eight states in 1990 as part of a project to stimulate development of interagency systems of care for children with emotional and behavioral disorders.

2.4. Key Features of Systems of Care

In this section, we briefly discuss key concepts and component services involved in systems of care programs. We examine organizational aspects of systems of care and explore how the generic model has been applied at several levels of organization.

2.4.1. Individualized Treatment Planning

At the core of any systems of care model is the assumption that treatment services and interventions must be tailored to the specific needs of the child and his or her family. Although an established tenet in mental health and special education circles, individualized treatment planning has taken on new forms in the context of systems of care. Service providers have begun to ask what interventions, opportunities, or tangible goods the child and family most need and how the available resources can be marshaled to meet those needs. A key to the success of individualized treatment planning appears to lie in the concept of flexible funding (England & Cole, 1992; Quinn & Cumblad, 1994). In general, flexible funding is a practice intended to forestall duplication of services across agencies and to provide easier access to nontraditional services needed by the children. For example, as used in the Idaho program, flexible funding expenses may include rent payments, school fees, behavior modification rewards, family camping trips, eyeglasses, birthday gifts, and so on (Dollard, Evans, Lubrecht, & Schaeffer, 1994).

2.4.2. Intensive Case Management

Children and their parents often cannot access needed services efficiently without assistance. It is necessary to take an aggressive approach to case management in order to help connect families with services and providers, to help providers and families to coordinate their efforts, and to initiate problem solving when crises threaten to disrupt the child's care and family life. Intensive case management involves teaching people the intricacies of the community child service system and supporting them in their mission to make that system responsive to the needs of individual children and their families.

2.4.3. Family-Centered Services

The concept of family-centered services has evolved considerably in recent years. The genesis of the idea to maximize family involvement in mental health services for children goes back to issues of place. For example, one of the assumptions of the Willie M. program was that "children are best served close to their own communities to maximize the possibility of family involvement in services and to allow for reintegration of the child into his or her natural environment" (Behar, 1985, p. 191). The level of commitment to family participation reflected in this assumption can be described as "family-allied." In the schema proposed by Dunst, Johanson, Trivette, and Hamby (1991), a family-allied program enlists the support of families to carry out interventions prescribed by professionals; families are seen as largely ineffectual in producing change in their lives and as requiring professional guidance.

Two further levels of family-oriented services reflect an increasing commitment to family participation. Family-focused programs are those in which families and professionals collaborate to define the families' needs. Finally, family-centered programs are those in which the families' needs drive all aspects of service delivery, and resource provision and interventions are designed to promote family decision making, capabilities, and competencies.

While there have been many efforts to make mental health services more family-centered, important barriers remain. Such barriers include the tendency to focus on the child rather than the family as the unit of service, the tendency to focus on traditional mental health services rather than on the full range of services that may be needed, the tendency to emphasize formal services to the exclusion of informal networks, and the failure to use the resources and expertise of parents and other family members (Friesen & Koroloff, 1990). That such barriers continue to require discussion suggests that child mental health service systems have some distance to go to become truly family-centered.

2.4.4. Interagency Collaboration

Duchnowski and Friedman (1990, p. 7) identified the development of efforts to improve interagency coordination as "one of the major challenges of the next decade." Developing organizational structures that support interagency collaboration is one of the chief ways that systemic reform has proceeded in recent years. Among the most common of such structures is the interagency team, a group of persons that includes representatives from each of the agencies involved. The concept of an interagency team has been implemented at all levels of state and local administration. Collaboration at the highest levels of government has been essential in the initial restructuring of some states' service systems. The most visible manifestation of the interagency team is the local team that is charged with the mission of designing an individualized set of services for each child.

Interagency collaboration efforts have shown promise in providing effective and efficient community-based services, yet any such efforts are bound to encounter significant barriers and substantial resistance to change. MacBeth (1993), for example, described some of the problems encountered in Virginia with the integration of services across agencies, including language barriers, segmenting services by agency, and maintenance of the status quo. In Illinois, service providers acknowledged interagency collaboration barriers that included agency-specific funding mechanisms and service mandates and a lack of effort on the part of the system to eliminate ineffective community programs (Quinn & Cumblad, 1994).

2.5. Applications of the Systems of Care Approach

There have been numerous applications of the systems of care approach, and a comprehensive documentation of these applications is beyond the scope of this chapter. We present brief descriptions of a few of these applications.

2.5.1. North Carolina's Willie M. Program

North Carolina got an early start on implementation of integrated systems of care with its Willie M. Program. By 1983, the state had been divided into 16 zones, and in most cases, each zone had developed its own capacity to provide a full range of treatment, educational, residential, and support services. The program included active case managers who steered children and families through the system. In 1985, after 4 years of experience, communities were able to serve most emotionally disturbed children locally. In addition, a wider continuum of services was emerging, characterized by flexible management and a no-exclusion policy (Behar, 1985).

2.5.2. California's Ventura Planning Model

The Ventura Planning Model (Jordan & Hernandez, 1990) was a proposal for mental health services reform that supported the development of local systems of care for disturbed children. The Ventura model, initiated as a demonstration project in 1984, has been extended to other sites and client populations. Although the model does not specify goals or services, it does define a planning process whereby communities can create systems of care tailored to their local needs and programs.

2.5.3. Alaska Youth Initiative

The Alaska Youth Initiative provided a model for individualized services for children and adolescents with emotional disabilities. Features of the model include unconditional care (meaning the child cannot be expelled from the system of care), client-centered services, flexible funding, and accountability (VanDenBerg, 1993). Decisions regarding services are made by an individualized multidisciplinary core service team that includes professionals, family members, and family support persons (Braveman, Craft, & Blair, 1993).

2.5.4. Illinois Initiative

In 1990, the Illinois State Board of Education established the Illinois Initiative to set guidelines for the development of family-centered, community-based, individualized, effectively linked, and readily accessible services for children with emotional and behavioral disorders. The Illinois Initiative resulted in the creation of six model community-based treatment programs targeting children who would otherwise have been placed in residential treatment centers. Each program began with a local needs and resources assessment and then sought to create a continuum of services in the community that would meet the child's individual needs. In addition, an interagency case management system was established to enhance communication and coordination among agencies and between agencies and families (Epstein, Cullinan, Quinn, & Cumblad, 1994).

2.5.5. Vermont's Project Wraparound

The Vermont program, Project Wraparound, emphasizes individualized care to prevent children from being removed from their families. Burchard and Clarke (1990) described Project Wraparound as services that are unconditional, provided in the least restrictive setting possible, flexible, child- and family-centered, and interagency-coordinated. The individualized care provided by the project may mean that a family intervention specialist initially spends substantial amounts of time in the child's home. As the situation stabilizes, a variety of other support services for the family and the school are brought to bear. Located in a small, rural community in northern Vermont, Project Wraparound represented a unique collaboration between state service agencies and a university clinical psychology training program (Burchard, Clarke, Hamilton, & Fox, 1990).

2.5.6. Ohio's Children's Project Implementation Plan

With the closing in 1982 of a state psychiatric hospital for children, six Ohio local mental health authorities collaborated to create a regional community mental health system for children. In 1988, a comprehensive case management program based on the Stroul and Friedman (1986) system of care model was instituted in the region. The goal of the project was to provide a range of treatment options in the least restrictive setting possible (Polivka & Clark, 1994).

2.5.7. Virginia's Comprehensive Services Act

In 1993, the Virginia General Assembly enacted the Comprehensive Services Act (CSA), an ambitious statewide effort to develop responsive local systems of care for children with emotional and behavioral disorders. The CSA mandated the establishment of community interagency service planning units, called Family Assessment and Planning Teams, which include parent representatives. In addition, the CSA dramatically restructured funding for services by consolidating several funding streams into a single pool that was then made available to local communities, thereby markedly increasing the flexibility of these communities' purchasing authority (MacBeth, 1993).

2.5.8. New York's Children and Youth Intensive Case Management Program

The state of New York has implemented an intensive case management program designed to maintain children in the least restrictive appropriate treatment setting. Evans, Banks, Huz, and McNulty (1994) reported that the program resulted in fewer hospital admissions and fewer days spent in the hospital.

2.6. Evaluation of Systems of Care

The move toward the establishment of community-based systems of care has been driven by advocacy challenges (Knitzer, 1982), litigation (Behar, 1985), financial incentives (Burns et al., 1993), and common sense. Notable for its absence is an empirical research base demonstrating the differential effectiveness of applications of the systems of care concept. Among the eight criteria for evaluating the quality of mental health programs for children and adolescents proposed by Knitzer (1982), not one refers to the investigation of clinical or social outcomes. The literature reveals no systematic, experimental investigations of systems of care models (Kutash, Duchnowski, Johnson, & Rugs, 1993). Systems of care reform has forged ahead in this country, largely without the benefit of program evaluation based on clinical and social outcome data. Data are emerging on some aspects of the various models, however, and a commitment to data-based evaluation may be found in at least some programs (Burchard & Schaefer, 1992).

One type of evaluation relevant to the current reforms is at the level of organizational change. At this level, the evaluation focuses on whether the organizational structure of the service system has made meaningful changes in the direction prescribed by planners. Morrissey, Calloway, Bartko, Goldman, and Paulson (1994) demonstrated this focus in their evaluation of the outcome of the demonstration projects funded by the Robert Wood Johnson Foundation to reform community services for the chronically mentally ill.

One form of evaluation that focuses on organizational change is the assessment of relevant participant attitudes. A limited effort to examine attitudes toward organizational change was included in the evaluation of Virginia's CSA Demonstration Sites. Although the results of that evaluation suggested a generally more positive approach to interagency teamwork, perceived negative findings included increased time demands for interagency team meetings and increasingly negative attitudes about collaboration (Commonwealth Institute for Child and Family Studies, 1992).

Evaluation of organizational change is not, however, the sole level of evaluation needed in mental health services reform. As demonstrated in the Robert Wood Johnson program on chronic mental illness, structural change in the reform of mental health service systems may not be sufficient to produce improvements in the quality of life of the patients served (Goldman, Morrissey, & Ridgely, 1994). A second level of evaluation is the assessment of the extent to which goals related to the range, mix, and cost of services are met.

Comparisons of cost and residential placement data have been an important part of the evaluation of the community-based intervention program in Ventura County, California. Evaluation findings offer clear evidence that systemic reform can yield economic savings while reducing restrictive placement of youth with serious emotional disturbance (Ichinose, Kingdon, & Hernandez, 1994; Jordan & Hernandez, 1990). Further, in comparison to rates for the state as a whole, replications of the Ventura program in several other model sites demonstrated lower rates of foster home and state hospital utilization and expenditure along with lower per capita rates for group home placements and expenditures (Rosenblatt & Attkisson, 1993; Rosenblatt, Attkisson, & Fernandez, 1992).

A third form of evaluation of child mental health services is the description of clients served by the programs. For example, the Alternatives to Residential Treatment Study (ARTS) (Duchnowski, Johnson, Hall, Kutash, & Friedman, 1993) provided descriptive data on children and families that entered five CASSP-nominated, state-of-the-art programs around the country. Baseline data included measures of family characteristics, as well as several child variables such as IQ and achievement, behavior problems, social skills, functional impairment, and self-esteem. These ARTS data form the baseline for a longitudinal study that will describe service program outcomes.

Finally, evaluation of child mental health systems of care must include assessment of clinically and socially relevant outcomes for children and their families. It is this level of evaluation that is most notably deficient and urgently needed. Although increasing quantities of resources are being devoted to the implementation of systems of care, there are only limited data to show long-term positive clinical and social outcomes for the children and their families. In one example of such an evaluation, Clarke, Schaefer, Burchard, and Welkowitz (1992) assessed changes in 19 children served by a wraparound project. Results indicated that while clinician ratings of child and family characteristics demonstrated significant improvement following the onset of the intervention, teacher ratings also showed improvements in the children, but the changes failed to achieve significance. In another example, implementation of the model program in Ventura County resulted in outcomes that met or exceeded the treatment-oriented goals set for the project, including reduced recidivism by juvenile offenders and improved school attendance and performance (Jordan & Hernandez, 1990).

However, not all the findings are encouraging. For example, in

1986, a model continuum of care was implemented in the area surrounding an army post in North Carolina. The service operated as a managed care program, offering traditional inpatient, outpatient, and residential treatment services, as well as intensive outpatient treatment and an intermediate level of wraparound services. A quasi-experimental evaluation of this continuum of care compared it to two matched sites at which children received standard treatment offered by the Civilian Health and Medical Program of the Uniformed Services (CHAMPUS). On measures collected 6 months after admission to treatment, the demonstration program did not exhibit general superiority over comparison sites. The few differences that existed were mixed, with some measures showing better results in the experimental program and some in the control groups. In the short term, the model program yielded no identifiable treatment effects (Bickman, Heflinger, Lambert, & Summerfelt, 1995).

One reason that empirical studies of the clinical and social impact of systems of care interventions have been slow to emerge is that there has been a dearth of appropriate instruments to measure their impact. However, assessment technology in this area has advanced in recent years. The Vermont System for Tracking Client Progress (VSTCP) offers an example of a set of comprehensive client outcome measures specifically designed for children involved in local systems of care. The VSTCP includes measures of client behavior, residential and educational restrictiveness, life events, and daily costs (Burchard & Schaeffer, 1992).

Participant satisfaction and general perception of the treatment program are emerging as a focus of outcome evaluation. For example, one study examined relationships among children's satisfaction with treatment, their sense of involvement in decision making, the restrictiveness of their placement, and the severity of their negative behaviors (Rosen, Heckman, Carro, & Burchard, 1994). Another study reported parent perceptions of their children's problems, service histories, unmet needs, and barriers to timely and effective treatment (Tarico, Low, Trupin, & Forsyth-Stephens, 1989).

3. Alternative Approaches

In addition to the evolution of the key concepts represented in most community-based systems of care for children with emotional and behavioral disorders, there are recent developments in specific service components that warrant discussion. These alternative approaches are typically integrated into a comprehensive system of care and do not have the widespread application of the key concepts discussed above.

Nonetheless, they demonstrate additional directions in which child mental health service systems are evolving.

3.1. Therapeutic Foster Care

The goal of therapeutic foster care, also described as specialized foster homes, therapeutic foster homes, and treatment homes, is to keep children in a family setting while providing their foster parents with the training and support services necessary to meet the child's special needs. A leading example of a therapeutic foster care program is the treatment foster care (TFC) model developed at the Oregon Social Learning Center (see Chapter 2). Based on Patterson's social learning parent training model (Patterson, Reid, & Dishion, 1992), the TFC program provides foster parents with preservice training emphasizing behavior management, developmental issues, communication and problem solving skills, and collaboration. Daily telephone contacts, along with weekly consultation groups and support groups, are part of the ongoing support system offered to foster families (Moore & Chamberlain, 1994). A similar program was evaluated as an alternative to psychiatric hospitalization, and 3-month follow-up data supported claims that the program was safe, effective, acceptable to consumers, and inexpensive, as compared to inpatient treatment (Mikkelsen, Bereika, & McKenzie, 1993). Although therapeutic foster care programs are proliferating around the country, outcome data are limited and controlled studies are nonexistent.

3.2. Day Treatment Programs

Day treatment programs add a strong mental health treatment component to a child's school program. These services are underdeveloped in most communities, however, and national data on the use of day treatment, or partial hospitalization, suggest that it is relatively uncommon. In 1986, only 3% of the adolescent admissions to mental health treatment were to partial hospitalization programs (Burns, 1991), even though communities have moved away from inpatient hospitalization toward less restrictive care (Burns et al., 1993). Although the sparse literature on day treatment is generally positive (Baenen, Stephens, & Glenwick, 1986), it tends to lack methodological rigor. In a recent example, Grizenko, Papineau, and Sayegh (1993) described the effects of a multimodal, psychodynamically oriented day treatment program for preadolescents with disruptive behavior disorders. The program included daily special education, a wide variety of psychotherapeutic activities, weekly family therapy, and medication when indicated. Participants were reported to improve on measures of behavior and self-perception as compared to waitlist controls.

3.3. Prevention Programs

School-based prevention programs have focused on aggressive, violent behavior and drug use (Kellam, Rebok, Ialongo, and Mayer, 1994), injury prevention (Englander, Cleary, O'Hare, & Hall, 1993), use of smokeless tobacco (Stevens, Freeman, Mott, & Youells, 1993), coping with stressful experiences (Dubow, Schmidt, McBride, & Edwards, 1993), dropout prevention (Mayer, Mitchell, Clementi, & Clement-Robertson, 1993), adjustment to divorce (Pedro-Carroll, Alpert-Gillis, & Cowen, 1992), sex abuse prevention (Madak & Berg, 1992), and transitioning to a new school (Jason, Weine, Johnson, Danner, Kurasake, & Warren-Sohlberg, 1993). Other prevention programs, based outside the school, have sought to include families. These programs have targeted such issues as substance abuse prevention (Jason, Pokorny, Kohner, & Bennetto, 1994; Van Hasselt, Hersen, Null, & Ammerman, 1993), parenting dysfunction (Huxley & Warner, 1993), children of divorce (Wolchik, West, Westover, & Sandler, 1993), and children of parents with affective disorders (Beardslee, Hoke, Wheelock, & Rothberg, 1992).

Primary prevention programs designed to prevent the development of emotional and behavior disorders are relatively rare. In a notable exception, Aronen (1993) reported a prospective, longitudinal study of the effects of a program in which psychiatric nurses conducted counseling visits in the homes of young children about ten times a year for 5 years. The aim of the visits was to provide counseling regarding child-rearing attitudes and practices and suggest ways to improve family interaction. Aronen reported that when the children were about 10 years old, fewer children in the counseling group were found to be mentally disturbed than in the control group.

3.4. Developments in Inpatient Care

The inclusion of parents as partners in clinical decision making represents one of the recent trends seen in some child inpatient treatment settings. For example, Byalin (1990) described a model of inpatient treatment in which parents were maximally involved in the identification of target behaviors, development of treatment strategies, implementation of interventions, and timing of discharge. The program resulted in an enthusiastic consumer response and a reduction in the length of hospitalization.

3.5. Beyond Systems of Care

A key feature of the systems of care reform movement has been the focus on organizational aspects of service systems. Organizational reform emphasizes restructuring the way in which agencies and systems work together to coordinate services and remove barriers that are inherent in a fragmented system. This focus on organizational structure may also be the chief weakness of the systems of care reform in that, for the most part, proponents have failed to offer a conceptual framework that integrates, develops, and improves the clinical and social services provided. Arising from the advocates' philosophical stance, and carried forward by a federal (CASSP) emphasis on organization, systems of care reform has plunged ahead in the absence of a coherent conceptual framework.

One notable exception is the Henggeler and Borduin (1990) multisystemic treatment (MST) model. Grounded in family systems theory and drawing on the social ecology literature, MST views individual patients as nested within interconnected systems that include self, family, peers, neighborhood, and school. Interactions between or within any of these systems may develop dysfunctional aspects. MST consists of problem-focused interventions drawn not only from the family therapy literature, but also from nonsystemic cognitive–behavior therapy. The strengths of MST include a systematic, theory-driven approach to the development of the treatment model and a firm commitment to empirical testing of the model at each stage of development. Recently, studies to establish the conceptual integrity and clinical and social impact of MST in the treatment of adolescents with antisocial behavior have been initiated. An explication of the conceptual basis, central features, and implementation details has been followed by a treatment manual that provides guidelines for implementing MST with adolescents and their families (Henggeler, 1991).

Henggeler, Melton, and Smith (1992) compared juveniles at risk for out-of-home placement because of criminal behavior treated with MST with those provided the usual juvenile justice system approach. Both groups were assessed pre- and postintervention, and youths in the MST program were found to have had fewer arrests, fewer days of incarceration, and less self-reported criminal behavior. Further, their parents reported reduced peer aggression and more family cohesion.

Henggeler, Melton, Smith, Schoenwald, and Hanley (1993) reported a controlled clinical trial of the MST model of family preservation in a sample of juvenile offenders and their families. Follow-up results measured an average of 2.4 years after initial referral indicated that youths who received the family preservation intervention were less likely to be arrested in comparison to those who received the usual treatment.

One aspect of MST requiring further elaboration is the translation of theory into practice at the organizational level. While systems theory offers a broad conceptual base for understanding the behavior of agencies and organizations, less attention has been paid to elaboration of the principles that can guide organizations in the development of structures and practices to capitalize on the strengths of systems and overcome barriers to collaboration.

4. Emerging Issues

4.1. Impact of National Health Care Reform

A major unanswered question regarding the future of child and adolescent mental health services relates to the impact of national health care reform. Substantial change in the United States health care system appears inevitable and promises to affect the delivery of mental health services for a large portion of the population. Such reforms are unlikely, however, to strike out in totally new directions; recent trends in the health care system offer indicators of likely directions, even though the end product of the reforms may not be resolved for years to come.

4.2. Managed Care and Mental Health Services

Managed care most commonly refers to a system that uses some form of peer review to limit utilization. Less commonly, it refers to a system of case management to coordinate treatment and assure continuity of care (Broskowski, 1994). Application of the managed care approach to mental health treatment is a relatively recent phenomenon, but such applications have multiplied rapidly in response to skyrocketing mental health treatment costs (DeLeon, VandenBos, & Bulatao, 1994). Managed care has the potential for safeguarding or even enhancing the quality of mental health care. Although cost containment has generally been the driving force behind the explosion of managed care programs, emerging competition between provider groups may also increase the demand for demonstrably positive treatment outcomes and consumer satisfaction.

4.3. The Role of the Private Sector

Among the most striking trends in recent years is the upsurge of private sector interest in children's mental health services. For example, between 1975 and 1980, private psychiatric hospitals doubled their share of the inpatient services market (Burns, 1991). Currently, the vast majority of residential treatment centers for children are private, generally not-for-profit, enterprises. As pressure builds to decrease the utilization of inpatient and residential treatment settings, private providers will be looking for other approaches to replace these increasingly unpopular restrictive treatment services.

4.4. School-Based Services

The number of children identified as seriously emotionally disturbed by the special education system has grown steadily in recent years. This population increased by 48% between 1976 and 1991 and, in 1993, constituted 8.9% of the entire special education population (U.S. Department of Education, 1993). Mental health services, when they are provided in educational context, are generally made available only to children who are classified as seriously emotionally disturbed. Recent data suggest that children with certain psychiatric diagnoses, such as conduct disorder, are not classified as seriously emotionally disturbed and frequently are not considered eligible to be served by special education programs. In fact, for children with a primary or secondary diagnosis of conduct disorder, the chances of being found eligible for special education services are 1 in 3 (Forness, Kavale, & Lopez, 1993). One resolution to this problem is to make the definition of serious emotional disturbance more behaviorally oriented, encouraging special education to serve children with conduct disorders as well as those with emotional disorders (Knoff & Batsche, 1990).

For children identified as seriously emotionally disturbed, the services they receive show considerable variation across school systems. Some systems have taken the position, at least unofficially, that mental health treatment does not come within the purview of educational institutions and must be sought elsewhere. Recent child mental health services reformers, on the other hand, have offered examples of ways in which school-based programs can meet the needs of seriously emotionally disturbed students, including providing enriched behavior management systems and curricula, group therapy in the classroom, and increased support services to students able to learn in regular education classrooms (Knitzer, Steinberg, & Fleisch, 1991).

4.5. Meeting the Mental Health Needs of Children in Primary Care Settings

Primary care providers have long played an important role in meeting the mental health needs of children and their families. Professionals in primary care settings, however, face the problem of identifying which patients need mental health services, setting aside time to address those needs through consultation or referral, and following up on recommendations or referrals. In an effort to address the problem of identification, Simonian, Tarnowski, Stancin, Friman, and Atkins (1991) developed a multistage screening model for use in pediatric primary care settings that increases the likelihood that mental health issues will be evaluated as a part of routine pediatric care. Bolstering the mental health services capacity in primary care holds considerable promise for addressing unmet needs in child mental health. Movement in this direction could be particularly effective in serving disadvantaged children whose families are less likely to seek out and use traditional mental health services (Tarnowski, 1991).

4.6. Focus on Severe Emotional Disturbance

Much of the attention in child and adolescent mental health services in recent years has been focused on children with relatively severe emotional and behavioral problems. The assertion by Knitzer (1982) that many of the most seriously disturbed children and youth are among the least adequately served has been often repeated and elaborated. The emphasis on relatively severe pathology in children was included in the policy focus of CASSP and in the wording of the requirement for state mental health plans (Duchnowski & Friedman, 1990). This emphasis is not without empirical basis. For example, children with conduct disorder show strong persistence of externalizing behavior problems and a relatively poor outcome (Offord et al., 1992). It is of concern, however, that in this period of declining resources, the field has been remarkably quiet about the mental health service needs of other affected children. Recent data indicate that internalizing disorders are common in children, are frequently comorbid with other internalizing or externalizing disorders, and, in some children, are quite persistent (Ollendick & King, 1994). Yet these children are less likely to receive treatment, as children with highly visible and highly disturbing behaviors consume an ever-increasing proportion of mental health resources. In addition, the expanding emphasis on severely disturbed children threatens to undermine attention to and support for prevention and early intervention programs (Friedman & Duchnowski, 1990). As noted by Knitzer (1993), there is a need for early intervention, particularly with urban children living in poverty who are at substantial risk for the development of serious emotional or behavioral disorders.

4.7. Awareness of Diversity and Cultural Sensitivity

Duchnowski and Friedman (1990) identified the establishment of cultural competence in systems of care as one of the key challenges in building the system. About a third of the population of this country is comprised of minority groups, and it is estimated that by the turn of the century, over 50% of the school-age population will be minority students (Hodgkinson, 1985). In terms of systems of care, this demographic trend means that increasing numbers of children and adolescents seeking mental health services will be from minority families. It will be a challenge for the system to provide enough well-trained professionals who are competent in providing services to people of diverse cultural backgrounds. Even something as basic as a mental health needs assessment can pose major problems if the professional does not understand the child's cultural and religious beliefs, values, and behavior. Further, if the professional does not share the child's culture, the potential for misunderstanding and misinterpreting the nature of the problems exhibited by the child with emotional or behavioral problems is increased. A related problem is the lack of culturally sensitive assessment instruments that have been normed with different cultural groups. Assessment instruments that have been standardized on middle-class white American children may not be valid for children of other cultures. Clearly, there is an urgent need for cross-culturally trained mental health professionals and for psychometrically robust assessment instruments that will provide valid assessments of the mental health status of children from diverse cultures.

4.8. Development of Transition Services

The transition from child services to adult services for children with emotional and behavioral disorders has received little attention in the mental health literature. The special education system has responded to the issue of transition at a policy level by mandating the inclusion of transition goals and objectives for all students with disabilities as they approach their exit from the education system. Mental health has been somewhat slower to respond, and even within the education system, relatively less attention has been paid to the transition needs of seriously emotionally disturbed students, as compared to students with other disabilities. Koroloff (1990) has described nine components of an exemplary transition policy that would address these deficiencies (see Table 3). Some of these components may be found in some states' policies regarding the transition of seriously emotionally disturbed students, but there has not yet been a demonstration of a comprehensive, effective transition program, implemented on a statewide level.

4.9. Implications for Child Mental Health Training Programs

The 1988 National Conference on Clinical Training in Psychology, entitled *Improving Psychological Services for Children and Adolescents with*

TABLE 3
Components of an Exemplary Transition Policy[a]

1. There must be a strong mechanism for interagency planning and coordination at the local level.
2. Adult-serving agencies must be involved prior to the time the youth leaves the child-serving system.
3. There must be a process for identifying or initiating transition planning for the child at an early age.
4. The process for initiating transition planning should be automatic and not dependent on a unique request for each individual youth.
5. A variety of settings should serve as the point of identification and initiation of transition planning.
6. A person or system must be identified to take responsibility for planning and delivering services over a period of time, specifically past the age at which the youth must leave special education.
7. Parents and youth should be explicitly included in the planning and implementation of the transition process.
8. There must be an interdepartmental mechanism at the state level for the planning and coordination of services, as well as resolution of disputes.
9. The concept of transition services must be broadly construed to include all aspects of successful independent adult living.

[a]From Koroloff (1990). Used by permission.

Severe Mental Disorders, resulted in a set of recommendations to NIMH that included (1) attracting more students, especially ethnic minorities, to clinical child psychology and related fields; (2) strengthening links between training programs and state/community service settings; (3) encouraging training faculty to develop skills in community-based treatment; and (4) encouraging broad clinical training, not only focusing on severe emotional and behavior disorders but also emphasizing treatment of less severe impairment and prevention interventions (Magrab & Wohlford, 1990).

Knitzer (1993) echoed these concerns as she outlined an agenda for addressing deficits in training programs for child mental health professionals. Her recommendations included increasing the experience of faculty members in community systems of care, providing broader clinical experience for trainees that includes in-home and in-school services, bolstering minority recruitment efforts in mental health fields, and ensuring that a family-centered perspective pervades child mental health training.

Duchnowski and Friedman (1990) identified the reform of university-based training programs and services as one of the major challenges to the children's mental health field in the 1990s. Their central concern was that the considerable innovation in service delivery models and the new knowledge generated by the application of these models were not being incorporated into university training programs. Duchnowski and Friedman (1990, p. 5), describing the approaches that work as "psychosocial, multi-agency, family-focused, and often crisis-oriented," maintained that these approaches are not the focus of university training programs and that, as a result, fewer appropriately trained clinicians are entering the field. Thus, more retraining is required and there is a greater conceptual distance between mental health professionals and policy makers.

One solution to some of these training issues is to increase contact between training programs and local service agencies. Such contact can provide service agencies access to research and evaluation expertise and up-to-date clinical findings while keeping academic programs in touch with the realities of applied-service settings. For example, one community initiated a collaboration with a school of professional psychology to conduct a child mental health needs assessment. The resulting effort not only provided the service agencies with information for program development and long-range planning but also led to modifications and enhancements of the psychology training program (Wolf, Yung, & Cotton, 1994). Vermont's Project Wraparound offers another outstanding example of collaboration between a university training program and the child services system (Burchard et al., 1990).

4.10. Where Does the Future Lie?

Events leading up to the beginning of the CASSP program and the subsequent activity stimulated by CASSP have resulted in substantial progress in the child mental health system. In their review of the accomplishments of the CASSP program, Day and Roberts (1991) found the following: a recognition of lack of services; a conceptual shift to community-based, multiagency systems of care with individualized service approaches; a redefined role for parents, including parental empowerment; a network of information sharing; an increased base of knowledgeable leadership; mental health services for children being brought into public and political arenas; rights and needs of parents being brought into discussion; a recognition of the importance of cultural considerations; the requirement that services for children be included as part of the state plan; and the increased availability in most states of additional services that are more community-based and less restrictive.

In their report, however, Day and Roberts (1991, p. 347) noted that federal CASSP funding was never intended to be used for direct services and stated that "the reality of implementation is that it is extremely difficult to advocate for, and improve the coordination of, services which are nonexistent and generally unfamiliar." This problem is especially critical in rural areas with low-density populations (Petti, Cornely, & McIntyre, 1993). A related problem is that where services do exist, they are frequently derived from widely divergent or even contradictory theoretical/conceptual models. The coordination of such divergent services poses a formidable problem that no current model of systems of care adequately addresses. The prospects for validation of present systems models are exceedingly dim unless the conceptual models driving the clinical interventions are clearly explicated, effectively communicated to the participants, and universally applied within the system.

Although there is mounting evidence that recent efforts to integrate systems of care have produced change at the organizational level, such change is not necessarily associated with improvement of patients' mental health status or quality of life (Goldman et al., 1994). It has been suggested that systemic change of the sort envisioned by the Robert Wood Johnson Foundation is a necessary but in itself insufficient condition for positive patient changes. Goldman et al. (1994, p. 44) note that the focus of the Robert Wood Johnson project was on structural change and continuity of care with the assumption ". . . that the state of the art in clinical and social care was available in each of these communities." However, patient outcomes led the authors to question this assumption. Similar questions might also be raised with regard to the child mental health services systems of care models sweeping the country. Systemic structural reforms may have intrinsic value, but unless there are effective clinical and social interventions available to the community, even the best organization will fail to achieve significant gains in children's quality of life.

A key task for the immediate future of children's mental health services is to move beyond the vociferous endorsement of values to the experimental evaluation of interventions. We should be clear that values are influenced by many ethical and philosophical factors not subject to empirical validation; the day-to-day practices that derive from those values, however, must be empirically validated or discarded.

Another issue that deserves consideration is the importance of developmental issues in providing services for children with emotional and behavioral disorders. With the increase in sophistication in the assessment of children's service needs has come the realization that these needs differ across the developmental spectrum of childhood. Trupin, Forsyth-Stephens, and Low (1991) reported that substantial unmet needs for mental health services could be documented, on the basis of behavior and risk characteristics, among children considered seriously emotionally disturbed. Further, they reported that these needs differed depending on the age of the child. Among their other findings, children (ages 6–11) were reported to have a greater need for respite care and therapeutic camp services, while young adolescents (ages 12–16) demonstrated a greater need for foster home placement.

Increasing interest in child mental health services research is an essential component if the field is to continue to move forward. The lack of well-controlled studies of clinical, social, and cost outcomes is a major problem. Burns and Friedman (1990) discussed a need for research on how to integrate and coordinate the range of services required by emotionally and behaviorally disturbed children and their families. The field has made some progress in this area, but little attention has been given to investigation of the factors that foster and support or, conversely, inhibit and undermine integration and collaboration efforts. Further, the task is not complete until the questions regarding the relationship between these factors and clinical and social outcomes have been adequately answered.

5. References

Aronen, E. (1993). The effect of family counselling on the mental health of 10–11-year-old children in low- and high-risk families: A longitudinal approach. *Journal of Child Psychology and Psychiatry, 34,* 155–165.

Baenen, R. S., Stephens, M. A. P., & Glenwick, D. S. (1986). Outcome in psychoeducational day school programs: A review. *American Journal of Orthopsychiatry, 56,* 263–270.

Beachler, M. (1990). The Mental Health Services Program for Youth. *Journal of Mental Health Administration, 17,* 115–121.

Beardslee, W. R., Hoke, L., Wheelock, I., & Rothberg, P. C. (1992). Initial findings on preventive intervention for families with parental affective disorders. *American Journal of Psychiatry, 149,* 1335–1340.

Behar, L. (1985). Changing patterns of state responsibility: A case study of North Carolina. *Journal of Clinical Child Psychology, 14,* 188–195.

Behar, L. B., & Munger, R. L. (1993). Children's mental health administration. *Administration and Policy in Mental Health, 20,* 209–213.

Bickman, L., Heflinger, C. A., Lambert, E. W., & Summerfelt, W. T. (1995). The Ft. Bragg managed care experiment: Short term impact on psychopathology. *Journal of Child and Family Studies* (in press).

Braveman, P., Craft, K., & Blair, S. (1993). Alaska Youth Initiative: Core service teams and "bubble planning." In C. R. Ellis & N. N. Singh (Eds.), *Children and adolescents with emotional or behavioral disorders: Proceedings of the Third Annual Virginia Beach Conference* (p. 14). Richmond, VA: Commonwealth Institute for Child and Family Studies.

Broskowski, A. (1994). Current mental health care environments: Why managed care is necessary. In R. L. Lowman & R. J. Resnick (Eds.), *The mental health professional's guide to managed care* (pp. 1–18). Washington, DC: American Psychological Association.

Burchard, J. D., & Clarke, R. T. (1990). The role of individualized care in a service delivery system for children and adolescents with severely maladjusted behavior. *Journal of Mental Health Administration, 17,* 48–60.

Burchard, J. D., Clarke, R. T., Hamilton, R. I., & Fox, W. L. (1990). Project Wraparound: A state–university partnership in training clinical psychologists to serve severely emotionally disturbed children. In P. R. Magrab & Wohlford (Eds.), *Improving psychological services for children and adolescents with severe mental disorders: Clinical training in psychology* (pp. 179–184). Washington, DC: American Psychological Association.

Burchard, J. D., & Schaefer, M. (1992). Improving accountability in a service delivery system in children's mental health. *Clinical Psychology Review, 12*, 867–882.

Burns, B. J. (1991). Mental health service use by adolescents in the 1970s and 1980s. *Journal of the American Academy of Child and Adolescent Psychiatry, 30*, 144–150.

Burns, B. J., & Friedman, R. M. (1990). Examining the research base for child mental health services and policy. *Journal of Mental Health Administration, 17*, 87–98.

Burns, B. J., Thompson, J. W., & Goldman, H. H. (1993). Initial treatment decisions by level of care for youth in the CHAMPUS Tidewater demonstration. *Administration and Policy in Mental Health, 20*, 231–246.

Byalin, K. (1990). Parent empowerment: A treatment strategy for hospitalized adolescents. *Hospital and Community Psychiatry, 41*, 89–90.

Chin, J. L. (1990). Training to meet the needs of Asian-American children, youth, and families. In P. R. Magrab & P. Wohlford (Eds.), *Improving psychological services for children and adolescents with severe mental disorders: Clinical training in psychology* (pp. 173–176). Washington, DC: American Psychological Association.

Clarke, R. T., Schaefer, M., Burchard, J. D., & Welkowitz, J. W. (1992). Wrapping community-based mental health services around children with a severe behavioral disorder: An evaluation of Project Wraparound. *Journal of Child and Family Studies, 1*, 241–261.

Cohen, R., Harris, R., Gottlieb, S., & Best, A. M. (1991). States' use of transfer of custody as a requirement for providing services to emotionally disturbed children. *Hospital and Community Psychiatry, 42*, 526–530.

Cohen, R., Preiser, L., Gottlieb, S., Harris, R., Baker, J., & Sonenklar, N. (1993). Relinquishing custody as a requisite for receiving services for children with serious emotional disorders: A review. *Law and Human Behavior, 17*, 121–134.

Collins, B. G., & Collins, T. M. (1994). Child and adolescent mental health: Building a system of care. *Journal of Counseling and Development, 72*, 239–243.

Commonwealth Institute for Child and Family Studies (1992). *Council on Community Services for Youth and Families Demonstration Projects: Final Report on Evaluation.* Richmond, VA: Author.

Costello, E. J. (1989). Developments in child psychiatric epidemiology. *Journal of the American Academy of Child and Adolescent Psychiatry, 28*, 836–841.

Costello, E. J., Burns, B. J., Angold, A., & Leaf, P. J. (1993). How can epidemiology improve mental health services for children and adolescents? *Journal of the American Academy of Child and Adolescent Psychiatry, 32*, 1106–1113.

Day, C., & Roberts, M. C. (1991). Activities of the Child and Adolescent Service System Program for improving mental health services for children and families. *Journal of Clinical Child Psychology, 20*, 340–350.

DeLeon, P. H., VandenBos, G. R., & Bulatao, E. Q. (1994). Managed mental health care: A history of the federal policy initiative. In R. L. Lowman & R. J. Resnick (Eds.), *The mental health professional's guide to managed care* (pp. 19–40). Washington, DC: American Psychological Association.

Dollard, N., Evans, M. E., Lubrecht, J., & Schaeffer, D. (1994). The use of flexible service dollars in rural community-based programs for children with serious emotional disturbance and their families. *Journal of Emotional and Behavioral Disorders, 2*, 117–125.

Dubow, E. F., Schmidt, D., McBride, J., & Edwards, S. (1993). Teaching children to cope with stressful experiences: Initial implementation and evaluation of a primary prevention program. *Journal of Clinical Child Psychology, 22*, 428–440.

Duchnowski, A. J., & Friedman, R. M. (1990). Children's mental health: Challenges for the nineties. *Journal of Mental Health Administration, 17*, 3–12.

Duchnowski, A. J., Johnson, M. K., Hall, K. S., Kutash, K., & Friedman, R. M. (1993). The Alternatives to Residential Treatment Study: Initial findings. *Journal of Emotional and Behavioral Disorders, 1,* 17–26.

Dunst, C. J., Johanson, C., Trivette, C. M., & Hamby, D. (1991). Family-oriented early intervention policies and practices: Family-centered or not? *Exceptional Children, 58,* 115–126.

England, M. J., & Cole, R. F. (1992). Building systems of care for youth with serious mental illness. *Hospital and Community Psychiatry, 43,* 630–633.

Englander, J., Cleary, S., O'Hare, P., & Hall, K. M. (1993). Implementing and evaluating injury prevention programs in the traumatic brain injury model systems of care. *Journal of Head Trauma Rehabilitation, 8,* 101–113.

Epstein, M. H., Cullinan, D., Quinn, K. P., & Cumblad, C. (1994). Characteristics of children with emotional and behavioral disorders in community-based programs designed to prevent placement in residential facilities. *Journal of Emotional and Behavioral Disorders, 2,* 51–57.

Evans, M. E., Banks, S. M., Huz, S., & McNulty, T. L. (1994). Initial hospitalization and community tenure outcomes of intensive case management for children and youth with serious emotional disturbance. *Journal of Child and Family Studies, 3,* 225–234.

Feldman, S. (1993). Children's mental health administration: A note from the editor. *Administration and Policy in Mental Health, 20,* 207–208.

Forness, S. R., Kavale, K. A., & Lopez, M. (1993). Conduct disorders in school: Special education eligibility and comorbidity. *Journal of Emotional and Behavioral Disorders, 1,* 101–108.

Frank, R. G., & Dewa, C. S. (1992). Insurance, system structure, and the use of mental health services by children and adolescents. *Clinical Psychology Review, 12,* 829–840.

Friedman, R. M., & Duchnowski, A. J. (1990). Service trends in the children's mental health system: Implications for the training of psychologists. In P. R. Magrab & P. Wohlford (Eds.), *Improving psychological services for children and adolescents with severe mental disorders: Clinical training in psychology* (pp. 35–41). Washington, DC: American Psychological Association.

Friesen, B. J., & Koroloff, N. M. (1990). Family-centered services: Implications for mental health administration and research. *Journal of Mental Health Administration, 17,* 13–25.

Goldman, H. H., Morrissey, J. P., & Ridgely, M. S. (1994). Evaluating the Robert Wood Johnson Foundation program on chronic mental illness. *Milbank Quarterly, 72,* 37–47.

Grizenko, N., Papineau, D., & Sayegh, L. (1993). Effectiveness of a multimodal day treatment program for children with disruptive behavior problems. *Journal of the American Academy of Child and Adolescent Psychiatry, 32,* 127–134.

Henggeler, S. W. (1991). *Treating conduct problems in children and adolescents: An overview of the multisystemic approach with guidelines for intervention design and implementation.* Columbia: South Carolina Department of Mental Health.

Henggeler, S. W., & Borduin, C. M. (1990). *Family therapy and beyond: A multisystemic approach to treating the behavior problems of children and adolescents.* Pacific Grove, CA: Brooks/Cole.

Henggeler, S. W., Melton, G. B., & Smith, L. A. (1992). Family preservation using multisystemic therapy: An effective alternative to incarcerating serious juvenile offenders. *Journal of Consulting and Clinical Psychology, 60,* 953–961.

Henggeler, S. W., Melton, G. B. Smith, L. A., Schoenwald, S. K., & Hanley, J. H. (1993). Family preservation using multisystemic treatment: Long-term follow-up to a clinical trial with serious juvenile offenders. *Journal of Child and Family Studies, 2,* 283–293.

Hodgkinson, L. (1985). *All one system: Demographics of education.* Washington, DC: Institute for Educational Leadership.

Huxley, P., & Warner, R. (1993). Primary prevention of parenting dysfunction in high-risk cases. *American Journal of Orthopsychiatry, 63,* 582–588.

Ichinose, C. K., Kingdon, D. W., & Hernandez, M. (1994). Developing community alternatives to group home placement for SED special education students in the Ventura County system of care. *Journal of Child and Family Studies, 3,* 193–210.

Jason, L. A., Pokorny, S. B., Kohner, K., & Bennetto, L. (1994). An evaluation of the short-term impact of a media-based substance abuse prevention program. *Journal of Community and Applied Social Psychology, 4,* 63–69.

Jason, L. A., Weine, A. M., Johnson, J. H., Danner, K. E., Kurasake, K. S., & Warren-Sohlberg, L. (1993). The School Transitions Project: A comprehensive preventive intervention. *Journal of Emotional and Behavioral Disorders, 1,* 65–70.

Joint Commission on Mental Health of Children (1969). *Crisis in child mental health: Challenge for the 1970s.* New York: Harper & Row.

Jordan, D. D., & Hernandez, M. (1990). The Ventura planning model: A proposal for mental health reform. *Journal of Mental Health Administration, 17,* 26–47.

Kauffman, J. M., & Lloyd, J. W. (1995). A sense of place: The importance of placement issues in contemporary special education. In J. M. Kauffman, J. W. Lloyd, T. A. Astuto, & D. P. Hallahan (Eds.), *Issues in the educational placement of pupils with emotional or behavioral disorders* (pp. 3–19). Hillsdale, NJ: Erlbaum Associates.

Kavanagh, K. H., & Kennedy, P. H. (1992). Promoting cultural diversity. Newbury Park, CA: Sage Publications.

Kellam, S. G., Rebok, G. W., Ialongo, N., & Mayer, L. S. (1994). The course and malleability of aggressive behavior from early first grade into middle school: Results of a developmental epidemiology-based preventive trial. *Journal of Child Psychology and Psychiatry, 35,* 259–281.

Knitzer, J. (1982). *Unclaimed children.* Washington, DC: Children's Defense Fund.

Knitzer, J. (1993). Children's mental health policy: Challenging the future. *Journal of Emotional and Behavioral Disorders, 1,* 8–16.

Knitzer, J., Steinberg, Z., & Fleisch, B. (1991). Schools, children's mental health, and the advocacy challenge. *Journal of Clinical Child Psychology, 20,* 102–111.

Knoff, H. M., & Batsche, G. M. (1990). The place of the school in community mental health services for children: A necessary interdependence. *Journal of Mental Health Administration, 17,* 122–130.

Koroloff, N. M. (1990). Moving out: Transition policies for youth with serious emotional disabilities. *Journal of Mental Health Administration, 17,* 78–86.

Kutash, K., Duchnowski, A., Johnson, M., & Rugs, D. (1993). Multi-stage evaluation for a community mental health system for children. *Administration and Policy in Mental Health, 20,* 311–322.

MacBeth, G. (1993). Collaboration can be elusive: Virginia's experience in developing an interagency system of care. *Administration and Policy in Mental Health, 20,* 259–282.

Madak, P. R., & Berg, D. H. (1992). The prevention of sexual abuse: An evaluation of "Talking About Touching." *Canadian Journal of Counseling, 26,* 29–40.

Magrab, P. R., & Wohlford, P. (1990). Recommendations to NIMH from the 1988 National Conference on Clinical Training in Psychology: Improving psychological services for children and adolescents with severe mental disorders. In P. R. Magrab & P. Wohlford (Eds.), *Improving psychological services for children and adolescents with severe mental disorders: Clinical training in psychology* (pp. 5–6). Washington, DC: American Psychological Association.

Maluccio, A. N., & Marlow, W. D. (1972). Residential treatment of emotionally disturbed children: A review of the literature. *Social Service Review, 46,* 230–250.

Mayer, G. R., Mitchell, L. K., Clementi, T., & Clement-Robertson, E. (1993). A dropout prevention program for at-risk high school students: Emphasizing consulting to promote positive classroom climates. *Education and Treatment of Children, 16*, 135–146.

Mikkelsen, E. J., Bereika, G. M., & McKenzie, J. C. (1993). Short-term family-based residential treatment: An alternative to psychiatric hospitalization for children. *American Journal of Orthopsychiatry, 63*, 28–33.

Moore, K. J., & Chamberlain, P. (1994). Treatment foster care: Toward development of community-based models for adolescents with severe emotional and behavioral disorders. *Journal of Emotional and Behavioral Disorders, 2*, 22–30.

Morrissey, J. P., Calloway, M., Bartko, W. T., Goldman, H. H., & Paulson, R. I. (1994). Local mental health authorities and service system change: Evidence from the Robert Wood Johnson program on chronic mental illness. *Milbank Quarterly, 72*, 49–80.

National Center for Education Statistics (1993a). *Projections of education statistics to 2004.* Washington, DC: U.S. Government Printing Office.

National Center for Education Statistics (1993b). *Digest of education statistics.* Washington, DC: U.S. Government Printing Office.

Offord, D. R., Boyle, M. H., Racine, Y. A., Fleming, J. E., Cadman, D. T., Blum, H. M., Byrne, C., Links, P. S., Lipman, E. L., MacMillan, H. L., Grant, N. I. R., Sanford, M. N., Szatmari, P., Thomas, H., & Woodward, C. A. (1992). Outcome, prognosis, and risk in a longitudinal follow-up study. *Journal of the American Academy of Child and Adolescent Psychiatry, 31*, 916–923.

Ollendick, T. H., & King, N. J. (1994). Diagnosis, assessment, and treatment of internalizing problems in children: The role of longitudinal data. *Journal of Consulting and Clinical Psychology, 62*, 918–927.

Patrick, C., Padgett, D. K., Burns, B. J., Schlesinger, H. J., & Cohen, J. (1993). Use of inpatient services by a national population: Do benefits make a difference? *Journal of the American Academy of Child and Adolescent Psychiatry, 32*, 144–152.

Patterson, G. R., Reid, J. B., & Dishion, T. J. (1992). *Antisocial boys.* Eugene, OR: Castilia Publishing.

Pedro-Carroll, J. L., Alpert-Gillis, L. J., & Cowen, E. L. (1992). An evaluation of the efficacy of a preventive intervention of 4th–6th grade urban children of divorce. *Journal of Primary Prevention, 13*, 115–130.

Petti, T. A., Cornely, P. J., & McIntyre, A. (1993). A consultative study as a catalyst for improving mental health services for rural children and adolescents. *Hospital and Community Psychiatry, 44*, 262–265.

Polivka, B. J., & Clark, J. A. (1994). A collaborative system of care for youth with severe emotional disturbances: An evaluation of client characteristics and services. *Journal of Mental Health Administration, 21*, 170–184.

President's Commission on Mental Health (1978). *Report to the President* (4 vols). Washington, DC: U.S. Government Printing Office.

Quinn, K., & Cumblad, C. (1994). Service providers' perceptions of interagency collaboration in their communities. *Journal of Emotional and Behavioral Disorders, 2*, 109–116.

Rosen, L. D., Heckman, T., Carro, M. G., & Burchard, J. D. (1994). Satisfaction, involvement, and unconditional care: The perceptions of children and adolescents receiving wraparound services. *Journal of Child and Family Studies, 3*, 55–67.

Rosenblatt, A., & Attkisson, C. C. (1993). Integrating systems of care in California for youth with severe emotional disturbance. III. Answers that lead to questions about out-of-home placements and the AB377 evaluation project. *Journal of Child and Family Studies, 2*, 119–141.

Rosenblatt, A., Attkisson, C. C., & Fernandez, A. J. (1992). Integrating systems of care in California for youth with severe emotional disturbance. II. Initial group home expenditure and utilization findings from the California AB377 evaluation project. *Journal of Child and Family Studies, 1,* 263–286.

Simonian, S. J., Tarnowski, K. J., Stancin, T., Friman, P. C., & Atkins, M. S. (1991). Disadvantaged children and families in pediatric primary care settings. II. Screening for behavior disturbance. *Journal of Clinical Child Psychology, 20,* 360–371.

Stevens, M. M., Freeman, D. H., Mott, L. A., & Youells, F. E. (1993). Smokeless tobacco use among children: The New Hampshire study. *American Journal of Preventive Medicine, 9,* 160–167.

Stroul, B. A., & Friedman, R. M. (1986). *A system of care for seriously emotionally disturbed children and youth.* Washington, DC: CASSP Technical Assistance Center at Georgetown University.

Stroul, B. A., & Goldman, S. K. (1990). Study of community-based services for children and adolescents who are severely emotionally disturbed. *Journal of Mental Health Administration, 17,* 61–77.

Tarico, V. S., Low, B. P., Trupin, E., & Forsyth-Stephens, A. (1989). Children's mental health services: A parent perspective. *Community Mental Health Journal, 25,* 313–326.

Tarnowski, K. J. (1991). Disadvantaged children and families in pediatric primary care settings. I. Broadening the scope of integrated mental health services. *Journal of Clinical Child Psychology, 20,* 351–359.

Trupin, E. W., Forsyth-Stephens, A. F., & Low, B. P. (1991). Service needs of severely disturbed children. *American Journal of Public Health, 81,* 975–980.

U.S. Department of Education (1993). *To assure the free appropriate public education of all children with disabilities: Fifteenth annual report to Congress on the implementation of the Individuals with Disabilities Education Act.* Washington, DC: Author.

U.S. Office of Technology Assessment (1986). *Children's mental health: Problems and service—a background paper.* Washington, DC: U.S. Government Printing Office.

VanDenBerg, J. E. (1993). Integration of individualized mental health services into the system of care for children and adolescents. *Administration and Policy in Mental Health, 20,* 247–257.

Van Hasselt, V. B., Hersen, M., Null, J. A., & Ammerman, R. T. (1993). Drug abuse prevention for high-risk African-American children and their families: A review and model program. *Addictive Behaviors, 18,* 213–234.

Ward, J. G. (1992). The power of demographic change: Impact of population trends on schools. In J. G. Ward & P. Anthony (Eds.), *Who pays for student diversity?: Population changes and educational policy* (pp. 1–20). Newbury Park, CA: Corwin Press.

Willie M. et al. v. James B. Hunt, Jr. et al., Civil No. C-C-79-294-M (W.D.N.C. 1980).

Wohlford, P. (1990). National responsibilities to improve training for psychological services for children, youth, and families in the 1990's. In P. R. Magrab & P. Wohlford (Eds.), *Improving psychological services for children and adolescents with severe mental disorders: Clinical training in psychology* (pp. 11–34). Washington, DC: American Psychological Association.

Wolchik, S. A., West, S. G., Westover, S., & Sandler, I. N. (1993). The children of divorce parenting intervention: Outcome evaluation of an empirically based program. *American Journal of Community Psychology, 21,* 293–331.

Wolf, E. M., Yung, B. R., & Cotton, K. L. (1994). Collaborative needs assessment for child mental health program development. *Journal of Mental Health Administration, 21,* 161–169.

Index

Adolescent substance abuse
  conceptual models, 93–100
  and coping, 105–111
Attention-deficit hyperactivity disorder
  compatibility equations, 207–209
  implications
    for applied research, 222–224
    for school-based assessment and inter-
      vention, 220–222
    for teacher training, 224–225
  student–teacher compatibility, 209–214
  student–treatment compatibility, 216–
    220
  teacher–treatment compatibility, 214–
    216

Behavioral family intervention
  for childhood anxiety disorders, 298–300
  combining individual and family inter-
    ventions, 315–316
  conceptual framework, 285–286
  for conduct problems, 300–304
  and consultation skills, 288
  definition, 284–285
  enhancing treatment outcome, 304–307
  for health-related problems
    acute pain, 293
    chronic food refusal, 293–296
    infant sleep disturbance, 296–297
    pain management, 288–293
  high-powered applications, 314–315
  intervening across multiple settings, 313–
    314
  and learning problems, 315
  for maritally distressed and remarried
    families
    children in conflictual marriages, 307–
      309
    children in remarried families, 309–
      310
  process variables, 310–313
  public health perspective, 316–317
  role of media, 317–318
  with rural and isolated families, 316
  and therapeutic options, 286–287

Children's health status
  associated child variables
    child psychopathology, 237–239
    coping and stress, 235–237
    perceptions of control, 234
  definitions, 231–233
  and health care utilization, 239–240
  learned illness behavior, 266–273
  maternal negative affect, 262–266
  parental influences
    family functioning, 247–248
    health beliefs and behaviors, 246–247
    parental psychopathology, 248–250
    utilization patterns of health care, 250–
      252
  recurrent abdominal pain
    and child psychopathology, 267–268
    and coping and control, 269–270
    and maternal negative affect, 266–267
    and primary care utilization, 268–269
    and social learning, 266
    theoretical model and intervention,
      270–272
  relationships among variables, 243–245
  secondary associated variables
    concepts of health and illness, 241–
      242
    symptom appraisal, interpretation,
      and labeling, 240–241
  social learning processes
    and control perceptions, 261
    and coping responses, 257–261
    and the coping–control relationship,
      261–262
    direct modeling of health behaviors,
      254–257
    reinforcement of illness behaviors,
      253–254
    socialization of health behaviors, 252–
      253
Conduct problems
  in childhood
    families under siege, 13–34
    family experiences after intervention,
      47–58
    parents' therapy experiences, 34–47

Conduct problems (*cont.*)
  conduct disorder in adolescence
    association with peers, 66–67
    environmental mediators, 65–66
    foster care treatment, 70–85
    OSLC treatment foster care model, 67–70
    and temperament, 118–119

Ethnicity
  African-American children, 140–142
  Anglo-American children, 144–145
  Asian-American children, 142–144
  attributions, 146–147
  defining and measuring, 135–137
  and friendship
    correlates of acceptance and rejection, 156–162
    interactional preferences, 153–156
  Hispanic children, 138–140
  social values and practices, 137–138
  stereotypes, biases, and attitudes, 147–152

Foster care treatment
  for delinquency, 70–71
  gender considerations, 73–77
  program practices, 81–83
  for severe emotional disturbance, 71–73
  staff assumptions, 79–81
  supervision and discipline, 83–85
  vs. group care, 78–79

Mental health services for children and adolescents
  alternative approaches
    day treatment programs, 350–351
    inpatient care, 351
    multisystemic treatment, 352–353
    therapeutic foster care, 350
  applications of systems of care
    Alaska Youth Initiative, 345
    California's Ventura Planning Model, 345
    Illinois Initiative, 345
    New York's Children and Youth Intensive Case Management Program, 346–347
    North Carolina's Willie M. Program, 344
    Ohio's Children's Project Implementation Plan, 346
    Virginia's Comprehensive Services Act, 346

Mental health services for children and adolescents (*cont.*)
  barriers to services, 333–335
  child mental health training programs, 356–358
  emerging factors
    diversity and cultural sensitivity, 355–356
    managed care and mental health services, 353
    national health care reform, 353
    primary care settings, 354–355
    related to severe emotional disturbance, 355
    role of the private sector, 353–354
    school-based services, 354
    transition services, 356
  estimates of need, 332–333
  evaluation of systems, 347–349
  home-based services, 338–339
  key features
    family-centered services, 343–344
    individualized treatment planning, 342
    intensive case management, 343
    interagency collaboration, 344
  location, 336–338
  social and demographic trends, 335–336
  system reform, 331–332
  systems of care in the community, 340–342

Neuromotor soft signs in children
  and behavior problems, 177–179
  and clinical psychopathology, 179–180
  determinants, 176
  developmental changes, 177
  and dysfunction, 174–176
  neurodevelopmental processes, 195–197
  neuromotor rating scale, 198–199
  precursors of adult psychopathology
    Emory Study, 180–191
    neuromotor functions and childhood affect, 191–193

Qualitative research methods
  coding
    axial, 8–9
    open, 7–8
    selective, 9–11

Qualitative research methods (*cont.*)
    implications, 31–34, 46–47, 58–60
    questions, 1
    reliability and validity, 4–6
    for studying conduct problems, 11–13
    types, 6–7
    vs. quantitative research, 2–4

Stress–coping model
    active and avoidant coping, 109
    assessment of coping, 105–108
    assessment of stress and substance use,
        103–104

Stress–coping model (*cont.*)
    buffering effects
        of academic and social competence,
            113–115
        of parental support, 111–113
    competence and resiliency, 97–98
    description of model, 93–97
    longitudinal effects of coping, 110
    negative life events, 104–105
    research methods, 100–103
    role of attitudes, 105
    and temperament, 115–119
    vs. deviancy model, 98